Radic(Lawrence

COSTERUS NEW SERIES 130

Series Editors:
C.C. Barfoot, Theo D'haen
and Erik Kooper

Radicalizing Lawrence

Critical Interventions in the Reading and Reception of D.H. Lawrence's Narrative Fiction

Robert Burden

 Amsterdam-Atlanta, GA 2000

ISBN 90-420-1303-6

© Editions Rodopi B.V.
    Amsterdam - Atlanta, GA 2000

Printed in The Netherlands

Acknowledgements

This book is the product of dialogue with colleagues and students over a long period of university teaching and research. I would like to thank in particular Professor Ben Knights at the University of Teesside, England for reading and commenting on the individual chapters in draft, and especially chapters 4 and 5, which benefited from his own work on "masculinities". He also kindly allowed me to read his chapter on Conrad and Lawrence in draft before the publication of his book, *Writing Masculinities: Male Narratives in Twentieth-Century Fiction* (1999). I am grateful to the University of Teesside for granting me sabbatical leave to work on the book during the second semester, 1998. I would also like to thank Professor Stephan Kohl at the University of Würzburg, Germany for his encouragement at the start of this project, when I was teaching in Germany. His comments on earlier drafts of chapters 1 and 2 have been instructive and enabling for the development of the whole study. Any faults that remain are of course the responsibility of the author alone.

Special thanks go to Shona Davie for her invaluable assistance with the final stages of copy-editing and proofreading.

An earlier version of part of chapter 1 was published as "Libidinal Structure and the Representation of Desire in *Sons and Lovers*" in *The Journal of the D.H. Lawrence Society* (Summer 1995). A revised and summary version of the theoretical survey in chapter 1 was published as "The Fate of Psychoanalytic Literary Criticism" in Rüdiger Ahrens and Laurenz Volkmann eds, *Why Literature Matters: Theories and Functions of Literature* (Heidelberg: Universitätsverlag C. Winter, 1996). Some of the implications of chapter 1 for Lacanian criticism have been developed into two papers: "Symbolization in Psychoanalysis and Literature: Lacanian readings of the 'poetic metaphor' in D.H. Lawrence" forthcoming in *The Hungarian Journal of English and American Studies* and "The Symptomatic Text: Symbolization in Psychoanalysis and Literature" forthcoming in *Symbolism: An International Journal of Critical Aesthetics*. An earlier version of part of the Foucauldian reading in chapter 2 was published as "The Discursive Formations of History in D.H. Lawrence, *The Rainbow*" in *Anglia: Zeitschrift für Englische Philologie*, 115/3 (1997). The bibliographic research for chapter 3 was published as "Lawrence and Germany: An Introduction", in: *Lawrence and Germany: A Bibliography*, compiled by Michael Weithmann and Regina Hoffmann (Passau: University of Passau Library, 1995).

To

H.T.

Contents

Introduction

The Critical Formations of Lawrence Studies

> But there is more to be said about Lawrence; much more than was usually said in the days when he was celebrated as a prophet of straight liberation and more than is often said when he is castigated from the vantage point of contemporary sexual politics.[1]

In the most dominant and persistent of critical formations, D.H. Lawrence has occupied a central place in the construction of an English literary tradition since the mid-1950s, coming at the end of F.R. Leavis's "Great Tradition" of English "moral realism". The importance of Lawrence was promoted by Richard Hoggart and Raymond Williams, carrying forward the original impetus of Leavis into the broader cultural study of regional literature (Lawrence's Nottinghamshire and Derbyshire), the working-class novel (his "autobiographical" fiction, *Sons and Lovers*, 1913), and the radical challenge to Edwardian and Georgian England of writing about sexual feelings, now reinscribed in a discourse of a newer morality, an openness to "true feelings" prefigured in Hoggart's spirited defence of *Lady Chatterley's Lover* before the official censor at the beginning of the 1960s. As a direct result of Leavis's Lawrence, the Lawrence of the early 1960s was the "sexual liberator" of men and women, the "priest of love". Yet the young women of 1969 were asking how their mothers could have so foolishly believed that Lawrence was on their side. Moreover, if such readers were feeling the need for a "new" Lawrence, then it was high time literary criticism argued their case. The women's movement of the 1970s, now espousing "sexual politics", and taking their lead from the attack on Lawrence by Kate Millett, recast him as the arch-misogynist. The former champion of the new morality, placed as such by a dominant English tradition of moral criticism, would now be the very example of everything patriarchy has done to women. Thus from about 1969 "our greatest living author" (Leavis) became unreadable.

---

[1] Jonathan Dollimore, *Sexual Dissidence: Augustine to Wilde, Freud to Foucault* (Oxford: Clarendon Press, 1991), 269.

Yet, the early feminist polemic against Lawrence and his supporters rarely gets beyond the transparent biographical reading, thus remaining broadly within the same critical practice as the Leavisites, even while opposing them on ideological grounds. Feminist criticism, though, has developed since the early 1970s, rejecting its early monologic and essentialist readings, with their generalizations about Lawrence's antipathy to women, to take account of the complexities of narrative, and the ironic contexts of the ideas in the fiction which problematize the relationship between the author and his characters. Indeed, more theory-based work on literature has also enabled a more thoroughgoing rejection of the Leavisite formation as well as the early feminist Lawrence criticism. But the impact of post-structuralist theory on Lawrence studies has been negligible. Even since the publication of the Centenary Essays in 1985, when there was, in fact, a general return to Lawrence, the challenge of the broader work being done on rereading or rethinking literature after the lessons of theory has only had a superficial effect on Lawrence. This now includes the latest turn in Lawrence studies sparked off by the belated publication of his comic novel, *Mr Noon*. Now Lawrence is read for the comic tone, the parodies, and the ironies, which dominate a frame of mind emerging around the time of the writing of *Women in Love* (1916). But this newer reading is without any substantive theorizing.

Thus, it is an important task for literary and cultural studies to bring Lawrence and post-structuralist theory together. This work should begin by deconstructing the single-minded positions on Lawrence and their partial literary histories, placing their iconography and demonology in a cultural history of discursive practices in order to analyse the relationship between these methodologies of criticism and their objects. In this way, the works of literature themselves, in their aesthetic complexities, may enable us to read the works of literary criticism. In other words, we should not allow things to be a one-way passage, only testing the adequacy of a specific theory to a specific novel. Thus, by bringing Lawrence and theory together in this study, I will investigate to what extent theory is transfigured in the process by the levels of resistance to it in Lawrence's writing. Indeed, his modernist experiments in style and structure offer degrees of resistance to the tendency of any one theory to reduce the text to the limits of its respective master code. I shall, therefore, be concerned with the extent to which interpretive strategies need reformulating before they can accommodate the poetic in Lawrence's writing, especially in its specific developments of an "aesthetic structure" in the form of the ambivalent symbol as recurrent motif in *Sons and Lovers* and *The Rainbow*; in parody and satire in *Women in Love, The Lost Girl*, and *Mr Noon*; in the deconstructive effects which enable us to read the phallocentricism of *Aaron's Rod, Kangaroo, The Plumed Serpent*, and *Lady Chatterley's Lover* against itself.

Lawrence has always been provocative of extreme responses in his critics. He has been read as representing quite opposed and seemingly incompatible positions: for some a moralist, for others an offender of public morals and taste; the first working-class writer and yet ambivalent towards his class origins; deeply religious vitalist and proto-fascist; a crucial force in the struggle for sexual emancipation, and a persistent misogynist. The struggle over Lawrence has been long and hard. It was for a long time difficult to say simply that Lawrence was a modernist, just as it has become impossible to agree with Leavis that he was exclusively in the tradition of the great moralist-realists of English literature. As I argue in this study, the polarization of critics into the pro-modernist and pro-realist camps has been at best reductionist. Lawrence's writing is structured by a number of different and often contradictory representative codes; and recent critical theories have produced a much more elastic understanding of Modernism than has hitherto been in circulation in Lawrence studies.

Even though strong readings have dominated Lawrence's work from the earliest assessments to the dispute within feminist criticism over his representation of women, there has surprisingly been a singular reluctance to approach Lawrence through theory as it is understood in post-structuralism. The exceptions are few and far between. Doherty has drawn attention to the predominance of the force of older critical paradigms: "Clearly Lawrence still attracts mainly traditional critics who focus on themes, evaluations and sources, and who find in his work precisely the kind of bulwark for those values which seem threatened by those theoretical approaches which they reject."[2] You do not have to go back too far in the history of reception for an example. Bell, in an otherwise intelligent, philosophical study of Lawrence's ontology, explicitly rejects French critical theory as irrelevant to Lawrence. Instead, he approaches Lawrence through Heidegger and Cassirer because they are his "near contemporaries". This is a strange use of historicism to undermine the more recent critical reception (and Doherty's in particular), which attempts rereadings through the newer critical paradigms. Theory is rejected on the grounds that it works from totally different premises to those of Lawrence and his contemporaries: "Lawrence's sense of language needs to be understood in its own terms before it can

---

[2] Gerald Doherty, "White Mythologies: Lawrence and the Deconstructive Turn", *Criticism*, XXIX/4 (Fall 1987), 477.

usefully be seen through Derrida's."[3] But Derrida would agree that we begin with the terms proposed by the author, before going on to read them against themselves. Yet, despite his anti-theory stance (and especially his rejection of feminism), Bell mentions Bakhtin and Foucault when it suits his purpose — even though there is no substantive discussion.

Reading Lawrence only "in his own terms" has been the key proposition by those who see every other reading as a false reading. However, this proposition relies on a limited notion of context. Texts are indeed radically situated, in their writing and rewriting, first reading and subsequent rereadings, within different and changing critical formations. Thus, the text does not exist on its own as a transcendent essence. It is always open to new contexts, which include those of the author and his readers. Moreover, if you really read Lawrence "in his own terms" then you would be more on the side of Derrida than traditional Lawrence criticism has acknowledged. For Doherty, "Lawrence in certain contexts ... like Derrida, is an ardent deconstructor of logocentric modes of completion and closure". They both envisage "a disarticulation from within the Western ontotheological tradition which determines how the human mind constitutes itself and how things are known. In this context both the novelist and the philosopher have Nietzsche as a strong precursor". More recently, the recognition of this common Nietzschean affinity between the Modernism of the early twentieth century and the post-structuralism of today has argued for a quite different relevance between contemporary theory and the early writing. As I argue in this study, Lawrence's deconstruction of the old stable ego reinscribes newer fragile senses of self in the narrative fiction, which then have epistemological implications for the form of the novel. The instabilities of writing, from *Women in Love* onwards, transform the novels into sites for the play of meaning. Therefore, just as Lawrence was becoming more doctrinaire, especially in his turn against women and his advocacy of male leadership, the fiction was becoming more experimental.

A principal claim of my study, then, is that the fiction writing has deconstructive effects on the doctrine. To quote Doherty once more: "One could demonstrate ... that those discursive structures in which difference is liquidated in the drive towards an ultimate wholeness are traversed by rhetorical forces which at once ground and dissolve all such movement towards synthesis."[4] I am not simply claiming that Lawrence

---

[3] Michael Bell, *D.H. Lawrence: Language and Being* (Cambridge: Cambridge University Press, 1991), 234.
[4] Doherty, 477, 485.

was a profoundly contradictory writer. What I want to argue is that, first, post-structuralist criticism reinstates the textuality of Lawrence's writing, enabling us to see it as much more radically modernist than traditional criticism allowed. And, second, that the theory approaches called upon in this study do justice in their different methods to Lawrence's own claims that his fiction was a testing out of his doctrine (a "thought-adventure"), and that we should trust the tale not the author. Middleton, in writing about *The Rainbow*, says, "I doubt whether anyone has plans for a post-structuralist Lawrence".[5] My book assesses the possibilities of radicalizing Lawrence through recent theory.

Doherty has not been alone in making deconstructive claims for Lawrence. Fernihough is exemplary: "Paradoxically enough, in view of Lawrence's current reputation, his attack on logocentrism and on a model of language which assumes a bounded, coherent self in mastery of an objective, outer world, links him to contemporary French feminist theory." Precisely what that link might be I explore in chapter 6. Fernihough goes on to suggest that, as Lawrence's "strident didacticism is notorious", we should accept his invitation "to read against the grain", because it should be "ultimately, both productive and liberating".[6] She speaks for Lawrence and Derrida here. When Derrida writes about the deconstructive effects of texts he might as well have been writing directly on Lawrence:

> For instance, some works which are highly "phallocentric" in their semantics [he has Joyce in mind], their intended meaning, even their theses, can produce paradoxical effects, paradoxically anti-phallocentric through the audacity of a writing which in fact disturbs the order or the logic of phallocentrism or touches on limits where things are reversed: in that case the fragility, the precariousness, even the ruin of order is more apparent.[7]

In chapters 4 and 5, I put Derrida's claims about the deconstructive effects of texts to work on the "leadership" novels, demonstrating in detail that it is because textual signification is in excess of originary intention that texts can have deconstructive effects, and can be read

[5] Peter Middleton, *The Inward Gaze: Masculinity and Subjectivity in Modern Culture* (London: Routledge, 1992), 68.
[6] Anne Fernihough, *D.H. Lawrence: Aesthetics and Ideology* (Oxford: Clarendon Press, 1993), 14.
[7] Jacques Derrida, "That Strange Institution Called Literature: An Interview with Jacques Derrida", in *Acts of Literature*, edited and introduced by Derek Attridge (New York and London: Routledge, 1992), 50.

differently according to the changing contexts of critical formations. It is the greatest weakness of the so-called "anti-theorists" in Lawrence studies that they refuse to recognize these complex and creative processes of text, contexts and reading. As Burke has argued, there is an enabling difference between "the programmatic intention (what the author set out to say) and the operative intention (what his text ends up saying)".[8] And as if that process were not complex enough, there is the further complication of interpretation: the text as an object of criticism. In deconstructing the history of reception, competing interpretations are interrogated for the critical assumptions which frame the way the text is read. The reading and reception of Lawrence's narrative fiction plays a major role in this study. Criticism which claims to read Lawrence "in his own terms" is highly problematic.

In 1985, Lodge claimed that post-structuralist theory had ignored Lawrence. In trying to account for this Lodge writes the following: "a writer whose work is so intensely personal, expressive and polemical as Lawrence's doesn't attract critics who maintain that the idea of the author is a fiction, a mere 'function of discourse'."[9] Lodge goes on to read Lawrence through Bakhtin, and with some relief as the latter reinstates the author in the creative process after he had long been declared dead. I discuss the uses of Bakhtin in recent Lawrence studies in chapter 3. But Lodge's understanding of "the death of the author" is inadequate. It is a misunderstanding that, once recognized as such, takes the force out of the anti-theorist arguments. We need to turn to Burke's discussion to see how misinformed Lodge and many others have been about "the death of the author".

Clearly, in the 1960s and early 1970s, when reference to the author as originating authority had been discredited, structuralism made dealing with texts that demonstrate a lively authorial presence problematic. But even since the end of structuralism, theorists have continued to look on Lawrence studies as a largely enclosed specialism with its continuing bibliographic and biographic work, exemplified in the Cambridge University Press editions of Lawrence's works. However, there, the editors have produced texts that demonstrate the complex relationship between author and publisher's editor at times when Lawrence's idea of the novel was not widely understood. What this implies are notions of an author-function and an authorial inscription which post-structuralist

[8] Seán Burke, *The Death and the Return of the Author: Criticism and Subjectivity in Barthes, Foucault and Derrida* (Edinburgh: Edinburgh University Press, second edition, 1998, first published 1992), 141.
[9] David Lodge, "D.H. Lawrence: Genius, Heretic, Classic", reprinted in *Write On: Occasional Essays 1965-1985* (London: Penguin, 1986), 192.

theory — in the work of Barthes, Foucault and Derrida — has already theorized; a theory that has had little purchase on Lawrence scholarship. When Barthes wrote his seminal paper "The Death of the Author" (1968), it was not to be taken literally. The author was not henceforth banned from literary studies. Barthes was actually opposing conventional biographicist criticism, which assumed the work's meaning was traceable to the author's intention, and the unity and coherence of the work derived from the unity and coherence of the writer's self (a notion derived from the Romantic tradition with its propositions of authorial "genius" and "original composition"). The obsession with biography, both in the public sphere and in academic scholarship, necessarily leads Barthes to overstate his case. Yet, clearly, the author's intention and his own reading of his fiction are only part of the greater semiotic process of text, context and reading. In any case, Lawrence's writing-life does not offer us a stable point of reference for the interpretation and significance of his works, as the three-volume Cambridge biography has demonstrated. Linda Ruth Williams' warning should be heeded: "It is easy to slip into unthinking psychobiography with Lawrence's work because he is such a polemicist, writing from a central 'I' subject position despite the glaring contradictions of that 'I', and despite its own famous protestation, 'Never trust the artist, trust the tale'."[10] We should not assume that the author-ego of Lawrence's essays or his literary criticism is the same as that of the travel writing, or the poetry, or the fiction. Moreover, Lawrence's writing-life is characterized by discontinuities and contradictions too.

As I argue throughout this study, the biographic-minded critics who dominate Lawrence studies ought to appreciate the senses in which the complex semiotic and aesthetic processes of signification in the fictional texts take us a long way from the autobiographical, even when the latter is one of the textual codes in Lawrence's case. Eggert, adopting Foucault's concept,[11] writes of the "author-function", "Lawrence", suggesting ways to get beyond the "unignorable presence" of the author, Lawrence, in his writings. Eggert is not just referring to the many Lawrences constructed by the biographies, personal reminiscence, anecdotes, rumours or gossip — like the popular legends of sexual scandal, demonography, or the "priest of love" — as "the text *Lawrence* is variously constituted and reconstituted". But, rather, what is at stake is that authorial intrusiveness, often only thinly disguised as implied author

---

[10] Linda Ruth Williams, *Sex in the Head: Visions of Femininity and Film in D.H. Lawrence* (New York and London: Harvester Wheatsheaf, 1993), 18.
[11] See Michel Foucault, "What is an Author?", reprinted in Donald F. Bouchard ed., *Michel Foucault — Language, Counter-Memory, Practice: Selected Essays and Interviews* (Ithaca, New York: Cornell University Press, 1977).

or a character speaking for the author in the doctrinal passages of writing, which continues to mislead critics and editors alike into transparent readings of the author's "original word". Such critics and editors — and Eggert numbers the editors of the Cambridge editions of the works amongst them — continue, therefore, to work with a conception of the author as the sole authority for the text's meaning and significance, returning the edited and cut texts to Lawrence's original version, and calling this then the "authentic" work. However, as Eggert claims, this argument overlooks the more complex copy produced by the collaboration of publisher's reader and author (and we might add the other collaborators in Lawrence's writing-life — all of them women). Restoring the cuts to texts like *Aaron's Rod*, as I demonstrate in chapter 4, has been crucial. But editorial reading, and further draft work, was always important, and Lawrence must have worked hard at it — as the rather unfinished quality of *Mr Noon* makes clear. For Lawrence in particular, authorship should be understood as a participatory activity. As Eggert rightly insists: "In an age when textual meaning is held by some theorists to be plural and constantly reconstituted, and by others to be radically indeterminate, for editors to seek to confine textual possibilities to those the author intended may seem antediluvian." Such questions concerning the genesis of the text need to be taken into account: "Clearly, for Lawrence the activity of authorship was a continuum: always subject to new stimulus, influence and experiment. His published volumes only partially represent this continuity, their inadequacy accentuated by a publisher's reader's extensive involvement."[12]

   As Barthes formulated it, "[t]o give a text an Author is to impose a limit on that text, to finish it with a final signified, to close the writing".[13] It might, though, be more enabling, and closer to the process of textualization, to propose the "dialogic author".[14] Like the *"bricoleur"* of structuralism, Bakhtin's artisanal writer is allowed more creative agency in the "architectonics" of textual construction (see chapter 3 for detailed discussion) than Barthes' author-scribe who is only a "cipher of codes". Designating Lawrence as "dialogic author" allows us to grant him agency in the production of text, in a return to first contexts, even while bringing into play subsequent contexts of reading, and continuing to work with Barthes' definition of a text as "a multidimensional space in which a variety of writings, none of them original, blend and clash. The text is a

[12] Paul Eggert, "Opening up the Text: the Case of *Sons and Lovers*", in Keith Brown ed., *Rethinking Lawrence* (Buckingham: Open University Press, 1990), 39, 40, 51.
[13] Roland Barthes, "The Death of the Author", reprinted in Stephen Heath ed., *Image-Music-Text* (Glasgow: Fontana, 1977), 147.
[14] Burke, 24.

tissue of quotations drawn from the innumerable centres of culture".[15] In chapter 2, I read *The Rainbow* through Foucault's notion of the discursive formation of history, drawing out the contradictory structure of discourses that underpin the text even while enabling the construction of a cultural history (a history of sexuality). In chapter 3, the author emerges as a "carnivalized subject", as the fiction turns to a "furious comedy" exemplified in *Mr Noon*.

This discussion of authorship is further complicated by the modernist aesthetic of impersonality (T.S. Eliot) and its development into the anti-intentionalism of the American New Criticism, in the one formation; and the Russian Formalist priority of textual structure and reading-effect over biography, and its development into the typologizing work of structuralism, in the other formation. While, clearly, Lawrence needs to be read against Eliot's impersonality aesthetic, additionally the return to the author and signature in post-structuralism should be brought into play. As Burke argues, after Derrida, the boundary between life and work has become much more fluid and "enigmatic". In a neat reversal of Barthes' seminal formulation, Burke asks: "Yet might we not venture that the birth of the reader is not achieved at the cost of the death of the author, but rather at that of showing how the critic *too* becomes an author?"[16] Since his 1960s philosophical work, Derrida has taken up a position on signature and intentionality that has seldom been acknowledged. In "Signature, Event, Context" he argues that, in Burke's words:

> Intention is to be recognized, and respected, but on condition that we accept that its structures will not be fully and ideally homogenous with what is said or written, that is not always and everywhere completely adequate to the communicative act .... [I]ntention itself is not thereby cancelled but rather lodged within a broader signifying process.[17]

Textual signification is in excess of originary intention and is one of several inscriptions in a textualization that it no longer dominates. Lawrence is close to Derrida when he claims that his fiction writing is a "thought-adventure" where the doctrine is exposed for its contradictions. (I discuss the deconstructive effects on phallocentricity in the "leadership" novels in chapters 4 and 5.) For, as Burke puts it: "It is only in

---

[15] Barthes, 147. Barthes notoriously reinstates the author in *S/Z*, where Balzac emerges as the "*bricoleur*" and the "dialogic author" at one and the same time.

[16] Burke, 61. Emphasis in original.

[17] Burke, 140.

terms of this reconstruction that the deconstructor can begin to separate
that which belongs to authorial design from that which eludes or unsettles
its prescriptions." Lawrence, though, encourages the deconstruction —
and most Lawrence critics have not read his fictional texts in their own
terms at all. We need to account for the creative disjunction between what
the author set out to say (accessed through the letters, for instance), and
what the text ends up saying (to us and to others in given contexts and
critical formations). This is what Burke means by the disjunction
between the "programmatic intention" and the "operative intention".
However, we should not leave out of account the critic's intention —
which would range from the early feminist attacks to those who seek to
"rescue" Lawrence from accusations of pornography, fascism and
sexism.

There is, therefore, a new theorizing about the relationship between
the author and the work that does not return to older forms of biographical positivism, yet gets beyond the programmatic limits of American
New Criticism and French structuralism to attempt a post-semiotic
reworking of the "connection between *bios* and *graphé*".[18] Additionally,
the New Historicism, Cultural Materialism, and Postcolonial theory have
insisted on a return to context and history which situate text and authorial
subjectivity in the shifting contexts of production and reception. Critics
who have worked with older notions of author, context and history have
not done justice to Lawrence. Post-structuralist theorizing, as this study
will attempt to demonstrate, should radicalize Lawrence while reassess-
ing his significance in the cultural history of Modernism. In Derrida's
words: "Like all valuable readings of literature, they seek to make the
text strange (or perhaps strangely familiar), offering not a reduced and
simplified version of the text but one which operates at its own level of
difficulty."[19] Thus bringing theory to Lawrence is an affirmative strategy,
radicalizing what has hitherto been reduced to the transparencies and
positivisms of traditional, anti-theoretical criticism. The terms in which
Lawrence's work has been praised or dismissed have denied it its
potential radical force. The newer notions of textuality deconstruct the
older concept of unity and meaning. To quote Derrida once again:
"'Good' literary criticism, the only worthwhile kind, implies an act, a
literary signature or counter-signature, an inventive experience of
language, an inscription of the act of reading in the field of the text that is
read."[20]

---

[18] Burke, 141, 188.
[19] Derrida, cited in Attridge, 17.
[20] Derrida, 52.

Surveying the history of the reception of Lawrence, Widdowson proposes a couple of crucial dates which then act as watersheds — that is to say, significant moments in recent history where literary criticism took a radical turn in direction, in general and in Lawrence studies. Up to 1968, literary criticism was largely celebratory of Lawrence and his works. The critics were divided into two camps: there was the Leavis/Spilka camp, exemplified in Britain by F.R. Leavis, *D.H. Lawrence: Novelist*; and in the USA with the essays collected in the widely read *Twentieth Century Views* series. Then there was the Kermode/Clarke camp, exemplified in Kermode's *Fontana Modern Masters: Lawrence* (1973), and Clarke's *River of Dissolution: D.H. Lawrence and English Romanticism* (1969), and especially in the widely read collection of essays in Clarke ed., *Macmillan Casebook Series: The Rainbow and Women in Love* (1969). The first camp (Leavis/Spilka) read Lawrence as the critic of modern industrial civilization, celebrating a return to the traditional moral and the spiritual virtues of a healthy attitude to life; the last of the great English Realists. The second camp (Kermode/Clarke) read Lawrence as the prophet of doom and apocalypse, the promoter of the demonic and Dionysian in his rage against the conformities of modern civilized existence. In this formation, Lawrence is the last of the Romantics, and part of European Modernism. After 1968, Lawrence is constructed and reconstructed as a cultural figure, a product of one cultural effect or another, demon or icon, in a struggle over his meaning and significance. And for Widdowson, it is the Marxist and the Feminist readings from the late 1960s onwards which set the agenda for that political struggle over Lawrence. Moreover, there was, of course, a lot more at stake than the fortunes of one writer: nothing more nor less than English Studies itself. Lawrence had been central to the "Rise of English" from the start, and his canonical and iconic status was to become central to the battle over Patriarchy and Theory at one and the same time. Indeed, Lawrence offers us a focus for a cultural history.

By the late 1980s, things become less polarized, as post-structuralist thought about the instability of language and the indeterminacy of meaning causes a shift towards more relativist criticism. Now meanings are determined by positions taken, and texts are recognized for their indeterminacies. The upshot of this latest shift in the fortunes of literary criticism has been that Lawrence's texts are now seen for what they always were: objects of critical practices and not the unmediated essence that pre-post-structuralist criticism assumed. Reading Lawrence should now always be tied up with reading the conflicting critical constructions in a history of reception, which is not a smooth development, but a series of discontinuities. Criticism has finally lost its innocence.

Widdowson's history makes a lot of sense. It justifies, of course, his selection of representative criticism, which covers that post-1968 struggle over Lawrence. His own leanings are decidedly on the New British Left, with its advocacy of a broader Cultural Materialism for English Studies; and in this it has shaped the way things are today in the British Universities. However, Widdowson is at pains to stress the key role played by feminism in general and particularly in Lawrence studies. He writes: "If sex and sexuality had been a key issue in the sixties — both generally and in relation to Lawrence — it was rapidly reinflected thereafter as gender, and Lawrence who had been perceived as a guru of sexual liberation became the phallocratic oppressor of gender politics." Lawrence is "indelibly feminized".[21] At the same time, on the political Left, the recognition of the importance of class in the novels was transformed into the claims for the fascist mythologizer of the newer cultural politics of the 1970s.

Now, I think that the exclusive Left emphasis of Widdowson's position leads him to neglect two major radical strands in the reception of Lawrence, namely the Freudian and the Bakhtinian. His only gesture towards psychoanalysis is the inclusion of Eagleton — a fellow Marxist — on *Sons and Lovers*. And I demonstrate in chapter 1 just how limited that reading is for psychoanalytic criticism. It would seem that in order for Widdowson to be able to say that gender replaces sexuality he has to suppress the presence of psychoanalytic criticism which would demonstrate a different history, where sexuality is always prior to gender because it is more fundamental to the unconscious forces of being, in the first instance. Gender difference is precisely the tip of the sexual iceberg. Gender difference is questioned in any case by Lawrence's theories and representations of sexuality. Drawing attention to Widdowson's exclusion of psychoanalytic criticism, in his introductory history and his selection of critics, enables me to take his main point about the cultural-ideological construction of readings and turn it back on his own history of Lawrence, thus making central precisely what he has marginalized. As he so rightly puts it:

> For we may now perceive that all that critical praxis ever is, is the continual production of past writing within and on behalf of present cultural history; that literature exists only to be shaped and recuperated by and for its moment of consumption ... that every historical moment "writes" the literature it wishes to read largely

---

[21] Peter Widdowson, "Post-Modernizing Lawrence", Introduction to the *Longman Critical Reader: D.H. Lawrence* (Harlow: Longman, 1992), 10, 16.

by way of the ceaseless flow of ephemeral monographs and col-
lections of critical essays.[22]

Widdowson is not wrong about that radical history since the late 1960s. It
just seems incomplete to me.

The next major point in his argument is that the cultural politics of
the 1970s and 1980s paved the way for post-structuralism and its
deconstructive readings, by recognizing that "meaning only exists within
history, is not permanently fixed, is contingent and determinate, is not
owned by any one interest". Now we see just how unstable and self-
deconstructing Lawrence's texts are. But are they unstable and self-
deconstructing because they are the objects of those post-structuralist
theories of shifting and unstable signifiers, and the indeterminate play of
meaning? Or do Lawrence's texts have a necessary instability as
modernist writing? In any case, one thing we should find ourselves
agreeing with is that developments in critical theory over the last twenty
years which "thoroughly inform critical practice ... can re-present
Lawrence in a guise quite unlike that which he bore some twenty years
earlier".[23]

Of course, Lawrence always existed in several versions. As Raymond
Williams argued in his 1985 foreword to a collection of centenary essays,
we can identify three dominant versions of Lawrence: (i) the last novelist
of the great English tradition of moral realism (with his individualist
critique of industrial civilization); (ii) the first major working-class writer
who establishes a tradition that leads to the work of Alan Sillitoe and
David Storey (among others); (iii) the "pioneer of a new kind of
understanding and presentation of sexuality" which is meant to go
beyond class. The question is: can all these versions be correct?[24] In this
study, I argue that they can.

The next question is: can Lawrence's work be seen as a whole?
Should we not, rather, give credit to the view that his work is predominantly discontinuous, restlessly unsettled? The cultural impact of
Lawrence is important now to any study of his works. Referring to
Widmer's 1987 paper, "Lawrence's Cultural Impact", Widdowson
suggests three principal areas of impact: "the feminist-misogynist
disputes; the obscenity-censorship conflicts; and the problematic role as a
prophet of enlarged eroticism." Are any of these wrong? The answer

---

[22] Widdowson, 11.
[23] Ibid., 17.
[24] Williams, foreword to *The Spirit of D.H. Lawrence: Centenary Essays*, edited by
Gamini Salgado and G.K. Das (London: Macmillan, 1988), vii.

seems to be that Lawrence was indeed "both sensitively sympathetic to women and an extreme male chauvinist". But this is only a problem if you think you must have a single unified view, based on an older paradigm of textual unity, and one that demonstrates the author's consistency on such important matters. These versions of Lawrence are constructed by strongly opposed positions in a cultural history of reception. But they are also provoked to a certain extent by "the radically unstable discourse that Lawrence's work seems to be".[25]

The full consequence of post-structuralist criticism leads us into the bind of the text as object of deconstructive reading and at the same time as a mirror reflecting the concerns of the critic. Indeterminacy turns out to be a function of Lawrence's writing, "a function of its own 'impossible' desire to achieve both 'the passionate struggle into conscious being' and 'the struggle for verbal consciousness'". So Lawrence is now a proto-deconstructionist: his novels deconstruct themselves, because everything that is asserted is then denied, where the constructedness of everything is laid bare in that defamiliarizing way of Modernism. Lawrence creates discourses of love and sex out of the available languages, but then shows them to be limited — because he has to get beyond words, which of course is impossible. If we cannot trust the writer, it seems that we cannot trust the tale either. But, as post-structuralists, we always already knew that. The more Lawrence's writings become the objects of newer theoretically informed literary criticism, the more complex they become. Reading the old traditional criticism shows us how it misses so much in Lawrence. However, to do justice to Lawrence we need a criticism that is not only a deconstructive play of meaning, as if anything goes.[26] What we need is interplay between text, history and criticism that accounts for the changing contexts of production and reception in their critical formations, including the first contexts.

In the chapters that follow, I argue that the provisionality of even forceful positions on Lawrence is already reflected in Lawrence's fictional texts, which are characterized by stylistic and narrative experiment even while trying to insist on forms of ontological essentialism. The different critical theory approaches in this study enable a reassessment of Lawrence's relationship to Modernism, first because the newer textual theories are able to draw out the radical experiments in Lawrence's writing that have often gone unnoticed by critics working

---

[25] Widdowson, 19, 20.
[26] Cf. John Worthen's critique of Linda Ruth Williams for her lack of understanding Lawrence's polemical position in his day, in his review of *Sex in the Head*, in the *Journal of the D.H. Lawrence Society*, (1996), 75.

with older critical paradigms; and second, because critical theory has produced a more elastic concept of Modernism of which traditional Lawrence scholars seem largely unaware.

In this study, I use the term "critical theory" in its loose sense of theories of criticism (as opposed to the stricter sense of the *Kritische Theorie* of the Frankfurt School), and in particular post-structuralist theory. I avoid the confusion with the term "literary theory" because it carries with it connotations of theories of literature (even when there is a discussion running through this study of Lawrence's theory of the novel).

In chapter 1, I approach *Sons and Lovers* through psychoanalytic criticism, which has played a principal role in its reception. Indeed, it was celebrated by the early Freudians as an "Oedipal novel". I examine that reception in the light of developments within psychoanalytic criticism. My two claims are that, first, the fate of psychoanalytic criticism is mirrored in the reception of *Sons and Lovers*; and second, that the potential of psychoanalytic theory — in Freud and Lacan — has never really paid off in the practice of psychoanalytic readings of Lawrence's text. The chapter, thus, consists of: (i) a historical and conceptual description of the fate of psychoanalytic criticism; (ii) a critical survey of the Freudian and post-Freudian reception of *Sons and Lovers*; (iii) a Lacanian reading of the "libidinal text". In this reading, working in some detail with the text of *Sons and Lovers*, I argue that Freud's "family romance" should be reread through the Lacanian ontology of the Imaginary, the Symbolic, and the Real. Then, I look at the tropes of metaphor and metonymy as symptom and desire, respectively, which enable a psychoanalytic reading of the textual representation of sexuality. There are many instances in Lawrence's writing of the metonymic displacement of unconscious desire onto the body of the other, formally incorporated in the text through the technical process of focalization, whereby desire fetishizes parts of the body as they come into the focus of the gazing subject. Perception is invaded by unconscious desire, the object-body broken into bits and pieces in a libidinized representation. Aesthetic structures and unconscious forces are brought together through the "creative metaphor" in Lawrence — often in the form of expression-ism. This chapter concentrates on examples of such writing, and the possibilities for their psychoanalytic explanation.

In chapter 2, I attempt a Foucauldian reading of *The Rainbow*. His-tory plays a major role in its critical reception. The real historical reference and the family history are complicated by their framing in an archetypal or mythic history. The critical reception has been dominated by two other, opposed kinds of history: F.R. Leavis' "essential English history", and Frank Kermode's apocalyptic history, a vision of spiritual decline that, through the catastrophe of the Great War, would lead to spiritual regeneration. In order to enable a constructive mediation between these different theories of history, this chapter draws on the work of Michel Foucault. Instead of discussing the novel and history as discrete entities with history serving as background, context, or influence, as much of the critical reception has it, Foucault enables such static distinctions to be problematized by turning the discussion towards discourse, thus keeping things close enough to the texts of fiction and history while seeing the traces of history in the discursive practices represented in the novel. The discourses that emerge from such a reading are: the myth of origins; evolution and its modern inversion in spiritual decline; organicism, an aspect of Lawrence's neo-Romanticism and his ontological essentialism; the scientific metaphors deriving from electromagnetism for the representation of a polarized sexual relationship; the Christian discourse of the Flesh; and the Nietzschean will-to-power. Foucault's theories of discourse and discursive practice enable an historical analysis of subject formations that has broader social and political implications. Here, the fictional subject is constituted in and by discourses, so that it is less an essence more an effect, or series of paradoxical effects, of diverse discourses. Indeed, Foucauldian theory is appropriate to the analysis of a Lawrence novel in which the character represents a disunified, complex subjectivity; a modernist representation which displaces the old stable ego of the autonomous subject.

Foucault also enables us to theorize the extent to which Lawrence's works are themselves subject to the force of the available discourses of sexuality. How original is Lawrence's representation of sexuality? His writing belongs to the entire modern discursive formation of the sexual — the construction of what is called "sexuality" — not least because his works consist of a set of representations (images, discourses, ways of describing the sexual). As Foucault argues in *The History of Sexuality*, bodies become saturated with sexuality, just as desirability becomes increasingly important in the construction of subjectivities. Lawrence reinforces the sexual as discourse, as principal characters write their desire on the body of the other. Yet, whereas I approach such a relationship between self and other through a psychoanalytic theorizing in chapter 1, here I apply Foucauldian theories of the subject formed in discourse to emphasize the differentiated, historicized sexual subject — and especially that of the "New Woman". Finally, I put Foucault's theory of literature as transgression to work on Lawrence's text. Although "transgression" belongs to Foucault's early work of the 1960s, typified by his book on Raymond Roussel, and his canon of mad poets, artist and philosophers in *Madness and Civilization* (1961) and *The Order of Things* (1966), it continues to play a role in his later ethics. I believe that the Foucauldian aesthetics of transgression has general implications for assessing Lawrence's Modernism. Lawrence's principal transgression is both linguistic and ethical, as seen in his poetic and audacious (for 1915) representation of sexuality and sex.

Chapter 3 approaches *Women in Love*, *The Lost Girl* and *Mr Noon* through Bakhtin. Since the belated publication of *Mr Noon* in 1984, and the Cambridge University Press *Letters*, there has been a significant shift in Lawrence studies that hinges on an attitude or mood detected in the letters, and corroborated in *Mr Noon*, that emerges around the time of the completion of *Women in Love*. A more self-ironical, cynical attitude towards his work, and especially towards his English reading public, seems to have been set in train by the continual difficulties Lawrence experienced after the banning of *The Rainbow* in 1915. What has emerged is a new sense of the comic in Lawrence, and *Women in Love* and *The Lost Girl* have undergone a retrospective rereading from the standpoint of the burlesque, parody form of *Mr Noon*. Coincidental with the turn towards the comic in Lawrence studies has been the attempt, since 1985, to theorize it through the work of Mikhail Bakhtin. In 1996, Lydia Blanchard confidently declared that, "the approach taken by Bakhtin, with its emphasis on dialogics, dramatizes the inadequacy of most other critical theories of the novel for discussing Lawrence".[27] In this chapter, I engage with the arguments for this new Lawrence and its Bakhtinian theorizing, by tracing this recent history of Bakhtinian Lawrence criticism, and assessing whether Blanchard is justified in her major claim about Lawrence and critical theory. But also, whether we can say, as Widdowson has of Lodge, that Lawrence critics have been "drawing opportunistically" on Bakhtinian theory, neutralizing its radical effects by the adventitious, empiricist "testing" of it on the works.[28] I argue that, indeed, the recent work of Lodge, Fleishman, Blanchard and others, while demonstrating an increasing use of Bakhtin in Lawrence criticism, have not drawn the full implications of Bakhtinian poetics.

The carnivalesque and the dialogic are the two crucially interconnected ideas in Bakhtin. He argued that a novel is a medley of many styles, many languages and voices. The novel contains discourses of various types — as Foucault also argued; but for Bakhtin these discourses cannot be reduced to a single common denominator (Foucault's "episteme"; Lacan's "desire"). The novelist works with "a very rich

---

[27] Lydia Blanchard, "D.H. Lawrence and his 'gentle reader'", reprinted in Paul Eggert and John Worthen eds, *Lawrence and Comedy* (Cambridge: Cambridge University Press, 1996), 107.
[28] Widdowson, 11-12.

verbal palette" (Bakhtin).[29] In "Why the Novel Matters" (1925) Lawrence unwittingly speaks of a Bakhtinian novel. As Lodge puts it (paraphrasing Lawrence): "Of all the forms of human discourse ... [the novel] was the only one which could embrace the totality of human experience, the whole man alive."[30] In *Women in Love, The Lost Girl* and *Mr Noon* Lawrence tries to live up to this ideal, and in doing so produces serio-comic fictions, polyphonous in their discourses and voices, dialogic in their play of ironies. The main thrust of Bakhtin's claim for the novel is precisely its potential for a discursive polyphony, doing justice to the inherent dialogism of language with its complex interweaving of various types of speech — direct, indirect, or doubly-oriented (as in parody); and with its irreverent attitude towards authority and monologistic thought exposed to ridicule in the carnivalesque. Nothing is more irreverent than the "furious comedy" and assault on the reader in *Mr Noon*. Bakhtin's point is that the variety of discourses and the views they propose always serve to dialogize each other, so that any single monologistic argument or world-view in the novel would not evade its ironic or deflationary context. The speech genres in *Women in Love* are dialogized in their situations of context and reception in the novel, thus effecting a play of irony. The dialogic is an essential source of a humour that takes social satire to new levels of bitterness directed at the English aristocracy, the "New Woman", and the chic, metropolitan modern art world. In this chapter, I look in some detail at the stylization of speech genres through the play of intonation and addressivity; and the parodies and self-parodies which reveal a hidden polemic in the internal dialogics of the texts — a polemic that has been emerging through recent Lawrence scholarship as a crisis in his writing-life. A Bakhtinian approach enables that crisis to be seen reflected in the play of style and narrative to different degrees in the three novels, through a closer textual analysis, which also recognizes the historical and biographical frames and contexts. Moreover, it enables a reassessment of Lawrence's relationship to Modernism, which goes beyond the simple choice between his work (serious, philosophical) and that of Joyce (playful, parodic). The Modernism of *The Rainbow* is not the same as the Modernism in the three novels discussed in this chapter.

In chapters 4 and 5, I discuss Lawrence's "leadership" novels in the light of theories of masculinity. The consensus view that Lawrence

---

[29] Mikhail Bakhtin, *Problems of Dostoevsky's Poetics* (London and Minneapolis: University of Minnesota Press, 1984), 201.

[30] David Lodge, *After Bakhtin: Essays on Fiction and Criticism*, (London and New York: Routledge, 1990), 20. D.H. Lawrence, "Why the Novel Matters", in *Phoenix: The Posthumous Papers of D.H. Lawrence,* (London: Heinemann, 1967, first published 1936).

promoted masculine supremacy in phallocentric and phallocratic fictions
has been variously challenged in recent criticism by claiming that it is
precisely here, in these novels of the 1920s, that Lawrence was at his
most experimental, his most modernist. The masculinist doctrine
undergoes degrees of deconstruction in fiction characterized by Lawrence
as "thought-adventure". The ideas expressed categorically in the essays
are tested out in the fiction. However, I go further than the author's own
view by reading the adventure of thought as an adventure of writing, in
which the theories of masculinity are promoted in texts which in their
play of linguistic and representational codes implicitly question fixed
meaning and grand narratives. I argue that a deconstructive approach
enables us to draw out the characterological and textual instabilities
which function to undermine the doctrinaire assertions of male leadership. What is now becoming clearer in Lawrence studies is that the post-
war cultural crisis was also a crisis of the novel. However, nobody would
deny that Lawrence turned more explicitly against women after the First
World War. The essays, fiction, and letters from about 1918 are filled
with what has often been called a hysterical masculinity. It is also now
becoming clearer, though, that the misogyny and the phallocratic beliefs
of the post-war period are, first, emergent already in the earlier fiction,
albeit in less strident form; second, that they belong not only to Lawrence's personal philosophy, but are also part of a general post-war
reaction against the extent of female emancipation; and third, they are
represented in fictional texts characterized by degrees of formal
instability. Lawrence's ongoing quest is not just philosophically utopic,
and predominantly reactionary; it is also a formal enquiry into the future
of the novel. In chapter 4, I discuss Lawrence's ideas for a new masculinity, which emerged from the non-fiction writing in the 1920s, and then
place those ideas in the context of some of the major propositions from
masculinity theory. This is followed by a general discussion of masculinity in recent Lawrence criticism. Then I look in some detail at *Aaron's
Rod*, and then at *Kangaroo* and *The Plumed Serpent* in the next chapter.
In both chapters 4 and 5, I demonstrate the differing extents to which the
masculinist ideas in the "leadership" novels are questioned by the texts
that try to promote them. Lawrence is at his most sceptical in parts of
Aaron's Rod and practically all of *Kangaroo*, his most adventurous and
experimental writing. The doubts are played down in *The Plumed
Serpent*, yet the deconstructive approach teases out the contradictions in
the text to an extent that the earlier feminist readings could not achieve
by their exclusive concentration on the sexual politics. What emerges
from this approach is that, even while seeking to express a doctrinaire
masculine supremacy in reaction to the perceived wilfulness of modern
women and the general post-war cultural disintegration, Lawrence's

writing is much more radical in its modernist experiments than the critical consensus has noticed. Thus, it is that textual instabilities undermine the assertions of ideology. In this, the "leadership" novels belong to the whole play of writing that began with *Women in Love*, and includes *The Lost Girl* and *Mr Noon*, which I discuss in chapter 3. Post-structuralist criticism brings out the warring contradictions in the text because it is not hampered by an older paradigm of textual unity, as so many Lawrentian critics have been. Therefore, following the principle, consistent throughout this study, that Lawrence's writing can only be fully appreciated when scrutinized in detail, I look at the effects of dissemination and play, the textual instabilities which enable a decon-struction of the gender oppositions even while they attempt to establish a new masculine essentialism.

In chapter 6, I revisit the feminist critique of Lawrence with the aim of showing that the more radical literary critical positions within feminism have had little purchase on Lawrence studies. While American and British feminist critics have approached the works through sexual politics, they have generally relied on older critical paradigms. Thus, the author's reputation and his views from the non-fiction have been the starting point for transparent readings of the fictional texts, so that while the approach has been radical as sexual politics, it has been conservative as textual criticism. Kate Millett's sexual politics derived from Simone de Beauvoir's reading of Lawrence. They are both characterized by an unhistoricized approach to the development of Lawrence's work. A quite different French feminism than that of de Beauvoir's, represented by Cixous and Irigaray, has reread sexual politics through the radical textual theories of post-structuralism. I put their concepts of *"écriture féminine"*, *"jouissance"*, and the insistence on a new language of the body to work on *Lady Chatterley's Lover*. I argue that it is here, in post-structuralist French feminism, that we find a critical approach that does justice to Lawrence's poetic representation of female sexuality. Moreover, in the textualization of *"jouissance"*, Lawrence gives female sexuality a moment of autonomy and a value that serve to prioritize it over male phallicism, even while the phallus remains the transcendental signifier. Reading such moments as instances of *"écriture féminine"* avoids the ideological reductionism of American and British sexual politics. However, I take things one step further by bringing the problem of class into the discussion of sexuality. Indeed, a major criticism of post-structuralist French feminism is its general lack of politics, preferring instead to remain within the closed complexities of textual criticism and the cultural generalizations of semiotics. I suggest ways in which *Lady Chatterley* problematizes the relationship between class and sexuality. This involves revisiting the instances of the problematic in *Sons and*

Lovers, *The Rainbow*, and *Women in Love*. I conclude that we need a more post-Althusserian approach to the relationship between text and ideology which insists on the ways in which the workings of ideology become visible in the narrative forms of literature and myth. This should enable a better understanding of the complex relationship between the class ideologies and the sexual ideology that seeks to abolish them, as Lawrence attempts to write class out of the text and mythologize history and social relationships — a process clearly visible in the differences between the three versions of *Lady Chatterley's Lover*, which I discuss in some detail. But also there are complexities between the text and ideology which go beyond the description of its internal contradictions towards its future, a future which lasts a long time, as text-for-criticism and cultural object: the scandal in the text has become a scandal of the text.

In this chapter — and throughout the study — I work with the assumption that a sexual politics without a textual theory is no better than a post-structuralism without politics. My conclusion is that, in *Lady Chatterley's Lover*, class and the force of social conventions hover around in the margins of the text refusing to go away. In the sexual ideology, Connie's sexuality is simplified more and more into an essence to fit better the new phallic tenderness. To do this Lawrence has to abolish her critical consciousness, and her feminism. But the moments of "*jouissance*" defy her reduction to the second sex, as they are high points of aesthetic as well as sexual value. The female imaginary is foregrounded in the text because Connie is so often the focalizing agent. The feminist critique is already articulated in the text. Lawrence does not convince us that the future perfect is masculine. It seems more likely to be feminist: the newly born, blissful woman; the feminized culture; and the feminist reader.

In the conclusion, I argue that, contrary to the fears of those who resist theory because it has its own agendas, and therefore would use Lawrence for its own purposes, once the fictional narratives become texts-for-criticism in the newer paradigms of post-structuralism, their coherences are understood differently. The older notion of textual unity is displaced by aesthetic structures of degrees of generic and linguistic destabilization. I characterize Lawrence's writing as expressionist in *Sons and Lovers* and *The Rainbow*, but more "writerly" in the fiction from *Women in Love* onwards. Thus, I take up a position contrary to those who see *The Rainbow* as *the* Lawrentian novel, with its prose rhythms and repetitions, and its intricate organic form, and who then subsequently declare the writing in the early 1920s chaotic and incomprehensible. What I hope to have shown is that post-structuralist critical paradigms — the psychoanalytic, the discursive, the dialogic, the deconstructive, and the poetry of *"jouissance"* — in producing different senses of coherence than those that have dominated Lawrence studies, have done greater justice to Lawrence's writing.

Because of Lawrence's complex processes of textualization, nothing is achieved without textual detail. And the conclusion I come to is that that detail has displaced the monolithic relationship of Lawrence to Modernism, not least because critical theory has problematized the concept of Modernism itself. Therefore, in this concluding chapter, I offer a few suggestions about an expanded relationship between Lawrence and the problematics of Modernism which go beyond the formal experiments of the narrative fiction to include the question of modernity itself. Here, I compare Lawrence's own ideas about modernity which emerge in the main body of this study with those prominent at the time. Modernity has been described as the experience of the fleeting, the transitory, and the arbitrary. Society is unstable, values are being questioned, conventions seem an empty shell, social relations are subject to instrumentalization or reification. Much of this critique seems to have been registered by Lawrence, as the main body of this study shows. Indeed, as I argue in summary here, Lawrence's aesthetic and his tendency to turn to mythic solutions for the cultural crisis seems to be a compensation for fragmentation in life. At such moments, he has a darker, apocalyptic reaction to modernity, and one that may be characterized as post-Nietzschean and neo-Romantic. As I hope this study demonstrates, Lawrence's modernist writing, in its various forms, has deconstructive effects on his myth-making and his essentialist notions of the self — a creative contradiction, which I seek to elucidate in bringing together Lawrence and critical theory.

1

Sons and Lovers and the Possibility of a Psychoanalytic Criticism

1. Introduction

The reception of *Sons and Lovers*[1] has been dominated by two kinds of reading: the biographical and the Freudian. The latter has so often been called upon to illustrate the former.[2] Both kinds of reading have been through periods of discredit. It has for a long time been considered naive, at least in academic scholarship, to search for the meaning and significance of the text in the life and intentions of the author. Lawrence studies, however, have been dominated by biographical and source studies, not least because the works are exceptionally infused with the life of the author.[3] Indeed, it has recently been suggested that critical theory has largely left Lawrence alone precisely because of that authorial presence in the writing.[4] The hunting for clues to the author's original intentions in the documented life and letters is an ever growing industry,[5] despite the limits to such knowledge for the reader of structurally and aesthetically complex novels. The exclusively biographical reading is reductive.

---

[1] First published by Heinemann, 1913. Page references in text [SL] are to the Penguin edition of the Cambridge D.H. Lawrence (London, 1994).
[2] A tradition which began with Alfred Kuttner's review in *New Republic* (10 April 1915), reprinted in R.P. Draper ed., *D.H. Lawrence: The Critical Heritage,* (London: Routledge, 1979), 76-80. This was then developed into an article, *"Sons and Lovers*: A Freudian Appreciation", *Psychoanalytic Review* (July, 1916), reprinted in Gamini Salgado ed., *Casebook: Sons and Lovers* (London: Macmillan, 1979).
[3] Examples are many and varied: Jessie Chambers, *D.H. Lawrence: A Personal Record* (London: Frank Cass, 1977. First published 1935); cf. xxvi and 184-85, 202-203 for the autobiographical reference to the mother-son relationship in SL. John Middleton Murry, *Son of Woman* (London: Jonathan Cape, 1931). Kate Millett, *Sexual Politics* (London: Virago, 1969).
[4] Paul Eggert, "Opening up the text: the case of *Sons and Lovers*" in Keith Brown ed., *Rethinking Lawrence* (Milton Keynes: Open University Press, 1990), 38-9.
[5] Cf. The Cambridge University Press *Collected Letters*, and editions of the novels and stories with their claim to reinstate Lawrence's original copy. Even the new Penguin editions of the Cambridge University Press editions continue to maintain the claim that these texts are "authoritative", "authentic productions of [Lawrence's] genius" (see "Note on the Penguin Lawrence Edition"). For a critique of their underlying notion of authorship, see Eggert.

Recently, however, there have been signs of change. In the three volumes of the Cambridge biography the authors insist on demonstrating the limits of the fiction as reliable biographical source.[6] Such caution did not characterize the earliest memoirs, or the first Freudian readings.

Sons and Lovers has been identified, from its first reception, with the Oedipus complex, Freudians enthusiastically celebrating it as an "Oedipal novel"[7] — much to Lawrence's public irritation.[8] What has attracted psychoanalytic criticism to the novel has been its intense preoccupation with the mother-son relationship, and this has inevitably lead to speculation about the author's relationship with his mother.[9] The Freudian and post-Freudian psychoanalytic reading has a long history, and in this chapter I shall be looking at some of the key examples.[10]

There is also a history of psychoanalytic criticism. What I shall call the fate of psychoanalytic criticism needs careful understanding: Freudian criticism, once accused of reductionism, was to transform itself into what has best been described as "psycho-textual criticism" (which I shall explain in some detail below). But in its transformation it has become no longer identical with itself. It is now being claimed that, despite all the enthusiasm for Lacan's return to Freud in critical theory,

---

[6] John Worthen, *D.H. Lawrence: The Early Years* (Cambridge: Cambridge University Press, 1991); Mark Kinkead-Weekes, *D.H. Lawrence: Triumph To Exile, 1912-1922* (Cambridge: Cambridge University Press, 1996); David Ellis, *D.H. Lawrence: Dying Game 1922-1930* (Cambridge: Cambridge University Press, 1998).

[7] Kuttner being the first; Eagleton offering a recent critique in *Literary Theory: An Introduction* (Oxford: Blackwell, 1983), ch. 5.

[8] I shall be dealing with Lawrence's quarrel with Freud below.

[9] Kuttner, Chambers, Murry, for instance.

[10] Besides Kuttner, a few examples from a long list would include Frederick J. Hoffmann on Lawrence's quarrel with Freud in *Freudianism and the Literary Mind* (Baton Rouge, Louisiana: Louisiana State University Press, 1957); Daniel A. Weiss, *Oedipus in Nottingham: D.H. Lawrence* (Seattle: University of Washington Press, 1962); A. Kazin, "Sons, Lovers, and Mothers", *Partisan Review*, 29 (1962); Shirley Panken, "Some Psychodynamics in *Sons and Lovers*: A New look at the Oedipal Theme", *Psychoanalytic Review*, 61 (1974); Marguerite Beede Howe, *The Art of the Self in D.H. Lawrence* (Athens Ohio: Ohio University Press, 1977); Giles Mitchell, "*Sons and Lovers* and the Oedipal project", *The D.H. Lawrence Review*, (Fall 1980); Ann Benway, "Oedipus Abroad: Hardy's Clym Yeobright and Lawrence's Paul Morel", in *The Thomas Hardy Yearbook*, 13 (1986); T.H. Adamowski, "The Father of All Things: The Oral and the Oedipal in *Sons and Lovers*", *Mosaic* (Fall 1981); Anne Fernihough, *D.H. Lawrence: Aesthetics and Ideology* (Oxford: Clarendon Press, 1993), ch. 3; Ben Stoltzfus, *Lacan and Literature: Purloined Pretexts* (Albany, New York: State University of New York, 1996), chs 1 and 2; Fiona Becket, *D.H. Lawrence: The Poet as Thinker* (London: Macmillan, 1997), chs 4 and 5.

psychoanalytic criticism as such is no longer possible.[11] This chapter engages with that claim, tying together the fate of psychoanalytic criticism with the Freudian and post-Freudian reading of *Sons and Lovers*. I shall argue that Lacanian criticism has had little purchase on Lawrence studies, despite the fact that it offers an approach that does justice to the figurative complexities of the text even while rereading it as an object of psychoanalysis. Having prepared the theoretical ground, my psychoanalytic reading of *Sons and Lovers* as libidinally structured text will demonstrate how the whole text reworks its material — albeit material deriving from the life and times of the author — onto an aesthetic plane through the device of recurrent motifs which then acquire symbolic and psychoanalytic value. In this way, the experiences that are singled out for such treatment in the fiction are no longer transparently autobiographical. They are made significant within structural and figurative schemes, and generalized from the individual case histories of the characters to give the novel a greater universal impact which locates Lawrence in the age of Freud and the discontents of early twentieth-century "civilization".

2. The fate of psychoanalytic criticism

i. Psychoanalysis and literature
The relationship between psychoanalysis and literature is a disputed one. Psychoanalytic understanding of the literary text requires the mediation between a scientific discourse, itself subject to theoretical and methodo-logical dispute, and the discourses of literature. The process of mediation can not be taken for granted, as Freud insisted in 1930:

> I would not say that an attempt of this kind to carry psychoanaly-sis over to the cultural community was absurd or doomed to be fruitless. But we should have to be very cautious and not forget that, after all, we are only dealing with analogies and that it is dangerous, not only with men but also with concepts, to tear them from the sphere in which they have originated and been evolved.[12]

While bearing Freud's warning in mind, we should also acknowledge that the analogical relationship between psychoanalysis and literature is one

---

[11] Robert Young "Psychoanalysis and Political Literary Theories", in James Donald ed., *Psychoanalysis and Cultural Theory: Thresholds* (London: Macmillan, 1991), 140.
[12] *Civilization and its Discontents* (London: The Hogarth Press, 1975), 81.

that is already proposed by psychoanalysis itself in the form of the case history or the dream-work. Storytelling and narrative, as well as the devices of rhetoric — metaphor and metonymy — have an important function in Freud's science. As Culler explains:

> Psychoanalytic understanding involves reconstructing a story, tracing a phenomenon to its origin, seeing how one thing leads to another. Freud's case histories themselves are indeed narratives with a *fabula* and a *sjuzhet*: the *fabula* is the constructed plot, the sequence of events in the patient's life, the *sjuzhet* is the order in which these events are presented, the story of Freud's conduct of the case.[13]

It is, moreover, the bringing together of narrative theory and psychoanalytic explanation that seals the fate of psychoanalytic criticism. Texts have lost their transparency; the person has become a text, or, like history itself, is only available for analysis in the form of a text. Now to turn a text into a person, forgetting the textual altogether, as in the earliest biographic or Freudian criticism, so that the characters are mistaken for real people and narrators for the author, has become the sign of the greatest naivety.

Because a book is not a person, psychoanalysis had to become textual analysis in order to be acceptable as literary criticism. But once it is literary criticism, then it is no longer strictly psychoanalysis; and psychoanalytic criticism now becomes a contradiction in terms. Indeed, it has recently been claimed that there is no longer such a thing. Once it became textual analysis, and, through the complex and often mystifying office of Lacan, mediated the psychoanalytic and the cultural-literary on the page, it forfeited its claim to being psychoanalysis. As Robert Young has put it, "indeed, nowadays the politicization of psychoanalysis, in direct contradiction with its former identity ... means that a *pure* psychoanalytic criticism is no longer possible". It was "always something of an embarrassment", and it is "a relief to announce that psychoanalytic criticism, as an autonomous critical method, no longer exists".[14] There is something inevitable, even circular, in the fate of psychoanalytic criticism: it has apparently argued itself out of existence. If it began its career in Freud's essays on art and literature, only to be accused of sheer reductionism (turning the text into a person-for-analysis), it has now

---

[13] Jonathan Culler, *The Pursuit of Signs* (London and New York: Routledge, 1981), 178-79.
[14] Young, 142-43.

ended its long and disreputable career because it strenuously sought to mediate a more effective relationship between literature and psychoanalysis.

ii. The Freudian reading

Freud's case histories, as Culler suggests, may have been intended as the practice and the proof of his psychoanalytic theories. Today, however, they are sources for a theory of storytelling. Freud, though, also wrote about art and literature.[15] Lis Møller has raised important questions about Freud as art and literary critic.[16] She takes a close look at his reading of Jensen's novella, *Gradiva*, and Hoffmann's story, "The Sandman", and the case history of the "Wolfman", and asks what happens when Freud applies his theories? This raises further, fundamental questions about the Freudian hermeneutic: "What kind of knowledge (or *truth*) does it produce?" And: "How should we conceive of the relationship between his object of investigation and the interpretive discourse of psychoanalysis?" (Møller, x) Freud's reading of Jensen and Hoffmann, and the case histories, should provide the answers.

Freud has two models of reading. The first was profoundly questioned by the second. In Jensen's *Gradiva* he discovered that archaeology was the analogy for psychoanalysis itself. The excavation of the lost city and its reconstruction becomes "inextricably bound up with the very idea of psychoanalysis as depth hermeneutics" (Møller, xi-xii). *Gradiva* is thus read as a specimen story for psychoanalysis. The second model derives primarily from the "Wolfman" case, and involves the idea of "construction in analysis" whereby the decisive "primal scene" of the trauma turns out to be an unconscious fantasy instead of the discovery of some deeply buried memory of a real event in childhood. Freud gave this mode of understanding the trauma after the "event" the epithet, "*nachträglich*", which has been variously translated as deferred action, retroactive fantasy, and retroactive causality. In this sense, he could argue that the "primal scene" was produced in the dream-work — the narrative account of the dream. Everything is understood subsequently, and is therefore an interpretation. The analysand is subject to the logic of the "*nachträglich*". This bears out Freud's early claim (1896) that, "hysterical symptoms can only arise with the co-operation of memories".[17] Culler has appropriately renamed the "primal scene" the "primal fantasy". For

---

[15] Cf. *Art and Literature: The Penguin Freud Library*, 14 (London: Penguin, 1990).
[16] *The Freudian Reading: Analytical and Fictional Constructions* (Philadelphia: University of Pennsylvania Press, 1991). Page references in text.
[17] "The Aetiology of Hysteria", cited in *The Freudian Reading*, 79.

what is at stake here is the functioning of an undecidability which is the "effect of the convergence of two narrative logics that do not give rise to a synthesis". Freud's problem is that if the dream-work, or analysis itself, produces the latent content it is looking for, how can the model of psychoanalysis as "archaeology of the soul" continue to have any credibility? What is being excavated and reconstructed seems to be · nothing other than the product of a fantasy in the moment of thinking about the past. The archaeological metaphor, that "alluring spatial model of the unconscious", and its methodology of excavation, deciphering, decoding, and reconstructing, is challenged by a "figure of temporal spacing" (Møller, 42, 58) the "*nachträglich*" or retroactive fantasy. These models are diametrically opposed theories of reading.

The Freudian hermeneutic is, then, complex and problematic:

> Construction is also the mark of the fictionality of psychoanalytic interpretation. The analytic construction belongs in the realm of the "as if" or the "as though". It is a hypothesis, suggested by the analyst, that occupies an empty space in the patient's narrative about the past, but which is verifiable only in the present. How should we then conceive of the analyst's work of construction? Does analysis produce narratives "from" the analysand's past, or rather narratives "relating to" the past? (Møller, xi)

Do meanings come from the buried memories of the past, excavated in analysis, or is that meaning only provoked, prompted by the situation of being in analysis? Freud's answer is to accept both processes, and to oscillate between the two models. What he is left with is a space in between, a "*Zwischenbereich*", which "encompasses the dialogic space of analysis" (Møller, 84). Not that Freud would ever really abandon his belief that there is a past buried deeply in the unconscious which psychoanalysis would recover. Indeed, he thought that the two models might well be the two sides of the same coin. It might after all be the point of analysis to get the patient to understand the relationship between the fantasy and the event in the past, real or imagined. John Forrester discusses this very point. For when Freud discovered the importance of fantasy, "he opened up the way to the recognition [of] infantile sexual fantasy",[18] and thus undermined his early seduction theory. It is not just that the past has a deeply causal relationship to the present, but rather that the present appears to affect our understanding of the past. Freud's case

---

[18] *The Seductions of Psychoanalysis* (Cambridge: Cambridge University Press, 1990), 75.

histories (the "Wolfman", "Emma") tell of the gradual revelation of traumatic, sexual "events" in childhood, which only come to light after the onset of puberty. Belated understanding is always motivated. The "Wolfman" reads his past as a projection of his later fantasy which has an adult sexual motivation.

Now it seems to me that the conflict between the theory of psycho-analytic reading as archaeology and that as construction in analysis rehearses the very critique that would be levelled at Freudian literary criticism. The surface-depth paradigm, the model of latent and manifest content, belongs to the dominant tradition of art-appreciation,[19] as well as the great archaeological studies of the excavations in the nineteenth century. Indeed, the surface-depth paradigm seems to have been an obsession in the period, like the quest for or return to origins in archae-ology, anthropology, and evolution.[20] Meaning is buried in the site or text. The archaeologist or literary critic has the task of discovering it. Traditional literary criticism has presupposed the self-evidence of this hermeneutic model. The construction in analysis model, however, implies that meaning is produced, not simply discovered, by a specific mode of questioning deriving from a set of theoretical presuppositions. The text, or the patient, is an object of knowledge. Freud's reasoning, like any such reasoning derived from a master code, has power not least because it "creates inductive support for the kind of conclusions that it is used to draw".[21]

Freud the practising literary critic is far less credible, however, than Freud the theorist. The former soon forgets the hermeneutic problematic, and reverts to all the naiveties of which Freudian criticism will be accused. His reading of the *Gradiva* and "The Sandman" will seal the fate of psychoanalytic criticism. He believes that in recovering the latent meaning in Jensen's novella he is making the remarkable discovery that it is the proof of his theories of dreams — that dreams have a meaning, and that they reveal traces of sexual repression; and this, despite the fact that Jensen, by his own admission, had no prior knowledge of Freud's work. But while Freud nearly gets away with it here, he becomes terribly unstuck when he finds he cannot explain "the uncanny" in Hoffmann's story. And, it is here, at the moment of its attempt to deal with the literary text at its most intractable, that psychoanalytic criticism begins uncannily

---

[19] Described by Ernst Gombrich in "Freud's Aesthetics", which is discussed by Richard Wollheim in "Freud and the Understanding of Art", in Jerome Neu ed., *The Cambridge Companion to Freud* (Cambridge: Cambridge University Press, 1991), 256.

[20] Cf. Møller, 35-36.

[21] Hopkins, "The Interpretation of Dreams", in Neu, 116.

to predict the fate which awaits it.

Rand and Torok question what is now called "applied psychoanalysis", which they define as follows:

> Applied psychoanalysis uses a predetermined conceptual apparatus; it masters the unknown, it subdues the unforeseen through earlier discoveries. Even as it makes uses of genuine insights (for example the idea of sexual repression), this kind of psychoanalysis denies literary works the right to speak in their own voice.[22]

They offer a different psychoanalytic reading of *Gradiva*, rejecting Freud's insistence on sexual repression, and claiming instead that the story illustrates the "illness of mourning". After the young protagonist, Norbert Hanold loses his parents, he suffers from a delay in the process of the "maturation of erotic desire", but he is finally cured by his discovery of love for his childhood sweetheart. Norbert's sudden recovery of his psychic health also reminds us of Paul Morel's equally sudden recovery, as he clenches his fists and strides with a new determination towards the town. He also suffers the effects of a delayed sexual development, even if the reasons are different. But whereas mother-love in *Sons and Lovers* has been given by Freudians and non-Freudians alike quite plausibly as the cause of the boy's split personality, Rand and Torok insist that Freud's attempts to corroborate his theories have often failed because he chose the wrong examples and then forced them into his preconceived schema. They conclude that, "Freud's own desire to force his cases into his preconceived theoretical models has insidiously undermined the effectiveness of psychoanalysis as a whole".[23] The same has been said of the case histories, the "Dora" case being the most notorious.[24] However, what makes Rand and Torok's reading more valid than Freud's? They claim they are at least letting the text speak in its own voice, as if it has an autonomous, objective existence. Yet what they have done is contest Freud with a different psychoanalytic reading. So while they are right to accuse Freud of a doctrinaire reduction, are they any less reductionist themselves? If as they rightly insist the literary text should lead to "theoretical recasting, expansion, or refinement",[25]

---

[22] Nicholas Rand and Maria Torok, *Questions for Freud: The Secret History of Psychoanalysis* (Cambridge, Massachusetts, and London: Harvard University Press, 1997), 53.

[23] Rand and Torok, 66-67, 77.

[24] See Charles Bernheimer and Claire Kahane eds, *In Dora's Case: Freud — Hysteria — Feminism,* (New York: Columbia University Press, 1985).

[25] Rand and Torok, 94.

then their own reading is already under threat because they do not acknowledge that Jensen's *Gradiva* is always a text-for-criticism, and more obviously so when approached by a declared theory.

The desire to master the object of analysis, be it "dreams, the unconscious, the woman's body, sexual difference or narrative itself, was both the generating impulse and the Achilles' heal of the psychoanalytic project".[26] Freud reading *Gradiva* as specimen story of psychoanalysis is a classic example. Therefore, traditional Freudian literary criticism (applied psychoanalysis) stands accused of being "authoritarian, even imperialistic".[27] Freud would push his quest for complete understanding as far as he could, drawing all the consequences of the master code. His critical method is to analyse the dreams of the characters, always taking it for granted that characters are simply real people (the text is a person), and that dreams in literary texts (fictional dreams) are the same as the dreams of people in the real world (recounted in analysis). But methodological questions about the relationship of psychoanalysis to literature are apparently unimportant for Freud. The fact that dreams have a meaning is corroborated by Jensen's novella. Interpretation becomes an inquiry into the unconscious inspiration of the author. The literary text is always already an allegory of psychoanalysis, and, by the same token, an allegory of Freud's own reading.

What Freud overlooks is that, despite the fact that literature and psychoanalysis both explore the depths of the self, the relationship between psychic reality and the constructions of literary, fictional texts is not unproblematic. What is at stake here is formulated by Møller, and by Felman before her,[28] in the following way: "Is the literary text the place where knowledge ... of the mind resides? Or is literature rather the potential object of a psychoanalytic knowledge?" (Møller, 94) Without posing such complex questions, Freud turns ambiguities in the text into unequivocal statements. The still unresolved riddles of art and literature need explaining. In the case of *Hamlet*, for instance, Freud explains that:

> ... it was not until the material of the tragedy had been traced back by psychoanalysis to the Oedipus theme that the mystery of its effect was at last explained. But before this was done, what a mess of differing and contradictory interpretative attempts, what a vari-

---

[26] Suleiman, cited in Møller, 26.

[27] Peter Brooks, "The Idea of a Psychoanalytic Literary Criticism", *Critical Inquiry*, 13 (Winter 1987), 336, cited in Møller, 26.

[28] Shoshana Felman, "To Open the Question", in *Literature and Psychoanalysis: The Question of Reading: Otherwise* (Baltimore and London: Johns Hopkins University Press, 1982), 5-10.

ety of opinions about the hero's character and the dramatist's intentions![29]

Freud proceeds by way of summarizing the story, then analysing that summary; he finds nothing in the story that was not already there. But his reading is only a plot summary. It ignores the formal complexities of the literary text. Yet this dissociation of form and content is "inconsistent with the principles of psychoanalytic interpretation, according to which even marginal features must be taken into consideration" (Møller, 96). It was Freud, after all, who drew attention to the important access we get to the unconscious from slips of the tongue, jokes, and forgetfulness. The particular form of expressing the joke is the most important thing about it. Freud's hermeneutics proper and his method of literary criticism are quite at odds. Yet, he was not unaware of this:

> I have often observed that the subject matter of works of art has a stronger attraction for me than their formal and technical qualities, though to the artist their value lies first and foremost in these latter. I am unable rightly to appreciate many of the methods used and the effects obtained in art.[30]

Freud's literary criticism consciously limits itself to content analysis. Worse still, the subject matter of the work in question resides in his own summary — which is, of course, already an interpretation. We are, thus, reminded of Lawrence's summary of *Sons and Lovers* in a letter to Edward Garnett,[31] where in order to demonstrate that the novel has "form", Lawrence leaves much of its formal complexity out of account to concentrate on the overbearing and destructive relationship between the mother and the sons. It seems that, influenced by Frieda's reading of the manuscript, it is Lawrence himself who produced the first Oedipal reading of *Sons and Lovers*! (I shall return to Lawrence's reading later.)

The explanatory power of the Freudian hermeneutic does not stretch, where literature is concerned, to questions of form; so that it is powerless when faced with "the uncanny" in Hoffmann's "The Sandman". In Freud's reading, a complex narrative is reduced to its perceived psychic truths, while "the uncanny" itself remains unexplained. The psychoanalyst cures the text of its fictionality, as "it is translated into a psychiatric study" (Møller, 103). Although Freud is aware of what he is doing on one

---

[29] "The Moses of Michelangelo", in *Art and Literature: The Penguin Freud Library*, 14, 255.
[30] Ibid., 253, cited in Møller, 96.
[31] 19 November 1912.

level, he would not be forgiven by the literary critic for overlooking literature. For his interpretation of Hoffman's narrative "is an instance of psychoanalytic criticism in its most reductive and dogmatic form" (Møller, 112). "The uncanny" is the most fictional element in the story — at once a literary genre and the supernatural, both of which Freudian psychoanalysis is, by definition, unqualified to deal with: the first being a question of form; the second needing to be either located in the pseudo-science of the paranormal, or in the fantasy structure of narrators or characters. Freud, strangely enough, claims that the only way to explain it is to accept the existence of the supernatural; which for him as scientist means that it remains unexplained. We would expect the fantasy of characters to play a role in his criticism. The problem is in the text itself: the story is mediated through framing devices and different points of view, so that the act of telling is crucial to the meaning. But Freud's summary, as we have seen, consciously excludes questions of form. For him, the full import of the story must reside in its content, which it clearly does not. The same can be said of *Sons and Lovers*. Furthermore, the meaning of "The Sandman" is undecidable, not least for generic reasons: hesitation or undecidability is a basic premise of the effect of the uncanny as a literary genre.[32] Such a text resists, in its complexity, the Freudian master code.

A major premise in Lis Møller's *The Freudian Reading*, as well as in Felman's seminal reading of Henry James, *The Turn of the Screw*,[33] is that literature resists the psychoanalytic master code; indeed, it has always already anticipated the possible readings between which the critics will choose. Master codes are disempowered by the complex undecidability of the literary text, not because there is anything inherently untenable about psychoanalysis as such, but rather because the Freudian hermeneutic has tried to impose a univocal — and here, one-dimensional — reading on the text. It would be left to subsequent, post-Freudian psychoanalytic critics strenuously to discover ways of avoiding this trap.

In answer to the question, "what is a Freudian reading?", Felman has replied that it is an insistence on sexuality, on its "crucial place and role in the text".[34] Wright reinforces the point: "If there is a single key issue it is probably the question of the role of sexuality in the constitution of the

---

[32] As argued by Todorov, *The Fantastic: A Structural Approach* (Ithaca, New York: Cornell University Press, 1975, first published 1970). See also Rosemary Jackson, *Fantasy: The Literature of Subversion* (London: Methuen, 1981).
[33] "Turning the Screw of Interpretation" in Felman ed., 94-207.
[34] Felman, 103.

self, and crucially, how this sexuality is to be defined." [35] Both psychoanalysis and literature are concerned with the representative status of
metaphors, themselves designated as libidinally charged signifiers. The
unconscious speaks through its symbolism, and such psychoanalytic
effects are also at work in texts. (I shall be working with this crucial
proposition.)

According to Forrester, a psychoanalytic reading involves significant
reference to "the causal efficacy of sexuality". Not, though, the vulgar
Freudian reduction of imagery to phallic symbols. "Whose sexuality is at
issue?" It is not the sexuality of the author, nor that of the characters, but
the sexuality of the text itself. The reader is "the sexual object of the text:
quite simply, reading is being seduced by the text". The transference of
reading-effects is analogous to the transference in analysis proper. It is
not, however, simply a case of meaning or feelings enacted, nor of
readers in empathy. For Forrester — and for Felman — "the reading-
effects of the text are often as akin to love and hate as they are to
meaning: fascination, suspense, repulsion, satiation, frustration,
titillation, seduction". Moreover, the sexual is "what cannot be represented".[36] It appears in the text in distorted form as symptomatic imagery,
for instance. In this sense we might talk of the "textual unconscious", not
as the expression of the author's unconscious — although it would be
foolish to deny any such element, just as it would to try and prove it —
but as stylistic and structural effects that have a psychoanalytic explanation.

Assigning an unconscious to the text has been one of the principal
difficulties of "psychoanalytic reader-theory",[37] as Wright has described
it in her paper, with its appropriately ambiguous title, "The Reader in
Analysis". Returning us to the work of Iser, Jauss, and Holland in reader-
response theory[38] — but, regrettably neglecting the more politically
radical work on "reading formations" of Frow and Bennett — Wright
explains how the emphasis now falls not on the author, nor on the text,

---

[35] Elizabeth Wright, *Psychoanalytic Criticism: Theory in Practice* (London: Methuen, 1984), 3.
[36] Forrester, 263-266.
[37] In James Donald ed., page references in text.
[38] Wolfgang Iser, *The Act of Reading* (Baltimore and London: Johns Hopkins University Press, 1978; first published 1976); Hans Robert Jauss, *Aesthetic Experience and Literary Hermeneutics* (Minneapolis: University of Minnesota Press, 1982; first published 1977); *Toward an Aesthetic of Reception* (Minneapolis: University of Minnesota Press, 1982); Norman Holland, *The Dynamics of Literary Response* (New York: Oxford University Press, 1968); Robert Holub, *Reception Theory* (London: Methuen, 1984).

but on the reader.[39] Such criticism is concerned with the reader's fantasies. In order to generalize the theory of reader response, an ideal reader is proposed. The obvious problem with this is that readers do not read in the same way, nor may any one read with the same understanding and in the same mood at any time. Psychoanalytic reader theory took a more dramatic turn with the implications of Lacan's work that the signifying process is always in excess, always overdetermined, and that the unconscious speaks through its margins. For, it seems, the reader is at the mercy of this process, while at the same time, "the text is also at the mercy of the reader, because of the mediating effects of his [*sic!*] own unconscious". The question in traditional reader theory: "How does a text affect a reader?" becomes, in Lacan: "How does the unconscious read?" The answer is that it reads through the networks of images and key signifiers, a process through which meaning is never fixed, always in excess in the functioning of textual figures as the distorted expression of symptoms and desire. Thus: "It is neither the reader who is the prime mover of meaning (Holland), nor the author who controls the reader via the gaps in the text (Iser): both author and reader are controlled by the strategies of language." Meaning is mediated by "the effect of an (intersubjective) other — the public language shared by all", which is for Lacan the "Symbolic Order". Moreover, Symbolic Orders are subject to historical change, so that, for instance, reading literature from the past requires a "subsequent rereading of those rules" and the conventions that govern that Symbolic Order dominant at the time. We are, then, never the contemporary reader, the one addressed or implied in the text. We do not have the advantages (and disadvantages) of the first readers. Yet the text still continues to have an effect on generations of readers. We are still reading Lawrence, not however unmediated by the accumulations of readings and the more formal academic criticism which derives from them (a lesson learnt from Jauss's theory of reception). Readers today "will go on feeling the gap between the real of the world (contingent nature) and the referentiality of language" (Wright, 161-167).

iii. Psychoanalytic textual criticism

To go beyond the reductionism of the Freudian reading and do justice to the complexities of literature, Freudian criticism has been transformed into a psychoanalytic textual criticism. This newer method, as Peter Brooks claims, would strive to avoid the traps of applied psychoanalysis,

---

[39] John Frow, *Marxism and Literary History* (Cambridge, Massachusetts: Harvard University Press, 1986); Tony Bennett, *Outside Literature* (London: Routledge, 1990).

namely: "a study of the psychogenesis of the text (the author's unconscious), the dynamics of literary response (the reader's unconscious), or
the occult motivations of the characters (postulating an unconscious for
them)."[40] The newer critical method would not be found in Freud's own
essays on art and literature, but rather in the "dream-work" first explained
in *The Interpretation of Dreams* (1900), and in the dynamic drive theory
in *Beyond the Pleasure Principle* (1920). Brooks has characterized the
latter as, implicitly, "a theory of the very narratability of life", where
repetition and return function to bind textual energies: one textual
moment is bound to another by the tropes of similarity and substitution,
"rather than the mere contiguity of narrative sequence". And here we are
reminded of Lawrence's use of the "modified repetition" (as he explains
it in the Foreword to *Women in Love*).[41] Narrative thus "generates a
certain analytic force" (Brooks, 291) enabling a psychoanalytic
explanation of the text (Brooks, 285, 289-91). Not only can the narrative
be analysed in terms of the metonymic chain — the contiguity of events
and thoughts that make up the narrative syntagm; but also in terms of its
enfiguration of the force of desire — the axis of desire visible in its
insistent repetitions and returns.

In analysis, the patient is prompted to retrace a chain of associations.
The dream-work was characterized by Freud through figures of
representation: "condensation" as the overdetermined signifier of latent
wishes, to be known in a later terminology as metaphor; "displacement"
as the process of dream-censorship, disguising the unconscious material
in a chain of associations, later to be called metonymy. Freud drew
attention to the representability of dream-thoughts by images, certain key
words having significant associations; and that the verbal account — the
dream-work itself — was always, in any case, a secondary revision, or
interpretation.[42]

With the addition of recent developments in textual rhetoric and
narrative theory, psychoanalytic theory has developed into a more
plausible literary criticism. No longer will the text disappear under the
weight of the Freudian master code only to return as the repressed itself,
like Freud's atrophied reading of the uncanny. Indeed, the newer method
will stake its credibility on whether it is adequate to the task of explaining the textual itself. It was Lacan who developed the psychoanalytic

---

[40] Brooks, "Freud's Masterplot: Questions of Narrative", in Felman ed., 299.
Subsequent page references in text.
[41] Reprinted in the appendix to the Penguin edition of the Cambridge D.H. Lawrence.
[42] For a succinct account of Freud's dream-work and "strategies of desire" see Wright,
17-25. The best introduction to these ideas is Freud's (1915-1917) *Introductory
Lectures in Psychoanalysis* (*The Penguin Freud Library, vol. 1*).

potential of textual rhetoric.

Condensation (similarity, metaphoric shifts of association), and displacement (contiguity, metonymic shifts of association) are tropes or figures of the functioning of memory in the first instance. Metaphor and metonymy were singled out by Jakobson as "the two fundamental poles of language". It was he who brought Freud and linguistics together.[43] It was Lacan, though, who reworked Jakobson's, and Saussure's, linguistics for psychoanalysis. (I shall return to Lacan's use of Jakobson when I discuss the "poetic metaphor" in Lawrence's writing.) In 1957, having read Jakobson, Lacan declared that, "if the symptom is the metaphor, ... man's desire is a metonymy".[44] Freud maintained that the dream-work tended towards condensation: the meanings of dreams may be deciphered from the figures in the text of their re-presentation. Lacan, as Wilden explains, "goes much further towards systematizing Freud when he assimilates the dream mechanism of displacement (*metonymy*) to desire and that of condensation (*metaphor*) to the symptom or substitute".

Lacan has returned us, with a newer textual and linguistic emphasis, to one of Freud's fundamental ideas, namely: that language is invaded by the unconscious. Examples range from the repetition-compulsions of the neurotic, or forgetting, to the slips of the tongue of the speaker under pressure (who has, as we say, "something on his mind"). But also the unconscious speaks through the displacement of its desire onto part-objects (metonymies), and what Habermas has called the "deviant symbol-formation" whereby, as in parapraxes (slips of the tongue), what is indicated in this "intentional structure" is that:

> the faulty text both expresses and conceals the self-deceptions of the author. If the mistakes in the text are more obtrusive and situated in the pathological realm, we speak of symptoms ... [which] are part of intentional structures: the ongoing text of everyday language games is broken through not by external influences but by internal disturbances. Neuroses distort symbolic structures in all three dimensions: linguistic expression (obsessive thoughts), actions (repetition compulsions), and bodily experiential expres-

---

[43] "Two Aspects of Language and Two Types of Aphasic Disturbances", in Roman Jakobson and Morris Halle, *Fundamentals of Language* (Mouton: The Hague, 1956).
[44] Lacan, "L'instance de la lettre dans l'inconscient ou la raison depuis Freud", reprinted in *Ecrits 1* (Paris: Seuil, 1966); cited in Anthony Wilden, *Speech and Language in Psychoanalysis: Jacques Lacan* (Baltimore and London: Johns Hopkins University Press, 1981. First published 1968), 131, note 107. For a schematic version of the relationship between metonymy-desire in the syntagm, on the one hand, and metaphor-symptom in the paradigm, on the other, see Wilden, 246, 47.

sion (hysterical body symptoms).[45]

Habermas's crucial point is that although the process of interpreting such intentional structures is a kind of depth hermeneutics, it goes beyond hermeneutics as traditionally conceived by Dilthey, because it is not only concerned with what the distorted text means, but more significantly with "the meaning of the distortion itself".[46] And it seems to me that this is productive for a psychoanalytic reading of a literary text. For, when symptoms persist in compelling patterns in the text, they begin to unbalance its libidinal economy. Such symptomatic patterning is visible in the narrative text when unusual metaphors are the location for a psychoanalytic explanation which would not turn the text into a person. Indeed, as Brooks reminds us, the character and the author have now been turned into an effect of the text, "deconstructed into an effect of textual codes, a kind of thematic mirage". [47]

Brooks is keen to point out the extent to which other recent developments in psychoanalytic criticism have fallen short of the methodological rigour of text-analysis. Thus, for instance, some feminist criticism has continued to work on the psychoanalytic study of characters who represent the female psyche, in what at best is a "situational-thematic" method (Oedipal triangles as power structures, for example), but which, interesting as it is, stands accused of being "methodologically disquieting in its use of Freudian analytic tools in a wholly thematic way, as if the identification and the labelling of human relations in a psychoanalytic vocabulary were the task of criticism". The reader theories discussed by Wright are no better, for they (Holland, Iser) displace "the object of analysis from the text to some person, some other psychodynamic structure" (Brooks, 335).[48] Such displacements would be avoided if we insist on psychoanalytic criticism becoming rhetorics and text-analysis; a proposal, it should be stressed, which goes beyond mere formalism "to make that crossover between rhetoric and reference" which "ought to be the *raison d'être* for the recourse to psychoanalysis in the first place". This "erotics of form", defined as the interplay of form and desire, and

---

[45]*Knowledge and Human Interests* (London: Heinemann, 1968) 219. I take "author" here to mean the author of an utterance.
[46] Ibid., 220.
[47] Brooks, "The Idea of a Psychoanalytic Criticism", 335. Subsequent page references in text.
[48] I should add that Brooks' critique of feminism does not account for the work of the French feminists, like Cixous whose notion of "*écriture féminine*" enables a textualization of "*jouissance*". I shall return to this in chapter 6 in order to assess Lawrence's representation of female sexuality in the *Lady Chatterley* novels.

best exemplified in Barthes' *S/Z* (1970), is a dynamic process, and one that "unfolds and develops as texts are activated through the reading process". Thus what we now have is a "neo-formalist psychoanalytic criticism" (Brooks, 337, 340).

But does such a method solve the problem of the relationship between psychoanalysis and literature? Even in its modest proposals, Brooks' textual rhetorics can not, by his own admission, take for granted that psychic operations proper and tropes adequately fit together in written texts. They may offer a model or working analogy for the way human desire works, but we should not be in search of "mere metaphors", as it has "sometimes been the case with post-structuralist annexations of psychoanalytic concepts". There is a stake in the human — how we are constituted as human subjects — in the "convergent activities and superimposable forms of analysis of fiction-making and the study of the psychic process" (Brooks, 340-41).

Finally, it seems, it is the concept of the "transference" which defines the most productive relationship between psychoanalysis and literature. What others have called the collaboration of reader or critic in the production of meaning now becomes an act of intervention if not a kind of rewriting. The process has often been mirrored in the literary text: narrators or characters misreading or misapprehending, so that the fit between the narrative discourse and the story becomes problematic. An example would be the mediating devices of framing — different narrators passing on the story, as in Conrad's *Heart of Darkness* (1902), James' *The Turn of the Screw* (1898), Emily Brontë's *Wuthering Heights* (1847) — albeit through a defined situation of narrators and listeners, or through the writing and reading of letters. Here, we rely in large part on the storyteller. This process is transferred from the text, so that meaning is not simply a property of the text, found hidden there, nor is it, as Brooks explains, "wholly the fabrication of the reader (or community of readers) but comes into being in the dialogic struggle and collaboration of the two, in the activation of textual possibilities in the process of reading". Thus the reader is not fully authoritative, not the possessor of a master code, but, "caught up in the transference, he [or she] becomes analysand as well as analyst". The reader is active, and especially when he or she is the critic who construes "previously unseen networks of relations and significance", extending the narrative and "semantic web", so that parts of the story "seem to belong to the interpreter rather than to the person whose story it is, or was" (Brooks, 345-46).

Brooks' idea of constructive reading derives, as he himself points out, from Freud's late paper "Construction in Analysis" (1937) — which I discussed above. Freud discovered in analysis that (in Brooks' words) "hypotheses of interpretation ... open up ever wider and more forceful semantic patterns". The literary critic, even more so than the reader, effects changes in the text. Thus: "interpretation and construction are themselves most often dramas of desire and power." This goes for literature and for criticism (Brooks, 347).

Brooks is not however saying that psychoanalysis is — as it is for Felman — a kind of literature. Nor are they (literature and psychoanalysis) simply in a relation of intertextuality, as if between literary genres. Their relation "obliges the critic to make a transit through a systematic discourse elaborated to describe the dynamics of psychic process". As I have argued, psychoanalytic literary criticism has had a tendency to forget that psychoanalysis is a scientific discourse, just as Freudian literary criticism forgot the discourses of the literary text so that literature became a kind of psychoanalysis. What makes psychoanalysis important for the literary critic, however, is that "it stands as constant reminder that the attention to form, properly conceived, is not a sterile formalism, but rather one more attempt to draw the symbolic and fictional map of our place in existence" (Brooks, 348).

Lacanian psychoanalytic criticism has by and large rewritten or replaced Freudian criticism, not least because, in rereading Freud, Lacan has turned him into his mirror-image. Freud has also been a structuralist, is more latterly a post-structuralist, giving priority to the signifier, insisting that meanings are effects of texts, and interpretations are motivated constructions from hypotheses — a misrecognition to which Malcolm Bowie has strongly objected.[49] Yet Lacan's Freud is surely the best example we have of constructive rereading in Freud's sense.

iv. The politicization of psychoanalytic criticism

The consensus is, then, that if psychoanalytic criticism is anything at all it has to be a kind of textual analysis — a rhetoric of narrative, in Brooks' sense. But, as Young has insisted, there has been one more turn in the fate of psychoanalytic criticism, namely towards its politicization. Here, we should return to Jameson's seminal paper, "The Imaginary and the Symbolic in Lacan".[50] For, straightaway, we see that what is at stake is the whole problematic of the subject; and one through which Marxism will once again attempt to establish a dialogue with psychoanalysis.

Jameson takes up a position which may be characterized as post-

---

[49] *Lacan* (Glasgow: Fontana, 1991), 49-54.
[50] Fredric Jameson, "The Imaginary and the Symbolic in Lacan: Marxism, Psychoanalytic Criticism, and the Problem of the Subject", in Felman. Page references in text are to this edition. The paper is also reprinted in Jameson, *The Ideologies of Theory: Essays 1971-1986, vol. 1: Situations of Theory*, (New York and London: Routledge, 1988), chapter 3.

Marxist, mediating between the tripartite Lacanian scheme of the Imaginary, the Symbolic, and the Real, and the Marxian alienated subject of class and history. For Jameson's Lacan is also a materialist thinker for whom the dialectic consists in the antagonistic relation between sexuality (desire) and society (variously designated as the Other, the Symbolic Order, and the Real). The absent resolution or synthesis in Lacan will be provided by Jameson in the form of the Marxist master code itself.

It is important for his reading of Lacan that Jameson defines the Symbolic Order not only as the mechanism of familial, social and cultural prohibition — or Law, as Lacan designates it — but also that he should stress its function as mediation between the libidinal and the linguistic. The Freudian Oedipus complex is "transliterated by Lacan into a linguistic phenomenon", literally and symbolically as the moment of the entry of the subject into the Symbolic Order through the discovery of the Name-of-the-Father, a "menacing abstraction of the paternal role as the possessor of the mother and the place of the Law" (Jameson, 359). The subject first enters the realm of public language (the social) through the designation of the patronym (literally, the father's or family name), an identity through which the subject is called into being. It is at the same time the entry into the socio-cultural sphere, with its boundary conditions. This process of identity is a further alienation of the subject, and one similar to the castration anxiety discovered by Freud but here given, in Jameson's description, a socio-cultural explanation that draws heavily on Lévi-Strauss' influence on Lacan: that cultures and social formations are founded on the binding of kinship structures and taboos, and the ritualistic enactment of symbolic forms. This goes for both tribal and modern western societies. As Lacan explains: "obviously the Oedipus complex can appear only in the patriarchal form of the institution of the family ... [which as an] institution ... marks the intersection, in the cultural sphere, of the biological and the social."[51] And later in the *"Discours de Rome"* (1953):

> This law, therefore, is revealed clearly enough as identical to an order of language. For without kinship nominations [i.e. *le Non/Nom du Père*], no power is capable of instituting the order of preferences and taboos which bind and weave the yarn of lineage down through succeeding generations .... This conception [the Name-of-the-Father as "figure of the Law"] permits us to distinguish clearly, in the analysis of a case, the unconscious effects of this function from the narcissistic relations [i.e. the Imaginary Or-

---

[51] "Propos sur la Causalité Psychique", cited in Wilden, 126, note 94.

der], or even from the Real relations which the subject sustains
with the image and the action of the person who incarnates it.[52]

I have quoted Lacan at length here to illustrate that psychoanalysis is
immediately attractive to Marxist thought once it becomes more
anthropological. Yet as Lacan insists, we are not dealing with the
psychological determinism of a set of developmental stages in the life of
the subject. The Symbolic Order may resemble the Freudian Superego;
the Imaginary Order may have derived from the purely selfish drives of
the Freudian libido, combined with a kind of primary narcissism. But for
Lacan, the two orders are always co-present: the Imaginary persists even
after the subject's entry into the Symbolic and the alienating effects of the
otherness of language.[53] The Real, however, is more problematic in
Lacan.

For Jameson the Real is "simply History itself", sometimes also
called the "referent", or the "absent cause". And it is here in Jameson's
reading of the Lacanian Real that we come closest to Marxism: "for
psychoanalysis the history in question here is obviously enough the
history of the subject." We may want to question the ease with which the
Real is designated as the case history, if only to stress that Lacan often
defines it as literally that realm of events in the real world that resists the
subject's imaginary symbolizations, and which at best is only appropriated as misrecognition (*"méconnaissance"*). The problem of the subject
spills over from such theoretical considerations into literary criticism. For
one of the essential weaknesses of both psychoanalytic and Marxist
criticism has been their naive concepts of character in literature. What is
needed — and Lacan's scheme seems to offer a way forward — is (in
Jameson's words) "an instrument of analysis which will maintain the
incommensurability of the subject with its narrative representations — or
in other words between the Imaginary and the Symbolic in general — but
also one which will articulate the discontinuities between the subject's
various *representations* themselves". The problematic status of the
subject is a legacy of Modernism which sought "to eliminate the old-
fashioned subject from the literary text". (Jameson, 381-384) Jameson's
reworking of Lacan aims to replace the older study of individual
characters or point of view by "the study of those character systems into
which the subject is fitfully inserted". Thus, a fascist character system
would be based on the concept of the authoritarian personality. (Jameson,

---

[52] "The Function of Language in Psychoanalysis", in Wilden, 40-41.
[53] I shall discuss the resistances of the "female imaginary" to the Patriarchal Order in
Lawrence's late fiction in chapter 6.

346)[54]

If orthodox Freudian criticism has always worked with the assumption that "the logic of the wish-fulfilment (or of its more metaphysical contemporary variant, *le désir*)" is "the organizing principle of all thought and action", then what is needed for the reformulation of a psychoanalysis more compatible with Marxism is a dialectic "between individual desire and fantasy and the collective nature of language and reception" (Jameson, 341-42) — a formulation deriving from Freud himself. Adopting Lacan's three orders, we would avoid the naiveties of categories of the individual, of experience, and the representational transparency of the literary work so evident in Freudian literary criticism, as I described above.

Experiencing the Real is a complicated process in Lacan. It is at once never immediate, spontaneous, or instinctual. The Real can only be experienced through the mediation of the Imaginary and the Symbolic Orders. They exercise a simultaneous function on that mediation of the subject with the Real, defined by Wright as the field of brute existence "over which the Imaginary and the Symbolic range in their rival attempts to control".[55] And whereas the phallus as transcendental signifier is "one of the basic organizational categories of the Symbolic Order itself", the logic of the binary opposition is confined to the Imaginary. Thus the material of classical Freudian dream-symbolism and its vulgar form as the phallic symbol is radically reorganized. The old storehouse of universal symbols "will now be understood rather as part-objects in Melanie Klein's sense of organs and parts of the body which are libidinally valorised". These part-objects belong to the Imaginary (Jameson, 352). Here, as Wilden explains, Lacan's appropriation of Klein's object-relation theory depends on a radical reinterpretation of Freud's "*Fort! Da!*" in *Beyond the Pleasure Principle*. That is, for Lacan, the child's world — the world of the Imaginary Order — is now characterized in the terms of his psychoanalytic epistemology as (in Wilden's words), "the binary opposition of presence and absence".[56] The "*Fort! Da!*" is also the primary quest narrative, a story of the lost and the found.

What is radical here in Lacan is the dialectical presence of narcissism and identification, or the demand for the recognition of the Other, who is also a self making the demand, which persists into the later stages of the

---

[54] For further discussion see Fredric Jameson, *Fables of Aggression: Wyndham Lewis, the Modernist as Fascist* (Berkeley and London: University of California Press, 1979).

[55] Wright, 110.

[56] Wilden, 163.

life of the subject. It is a dramatic conflict between self and other first given its modern existential form in Sartre.[57] The ways in which the subject constitutes the Other, or is itself constituted by the Other, as object is central to Lacan. Wilden reminds us that the "pathological quest for the self in the other", and the "dialectic of love and hate", belong to a narcissism that was "known to psychologists of literature at one time as the Renaissance theory of love. *My soul is totally alienated in you* (Rousseau)".[58]

Lacanian theory becomes textual analysis when part-objects are identified as metonymies of desire, representing the bits and pieces of the body of the other *(le corps morcelé)*. This fragmentation is a projection of a perception learnt in the "mirror stage"[59] when, at the very moment of the birth of narcissism, the split between the consciousness of the self and the image of the body as other occurs, or is reflected back. The first instance of the objectification of the self will have a long afterlife, as it remains dynamically present in the Imaginary Order. Such a conception is not unknown to literature, as Wilden explains: "As others have said before Lacan, it is the notion of the *body image* which is involved rather than the notion of the body itself. The Romantic and existentialist heroes who face their mirrors know this." The mirror stage is not only an event in a psychic development, but also "a purely structural or relational concept", and one that theorizes the relationship between fantasy and the object of projection.[60]

Because desire is essentially selfish and narcissistic it is destructive. Malcolm Bowie describes this primary narcissism as "an inescapable structural imperative in the operation of all human desire". Desire is written on the body of the other, now designated as object and fragmented into part-objects. Moreover, as the "identification of oneself with another being is the very process by which a continuing sense of selfhood becomes possible",[61] the subject's self-image is inseparable from fantasy-projections or, as Lacan would formulate it, the misrecognition of the Real.

In his attempt to bring psychoanalysis and Marxism closer together in a theory of the subject, Jameson reinscribes the misrecognition of the

---

[57] Sartre, *Being and Nothingness* (1943); *The Roads to Freedom* (1947-1949); *In Camera* (1946).
[58] Wilden, 165. Emphasis in original.
[59] *Le stade du miroir* implies both a phase or stage and a stadium, encompassing the temporal and the spatial. Jacques Lacan (1949), "Le Stade du Miroir Comme Formateur de la Fonction du Je", reprinted in *Écrits* (Paris: Éditions du Seuil, 1966).
[60] Wilden, 173-74.
[61] Bowie, 31, 34, 35.

Real as collective class fantasy which works on the unconscious through the hegemonic processes of dominant ideology. Lacan claims that all reification "entails a confusion between the Symbolic and the Real".[62] Jameson, as Marxist, is more inclined to see things from the side of History — the capitalization signifying that which is already a reading of the past. Moreover, he has a strategy ready to hand in Althusser's definition of ideology as a representational structure to provide a theoretical link between the Lacanian subject and ideology. This discussion would be more thoroughly worked out in *The Political Unconscious* (1981). Here we find the following formulation:

> The Real is thus — virtually by definition in the fallen world of capitalism — that which resists desire, that bedrock against which the desiring subject knows the break-up of hope and can finally measure everything that refuses its fulfilment. Yet it also follows that this Real — this absent cause, which is fundamentally unrepresentable and non-narrative, and detectable only by its effects — can be disclosed only by Desire itself, whose wish-fulfilling mechanisms are the instruments through which this resistant surface must be scanned.[63]

In this respect, the Imaginary text consists of unconscious collective wish-fulfilments; the Symbolic text consists of the representation of the socio-cultural boundary conditions imposed on the Imaginary; while ideology would be, after Althusser, "the imaginary representation of the subject's relationship to his or her real conditions of existence".[64]

Now, as Young reminds us, Marxist theories of ideology are supposed to account for the reproduction of class relations. Althusser's controversial reformulation of ideology, through his partial appropriation of Lacan, is a theory of the subject in ideology which has enabled a shift away from class towards gender.[65] In other words, just as at the moment psychoanalytic criticism became textual analysis it forfeited its former identity as psychoanalysis, so as Marxism appropriated psychoanalysis it became post-Marxism. For, as Laclau has pointed out, the cumulative effects of the interventions of psychoanalysis and feminism on the categories of classical Marxism constitute post-Marxism; and this, despite the crucial

---

[62] Cited in Wilden, 124, note 86.
[63] Fredric Jameson, *The Political Unconscious: Narrative as a Socially Symbolic Act* (Ithaca and London: Cornell University Press, 1981), 183-84.
[64] Louis Althusser, *Lenin and Philosophy and Other Essays* (London: New Left Books, 1971), cited in Jameson, ibid., 181.
[65] A point made by Young, 144.

problem for Marxism proper of adding "a theory of subjectivity to the field of historical materialism, given that the latter has been constituted, by and large, as a negation of the validity and the pertinence of any theory of subjectivity (although certainly not of the category of *subject*)".[66] Moreover, for classical Marxism the subject of Freudian psychoanalysis should be understood as "the last refuge of bourgeois individualism".[67] Yet Althusser's appropriation of the Lacanian subject has been enthusiastically received on the Left in cultural and literary studies since the mid-1970s. Young dryly comments: "to everyone's convenience, suddenly it seemed as if Marxism and feminism could acquire a theory of the subject, and psychoanalysis a theory of the social."[68] The problem is that psychoanalysis has had, from the start, a basic theory of the relationship between the subject and the social: "if desire, for instance, is the desire for the Other, this means that desire is a social phenomenon. Furthermore, as the concept of desire itself suggests, psychoanalytic theory amounts to the argument that the structure of the relation of the psyche to the social is one of incommensurability." The psyche and the social do interact, but "they do so unhappily."[69]

I would not want to go along with the designation of the Lacanian Other as a purely social phenomenon, because that circumscribes the differentiation between the Other and the other and their complex functional value in and through the Symbolic Order.[70] Notwithstanding these difficulties, I merely make the point that thanks largely to Althusser's controversial use of Lacan, psychoanalysis has undergone a political turn, for which Jameson's post-Marxism articulates the theory for literary criticism. This newer psychoanalytic politics, and its influence on gender studies, has been most productive in cultural and literary studies. It has served as a middle ground between what Jameson has called "an overestimation of the Imaginary at the expense of the Symbolic" in psychoanalytic criticism, and "that veritable mapping of the Symbolic Order" which is semiotics. What is at stake is a theory which takes account of the referent by studying the limits of textual meaning, their historical preconditions. Thus, "the ideological representation must ... be seen as the indispensable mapping fantasy or narrative by which the individual subject invents a *lived* relationship with collective systems

---

[66] Ernesto Laclau, "Psychoanalysis and Marxism", *Critical Inquiry*, 13 (Winter 1987), 330. Cf. Young, 146.
[67] Young, 144.
[68] Ibid., 140. A classic example is Rosalind Coward and John Ellis, *Language and Materialism* (London: Routledge, 1977).
[69] Young, 141.
[70] Explained by Wilden, 263-4. See below where I discuss Lacan's "*objet petit a*".

which otherwise by definition exclude him" (Jameson's emphasis).[71]

Theories of the subject and the real as representational structures were always going to be productive for cultural and literary studies — the very realms of the representational and the symbolic forms of a culture. Ideological analysis was to become "symptomatic reading", revealing the distortions of History and the Real in their narrativized forms in "the political unconscious", by drawing attention to "discontinuities, rifts ... within a merely apparently unified cultural text".[72] The symptomatic reading relocates in its historical determinants what has had to be forgotten or repressed in order to create the illusion of coherence, completeness, or narrative unity. What appears in the text as the natural and as commonsense will henceforth be rewritten as the cultural and the ideological — which in the case of classic Marxism is the class struggle, or, in its newer gender version, patriarchy.

Literature for the Althusserians was a special case, playing its counter-hegemonic part, situated somewhere between science and ideology; the gaps, margins, the unsaid in the text unwittingly revealing its hidden ideological conditions.[73] Like Freud's analysis of the marginal forms of everyday life — jokes, forgetfulness, slips of the tongue; or the textual representation and concealment of symptoms and wish-fulfilment in the dream-work, the unconscious is concealed and exposed. So it is that the unconscious of the work of literature — be it the political or the personal — is revealed in the margins of the text. Psychoanalysis has known this process of representation since Freud; and Lacan has called it a mis-recognition of the real. As Gunn puts it: "For patient, as for analyst, language is necessarily symptomatic (especially language which establishes certainties and erects hierarchies)."[74] As I hope to show in my Lacanian reading of *Sons and Lovers*, the most enabling connections between psychoanalysis and literature are at the level of language. Following Lacan's claims that "the unconscious is structured like a language",[75] and "The unconscious is the discourse of the Other",[76] I shall argue that it is in the play of language, the metaphors and metonymies, the modified repetitions creating a structure of recurrent motifs, that psychoanalytic significance may be given to Lawrence's writing.

---

[71] Jameson, 380, 89, 94.

[72] Jameson, 35, 57.

[73] The seminal version being Pierre Macherey, *A Theory of Literary Production* (London: Routledge, 1979. First published 1966).

[74] Gunn, *Psychoanalysis and Fiction: An Exploration of Literary and Psychoanalytic Borders* (Cambridge: Cambridge University Press, 1990).

[75] *The Seminar. Book III. The Psychoses, 1955-56* (London: Routledge, 1993), 167.

[76] *Écrits*, 16.

The fate of psychoanalytic criticism, its attempts to improve its credibility, from the Freudian reading to psychoanalytic textual criticism, and finally to its politicization, is a lesson not too dissimilar from that of Marxist criticism: the conceptual framework for a psychoanalytic reading needs to take into account, in its theory and its practice, the limits that master codes face in their interpretive dealings with the complexities of texts. Such considerations will form the conceptual framework for a psychoanalytic reading of *Sons and Lovers*.

The history of psychoanalytic criticism may also be traced directly in the reception of *Sons and Lovers*.

3. The Freudian and post-Freudian reception of *Sons and Lovers*

i. The Oedipal novel 1: the first classic Freudian reading
The first classic Freudian reading claimed that *Sons and Lovers* illustrates the theory of the Oedipus complex that Freud was formulating at the time Lawrence was writing his novel. It was suggested by Alfred Kuttner in a review of the novel in 1915, and in the following year in a more extensive article.[77] *Sons and Lovers* is based on a commonplace of emotional life: a son loves his mother too dearly; the mother in return gives all her affection to him. Kuttner insists that the story does not only illustrate a theory. It is after all great art because the poet has transformed what the scientist has formulated in theoretical terms into personal conflicts based on human verities; which in this case is that of the struggle of a man "to emancipate himself from his maternal allegiance and to transfer his affections to a woman who stands outside the family circle" (Kuttner, 70). However, for Kuttner as for most of the early Freudians, the story originates in "the psychic conflicts of the author". Kuttner goes on to trace Paul Morel's attempts to emancipate himself from his mother through Miriam and Clara, (Kuttner, 74ff) and how unsuccessful he is even after the death of his mother. What has psychoanalysis to tell us about this?

On the surface, Paul is presented as a type of man who "seems to bear so many earmarks of degeneracy and abnormal impulse, who is alternatively a ruthless egotist and a vicious weakling in his dealings with women, and who in the end stoops to shorten the life of his mother". For Kuttner, in his Freudian reading, the whole thing has to be "deeper and due to profounder causes" (Kuttner, 82). To trace these causes we are taken briefly through the developmental stages of the child, in a more or less untechnical discourse. It is emphasized that the "evolution of the

---

[77] Kuttner, note 2 above. Page references in text.

mature love-instinct begins as soon as the child has sufficiently developed a sense of the otherness of its surroundings" (Kuttner, 83). This consists in first making the mother the object of his affections, then in alternating between affection and rivalry in his relations with the father and mother, until finally arriving at the mature adult stage characterized by the quest for a love-object other than the parents. We are reminded that education, socialization, taboos and repression have their function, not least in the developing sense of shame and guilt — all to which the "normal" child adapts in the course of growing up. Indeed, Freud, in postulating the norms of development, also attaches (Kuttner insists) "grave and far-reaching consequences to any deviations from this standard" (Kuttner, 86). Paul is, by definition, abnormal because of "the tremendous role that the abnormal fixation upon the parent plays in the psychic development of the individual". In his case it is the abnormal fixation on the mother (Kuttner 88). The expanding sense of self as we grow apart from our parents, and through which our identity develops, is not fully achieved by Paul: he cannot break away from his mother. In the novel, the trip to Lincoln cathedral with his mother is an example of his neurotic projection of a deep wish-fulfilment for the mother-imago — the youthful woman he loved as a child — and he as her perpetual child-lover: "there is a kind of bottomless childishness about him; life in a pretty house with his mother." Paul's breakdown at the end of the novel is caused by his inability "to accomplish the physical and emotional transfer" necessary to form a stable relationship with another woman, and by implication a stable, normal identity (Kuttner, 87-89).

Kuttner's conclusion is that Lawrence's novel "bears such unexpected witness to the truth of Freud's remarkable psycho-sexual theory". Many critics have since made that point. Not all of them have gone on to infer that the psychological problems described and dramatized in the novel must be autobiographical. Kuttner backs up his claims with the standard facts about the author's life: the death of his mother, after which Lawrence is released into artistic maturity, the result of which is *Sons and Lovers* where Lawrence proves he is a great artist by the extent to which he has transfigured what originated in his own psyche into a universal theme.

There are initially two points to make about Kuttner's Freudian reading. The first is that it is reductionist, seeing only the story and the characters in real-life terms, and forgetting the literature (turning the text into a person). In this we are reminded of Freud's own readings of art and literature which I discussed above. The second point to make is that it is also a reductionist understanding of Freudian theory. Judged with hindsight, it begins to look like that American development of Freudian theory which would later come to be known as ego-psychology, with its fixed notions of the normal and the deviant, and its prescriptions for a healthy life in adaptation-to-reality therapy. It will not be the last time the dimensions of Freud's theories will be misrepresented. Freudian literary criticism has a lot to answer for. Kuttner even resorts to a moral language: Paul is a childish, ruthless egotist and a vicious weakling; he is degenerate (a keyword in the lexicon about the sensitive artist in the late nineteenth and early twentieth century). What Kuttner neglects — perhaps for moral reasons too — is to give the technical name Freud would have given to what he is describing in *Sons and Lovers*, namely: the "incest taboo". Kuttner's reading is not strictly Freudian enough. And when Lawrence read the article in 1916 he thought it was a "half lie". As he would later write, "if you try to nail anything down, in the novel, either it kills the novel, or the novel gets up and walks away with the nail".[78] Yet Lawrence also overlooked the complexities of the novel when he felt obliged to explain and defend it in that letter to Edward Garnett in November 1912.[79]

Garnett had found that *Sons and Lovers* was too diffuse and lacked form. His assessment derived from the idea dominant at the time that a novel should be clearly structured around a controlling idea focussed on the central protagonist. Many reviewers at the time were to share this opinion. Lawrence protested: it has form, and it is based on a controlling idea. The mother transfers her passion from the husband to the sons, so that when they reach manhood, "they can't love, because the mother is the strongest power in their lives, and holds them .... As soon as the young men come into contact with women, there's a split .... The son loves the mother — all the sons hate and are jealous of the father". In the battle over the son with the lovers, the mother "gradually proves stronger .... The son decides to leave his soul in his mother's hands .... [He] goes for passion ... the split begins to tell again". As the mother is dying, the son abandons the lovers, and after her death he is left "naked of everything, with the drift towards death".

What Lawrence is describing here is the classic Oedipal story. It is a reading after the fact, promoted by Frieda who had a rudimentary knowledge of Freud through her association with Otto Gross.[80] And like Freud's own literary criticism (his reading of Jensen's *Gradiva*), even when generalized and untechnical in Lawrence, what is left out of

---

[78] "Morality and the Novel", *Calendar of Modern Letters* (December 1925), reprinted in Anthony Beal ed., *D.H. Lawrence: Selected Literary Criticism* (London: Heinemann, 1967), 110.
[79] Letter to Garnett, 14 November 1912, *The Selected Letters of D.H. Lawrence* edited by James T. Boulton (Cambridge: Cambridge University Press, 1997), 49.
[80] Kinkead-Weekes, 42ff.

account is the text itself: the dense and complex "web of metaphor", the shifting perspectives that play on the reader's sympathies, and the complex characterological oppositions and parallels, and so on.[81] Frieda's reading of *Sons and Lovers* as "sort of Oedipus" does not get us far.[82] However, what began its life as the semi-autobiographical novel *Paul Morel* had been developed into a plot, which although not based on a thorough knowledge of Freud, seems all the more remarkably close to Freud's ideas emerging at the same time, especially in those essays, "Family Romances" (1909), "A Special Type of Choice of Object Made by Men" (1910), and "On the Universal Tendency to Debasement in the Sphere of Love" (1912)[83], which seem at least superficially to be telling the same story about the family, the parent-child relation, and the sexual development of the young adult male, as Lawrence. However, we ought to acknowledge the origin of such stories in Sophocles' Oedipus tragedy and Shakespeare's *Hamlet*, common to both Lawrence and Freud.[84] Moreover, there was in the early twentieth century nothing unusual about the "Oedipus story"; as Rylance explains, it became "a consistent theme in English writing".[85] What ought not to be confused here is the designation of the text for a psychoanalytic reading and Lawrence's knowledge of Freud at the time of writing it. For, as Salgado points out, "Lawrence's sustained interest in Freudian psychology came only after the publication of *Sons and Lovers* and the keen interest it aroused among Freudians in England and America".[86]

ii. Lawrence's quarrel with Freud
The reductionist readings by the Freudians incensed Lawrence. He was to make several attempts to expound his counter-Freudian theory of the self, and it would not fully emerge until the 1920s. His quarrel with Freud is most explicitly argued in the pages of *Psychoanalysis and the Unconscious* (1921) and *Fantasia of the Unconscious* (1922). His ideas on

---

[81] Ibid., 44.
[82] Frieda's influence in 1912 is discussed by John Worthen in *D.H. Lawrence: The Early Years, 1885-1812* (Cambridge: Cambridge University Press, 1991), 441ff.
[83] Freud, *On Sexuality: The Penguin Freud Library, vol. 7* (London, 1977), 220-260.
[84] Knowledge of Freud in Britain at the time was sparse. A translation of *The Interpretation of Dreams* was published in 1913; and Strachey did not begin his translations until 1924. Freudianism did not reach the popular imagination until the late 1930s. Lawrence could hardly have read much Freud; but he did learn the rudiments of the early theories in 1914 from the British Freudians, Barbara Low and David Eder. For further discussion see Fiona Becket, 48-50.
[85] Rylance, *New Casebooks: Sons and Lovers* (London: Macmillan, 1996), 3-4.
[86] Salgado, *A Preface to Lawrence* (Harlow: Longman, 1982), 85. Subsequent references in text.

psychoanalysis and culture appeared the following year in *Studies in Classic American Literature* (1923). Lawrence was utterly convinced that, as Salgado so poetically explains, "a system is more like a river or a tree than a steam engine or the proof of a theorem". He strenuously wanted to clarify what differentiates his thought from that of Freud and the Freudians. The books of the early 1920s were explicitly polemical, arguing against what he believed to be the profoundly mistaken ideas of Freudian psychoanalysis. Lawrence wanted to make it clear that his notions of sexuality and the unconscious were very different from those of Freud. Lawrence's views derived from "a sustained reflection on his own individual case" (Salgado, 85, 87), as well as the lessons of his war experience and fiction writing. Similar claims have been made about Freud. The initial discovery of the Oedipus complex came from his self-analysis, although the vicissitudes of the theory were developed over a long period. As Nancy Chodorow points out, "we are becoming more aware of just how autobiographical the early writings often were".[87]

For Freud — and here to generalize for the sake of the comparison — the unconscious was selfish and ruthless in its drive to satisfy its wishes and desires, its pleasure principle. Such drives need to be controlled by the reality principle in order for social life, even "civilization" not to be brutally destroyed. At least these are the postwar theories found in the writings of the 1920s and 1930s (*Beyond the Pleasure Principle*; *The Future of an Illusion*; *Civilization and its Discontents*). For Lawrence, the unconscious was a fountainhead or well-head, more the source of the creative self than the location of repression (as Lawrence understood Freud to be saying) — a much more positive force than its Freudian counterpart. Indeed, Lawrence objected strongly, both in his fiction and essays, to the notion that conscious rational thought, and internalized ethical and social imperatives should control and censor the unconscious, spontaneous self. Life has a primal force, and this has its source in the Lawrentian unconscious. In *Psychoanalysis and the Unconscious* (1921) Lawrence put his objection to the Freudian unconscious thus: "the Freudian unconscious is the cellar in which the mind keeps its own bastard spawn."[88]

Later, Lawrence found support for his critique of Freud in the American psychologist, Trigant Burrow, whose book (which Lawrence reviewed in 1927), *The Social Basis of Consciousness*, argued that "the Freudian unconscious was merely the representation of *conscious* sexual life as it exists in a state of repression" (Salgado, 88). The other idea that

---

[87] Chodorow, "Freud on Women", Neu ed., 245.
[88] (London: Penguin, 1971), 207.

Lawrence gets from Burrow, and one that confirms his own thinking and writing about sexuality, is that the greatest sin is "sex in the head". It follows, then, for Lawrence as it does for Burrow, that the Freudian unconscious is nothing other than repressed ideas about sex, only a mental consciousness of sex.

For Lawrence, Freud's theories of sexuality are mechanistic and therefore limited. He (Lawrence) had believed from the outset in a deeper source for the self in a pre-mental unconscious life. For him, clinical Freudianism was an attempt by science to tie down through its cause and effect rationalizations what was essentially a unique life-principle. The individual was, in each instance, unique and mysterious, and a vital living organism. Lawrence's notion of the self, at once organicist and vitalist, is, even by his own admission, a broadly religious one.[89] Reading the *Fantasia* alone would testify to this, with its recourse to cosmology and eastern religious notions of non-mental centres of consciousness, and psycho-physiological theories of the processes of self-realization. In 1916 he was telling an English Freudian how the longer he lived the less he liked psychoanalysis;[90] and in 1928 he had not changed his mind:

> Science says it [sex] is an instinct; but what is an instinct? Apparently an instinct is an old, old habit that has become ingrained. But a habit, however old, has to have a beginning. And there is really no beginning to sex. Where life is, there it is. So sex is no *habit* that has been formed .... The deep psychic disease of modern men and women is the diseased, atrophied condition of the intuitive faculties. There is the world of life that we might know and enjoy by intuition, and by intuition alone.[91]

Lawrence's notion of the unconscious formed the basis of a moral imperative. Unlike the potentially selfish and destructive Freudian unconscious, it would lead, at least in theory, to a new relatedness. It lends a ready-made structural principle to the novels, which "explore the ebb and flow of the emotions and especially the rhythm of love and hate" (Salgado, 92). The Freudian split self would be healed by the ethical imperative: "be yourself!" It turns out to be a strenuous demand on the characters in the fiction; which goes to show that, although we may want to take Lawrence to task for his misreading of Freud — setting up a straw

---

[89] Cf. Black, *D.H. Lawrence: Sons and Lovers* (Cambridge: Cambridge University Press, 1992), *passim*, and especially 92.
[90] Talking to Barbara Low. A point made by Salgado (1982), 90.
[91] "Sex versus loveliness" (1928), reprinted in *Selected Essays* (London: Penguin, 1974), 13-15.

target for his own theories of the self — the novels themselves turn out to be spaces for the working through of crucial propositions which, in the writing and the reading, fortunately lose much of the programmatic naivety of the essays, and become in the process dramatizations of what it must have been like being a young man as Freud was devising his theory of the Oedipus complex.

Fernihough describes how Lawrence read widely in anthropology after the publication of *Sons and Lovers*. Like his knowledge of Freud and Jung, though, he assimilates certain general principles that would confirm his instinctual rejection of psychoanalysis as the science that reduced everything to sexual repression. Yet anthropology gives him the idea of an "aboriginal" memory which he reinscribes in *Kangaroo* (1923) and *The Plumed Serpent* (1926) as pre-Christian native instinct, and which Freud called the phylogenetic memory. Moreover, *Studies in Classic American Literature* (1923) is now generally recognized as an early example of psychoanalytic cultural criticism. Thus Lawrence avails himself of the concepts and language of psychoanalysis, reworking them for his own needs. In *Lady Chatterley's Lover* (1928) he reverses the teleology of the Oedipal story when Sir Clifford regresses emotionally to childhood as Mrs Bolton plays the mother.[92] Lawrence is much closer to Freud than his essays lead us to believe. In *Sons and Lovers*, for instance, he divides the psychology of Paul's relationships to the female lovers along Freudian lines: the affectionate and spiritual (his mother, and Miriam) is opposed to the sensual (Clara), as Freud outlined it in "On the Universal Tendency to Debasement in the Sphere of Love" (1912).[93] Lawrence even adheres to a Freudian aesthetic. As Lawrence admitted: "one sheds one's sickness in books — repeats and presents one's emotions, to be master of them".[94] Freud (1908) writes:

> The psychological novel in general no doubt owes its special na-
> ture to the inclination of the modern writer to split up his ego, by
> self-observation, into many part-egos, and, in consequence, to per-
> sonify the conflicting currents of his own mental life in several he-
> roes.[95]

---

[92] Fernihough, *D.H. Lawrence: Aesthetics and Ideology* (Oxford: Clarendon Press, 1993), 61-64.

[93] Ibid., 65-66. It should also be noted that literature already had a long tradition of dividing female sexuality along these lines. Freud drew on such popular ideas to corroborate his theories of sexual development. These binary divisions are the cause of the split in the adult male psyche.

[94] Letter to Arthur McLeod, 26 October 1913.

[95] Cf. *Art and Literature: The Penguin Freud Library*, Vol. 14, 138.

Freud's observations had shown him that this was common too in daily life, where the ego in our daydreaming "contents itself with the role of spectator" to our part ego-projections in our imagined future.[96] Writing is a form of psychotherapy, and as the Cambridge biography clearly shows, in all three volumes, Lawrence wrote to make sense of his life. *Sons and Lovers* is the most intensive version of this therapy as Lawrence masters his past, not as autobiography but as fiction, as he objectifies and generalizes his own case.[97] And perhaps this is the closest we can get to a psychobiography. Writing is a form of cure for the "sickness" because it requires the imagining of senses of otherness. For Paul Morel, like Norbert Hanold in Jensen's *Gradiva*, the illness of mourning is finally mastered.

So why did Lawrence attack Freud so vehemently, calling him "the psychiatric quack", and blaming him for imprisoning the instinctual self in a scientific rationality? Lawrence's attack is unusual because, as Fernihough explains, "Freud was more commonly seen by his own contemporaries to have subverted, not reinforced, this rationalist tradition".[98] Part of the answer is that Lawrence came to Freud via Nietzsche. He had understood Nietzsche to be saying that over-developed self-analysis was unhealthy. The spontaneous sources of being were subjected to a "horrifying mental tyranny". Thus Freudian thought was unhealthy. Too much self-consciousness and a coercive ego have led the modern self into a great loss of the natural, spontaneous centres of being. Much of Lawrence's work after *Sons and Lovers* is a working through of this proposition.

Despite his objections to the Oedipal reading of *Sons and Lovers*, by the 1920s, as Fernihough explains, Lawrence was proposing a similar theory to Freud's ego, id, super-ego structure. For Lawrence, the coercive ego will be threatened by the creative id. Lacan's rereading of Freud shows Lawrence to be unexpectedly prescient here: the Imaginary will be the place where the Law-of-the-Father may be resisted, as it lingers around, so to speak, as a creative potential. It will be the female characters in the fiction from *The Rainbow* onwards whose imaginary relation to their existence will act as a critical perspective on the "man's world". And it will be in the late cultural papers of Freud — too late for Lawrence — that a truly Lawrentian critique will emerge in the claim that "civilized" society has paid too great a price by repressing the sex-

---

[96] Ibid.
[97] As Worthen and others have demonstrated, the differences from his own family story outweigh the similarities if you look to the fiction for biographical evidence.
[98] Fernihough, 63.

drives.

The problem with Lawrence's attack on Freud is that, as I suggested above, it fails to appreciate the complexities of Freud's arguments, and the developments and changes they underwent. Indeed, many of the objections Lawrence levelled at Freud were ones already discussed in Freud's work. The most important one is the scientific status of psychoanalysis. More recent work, influenced in part by post-structuralism, has looked again at Freud's own doubts, tending to see, with Derrida, a self-deconstructing Freud whose work is not as positivist as Lawrence believed.[99] As I said above, with hindsight, Lawrence's Freud is a straw target to verify his own theories. Derrida, like Lacan, reads the Freudian unconscious as a text or discourse that speaks a kind of complex poetry. And again, this view brings Freud and Lawrence closer together than the Lawrence of the *Fantasia* would have wished. In *Studies in Classic American Literature* (1923), the concept of "art-speech" seems to be a form of poetry which allows the American cultural unconscious to speak the hidden truths which, in Lawrence's words, "the American plain speech almost deliberately conceals".[100] As I hope to demonstrate later in this chapter, the "poetic metaphor" (art-speech) is a point of location for the unconscious in the text. Fernihough takes the Derridean reading further by showing that "the modified repetition in Lawrence is inseparable from an endless *semantic* modification", unfixing the link between the signifier and the signified, and destabilizing the ego in what amounts to a "polysemy".[101]

Fernihough suggests that Lawrence is closer to the general principles of the British Object-Relations School. Influenced partly by Melanie Klein, Object-Relations theory assumes that "human beings are ... innately whole and already adapted to their environment (an assumption that Lawrence also makes), and that various psychic splits occur only in so far as they have experienced frustration, separation, or loss".[102] The Freudian idea of wish-fulfilling fantasy caused by the split is retained, as is the connection between creative writers or artists and childhood imaginative freedom which is retained in adult life. I would add that Lacan was also "influenced" by Melanie Klein, and his complex theories of the subject and the other are predicated on a reworking of object-

---

[99] Ibid., 69.

[100] *The Symbolic Meaning: The Uncollected Versions of Studies in Classic American Literature* edited by Armin Arnold (Fontwell, Arundel: Centaur Press, 1962), 18. Cited in ibid., 71.

[101] Fernihough, 73. In chapter 5, I attempt to show that *The Plumed Serpent* is characterized by a dissemination which serves to destabilize the doctrinal insistence.

[102] Ibid., 78.

relations (I shall return to the Other as object of desire in *Sons and Lovers*). Lacan's notion of the persistent Imaginary is also central to his reworking developments after Freud. D.W. Winnicott, as Fernihough explains, argued that object-relations were important for health and creativity because they functioned as an intermediary between internal, psychic reality, and the external world, and were a key to the relationship to otherness. Art and literature function in a similar way. Lawrence, too, describes art as displaying "the living conjunction between the self and its context", bringing together the impulses to merge and to separate — which are tensions in the psychological forces of *Sons and Lovers*, and ones which derive from the relationship with the mother. (Klein, the Object-Relations school, and Lacan all place more stress on the mother as the first object-Other, and her continuing influence, than the father in the Freudian Oedipus complex.) The importance of art for Lawrence — and the novel in particular — is that it "puts us curiously in touch with life": it can encompass the full complex psychology of the relationship between the self and the other. Fernihough's conclusion wittily captures the problem of Lawrence's quarrel with Freud: "Although the aesthetics of Lawrence and Freud, then, can be seen to coincide at several important junctures, Freud remains for Lawrence a Gerald Crich of the psyche."[103]

I would add that you should also remember that for Lawrence the centres of consciousness are relocated in the body; whereas for Freud and his followers the body is a location of pathological symptoms. Moreover, after Derrida's and Lacan's rereadings of Freud, the body is now the textual trace of the psyche just as the text incorporates unconscious tensions and motives symptomatically in distortions like modified repetitions and unexpected figures. As Lacan said, the symptom is a metaphor, and desire is a metonymy.

Becket brings us closer to such post-structuralist reading by reminding us that Deleuze and Guattari saw in Lawrence's quarrel with Freud a confirmation of their own anti-Oedipus stance. Thus, Lawrence is "more genuinely post-Freudian in his perceptions than many of the British writers of the time",[104] especially because he recognizes "the inadequacy of a 'technical' or conceptual language" to describe the emotional and sexual life of the individual. Lawrence finds other metaphors for the psychology of the self and the other; metaphors of "flows", "vibrations", and "currents", for instance, which dissolve the boundaries of psyche and body. I would add that here Lawrence is establishing an organicist discourse to displace Freud's mechanicist discourse of drives and

---

[103] Fernihough, quoting from *Apocalypse*, 81, 82.
[104] Becket, 50, 51-52.

pressures. (I shall return to Lawrence's discourses in the following chapter.) What attracts Deleuze and Guattari to Lawrence is that he understands sexuality as more creative and powerful than Freud does. Becket insists that the metaphoricity of the fiction also characterizes the non-fiction writing, like the *Fantasia*, which even in its title declares its impromptu and improvised approach. Lawrence's writing is radically metaphoric even when the figures derive from scientific discourses (a subject I approach through Foucault in the next chapter). Becket reiterates Fernihough when she concludes that Lawrence is increasingly being shown to challenge "logocentric modes in his writing. This is a response to the linguistic mobility of [his] texts".[105] It is, surely, also the outcome of approaching Lawrence's writing through post-structuralism. Deleuze and Guattari are on the side of Lawrence in their anti-Oedipus diatribe: "It is as if Freud had drawn back from this world of wild production and explosive desire, wanting at all costs to restore a little order there, an order made classical owing to the ancient Greek theatre." Lawrence, therefore, goes beyond Freud by finding a poetic language to expose the limits of scientific discourse while it inextricably connects (in Becket's words), "the body, language, and unconscious functioning".[106] This post-structuralist reassessment of Lawrence "is seen to nourish certain post-Freudian positions".[107] What is unusual about Becket's reading of Lawrence's quarrel with Freud is that, while she is prepared to adopt Deleuze and Guattari's radical position on Lawrence (without, I should add, following up the full consequences of their radical reflection on language in her own writing), she makes no mention of Lacan, in a study that is predominantly concerned with the "poetic metaphor" in Lawrence.

Clearly Lawrence availed himself of the language and thought of psychoanalysis, despite his hostility to Freud. He was himself working in the age of Freud, even when coming to Freud through Schopenhauer and Nietzsche. Richard Ellmann has called Lawrence an extraordinary example of "the writer who searches his own mind and jerry-builds a psychology".[108] As *Sons and Lovers* in particular demonstrates, and despite Lawrence's rejection of Kuttner's reading, the desires and traumas of the sons of possessive mothers are given both a psychoana-

---

[105] Becket, 66-67, 72, 95.
[106] Gilles Deleuze and Félix Guattari, *Anti-Oedipus: Capitalism and Schizophrenia* (London: The Athlone Press, 1988), 54, cited in Becket, 114-115. The problem here, though, is that Freud's writing was riddled with metaphor, and as Derrida has shown, is self-deconstructive. On this, see Fernihough's study, which I discuss above.
[107] Becket, 114.
[108] Richard Ellmann's foreword to Daniel A. Weiss.

lytic treatment (even when not a clinical one) and a moral explanation, but in a metaphorization that has opened up the text to post-Freudian readings. Nevertheless, the continuing tradition of Freudian readings has rarely been open to the radical developments in psychoanalytic criticism since Freud.

iii. The Oedipal novel 2: the continuing tradition

Daniel Weiss speaks for the whole tradition when he declares that *Sons and Lovers* is "provocative of psychoanalytic investigation". Although aware of the danger of "the reduction of literature to a limited number of pre-literary elements, and the reduction of all human motives to their first cause in some primordial family situation", his study of *Sons and Lovers* is guided by the conviction "that the Oedipal situation, as Freud describes it, prevails in the novel". Weiss' diluted form of psychoanalytic criticism leads, as it has so often done, to a thematic criticism that, in treating the characters as the real people they represent, tends to forget the text. [109]

Marguerite Beede Howe writes with more technical knowledge of both Freud and the conflicts and structures in Lawrence's novels. She places *Sons and Lovers* in an *oeuvre* which progressively refines and elaborates ideas about personality. In particular, it "deals explicitly with the origin of the mind-body dichotomy" which derives from the "sexual conflicts in the Oedipal personality".[110] This study also emphasizes the extent to which *Sons and Lovers* is indebted to Freud's theory of the Oedipus complex, despite Lawrence's own disclaimer. The incestuous mother-attachment causes "psychical impotence", which Freud described in the following formulation: "where they [such men] love they do not desire and where they desire they cannot love. They seek objects which they do not need to love, in order to keep their sensuality away from the objects they love."[111] This describes Paul's mother-incest, and the consequent relations with Miriam and Clara. It deranges the sexual self, causing a mind-body split, which leads him into "a terrible puritanism and denial of his own body". The psychological realism of *Sons and Lovers* is thus constructed on the Freudian premise that the Oedipus complex, in its pathological form, leads to the mind-body split. The structure of Part II of the novel is based on the underlying assumption of this split causing "ontological uncertainty".[112]

Terry Eagleton, in his psychoanalytic reading of *Sons and Lovers*,

---

[109] See Weiss, 5, 13, 16.
[110] Marguerite Beede Howe, *The Art of the Self in D.H. Lawrence*, 1.
[111] "The Tendency to Debasement in the Sphere of Love" reprinted in *On Sexuality: The Penguin Freud library vol. 7*, 251; referred to in Howe, 9.
[112] Howe, 9-10, 27.

begins by restating the consensus view that this is an Oedipal novel: the son loves the mother (incest taboo) and is in rivalry with the father (Oedipus complex); the son is then as adult unable to sustain a fulfilling relationship with another woman. For Eagleton, though, this is not just Freudian case history. Paul Morel's psychological development "does not take place in a social void".[113] Indeed, the social factors are complicated by the class distinctions prefigured in the divided family. Thematically, the father-son conflict is brought on by the mother. The mother is jealously possessive, the father has considerable difficulty articulating his feelings. The children are closer to the mother. She teaches them her middle-class values. Moreover, "to compensate for his inferior status at work, the father struggles to assert a traditional male authority at home, thus estranging his children from him even further" (Eagleton, 175). These social and class themes are crucial because for Eagleton a psychoanalytic reading "need not be an alternative to a social interpretation .... We are speaking rather of two sides of a single human situation" (Eagleton, 176). Paul has class and Oedipal problems.

To go beyond the confines of such a thematic reading we should, Eagleton suggests, discuss more formally the narrative structure, point of view, and characterization. For instance, Paul's point of view is largely if not entirely endorsed, and the receding of the father into the background as the son is foregrounded corresponds to the novel becoming more inward, as it does too when presenting the mother. Thus the narrative structure "to some extent conspires with Paul's consciousness" (Eagleton, 177), which may explain why the character of Miriam comes off badly (as Jessie Chambers was keen to point out).[114] But as we might expect, the novel is more complex than the simple presentation of a narrative bias. On this point Eagleton quotes H.M. Daleski: "The weight of hostile comment which Lawrence directs against Morel is balanced by the unconscious sympathy with which he is presented dramatically, while the overt celebration of Mrs Morel is challenged by the harshness of her character in action."[115] Paul's Oedipal relation to his father is an ambiguous one. He is at times aggressive towards him, yet at other times seeks to protect him from his hate, an ambiguous attitude which speaks of a kind of love-hate. Ambiguous too is Paul's attitude to class. Despite his rejection of working-class life prefigured in his father's work as coal miner, the middle-class alternative is not presented as something that can

---

[113] Terry Eagleton, "Psychoanalysis" in *Literary Theory*, chapter 5, 175. Subsequent page references in text.
[114] Chambers, 184-85, 202-03.
[115] H.M. Daleski, *The Forked Flame: A Study of D.H. Lawrence* (London: Faber and Faber, 1965), 43; cited in Eagleton, 177.

be wholly admired. Moreover, the father is not always characterized as dull and lifeless; a point which seems to account for the diminishing of him as having "much to do with its own narrative organization", as the emphasis shifts towards the son (Eagleton, 178). Herewith, Eagleton reinforces the consensus biographical view that in *Sons and Lovers* Lawrence was writing his way out of the working-class.

Finally, the claim that "the novel is not quite identical with itself" (Eagleton, 179), that its unconscious meanings reside in, and are made visible by, its marginal phenomena, has the full force of the Althusserian appropriation of Lacanian psychoanalysis behind it. Unfortunately, the theory slogans are not matched by appropriate critical comment on the text. It is tempting to suggest, indeed, that Eagleton's reading, far from being a psychoanalytic one, itself needs to be read symptomatically. For it is the recourse to social and class explanation, and the gestural comments about psychoanalytic and formal narrative analysis, that reveal an unconscious desire: as a Marxist he is bound to be more interested in the social explanation of class struggle than the psychoanalytic account of the Oedipal conflict. For the socio-political formation of the subject is bracketed off by the psychoanalysis of the self in the character. While claiming to offer a reading of *Sons and Lovers* as an application of psychoanalytic theory — indeed, in the chapter on the latter in his best selling primer on literary theory — Eagleton has argued that very theory into the margins of the broader socio-political understanding of texts. In doing so, he does not even acknowledge those attempts to mediate between Marxism and psychoanalysis by Jameson, which I discussed above.

Roger Poole, although not dealing with *Sons and Lovers* but rather with the novella *St Mawr* (1924), attempts a more strictly psychoanalytic reading, albeit with a certain scepticism about the wider implications of the theories of Freud and Lacan. It is a thought-provoking application of the newer textual variety of psychoanalytic criticism — adding a necessary rigour conspicuously absent in much of the tradition. Poole acknowledges that critical theory is saturated with Freud, and especially with Lacan's Freud. Psychoanalytic literary criticism, as we have seen, at best derives from the notion that mental process is at one and the same time a linguistic process. The literary text may be characterized by the libidinal economy of its tropes that are nevertheless over determined in their signifying function. Freud is interested in how the patient's story is told; the literary critic in "the play and slippage of rhetorical devices" in the fictional story.[116] Such are the devices through which the unconscious speaks.

Lawrence's symbolism has always been susceptible to a vulgar Freudianism and the attribution of "obvious phallic meaning". Freud himself admitted that there are certain symbols in the dream that have more explicit sexual meaning: ladders, hammers, swords, for instance. Yet, as Poole rightly maintains, symbols need not be only or simply phallic in this sense. For we are reminded that the horse symbol in *St Mawr*, and also earlier in *Women in Love*, could just as arguably be taken as symbolic of "energy, force and passion". This would not undermine its primary significance as "a symbol of phallic pride" — important to *Women in Love* (Poole, 94-96). Traditional meanings should not be overlooked either. Swift has horses representing noble rationalists in *Gulliver's Travels*, as Poole reminds us. I would add that surely what makes a mere signifier a symbol is that it contains, in its ambivalence and its ambiguity, more than one referent at more than one level. The horse, both traditionally and in Lawrence's text, at any one instance may signify force, power, passion, desire, drive, virility, masculinity; but also freedom, or nature versus culture. It also has a further structural significance in the weave of recurrent motifs, a feature common to much of Lawrence's writing, and one which is important when we read repetitions of motifs psychoanalytically.

The stallion symbol in *St Mawr* is over determined in the sense that it has a multi-symbolic function. Here a "complex motivation" represented by a single signifier alerts the reader to a certain deliberateness, an intentional scheme. The device is foregrounded — and is for Lawrence readers a stock-in-trade, so that its significance cannot be ignored. Lawrence's tendency towards "a certain rough literalness" also plays its part. For the psychoanalytic critic, such recurrent symbolism is the visible manifestation of an unconscious motivation. But as critics are beginning to notice more and more, the ambivalences of symbolic representation undermine univocal reading. It is here, with this point, that Poole proposes to read against the Freudian grain, while still granting validity to Freud's dream-work rhetorics. For as I have already argued, the strictures of the Freudian master code are deconstructed by literature. The text "tells its own story" through its aesthetic structure: the interconnectedness of recurrent motifs produces meaning-effects that insinuate a textual unconscious (Poole, 97, 99). But what is the textual

---

[116] Roger Poole, "Psychoanalytic Theory: D.H. Lawrence's *St Mawr*", in Douglas Tallack ed., *Literary Theory at Work* (London: Batsford, 1987), 92; subsequent references in text.

unconscious? It seems to be a complex and uneven mix of the author's, the characters', the reader's unconscious, together with sedimented history, collective fantasy, mythology. It is also that manifestation of a deep wish to aestheticize the passionate and the sexual which motivates the transliteration of brute images into the tropes of a poetic language which is consistent in Lawrence's writing.

Poole proposes the figure of "oscillation" for his psychoanalytic textual criticism. For it is a modernist textual effect in *St Mawr* which is at one and the same time "a reality in the unconscious". The novel oscillates between life and death, *Eros* and *Thanatos* as a sort of "*Fort!* *Da!*" narrative whose structural principle is the repetition-compulsion, which for Freud has therapeutic value:

> Freud comes to the conclusion that repetition-compulsions are useful in that they create retrospective anxiety in the psyche, such that the subject, by living again and again through his or her problems in the unconscious, be they recalled events or recurrent states, manages to build up, little by little, a sufficient defence against them. (Poole, 103-4)

Moreover, Lacanian significance may be attributed to the structures of the text. As Poole explains, "the object of desire is always deferred, belated or irretrievable, has a poetic suggestiveness that seems peculiarly well adapted to the sensibility of the contemporary western world" (Poole, 107).

Stoltzfus, attempts more committed Lacanian readings of Lawrence's novella, *The Escaped Cock (The Man Who Died)* (1929), and the story "The Rocking-Horse Winner" (1926). He follows the principle that, whereas Freudian reading (applied psychoanalysis) tends to look for the author behind the work, in Lacanian criticism the text "becomes a free-floating construct" of metaphors and metonymies in a play of language that is structured like the unconscious. In this respect, Lacan and Lawrence share the notion of a creative unconscious because the text records the discourse of the Other in its processes of writing. Indeed, there is a "remarkable congruity of his [Lawrence's] metaphors with Lacan's analysis of how unconscious discourse manifests itself". *The Escaped Cock* provides us with an answer to Lacan's question, "What does the unconscious want for me?" In Stoltzfus' words: "it wants me to live productively, and, in living, it overrides the death instinct that Freud formulated in *Beyond the Pleasure Principle*."[117] The last two sentences

---

[117] Stoltzfus, 19-20, 25.

of *Sons and Lovers* are also an affirmation of *Eros* over *Thanatos*.
Lawrence told Garnett that Paul Morel "drifts towards death".[118] The
novel, however, ends with the words, "But no, he would not give in ....
He walked towards the faintly humming, glowing town, quickly". And
this signifies a return to *Eros* after the long drift through the realms of
Thanatos. It is not a convincing, determined move; it is a spontaneous
and unexpected gesture.

   There is, though, one more point to make before I turn to my psychoanalytic reading of *Sons and Lovers*. I may be promoting a Lacanian
approach to Lawrence. But it should be noted that Lacan is just as guilty
as Freud is, in reading literature as allegory of his theory. Derrida accuses
Lacan of reducing the complexity of the literary text to psychoanalysis in
his *Seminar on "The Purloined Letter"* (1956): "the text is in the service
of the truth" — the truth of the psychoanalytic theory Lacan wishes to
illustrate through Poe's story. Therefore, even though Lacan is unusually
attentive to the letter of the text, and breaks with the Freudian tradition of
"naive semanticism and psychobiographism", in his reading of *The
Purloined Letter,* as Derrida claims, "we recognize the classical landscape
of applied psychoanalysis".[119] Lacan's own literary criticism, like Freud's,
will not be much help to us in devising a psychoanalytic approach to
Sons and Lovers that can do justice to the complexity of the literary text.
It will be the post-structuralist interventions in Freudian theory (and
Lacan's part in this), as I explained them above, which will be the basis
of the following readings.

4. Libidinal structure and the representation of desire in *Sons and Lovers*

i. Introduction
Here, I hope to demonstrate the extent to which Freud's "family
romance" is an appropriate description of *Sons and Lovers* once
reworked through the Lacanian schema of the Imaginary, the Symbolic,
and the Real. I shall then engage in a detailed symptomatic reading,
working with the Jakobsonian scheme of metaphor and metonymy
through its Lacanian re-appropriation as symptom and desire, respectively, in order to understand more formally the representation of the split
self. Finally, I shall discuss Jakobson's notion of the "poetic function" of

---

[118] Letter to Garnett, 14 November 1912.
[119] Derrida, "The Purveyor of Truth" reprinted in John P. Muller and William J.
Richardson eds, *The Purloined Poe: Lacan, Derrida, and Psychoanalytic Reading*
(Baltimore and London: Johns Hopkins University Press, 1988), 177.

language as it is reinscribed by Lacan and Lawrence in the form of the poetic metaphorization of the creative unconscious.

ii. A family romance

> He looked round. A good many of the nicest men he knew were like himself, bound in by their own virginity, which they could not break out of. They were so sensitive to their women, that they would go without them for ever rather than do them a hurt, an injustice. Being the sons of mothers whose husbands had blundered rather brutally through their feminine sanctities, they were themselves too diffident and shy. They could easier deny themselves than incur any reproach from a woman; for a woman was like their mother, and they were full of the sense of their mother. They preferred themselves to suffer the misery of celibacy, rather than risk the other person.   (SL, 323)

This passage has a level of generalizing truth which belongs to the overall scheme of the novel. It is a matrix for the mother-son story, and it is an explicit statement of such truths that have been revealed more indirectly through poetic and narrative devices. Paradoxically, while we see through Paul and his motivated perception, we also go beyond it into that universalizing of the particular so characteristic of the great novels of classic realism. Yet it contains a level of explicitness about the role of sexuality in personal development that would not have been possible in the nineteenth-century novel. Family relations are expressed in a psychological discourse that belongs to the age of Freud. It is a discourse that focuses our attention on the family story in more or less Freudian terms, and one similar to that used by Lawrence himself when he summarized the plot in that letter to Edward Garnett in 1912. Here he draws attention to the family story in terms of an intra-family struggle between the mother and the father, the sons and the father, and then the sons' lovers and the mother. This is the essential thematic structure of the Oedipal novel. Despite Lawrence's objections, Kuttner's Freudian reading, as we saw above, is close to Lawrence's plot summary. What is more significant though is the similarity between that summary and Freud's plot of the son's development in his paper, "Family Romances" (1909).[120] This is how Freud begins:

---

[120] "Family Romances" (1909) reprinted in *On Sexuality*, 219-225. All page references in text to this edition.

The liberation of an individual, as he grows up, from the authority of his parents is one of the most necessary though one of the most painful results brought about by the course of his development. It is quite essential that that liberation should occur and it may be presumed that it has been to some extent achieved by everyone who has reached a normal state. Indeed, the whole progress of society rests upon the opposition between successive generations. On the other hand, there is a class of neurotics whose conditions recognizably determined by their having failed in this task.

(Freud, 221)

The conditions for the gradual entry into the norms of social existence, described by Freud as the breaking away from the parents, are strenuously undermined in *Sons and Lovers* by the mother's conscious decision once she has turned against her husband to bring her children up to be the intellectual, emotional, and social-class rivals of the father.

A further stage in Freud's narrative of the "neurotic's family romance" (Freud, 222) is the desire for the mother. In Freud's formulation: "his desire to bring his mother (who is the subject of the most intense sexual curiosity) into situations of secret infidelity and into secret love-affairs" (Freud, 223). This desire is played out in the child's fantasy. Freud's claims remind us of Paul's relationship to his mother. Indeed, when Freud concluded that "the child's over-evaluation of the parents survives as well in the dreams of normal adults" (Freud, 225), we are reminded of Paul's longing for (in Freud's words) "the happy, vanished days when his mother (seemed to him) the dearest and loveliest of women". When Paul takes his mother to Lincoln he treats her as "his girl for an outing" (SL, 281). Her aging traumatizes him into fantasizing her as the beautiful young woman he idolized when he was a child. This may be characterized as the son's deep, unconscious incestuous desire for the mother. And in the novel this desire gets dangerously beyond a fantasy at times. Not only does he want to live with her in a cottage for ever instead of leaving home and getting married; they also kiss like lovers — and we assume this to be frequent when the father comments: "At your mischief again?" (SL, 252). There are pages of text drawing attention to the unusually intimate relationship between mother and son during the period of her illness and dying. As this is late in the novel, we are given the material to understand more about the problems the son has with his two female lovers. There is an obvious contrast between the easy tenderness of Paul's intimacy with his mother, and his often cruel and brutal treatment of Miriam, or unemotional sex with Clara. Paul has immense problems with the realizing of his sexual desire in physical lovemaking. Whenever sex enters into it — when the son is confronted by the female otherness of his lovers — he is no longer himself: "He shrank from the physical contact" (SL, 322). Paul's deep wish to live alone with his mother and not marry is also encouraged by Mrs. Morel's possessiveness,[121] which is rivalled only by Miriam's (a crucial feature of the tensions and drama in the plot). However, we ought to notice that Paul's relationship to his mother is not *consciously* sexual:

> Paul would have died rather than his mother should get to know of this affair [with Clara Dawes]. He suffered tortures of humiliation and self-consciousness. There was now a good deal of his life of which necessarily he could not speak to his mother. He had a life apart from her — his sexual life. The rest she still kept. (SL, 389)

It is the placing of the emphasis on "necessarily" that makes the reader reflect: does it tell us of the inevitability of this change in his life? Or, following a logic established in the narrative's essential oppositions, his not sharing his sexual life with his mother is consistent with the essence of their relationship: namely, that it is not *consciously* sexual; it is *unconscious*. As Helen and Carl Baron suggest, "Lawrence has inserted into a character's inner thoughts a degree of psychological complexity of which the character is unconscious".[122] In Freudian terms, if the neurotic son cannot break away from the parent and be free to love another woman, it is because of his mother's strong hold on him, even after her death. The power of that love engenders a split in the son's psyche between love and sex, so that Paul's libidinal attitude towards women is divided along quite conventional lines: the mother or Madonna figure is opposed to the figure of the whore — a gender opposition already emergent in Victorian literature. Paul cannot get beyond these stereotyped limits. (And we will have to wait till *The Rainbow* for the male characters to undergo a tougher sexual education, with the New Woman as their teacher.)

Just as the mother exacerbated the Oedipal rivalry between father and sons, so, once the sons reach sexual maturity, the mother and the sons' lovers become rivals. This goes for William as it does for Paul. In Lacanian terms, the entry into the Symbolic Order is presided over not by the Father, but the Mother.[123] Briefly put, the son takes over the linguistic

---

[121] Geoffrey Harvey (1987) suggests that "possessiveness" is the "controlling idea" of the novel. See *The Critics Debate: Sons and Lovers* (London: Macmillan), 38.

[122] Helen and Carl Baron, Introduction to the Penguin edition of the Cambridge D.H. Lawrence, xxxiii.

[123] This idea is indebted to Roger Fowler's analysis of socio-linguistic structure in *Sons and Lovers* in *Linguistics and the Novel* (London: Methuen, 1977), 113-122.

code (culturally, socially) of the mother ("the elaborate code") not the
working-class speech patterns and local dialect of the father (except in
moments of intimacy); and this also includes the mother's way of seeing
things, her puritanical view of the world, and her severe ambitions for her
son in class and cultural terms. The space in the house, the family, as well
as the internal emotional space is dominated by the mother: she becomes
the force of prohibition or Law. For Paul, that prohibition is internalized,
severely affecting his relations with others, and symbolically present as
"the Name-of-the-Mother" (*le non/nom de la mère*) — the name which
also prevents him from falling apart in his most desperate moment:
"'Mother!' he whimpered, 'mother!'" (SL, 464) The death of the mother
creates a profound loss, so that the son's desire can only circle around the
gap left by her absence, leaving him void of an essence because his sense
of identity was bound to hers. Nevertheless, he pulls himself together
suddenly, and determinedly strides towards the open future. However,
there is nothing in the psychology of the character that prepares us for
this ending.

Freud first used the actual term, Oedipus complex, in the paper "A
Special Type of Choice of Object Made by Men":

> He [the boy] begins to desire his mother herself in the sense with
> which he has recently become acquainted [i.e. knowledge of sex-
> ual relations between adults], and to hate his father anew as a rival
> who stands in the way of this wish; he comes, as we say, under the
> dominance of the Oedipus complex.[124]

The rivalry with the father in *Sons and Lovers* is a complex of love and
hate, as Paul seeks to protect his father from his unconscious aggressive
feelings towards him; but also from his conscious intellectual and class
superiority. The son's rivalry with the Father for the love of the Mother is
also complicated, as I have already suggested, by the part played by the
Mother, a part that takes the story back to the time before the son was
born. Structurally, as Helen and Carl Baron suggest, "Part I traces the
roots of Paul's psychology, while Part II follows the working out of that
psychological formation".[125] However, the sons do not slay the Father to
usurp his power, as the Oedipus plot requires. They are given that power
by the Mother. It is the power of education — both the intellectual and
the sentimental — so that they move out of the realm of the Father into
what is judged here to be the superior world of the Mother.

---

[124] Reprinted in *On Sexuality*, 238.
[125] Helen and Carl Baron, xx.

As Evans explains, Lacan more than Freud values the pre-Oedipal relationship to the mother, therefore the mother as object of desire and the father as rival render the Oedipal passage from the Imaginary to the Symbolic Order a confrontation of sexual difference. The father imposes the Law on the mother's desire ("At your mischief again?"), "forbidding the subject access to the mother".[126] But this castrating mediation in the child's desire for the mother should be the mother's discourse, respecting the Law of the father. The mother-son relationship in *Sons and Lovers* is, however, overdetermined, and Paul never transcends his imaginary aggression towards the father, and never identifies with him; so that the superego is not clearly established in the son. He is left drifting in a narcissistic void empty of value. As Lacan put it: "the Oedipus Complex is essential for the human being to be able to accede to a humanized structure of the real." Thus the subject's passage through the Oedipus Complex determines, (in Evan's words) "both his assumption of a sexual position and his choice of a sexual object".[127]

Lacan's rewriting of Freud opens up the text by drawing attention to the process of signification that the entry into the Symbolic Order presupposes. What is crucial about Lacan's scheme, however, is that the pre-Oedipal in Freud now becomes the Imaginary Order, itself not simply a developmental stage but one which remains co-present even after it has been superseded by the Symbolic Order. But does Paul get beyond his imaginary relationship to his existence, strongly characterized as it is by his unusually intimate relationship with his mother? Despite the sudden new determination at the very end of the novel, Paul faces an uncertain future.

A Lacanian reading shifts our focus towards the text itself, searching for the signs of traumatic causation in the earlier parts of *Sons and Lovers* in order to give a psychoanalytic explanation of the pathologies of Part II that does not leave the aesthetic dimension out of account — as was so often the case in applied psychoanalysis. Lawrence has prepared the ground well for a retrospective reading of Part I for the origin in childhood of the coming split in the subject. Here, there are two "primal scenes": the incident of the "blood on the child" (SL, 53); and the scene of "collecting the wages" (SL, 93-97). The former ("blood on the child") is the consequence of a violent encounter between father and mother when the drops of the mother's blood have "anointed" the baby boy. The latter is when the young Paul has to fetch the father's wages on a Friday

---

[126] Dylan Evans, *An Introductory Dictionary of Lacanian Psychoanalysis* (London: Routledge, 1996), 127-8.
[127] Jacques Lacan, *The Seminar. Book III*, 198; cited in Evans (1996), 129.

afternoon, thus being compelled to go amongst the working class and be exposed as the young snob. Here, his adopted middle-class attitudes are confirmed, and the signifier: "common" (SL, 97) takes on, in its recurrence throughout the text, a particular resonance in the subject's relationship to the other. Functioning as castration threat within the psychoanalytic reading, as the small boy is timidly lost in the sea of adults — "Paul was quite small, so it was often his fate to be jammed behind the legs of the men, near the fire which scorched him" (SL, 94) — the scene represents a kind of enforced entry into the Symbolic Order, as the "ringing voice" (SL, 95) of authority cries out his father's name (*le non/nom du père*, the prohibition and "Name-of-the-Father", which is literally the patronym). The whole scene is focalized through the boy as he suffers "convulsions of self-consciousness" (SL, 94) and can hardly utter an audible reply. His feelings of superiority because of his better education are severely undermined by a public exposure in which the so-called common people make a fool of him. When he blurts it out to his mother on returning home, it is the speech itself of the working classes that he accuses: "Mr Braithwaite drops his 'h's, an' Mr Winterbottom says 'you was'." The mother diagnoses the behaviour as symptomatic of his "ridiculous hypersensitiveness" (SL, 97). In the Lacanian reading, however, the scene signifies the boy-subject's refusal of the designated entry into the realm of the Father — here, the linguistic code, order, and rules of the mining community — to remain in that of the Mother. This will become problematic later in the novel when the incursion of the Imaginary into the Symbolic Order of the Mother will be the very sign of the pathological split.

The psychoanalytic reader should look carefully at the way the text presents its psychic material. The text is an intentional structure which carefully places its signifiers in a pattern of motifs, so that the process of signification is not transparent, nor do images simply have a single referent. In both primal scenes significance is reinforced by the aesthetic structure. Notice the signifier: "blood" in the first scene (SL, 52-53): "it'll make my *blood boil*"; "like a *flash of hot fire*"; "He *glowered* again"; "get the *flamin'* thing thysen"; "His face was *crimson*, his eyes *bloodshot*"; "Her left brow was *bleeding* rather profusely"; "*drops of blood* soaked into its white shawl" (emphasis added). The series of associations are: rising temper, fiery temper, bright red in contrast to white; the father's violent temper spilling the mother's blood that then stains the baby's white (innocent) shawl. The symbolism has conventional, Biblical connotations; and when the man's blood is roused, anger is confused with sexual excitement (a stock-in-trade in Lawrence's writing). Through the father's "fascinated" eyes we witness the baby boy's symbolic baptism. As she clasps her child to her he sees "a drop of blood fall from the averted wound into the baby's fragile, glistening hair .... Another drop fell. It would soak through to the baby's scalp." (SL, 54-55) The scene takes on a kind of religious significance as the child is baptized in the blood of the Mother.

The origin of traumatic causation, then, is marked in the text itself as primal scene through key signifiers which establish a pattern of recurrent motifs. This level of formal understanding allows us to go beyond the transparent psychoanalysing of the characters towards a reading of symbolic structures that have both psychoanalytic and aesthetic implications in the first instance, thus establishing character through signs in a structure of motifs. Similarly, the scene of the wage collecting establishes Paul's "*torture*" at the hands of "*patriarchal admonitions*": sometimes in winter the air in the closed room "*scorched* the throats of the people"; "the fire ... *scorched* him"; "Mr Braithwaite ... the *stern patriarch* in appearance", "*glowered*" over his spectacles, and has "a *large and magisterial voice*"; the cashier is "*large and important*"; Paul is "*pushed against*" the chimney-piece. His calves were *burning*"; he is trapped behind "the *wall of men*"; when called forward, he replies "*small and inadequate*"; and the "backs of the men *obliterated him*". Once he comes forward he is immediately admonished. The conclusion that the text has been confirming through its structure of repeated signifiers is that the subject is at the mercy of the discourse of the other. Paul's imaginary relation to his real conditions of existence means that he "suffered the tortures of the damned on these occasions" (SL, 94-96; emphasis added).

The dominant structural principle of the Imaginary Order is the binary opposition. The scene of the wage collecting is focalized through Paul's psychology as traumatic experience — his hypersensitive reaction to the other. Here, then, is a crucial example of the insistence of the Imaginary in the Symbolic Order. All that is in the Symbolic Order — the Name of the Father, patriarchal authority and admonition, and the communal social binding of a linguistic order or code — is translated into a series of binary oppositions to the small, inadequate, and threatened boy-subject. As such oppositions are hierarchies, he will relocate his place in them, finding a superior position for himself by inverting the hierarchy: he sees himself as superior in linguistic and educational terms, as he explains to his mother after the event. Both the Symbolic and the Imaginary Orders mediate the subject's relation to the Real, at the same time which makes the Real itself (as Jameson argued) the most problematic of the three orders. That is because "it can never be experienced immediately, but only by way of the mediation of the other two".[128]

Lacanian criticism grants priority to the signifier, and Lawrence reaches out beyond classic realism towards a more poetic structure so that acts of consciousness are represented in a recurrent pattern of signifiers which have further resonance in an aesthetic structure, and that meanings are often communicated indirectly by implication and not by transparent reference. A word does not simply correspond to a referent which is then re-imagined as an object in the real world. Rather, the text is a chain of signifiers for the Lacanian critic and for Lawrence.

iii. The psychoanalytic reading of metaphor and metonymy in *Sons and Lovers*

> The important part begins with the translation of the text, the important part which Freud tells us is given in the [verbal] elaboration of the dream — in other words, in its rhetoric. Ellipsis and pleonism, hyperbaton or syllepsis, regression, repetition, apposition — these are the syntactical displacements; metaphor, catachresis, antonomasis, allegory, metonymy, and synechdoche — these are the semantic condensations in which Freud teaches us to read the intentions — ostentatious or demonstrative, dissimulating or persuasive, retaliatory or seductive — out of which the subject modulates his oneiric discourse.[129]

In this section, I shall work with a psychoanalytic rhetoric in a reading of the representation of the metonymies of unconscious desire, and the metaphors of unconscious symptoms in Lawrence's writing. I will also broaden the discussion to include a notion of the "poetic metaphor" which will bring Lacan and Jakobson together to emphasize Lawrence's modernist representation of the crisis of the old stable ego.

The libidinal economy enabled by condensation and displacement, and first explained in Freud's *The Interpretation of Dreams* (1900), is now appropriated by literary criticism and understood as a binding of textual energies, a force or momentum given textual form in the narrative structure as repetition (Lawrence's "slightly modified repetition"), the full psychoanalytic explanation of which is to be found, as Peter Brooks insists, in *Beyond the Pleasure Principle* (1920). [130] If metaphor is symptom and metonymy desire, as Lacan insisted, then their psychoana-

---

[128] Jameson, 349.
[129] Lacan (1956), "The Function of Language in Psychoanalysis" in Wilden (1981), 31.
[130] Brooks, 289.

lytic interpretation is reinforced by their rhetorical function as the key signifiers that will bear the full force of an anxiety, a compulsion, an obsession. Thus the aesthetic structure will have a psychoanalytic explanation.

Metonymies of desire

In *Sons and Lovers*, unconscious desire is displaced onto the body of the Other. Paul appropriates the object of his desire, writes his desire on the woman's body by fetishizing parts of the body as they come into focus. Metonymy is defined as "a figure of speech in which the name of an attribute or a thing is substituted for the thing itself".[131] We should also distinguish between metonymy, strictly defined, and the figure synecdoche, "in which the part stands for the whole",[132] because when Paul's perception of the female Other is invaded by his unconscious desire, the object-body is broken into bits and pieces — which after Lacan we might designate as "*le corps féminin morcelé*".

Metonymic figures occur in *Sons and Lovers* at intense moments of sexual passion: "In the glow, he could almost feel her as if she were present, her arms, her shoulders, her bosom, see them, feel them, almost contain them." (SL, 316-17) The "as if" marks the point at which the body of the woman becomes a fiction for the sentient male, where it is broken into the bits and pieces, the fetishized part-objects of his desire. Thus the parts become single, libidinally charged attributes perceived by desire. An example of synecdoche, where the parts stand for the whole, is: "his vigorous, warm hands were playing excitedly with the berries." (SL, 226) Or: "Their two hands lay on the rough stone parapet of the castle wall … she saw nothing but his two hands, so warm and alive, which seemed to live for her." (SL, 316) In this last example, it is the woman's desire which is represented figuratively.

Wilden reminds us of what is at stake here for psychoanalytic theory: "The difference between the metonymic structure and the metaphoric structure corresponds to the task of displacement and substitution", both being crucial functions in the Freudian dream-work. The displacement of the object of "the subject's desire onto something apparently insignificant, represents the *manque d'être* (lack of being) which is constituent of desire itself". In *Sons and Lovers* the parts of the body are invested with desire so that it (unconscious desire) "becomes manifest as (conscious)

---

[131] J.A. Cuddon, *A Dictionary of Literary Terms*, (Oxford: Blackwell, 1991, Third edition) 545.
[132] Cuddon, 945.

but displaced demand".[133] Furthermore, if metaphor is associated with neurosis (representing it symptomatically), then metonymy is associated with schizophrenia (the split self).[134] The narrative of Part II generates an analytic force, as Peter Brooks would put it. The metonymic chain is constituted by the contiguity of represented thoughts and events, by definition. But it is also characterized psychoanalytically by the force of desire as the male subject, Paul, seeks to heal the split self by obtaining the recognition of the Other. However, as his perception is invaded by unconscious desire, his appropriation of the Other is a fundamental misrecognition, as it is for the Other as subject in its turn.[135] For Lacan, the phenomenon of delusional belief (*"le phénomène de la croyance délirante"*)[136] is a theory of psychic causality which seems productive in reading Lawrence's text. Although the tendency is to focus on the character of Paul in Part II, such analysis applies nevertheless to other characters as well. Indeed, it could be suggested that each of the main characters projects their deepest wish-fulfilments onto the Other. Mrs Morel's need to compensate for the love absent in her marriage is projected onto her sons; Miriam's saintly fantasies are projected onto Paul; Clara's desire for a man is projected onto Paul. Virginia Woolf was perceptive in her recognition that the textual instability that characterizes much of the Part II might be attributed to the "young man":

> The world of *Sons and Lovers* is perpetually in the process of co-hesion and dissolution …. Whatever we are shown seems to have a moment of its own. Nothing rests secure to be looked at …. The whole world … is broken and tossed by the magnet of the young man who cannot bring the separate parts into a unity which will satisfy him.[137]

Woolf describes here the structure of paradigmatic moments that constitutes the novel's realism; but also the dissolutions in Part II that may be attributed to the character of Paul (and which prompted Garnett

---

[133] Wilden, 242.

[134] Wilden, *System and Structure: Essays in Communication and Exchange* (London: Tavistock, 2nd ed., 1980; first published 1972), 49. For the full discussion of what Wilden calls "Freud's semiotic model" see chapter II: "Metaphor and Metonymy".

[135] Wilden, 96, note 12: "There is no simple equivalent for *méconnaissance* in English." Wilden suggests rendering it, depending on context, as "misconstruction" as in "something misconstrued", or as "failure to recognize". Hence my use throughout of "misrecognition".

[136] cf. ibid., 96-97.

[137] Virginia Woolf, *Collected Essays vol. 1* (London: Chatto and Windus, 1966), 354.

and the contemporary reviewers to claim that the novel lacked form, a criticism based on an older idea of textual unity). Psychoanalytic textual criticism seems to be able to theorize through the details of text analysis that process of "cohension and dissolution" noticed by Woolf.

Paul's body-watching is a figurative representation of his problematic relation to the female love-object. Once sexual desire enters into it, the dissolution and the separating of parts become dominant textual effects: "He saw the nape of her [Clara's] white neck, and the fine hair lifted from it." (SL, 269) Or: "He noticed how her breasts swelled inside her blouse, and how her shoulder curved handsomely under the thin muslin at the top of her arm." (SL, 270) Body-watching is common to both male and female characters: "Clara was conscious of his quick vigorous body as it came and went." (SL, 367) The signifier: "quick" will become associated in the Lawrence lexicon with the self alive and in fullness of being. Body-watching becomes a stock-in-trade in his writing, as the desired Other is always focalized through the misconstructions of the desiring subject. At such moments the unconscious is the discourse of the Other in both senses of affected by otherness, and being other to the conscious subject — what Freud called that other scene, and Lacan and Derrida insist is a scene of writing. The text thus has a dynamic force, and one which will confirm Lawrence's own claims for the deconstruction of "the old stable ego of the character".[138] The character is a construction of a complex array of forces, not least of which are the motivated perceptions of others, and the delusions and deepest fantasies of the self.[139] For Lawrence, as for Freud, these psychological phenomena are fundamentally sexual. The narrator sums up what the figurative effects of the text have been insinuating all along:

> He [Paul] was like so many young men of his age. Sex had become so complicated in him that he would have denied that he ever could want Clara or Miriam or any woman whom he *knew.* Sex desire was a sort of detached thing, that did not belong to a woman. (SL, 319, Lawrence's emphasis)

The last sentence could be adopted as a slogan for the Lacanian reading of the metonymic representation of desire: "a sort of detached thing" belonging to unconscious phantasy and, at best, displaced onto the part-objects of the Other in a libidinal epistemology. This desire is essentially

---

[138] Letter to Garnett, 5 June, 1914; in Beal ed, 17-18.
[139] A further example is: "He was Clara's white, heavy arms, her throat, her moving bosom. That seemed to be himself." (SL, 375).

destructive because it is partly under the control of what Malcolm Bowie has called, "an inescapable structural imperative [of the] ... ego's primary narcissism",[140] and Lacan has defined as the ever-present Imaginary with its tendency to reduce everything to childhood fantasies.

If, as Bowie claims, the full identification of the self with another being is "the very process by which a continuing sense of selfhood becomes possible", then the desiring subject is doomed to fail to achieve what is strenuously being demanded of her or him. This sense of self will re-emerge in *Women in Love* as the impossible ideal of a "oneness-in-separation". What I hope to have shown in the representation of desire in *Sons and Lovers* is neatly conceptualized by Bowie: "The drive, as it circles round the excavated centre of being, is pulled outwards towards the objects that promise gratification, but inwards too towards the completest form of loss that it already knows."[141] As Lawrence expresses it: "After all he was not himself, he was some attribute of hers, like the sunshine that fell on her." (SL, 351)

The other which desire appropriates is Lacan's "*objet petit a*", the other with the small 'o' (representing the object of desire, an imaginary part-object), which should be distinguished from the Other ("radical and irreducible alterity").[142] The object, or part-object is a kind of zone in between the subject and the Other, and it is as close as desire allows things to get. The drive (*der Trieb*) is a mental operation, manifest in the invasion of conscious perception by the unconscious. And for Lawrence mental operations especially in the form of conscious thought about sex ("sex in the head") are precisely why things go wrong. When Paul feels "*unconsciously* angry" (SL, 363, my emphasis) what is at stake here is that creative "fountain-head" of being, the Lawrentian intuitive and spontaneous ideal self, which resembles the Lacanian Imaginary. It is always in conflict with self-conscious rational thought, and Lacan's discourse of the Other because it brings the subject into the castrating sphere of the Symbolic Order.

In the end, Paul's inability to allow his spontaneous self to come through results in the split, which he clearly understands: he feels like "a man under chloroform .... Then there was this other self, in the distance, doing things ... and he watched that far-off him carefully to see he made no mistakes." (SL, 349) In a proto-Derridean moment, Paul perceives his own body in fragments through "a sort of disseminated consciousness", as he experiences the divorce between mind and body. And he is aware

---

[140] Bowie, 34-35.
[141] Ibid., 31, 163.
[142] Evans, 125.

that "you are what your unconscious self makes you, not so much what you want to be". (SL, 233) Substituting the attribute for the thing itself is, as we have seen, the definition of metonymy. Yet we are not trapped by Paul's self-image. For Clara, paradoxically, "he was a vigorous, slender man with exhaustless energy ... his eyes under the deep brows were so full of life, that they fascinated her" (SL, 351). She projects, in her turn, the man of her fantasy (her *objet petit a*), and the signifier, "fascinated" plays an important part, through its insistent recurrence in the text, in representing the conscious spell that the perceiving subject will be under when faced with the elusive object of its desire.

Symptomatic reading of poetic metaphors
The figurative representation of unconscious material is central to Lawrence's writing the sexual. In his work we find instances of what Lacan has called the "poetic metaphor": the creative spark of metaphor (*"l'étincelle créatrice de la métaphore"*). From the beginning, Lacan identifies metaphor with the poetic: "a definition of poetical style could be to say that it begins with metaphor, and that where metaphor ceases poetry ceases also."[143] The poetic metaphor is at its most striking in the Surrealist's incongruous juxtapositions (which were so attractive to Lacan that they even influenced his own style). The process of symbolization expressed in metaphor presupposes for Lacan, however, a positional as opposed to a semantic similarity. This is controversial because Lacan is defining metaphor in the terms conventionally attributed to metonymy; that is, not semantic substitutions, but positional coherence in the apparatus of enchained signifiers. He associates metaphor with condensation, and metonymy with displacement. In "The Insistence of the Letter in the Unconscious" Lacan reminds us that Freud's word for condensation in the dream-work is *"Verdichtung"* which serves in itself as an example of the process it signifies, condensing into a metaphor the riddle of the unconscious and poetry (*"Dichtung"*). Condensation is the process of the poetic metaphor, which demands deciphering yet resists transparent reading. *"Verschiebung"*, with its connotations of a putting-off or postponement of meaning, is Freud's word for displacement, and Lacan likens it to the process of metonymy whereby insignificant objects, events or minor attributes, displace the full presence of the subject, censoring the truth of its being.

Chaitin has produced a useful gloss on Lacanian rhetorics. As he rightly insists, the creative function of metaphor plays the key role in Lacan's psychoanalytic theory:

---

[143] Lacan, *The Psychoses*, 264.

Most psychoanalysts explain poetry by means of psychoanalysis; for many years, Lacan explained psychoanalysis by means of poetry. "The symptom is a metaphor". "Desire is a metonymy". "The primary processes of condensation and displacement are equivalent to the rhetorical tropes of metaphor and metonymy". "The subject is a poetic creation". "Love is a metaphor". "Transferential repetition is a poetic process". "Psychoanalytic interpretation is metaphoric".[144]

Moreover, as the last statement suggests, Lacan's style is itself poetic: allusive, intertextual, playful; a rebus demanding deciphering. His theory of language is non-representational, placing him in a lineage that goes back to the Symbolists and the Surrealists where the poetic has the creative power to unfix positive meaning, to give priority to the intuitive over the intellect, and confer new identities on the beleaguered subject: "Metaphor is somehow involved in creating and filling the place where the discourses of the family, society or theory have left a void."[145] Metaphor no longer has an essentially mimetic function based on the semantics of similarity, as it has in its tradition from Aristotle to Jakobson. That would entail a relative stabilizing of meaning which would not square with Lacan's theory of the contiguity of figures whose significance is primarily positional. "Juxtaposition automatically takes on syntactic significance".[146] Metonymy has priority over metaphor in this precise sense that positional surprises, like the striking object or the incongruous juxtaposition, function like defamiliarization.

Evans provides us with a succinct summary of the differences between Lacan and Jakobson:

> Whereas for Jakobson, metonymy is linked to both displacement and condensation, and metaphor to identification and symbolism, Lacan links metaphor to condensation and metonymy to displacement .... Lacan then argues that just as displacement is logically prior to condensation, so metonymy is the condition for metaphor.[147]

Furthermore, the provisionality of signifiers is fundamental to a theory of

---

[144] Gilbert D. Chaitin, *Rhetoric and Culture in Lacan* (New York and London: Cambridge University Press, 1996), 1.
[145] Ibid., 44.
[146] Ibid., 48.
[147] Evans, 113.

speech as metaphoric. Chains of signifiers cannot be settled on definitive signifieds. Metaphor is thus a constructive process:

> In sum, metonymy, the linguistic structure designed to name ourselves and the world, to designate the meaning of being, necessarily institutes the separation of the subject from predicate, meaning from being .... It is left to metaphor to fill the gap in being opened up by language, by knotting signifiers together.[148]

Metaphor, in other words, has the task of reattaching the subject to its attributes. The poetic metaphor creates new imaginary relations between the subject and the world. Lacan has adapted Jakobsonian rhetorics by bringing it together with a theory of being. Metaphor as condensation is a form of resistance to a metaphysics of the stable, autonomous self, to the pressures of assimilation to the social code, and the "collective pressure of patriarchal nominalization". Lacan's own programmatic resistance to the positivisms of ego psychology has led him towards the mapping out of new places for the subject, new "signifiers of desire" beyond the phallocentric.[149]

Grigg[150] also draws attention to the difference between Lacan and Jakobson. Metonymy is unproblematic: it is produced by means of substitution (of attributes for the thing, parts for whole in synecdoche) and has a syntactic explanation. Lacan and Jakobson agree on the structure and function of metonymy. But metaphor is much more problematic. Grigg explains that there are three principal types of metaphor: substitution, extension, and apposite metaphor. They all work by semantic and positional similarity. Thus, for example, a metaphor may depend on latent relations in the contiguous syntactic chain, first and foremost, before any connections with any signifier it may have replaced. Lacan seems to accept this idea, even while limiting himself to substitution metaphor. Jakobson, though, gives priority to semantics over syntax. Implicitly, he has returned to a pre-Saussurian theory of language, giving priority to identity over difference. Lacan, however, goes beyond both Jakobson and Saussure, while remaining in a creative affiliation with them both. He inverts Saussure's formula by giving the signifier primacy over the signified; and, as Samuel Weber argues, he favours "differential

---

[148] Chaitin, 53-4.
[149] Ibid., 246, 253.
[150] Russell Grigg, "Metaphor and Metonymy" in *Newsletter of the Freudian Field* 3/12, (1989), 58-75.

syntactical relations over semantic functions".[151] For Lacan, metaphor is positional not semantic substitution between signifiers, in the first instance. ("*L'inconscient est un concept forgé sur la trace de ce qui opère pour constituer le sujet.*"[152]) The subject constitutes itself in the "differential articulation" of language. While returning to Saussure, Lacan breaks out of the closed system of "*la langue*", and rewrites the theory of speech as articulation, thus finding a place for the subject in language. The subject now has the potential "to signify something entirely different from what it says".[153] And:

> If there is desire, it is only because there is the unconscious, i.e. a language, whose structure and effects escape the subject: because, at the level of language, there is always something that is beyond consciousness, which allows the function of desire to be situated.[154]

The unconscious is situated in the deviant sentence. The attention of the reader is first drawn to the placing of the unusual metaphor, before the levels of semantic allusiveness come into play.

Now, notwithstanding the above critical commentaries on Jakobson and Lacan's uses of his rhetorics, I suggest that what is more significant for psychoanalytic reading — and this is the point of my revisiting in some detail Lacanian rhetorics — is that we consider Lacan's theory of the poetic metaphor as a reworking of Jakobson's notion of the "poetic function" to correspond to his (Lacan's) ontology. "The creative spark of the metaphor" (Lacan) reminds us of the Russian Formalist concept of defamiliarization from which Jakobson derives his notion of a "poetic function" of language: "The poetic function projects the principle of equivalence from the axis of selection into the axis of combination."[155] Or, in Grigg's words: "striking metaphors make unexpected comparisons, and it is precisely the metaphor itself that makes us notice something new."[156] What the poetic function does, then, is to foreground the act of expression by drawing attention initially to the device itself and not the message or referent. The paradigmatic axis is also the place of metaphor,

---

[151] Samuel Weber, *Return to Freud: Jacques Lacan's Dislocation of Psychoanalysis* (London: Cambridge University Press, 1991), 53.
[152] Lacan, "Position de l'inconscient", cited in Weber, 10.
[153] Weber, 41.
[154] Lacan "Psychanalyse et médecine", cited in Weber, 54.
[155] Roman Jakobson (1958), "Linguistics and Poetics" reprinted in Lodge ed., *Modern Criticism and Theory: A Reader* (London and New York: Longman, 1988), 39.
[156] Grigg, 68.

the figure of similarity. The syntagmatic axis is the place of metonymy, the figure of contiguity. The poetic function is, thus, the incursion of the metaphoric into the metonymic chain.

I believe that such an account of Lacan's rhetorics clarifies his insistence on the priority of metonymy over metaphor, precisely in the sense that the syntagmatic chain is suddenly punctuated by signifiers of degrees of defamiliarity. Examples in Lawrence's *Sons and Lovers* are: "a white, virgin scent" (SL, 196) — describing roses, which at the same time is a projection of deep sexual feelings; "She flushed deeply, and he was covered with confusion" (SL, 301); "so that they knew they were only grains in the tremendous heave that lifted every grass-blade its little height" (SL, 398); "A grey, deathly dawn crept over the snow" (SL, 441); "Paul felt crumpled up and lonely" (SL, 451). Such tropes belong to an aesthetic structure of recurrent patternings of condensed or displaced motifs, in a significant play of unconscious forces.

I want finally to look at an extended example of the symptomatic text in *Sons and Lovers*. While Mrs Morel is pregnant with Paul she is locked out of the house by her husband after he has come home drunk and they have had a row. This passage (SL, 34-35) represents the eviction of the woman from the symbolic realm of the family house, a realm usurped by the man in a moment of drunken fury, but otherwise a matriarchal space. Once in the garden she is disoriented as her subjectivity is being reshaped by a different sense of otherness, and one that is a startling refiguring of her unconscious desire. The Lacanian subject is a configuration of degrees of imaginary positions in an articulation of desire constrained by symbolic alterity. Such a subject is represented in the text through a series of aesthetic strategies, which by their poetic defamiliarization, map out an imaginary space for resisting the symbolic with its patriarchal, social codes.

Symptoms are metaphors of the woman's immediate anxiety, as she goes over the ground of the traumatic scene: words spoken in anger are burnt into her consciousness "like a brand red-hot". The moment is worked through, repeating the essentially painful memory. The passion is transferred to the foetus which "boiled within her" — a trope that overdetermines the symptom of her delirium. She is no longer in conscious control, until, after a temporal lacuna which encompasses her loss of awareness, a completely new sense of otherness enforces her return to consciousness. The dark night is radiant with a luminous presence, implicitly offsetting the cold, sunless hovel of the inner, household space. The glaring white moonlight maps out the space for the hysteria of female sexuality — an imaginary lunacy as powerful resistance to the symbolic subject positioning. At this point, the symptomatic metaphor of the woman's anxiety is displaced by the metonymic as unconscious desire.

The woman is vertiginously engulfed by the moonlight in her front garden, "as if in an immense gulf of white light, the moon streaming high in her face". Here, the natural world is overdetermined in a series of displacements of unconscious forces: the images of otherness trying to penetrate her consciousness with their stark presence — "The tall white lilies were reeling in the moonlight, and the air was charged with their perfume, as if with a presence" — are the uncanny, poetic, mirror-images of her unconscious. And as the unconscious is the discourse of the Other, that is her estranged or as yet undiscovered sexuality, putting her hand into the "white bin" of the lily and getting golden pollen on her fingers (and on her face, as she later notices in the mirror) may be read as the ritual scene of the articulation of an auto-erotic female sexuality beyond the phallocentric.

In general, the forceful presence of natural images on the female subject effects a kind of return to consciousness, after the nausea of "a kind of swoon". The cold white light of the moon serves, in her appropriation of it, to extinguish "her inflamed soul", even though the scene in the house will remain "branded" on her soul.

This passage may be characterized as Expressionist, by which I mean a writing, which in attempting to project unconscious material necessarily entails a poetic distortion of language. Kandinsky defined Expressionism as "presenting nature not as an external phenomenon, but predominantly the element of inner impression". Here Lawrence seems close to the art of van Gogh, whose "capacity for experience grew to ecstatic heights, and his experiences were given visual form in flame-like lines and brilliant and radiant colours".[157] Here, too, in Lawrence's writing, waves of nausea and vertigo — in what seems an intense moment of agoraphobia — appear to be caused by the vast plenitude of nature, the immensity of its light, and the "deep draught" of its scent, when instead they emanate from the "delirious condition" of the sentient subject herself, as her unvoiced deep desire is transferred to the lilies that "were reeling in the moonlight".

Figurative associations attach themselves to character and states of consciousness, and they reverberate on through the narrative adding an extra level of significance, an aesthetic structure. This allows the image to leave its original context and be used in an associative function elsewhere in the text. Symbolism in Lawrence is predominantly bound up with a dynamic context, and therefore it defies single meaning. Lawrence

---

[157] Cited in Wolf-Dieter Dube, *The Expressionists* (London: Thames and Hudson, 1972), 15, 20.

himself insisted that, "symbols are organic units of consciousness with a life of their own, and you can never explain them away, because their value is dynamic, emotional, belonging to the sense consciousness of the body and soul, and not simply mental".[158] In the selected passage, the woman's unstable self is not represented in a metaphysical language — as it so often is in Lawrence. Instead, the unconscious is a physical sensation represented through poetic tropes whose implications reverberate on through the narrative to the extent that repetition and modulation, in an aesthetic structure of recurrent motifs, enable thematic correspondence to achieve an insistent psychoanalytic implication.

In Lawrence's writing things retain their concreteness and are associated with the character through a sentient intensity of perception, thereby allowing the metaphor to have primarily positional, and then, subsequently, semantic allusion. The experiences of reality and inner perception are divorced, except in the psychoanalytic form of projection. Such "sense-consciousness" is not dissimilar to Joyce's notion of "epiphany" in *A Portrait of the Artist as a Young Man* (1916). In Lawrence, though, it is less reflective, more intuitive. Nature is not only the symbolic parallel of Mrs Morel's emotional crisis. It may function in that scene in this way, expressionistically. Throughout the novel, the allusions to key figures reverberate in a non-reductive manner; while the otherwise repressed demands of unconscious drives are bound briefly in such crucial moments to an imaginary world otherwise estranged from the subject.

Another key passage (SL, 231) where metaphor can be read symptomatically is when Paul "coming home from his walks with Miriam, was wild with torture". Here the darkness is a "great hollow ... fronting him" as if he is walking into a "pit" in "the lowest trough of the night". She has made him feel insecure, uncertain of himself "as if he had not sufficient sheathing to prevent the night and the space breaking into him". The figures represent Paul's aggressive, phallic attitude towards Miriam, the female Other. They contrast sharply to his mother's vertiginous, or Miriam's ecstatic-religious projections. (SL, 255) Consistent with these associations, the spring is the season of dread for Miriam because Paul is then always hostile towards her. (SL, 322) As the mother's health deteriorates, the "gold wedding-ring shone on her white hand .... And she watched the tangled sunflowers dying" (SL, 428). She dies, and a "grey, deathly dawn crept over the snow" (SL, 441). After her death, the

---

[158] Lawrence cited in Johann N. Schmidt, *D.H. Lawrence: Sons and Lovers* (Munich: UTB-Verlag, 1983), 66. Much of this discussion of symbolism in Lawrence is indebted to Schmidt, 65-69.

son's emotional and mental breakdown is represented by the figures of the void, and the empty space that surrounds him and is inside him too. He only experiences space not time, as now deprived of the anchor of his mother "on every side the immense dark silence seemed pressing on him, so tiny a spark, into extinction" (SL, 464), because his understanding of himself, and his very being, has been inextricably bound up with that of his mother.

5. Conclusion

Sons and Lovers is in one sense thoroughly conventional: it tells a family story based in a specific region and locality, and concentrates on individuals who are breaking away from home. However, the story is modernist because it uses that conventional fictional situation to represent the crisis of the modern self. In this, psychology and sexuality required a new language, and Lawrence's invention now looks like a version of the Oedipal fiction that Freud was theorizing at the time. This is not surprising because both Freud and Lawrence came to Oedipus via Sophocles and *Hamlet*.

Lawrence's radical invention is, in Eggert's words, "an innovative language and idiosyncratic syntax that would plot the deeper movements of the subconscious".[159] Lawrence had an expression for the kind of writing that can represent the unconscious: he called it "art-speech". It is at best a process of symbolization that would not be esoteric and mystical as in the occult writings of the Symbolists, but would represent states of being as "pure experience, emotional and passional, spiritual and perceptual, all at once". Lawrence's rhetorics, his metaphors and metonymies, insists on paradox.[160] In the (1919) preface to the American edition of *Women in Love* he wrote that art should never neglect the "struggle for verbal consciousness", which was "the passionate struggle into conscious being".[161]

As I hope to have shown in this chapter, once the text becomes the object of a Lacanian criticism, then the coming into being of the Lawrentian self is more clearly read as a struggle with otherness. The focalizing agent is a narrating consciousness whose figurative language expresses what is unconscious to it — as Lacan said, "the unconscious is the discourse of the Other". It is not so much what images mean that is at stake, but more in what relation they are to the perceiving subject. Tropes

---

[159] Paul Eggert (1990), "Opening up the text: the case of *Sons and Lovers*", 50-51.

[160] Lawrence, "The Spirit of Place", *English Review* (November 1918), 321; cited in Mark Kinkead-Weekes (1996), 389, 449.

[161] Reprinted in Appendix 1 of the Penguin edition of the Cambridge D.H. Lawrence (London, 1995).

are more forcefully turned into symbols in *Women in Love*, as their meaning becomes more mythical. In *Sons and Lovers*, the poetic metaphor enables the dynamic representation of unconscious material. Lawrence, writing a poetry of desire in the age of Freud, appears more radical when read through Lacan because the creative unconscious and its linguistic representation is prescient of Lacan's Imaginary as the creative misrecognition of the Real which enables the subject to resist the prescriptions of the Symbolic Order. Moreover, Lacan enables us to bring the psychoanalytic and the poetic together and thus avoid the traps of Freudian applied psychoanalysis. The split subject undergoes a complex representation in Lawrence's writing. From Lacanian psychoanalytic criticism I have put the concepts of the Imaginary, the Symbolic, the Real, metonymy and metaphor to work on the text of *Sons and Lovers* in an attempt to bring psychoanalysis and literature more productively together. Such work will always be tentative, as the dynamics of the transference may only be understood in literary criticism as a one-way, or at best two-way rhetorical move. We should remember Freud's words that "after all, we are only dealing with analogies".[162]

---

[162] See note 12 above.

2

The Rainbow and the Discursive Formations of History: Towards a Foucauldian Reading

1. Introduction

The Rainbow (1915)[1] clearly marks its historical intention by a set of dates and references covering the period of English history from 1840 to 1905. It records the coming of the Industrial Revolution to the Midlands and the gradual erosion of rural England in the landmark events like the constructions of the canal, the railway, and the coal mine. There are also the changes in education, and the greater opportunities for women; and the imperial history, with its references to Khartoum, the Boer War, and the British rule in India. The novel also presents that history in its relation to the personal lives of the three generations of Brangwens. To a contemporary of Galsworthy whose *Forsyth Saga* (1906-1921) promoted a popular genre, it is a family chronicle of a familiar kind. The real historical reference and the family history are, however, complicated by their framing in an archetypal or mythic history established in the opening pages. In this chapter I shall discuss the complication of histories.

There are two other kinds of history that have been described in opposed critical receptions. First, F.R. Leavis's "essential English history", a forceful reading of English civilization in terms of a cultural-ideological, mythic version of England's past, and one that is not unlike Lawrence's.[2] Second, history as apocalypse, a vision of spiritual degeneration and the self-destruction of mankind prefigured in the real catastrophe of the Great War, yet supposedly leading to regeneration. This apocalyptic reading with its emphasis on the Biblical reference in Lawrence was first proposed, *contra* Leavis's culturalist reading, by

---

[1] References in text [R] are to the Penguin edition of the Cambridge D.H. Lawrence (London, 1994).
[2] F.R. Leavis, *D.H. Lawrence: Novelist* (London: Penguin, 1985. First published 1955). For a critique see G.M. Hyde, *D.H. Lawrence* (London: Macmillan, 1990), ch.3.

Kermode (1973) and revived by Fjagesund (1991).[3]

In order to enable a constructive mediation between these different theories of history, I shall draw on the theories of Michel Foucault. Instead of discussing the novel and history as discrete entities with history serving as background, context, or influence, as much of the critical reception has it, Foucault should enable us to problematize such static distinctions by turning the discussion towards discourse, thus keeping us close enough to the texts of fiction and history while seeing the traces of history in the discursive practices represented in the novel.

It is, though, by no means certain that Foucault would have agreed with the reading of Lawrence that I shall present in this chapter. Foucault himself only mentions Lawrence twice in passing. Once, when in the last pages of volume one of *The History of Sexuality* he quotes from *The Plumed Serpent* (1926) where Kate Leslie is extolling the wonders of sex, "when men keep it powerful and sacred". Then, he has Lawrence himself tell us that "the full conscious realization of sex is even more important than the act itself".[4] For Foucault, Lawrence is a symptom of that malaise that characterizes modernity: namely, breaking taboos by talking volubly about sex, while at the same time not having a liberating effect at all.[5] Lawrence belongs to the modern formation of sexuality, its emergent discourse. As sexuality was freed from Victorian morality — and Lawrence's part in this was significant — it only became more trapped in the greater unfreedom of the sciences and pseudo-sciences of sexology, psychoanalysis, pansexualism, and so on.[6] Foucault, however, curiously misreads Lawrence who was also against the scientific explanation of sexuality, and understood the limits of writing the sexual. But, like Foucault, Lawrence found writing the only medium in which to say that publicly.

I should stress from the outset, however, that there is no Foucauldian theory which can simply be applied to literature. He himself insisted, as Macey (1994) points out, "that his texts were a toolkit to be used or discarded by anyone and not a catalogue of theoretical ideas implying

---

[3] Frank Kermode, *Lawrence* (Glasgow: Fontana, 1973); Peter Fjagesund, *The Apocalyptic World of D.H. Lawrence* (London and Oslo: Norwegian University Press, 1991).

[4] *The History of Sexuality Volume 1: An Introduction* (London: Penguin, 1984. First published 1976), 157. Subsequent references in text [HS1].

[5] We ought not, though, to overlook the irony of Foucault's stance on the history of modern sexuality. After all, he himself "made a voluminous contribution to studies of sexuality while condemning *perpetual discourse* on sex". Domna C. Stanton, *Discourses of Sexuality* (Ann Arbor: University of Michigan Press, 1992), 1.

[6] For further discussion see Stephen Heath, *The Sexual Fix* (London: Macmillan, 1982) — a post-Foucauldian study which makes significant reference to Lawrence.

some conceptual unity".[7] In this spirit, I shall use Foucault's texts selectively and strategically as toolkits for radical rereadings of the relationship of *The Rainbow* to history. For this purpose, my Foucauldian reading is divided up into a sequence of units that correspond to the principal concepts in Foucault's main works: "the myth of origins"; "the historical archive"; "the modern episteme"; "power/knowledge"; "discipline and punish"; and, finally, "the aesthetics of transgression". This framework derives from the work beginning with *Madness and Civilization* (1961), *The Order of Things* (1966), *The Archaeology of Knowledge* (1969); and on through to the later works, *Discipline and Punish* (1975), and the three volumes of *The History of Sexuality* (1976, 1985, 1986). The exception to this chronology is the last section. Foucault's theory of literature as trangression belongs to the early work of the 1960s, although the notion of transgression continues to play a role in the later ethics. His idealist notion of the trangressive role of avant-garde literature and thought derives from his profound interest in the French *Nouveau Roman* (Robbe-Grillet) and the *Nouvelle Critique* (Roland Barthes), and is typified by his book on the obscure French Surrealist writer, Raymond Roussel (1877-1933).[8] Foucault's theory of transgression also plays a key role in *Madness and Civilization* (1961) and *The Order of Things* (1966). However, I believe that, although the radical critical practice of the *Tel Quel* journal to which the Roussel study belongs seems to have little ostensible use in reading Lawrence, its general implications for assessing Lawrence's Modernism should not be overlooked. As I hope to show in this chapter, Lawrence's principal transgression is both linguistic and ethical. It is seen in his poetic and, for 1915, audacious representation of sexuality and sex.

2. The reception of *The Rainbow* as historical novel

For Leavis (1955), *The Rainbow* was "essential English history", by which he meant Lawrence diagnosed the England of 1914 in terms of its "spiritual heritage".[9] However, Leavis (1976) insisted that what the old Brangwen civilization represented is not something Lawrence "would have wished to preserve".[10] The opening pages of the novel are "a necessary and potent presence", but, importantly, are "something to be

[7] David Macey, *The Lives of Michel Foucault* (London: Vintage, 1994), xx.
[8] *Death in the Labyrinth: The World of Raymond Roussel* (London: The Athlone Press, 1987. First published 1963).
[9] Leavis (1985), op. cit., 126.
[10] F.R. Leavis, *Thought, Words and Creativity: Art and Thought in Lawrence* (London: Chatto & Windus, 1976), 139.

transcended".[11] There are two points to make about Leavis's history: first, there is an agenda here to rescue Lawrence from the accusations current at the time of proto-fascism.[12] Second, Leavis privileges a history of civilization based on the values of the individual, and forgets the social and the historical in the process, and this even though he insisted that Lawrence was a social historian whose novel has "its historical depth".[13] In fact Leavis has selected one aspect of the novel — its emphasis on the loss of the spiritual dimension in modern life — precisely because Lawrence now confirms Leavis's own critique of modern civilization (i.e. "essential English civilization"). As many have pointed out before, this is a reductive reading. The contradictions of represented history are smoothed over. Nevertheless, Leavis's (1955) reading was to establish a critical consensus which runs something like: the gradual loss of the ideal organic community declines finally into the alienated, spiritually empty individual in the modern, mechanistic world. Raymond Williams' early work on Lawrence inherited this view for the Left, and Terry Eagleton kept it in circulation.[14]

Arguing against this consensus, Holderness (1982) questions whether the mythologizing tendency of the novel enables anything other than a strictly ideological view of history.[15] He argues that, although the novel is carefully dated, and the real historical references are mostly accurate, and the three generations are linked to the larger changes and events, progressively, history is presented reductively. The organic, pastoral life is contrasted sharply with "the nightmare" of Wiggiston colliery around 1880. This dualistic perspective will continue to dominate Lawrence's thinking about history. It is still there at the end of his life when he wrote the essay (1929), "Nottingham and the Mining Country".[16] This late essay clearly shows Lawrence's reduction of history and social relations to the opposition between an ideal organic past and a mechanistic present. Old

---

[11] Ibid., 117.
[12] Cf. Bertrand Russell, *The Autobiography of Bertrand Russell* (London: Unwin, 1975), 245-246: "He [Lawrence] had a mystical philosophy of the *blood* ... and I rejected it vehemently, though I did not know then that it led straight to Auschwitz. ... The world between the wars was attracted to madness. Of this attraction Nazism was the most emphatic expression. Lawrence was a suitable exponent of this cult of insanity."
[13] Leavis (1985), 173.
[14] Raymond Williams, *Culture and Society* (London: Penguin, 1958); *The English Novel from Dickens to Lawrence* (London: The Hogarth Press, 1984). Terry Eagleton, *Criticism and Ideology* (London: New Left Books, 1976).
[15] Graham Holderness, *D.H. Lawrence: History, Ideology and Fiction* (Dublin: Gill & Macmillan, 1982). Page references in text.
[16] *Selected Essays* (London: Penguin, 1974). Page references in text [SE].

rural England has gone for ever and with it the life of the organic
community (an ideology reinscribed in Leavis). Modern industrial Britain
has spoilt the country and the life of the people. The organic has given
way to the mechanistic. Man's true destiny, then, is to rediscover that lost
ideal. Holderness, however, insists that the mining communities were
both organic and mechanical, and that Lawrence's idealist totalities are a
symptom of his aestheticizing of history. For the old England of his youth
where "Robin Hood and his merry men were not very far away," (SE,
114) is that "old agricultural England of Shakespeare and Milton and
Fielding and George Eliot" (SE, 117). The people lived an almost
instinctive existence; the men brought with them from the mine a
"curious dark intimacy ... a lustrous sort of inner darkness, like the gloss
of coal in which we moved and had our real being". The conclusion to
this reminiscence is that frequently quoted passage: "The real tragedy of
England, as I see it, is the tragedy of ugliness. The country is so lovely:
the man-made world so vile" (SE, 119). The ugliness of industrialism
(real history) is contrasted with the loveliness of an ideal past (represented in literature). Thus Lawrence fails to offer a solution to the
problem of the contemporary England he diagnoses because, as
Holderness puts it, "he misconceives the problem itself" (Holderness,
38).

Now, notwithstanding the naiveties of Lawrence's essay, Holderness's critique of the novel cannot be simply corroborated by it. Novels
have a tendency to undo such simplistic oppositions in their complex
play of voices and symbolisms, a truth that Lawrence would have been
the first to acknowledge. Moreover, accusing Lawrence of offering "a
peculiarly pure and non-contradictory ideology ... as an alternative to
history", is largely beside the point and will not get us very far. When
was there ever a non-ideological representation of history? Holderness
even demonstrates, in his dispute here with Eagleton's[17] description of
Lawrence's ideological contradictions, that ideologies are non-
contradictory totalities by definition, but may be put into contradiction by
a critique deriving from another strong ideology. This kind of argument
was, of course, prevalent at the time Holderness was writing; and in it we
see a classic example of the dispute within Marxist criticism between an
Althusserian literary criticism represented in Britain at the time by
Eagleton, and Holderness's more orthodox Lukácsian criticism. He goes
on to insist that the "radically alienated perspective" (Holderness, 185) on
the process of industrialization, a perspective from the outside and from
above — Ursula's strident attack on the horrors of Wiggiston colliery is

---

[17] See note 14.

only opposed by her uncle Tom, the manager — is a blatant misrepresentation of history. *The Rainbow* is not a "realist totality", but an "evolving generational structure" without realism or history. The rainbow symbol at the end is its logical conclusion, as the new society will reproduce the old, and the sickness in the instrumental social life will be healed by being "incorporated into the individual and represented in her image". Thus it is that history completely disappears while ideology "descends from the heavens and unifies a fractured world" (Holderness, 186-9). If the irony is not intended here, then amazingly Holderness's recourse to figurative language mimics Lawrence's tendency towards aestheticization!

Leavis and Holderness, although coming from opposite ends of the political spectrum, both nevertheless represent particularly closed readings. Whatever their respective merits, such criticism reduces semiotic complexity to this or that aspect only, so that the novel seems to function merely as an object of a particularly narrow, restrictive criticism. By contrast, Kinkead-Weekes is more open to the textual complexities when he proposes three distinct senses of history in *The Rainbow*.[18] First, archetypal history with its Biblical and mythic reference. Second, real history recording the changes in English life from the rural to the urban, the agricultural to the industrial in the process of modernization. Third, the personal history of the three Brangwen generations. What we should notice is the interplay between the different histories. The personal lives become individually more and more connected to the wider circle of real history; the archetypal remains a conservative force, by definition, undermining the force of historical change by insisting on recurrent patterns in the perennial conflicts between men and women. In this it is an ahistorical structure. But, Kinkead-Weekes asks, how do the great changes of history affect the different generations of the Brangwen family, and how significant are the effects on the form and structure of the novel?

In the first generation, Marsh farm is relatively isolated from the events of history. The second gets progressively more involved. By the third, the novel presents "a fully historic world" (Kinkead-Weekes, 122). For Lawrence, though — as his "Study of Thomas Hardy" insists — the work is less about real events and more to do with "the evolutionary development of consciousness and selfhood" (Kinkead-Weekes, 136, note 1). However, *The Rainbow* is historical fiction because, besides the

---

[18] Mark Kinkead-Weekes (1985), "The Sense of History in *The Rainbow*" in Peter Preston & Peter Hoare eds, *D.H. Lawrence in the Modern World* (London: Macmillan, 1989). All page references in text.

level of archetype and myth, there is an "elaborate chronology" (Kinkead-Weekes, 123). Moreover, as one might expect from the logic of the plot and the development of the personal lives of the characters, the greater historical reference occurs in the third generation, as the world is largely perceived through the growing awareness of it by the characters. Here in the latter parts of the book we get references to *imperial history*: Khartoum (1885), the Boer War (1899-1902), and the British rule in India; *social history*: education reform, the Women's Movement, class inequality; *the history of science*: the new materialism and the empirical scientific attitude, but also the vastly improved conditions of life enabled by modern science and technology. It is the portrait of an age. And, as John Worthen also insists, some things really existed, actually happened in the places and to the families Lawrence knew, even though the names have been changed and some slight anachronisms are permitted for the sake of the plot (Kinkead-Weekes, 125).[19] In 1840, for instance, the canal-building age was coming to an end, but as the Midland Counties Railway opened, at about the time the beginning of the novel is set, the canal was extended,[20] just as new coal-seams were opened up. From the mid-1840s in both Derby and Nottingham industry underwent rapid expansion — the Nottingham lace factory (1846) — and the urban population increased by some twenty-fold by the 1890s, when the provision for wider access to education was established. It is important to notice, therefore, that the story also shows that Lawrence is not simply against modernity, as has often been claimed. The first generation is only half-educated, and the mother has educational ambitions for her son Tom who is sent to Nottingham Grammar school (which would have been unusual then, but not without precedent).[21] Thus she initiates a process of self-improvement, and one with clear historical and biographical reference. It belongs to a story also tried out in *Sons and Lovers* — as I described in chapter 1 — but with different emphases. Ursula's uncle Tom in the second generation goes to the Royal School of Mines (later Imperial College) in London. Will Brangwen benefits from the William Morris-inspired Arts and Crafts movement in education reform and becomes an

---

[19] Cf. John Worthen, "A Lawrence Biographer in Nottinghamshire" in Peter Preston ed., *D.H. Lawrence: The Centre and the Circles* (D.H. Lawrence Centre, University of Nottingham: Occasional Papers No.1, 1992), 21: "Lawrence wrote about the Nottinghamshire he knew, recreated it in detail ... drew on it, re-made it, revisted it in memory far more often than in fact. ... The families and landscapes ... were arguably by far the most important source for his writing, all his life."

[20] Kinkead-Weekes, 137, note 15: the actual spot of the canal still exists, "one can stand on it today."

[21] Worthen, 24-5.

instructor; and Ursula and Gudrun both receive a formal education, which would have been unimaginable for their grandmother's generation. Gudrun goes to Art College and Ursula becomes a teacher.

The most significant change, however, is the declining influence of the church and "the religious sense" (Kinkead-Weekes, 129). Victorian established religion had reduced the spiritual to morality; modern science and philosophical scepticism had cast doubt on the blind faith of earlier generations. Much has been written about this shadow over the Christian faith which appeared throughout the latter half of the nineteenth century. It is recorded in its best poetry. For Lawrence, too, modernity has gone wrong in "the very springs of human life". If this is Lawrence's message in *The Rainbow*, and the consensus says it is, then, as Kinkead-Weekes rightly says, we should read the beginning of the novel as establishing the archetype of a lost world: an allegorical reading of what is wrong with the England of 1914. The generations re-enact archetypal patterns, but each time under the newer demands and tensions of the changing historical circumstances (Kinkead-Weekes, 131). Salgado (1982) makes a similar point, but in a less structuralist language than that of Kinkead-Weekes.[22] Each of the main characters undergoes "the same struggle for fulfilment", enacting "the same story" while becoming more self-conscious.[23] The male and female principles, that dualistic structure worked out in the "Study of Thomas Hardy" and proposed at the beginning of the novel, may be a universalising impulse; but for Ursula, the representative New Woman, the pattern has become reductive for her "complex being". Thus it is that the archetypal and the personal history are related to the real history diagnostically. The message is: "through the decline in the religious sense, people have lost touch with the primary creative energies" (Kinkead-Weekes, 136).

Fjagesund[24] takes us much further than these three views of history. He takes up and expands Kermode's reading, arguing for an apocalyptic, millenarian history. *The Rainbow*, for him, is historical in the following senses:

---

[22] Kinkead-Weekes' "structuralism" may be a coincidence, writing as he does as late as 1985. The coincidence of course derives from Lawrence's own archetypal insistence. Anthropology — as Foucault would point out — belongs to the late nineteenth-century *episteme*, the *a priori* in thinking historically. I shall return to this point below. Kinkead-Weekes' method of criticism relies on describing objectively what he finds in Lawrence's novel.

[23] Gamini Salgado, *A Preface to Lawrence* (London: Longman, 1982), 112.

[24] Fjagesund, op. cit. Page references in text.

1. *Joachist* — an ancient form of spiritual cataclysm whereby the Biblical Flood gives way to the New Spring of God's Covenant with man, itself symbolized in the rainbow (Fjagesund, 16).

2. *Organical-Cyclical* — a complex reinscription of the Romantic and the mythological prefigured in the relationship between nature (the cycles of the seasons) and the generations, represented in patterns of essential oppositions: birth/death, growth/decay, light/darkness, for instance (Fjagesund, 14). Here is the basis of Lawrence's critique of the received History of Progress, and one that derives from Nietzsche's idea of the "eternal recurrence" combined with the general cultural pessimism prevalent at the time of writing (Spengler's *Decline of the West* was published in 1918). This view of history would play a greater part in *Women in Love* and *Lady Chatterley's Lover*.

3. *Heroic-Totalitarian* — expressing Lawrence's anti-democratic views, and receiving its fullest treatment in the "leadership" novels of the 1920s. Ursula is that special being who will demonstrate the way forward (Fjagesund, 22). Significantly, Lawrence's original blurb for the novel was about Ursula "waiting at the advance post of our time to blaze a path into the future" — so that in 1915 the women were to be the leaders; indeed, as Pinkney puts it, they were to "embody the potential utopian energies of the culture".[25]

4. *History as the Movement of Blind Forces* — in the light of the popular reception of Darwin (Evolution, Natural Selection) — but also the attack on rationalism in the philosophy of Schopenhauer, Nietzsche, and Bergson (irrationalism, nihilism, intuition, respectively) — and its literary representation in the naturalism of Zola and Hardy, the outbreak of the Great War in 1914 was confirmation that mankind was subject to cosmic forces beyond his control (Fjagesund, 23-4).

5. *The Renunciation of History* — the withdrawal from society to a Utopia is exemplified in Lawrence's various real or fictional alternative places during his quasi-nomadic life for which "Rananim" was the first.

---

[25] Tony Pinkney, *D.H. Lawrence* (Hemel Hempstead: Harvester Wheatsheaf, 1990), 71.

According to Fjagesund, the fiction mixes these five attitudes to history to varying degrees. Moreover, such an apocalyptic mind-set captures the mood of the early twentieth century, and Fjagesund usefully sketches its cultural history. The Edwardian period was characterized by doom and despair; its energies were focussed, especially through the popular press, on a growing *Germanophobia* (Fjagesund, 46). The popular literature of the time is typified by H.G. Wells' end-of-the-world and invasion stories (Fjagesund, 47). Signs of the end of civilization were imminent (the end of English civilization, of course). Ironically enough, though, the philosophy that gave such ideas credence came from Germany, and Lawrence was well read in it.[26] The dominant intellectual and artistic response, was a diagnosis of a general decadence and a call for a spiritual renewal. It is one for which Lawrence is representative. He proposes sex itself as the source of salvation, because it is the closest we get to a genuinely spiritual ontology. This is a return to an ancient idea, and one that is a necessary emphasis in Fjagesund's reading of Lawrence's apocalyptic notion of history.

3. Foucault, history and discourse
These various readings have in their different ways argued for a relationship between the novel and history. What difference does Foucault make when he assumes that all texts represent history in their letter because they are constructed from the multiplicity of discourses in circulation? A "discourse" in Foucault's sense is "a set of rules about what you can and cannot say. It insists on the connections between language, politics, and social practice".[27] Furthermore, if history is only available in textual form, Lawrence's novel, like any novel, philosophical or scientific treatise is bounded by the discourses contemporary with them, including what counted as history. It is to Foucault's discursive notion of history that we now turn.

Foucault has been appropriately described as a postmodern historian.[28] History consists of a series of practices deriving from discourses which the historian analyses in the available texts of a period. Thus the dominant way of seeing and understanding, the *episteme,* defines what a

---

[26] For information about secondary literature on Lawrence's connections with Germany see *Lawrence and Germany: A Bibliography*, complied by Michael Weithmann and Regina Hoffmann, with an introduction by Robert Burden (Passau: University of Passau Library, 1995).

[27] Michèle Barrett, "Discoursing with Intent" in *Times Higher Education Supplement* (12 May 1995).

[28] Flynn, "Foucault's Mapping of History" in Gary Gutting ed., *The Cambridge Companion to Foucault* (Cambridge: Cambridge University Press, 1994), 39-45.

period takes as given or *a priori*. This then informs the knowledges and the practices of science, medicine, psychology, and literature (precisely in its oppositional stance). Foucault's idea of history is not a traditional history of ideas which wants to demonstrate a sense of continuity by rewriting the past to justify the present in the terms of a development or the progress of civilization towards modernity (typical of an imperialist history, for example). The story of progress requires a smoothing over of discontinuities, contradictions, and the marginalization of texts that simply do not tell the same story. Moreover, such a history requires foundational principles, final causes and origins: the "civilizing mission" or "scientific progress", for example. In refusing such a history, Foucault has been its sharpest critic; and has been attacked in turn by traditional historians for it. His history is, instead, a discontinuous history, not so much explanatory, and certainly not teleological, but, rather, diagnostic. This is postmodernism by definition because of "its eschewal of foundations, origins, ultimates, and grand theories in favour of practical, moral (in the broad sense) concerns".[29] Therefore, the Foucauldian critique of the traditional nineteenth-century triumphalist history of progress would not locate, as that history itself did, "objectively" an origin in the past to explain the process of modernity. Instead it would insist that the origin and the consequent logic of its teleology is nothing more nor less than a fiction to justify the present. Indeed, teleologies always justify the present. Continuous history, that history of antecedents, is always a guarantee of progress. Foucault proposes radical discontinuity as a strategy to undermine conservative history. In *The Archaeology of Knowledge* (1969) he questions teleologies and totalizations, but also those other guarantees: evolution, influence, and tradition. Rorty captures Foucault's point well: "The urge to tell stories of progress, maturation and synthesis might be overcome if we once took seriously the notion that we only know the world and ourselves under a description."[30] Indeed, in order to make use of Foucault's critique of traditional history, we need to grant a strategic validity to his historical nominalism, not least because it concerns itself with the discourses that limit the description of the world in past social formations, be they scientific, philosophical, political, juridical, or literary.

   Another major point that we can derive from Foucault is that the causal process of a history of antecedents also guarantees the sovereignty of the subject. The subject is granted a stable foundation in its history —

---

[29] Ibid., 43-4.
[30] Richard Rorty, "Foucault and Epistemology" in David Couzens Hoy ed., *Foucault: A Critical Reader* (Oxford: Blackwell, 1986), 48.

a procedure especially apparent at the moment of high imperialism in Britain, for instance — so that a stage in civilization is given a coherence and unity through its History.[31] In Robert Young's words: "Continuous history and the subject are thus dependent on each other."[32] What Foucault does is investigate the specific conditions in any period in which the subject becomes a basis of knowledge. Subjects are produced by discourses — for example, the "hysterical woman" or "hypochondriac man" of psychiatric discourse in the nineteenth century; the "primitive savage" and "enlightened humanist" of the discourse of imperialism in the late nineteenth, and early twentieth centuries.

Foucault's historical research is "archival", by which he means not just the collecting of texts which have survived a given period, but the set of rules which define:

1. what has been designated as discourse and thus constitutes the limits of what can be said;

2. what discourses or statements were put into circulation, and what was repressed or censored;

3. what counted as memory — how the past was being understood;

4. what discourses from the past, or from other cultures are retained or imported or reconstituted;

5. what classes, groups, or individuals have access to discourses, which ones are institutionalized, and which have been appropriated by force.[33]

From the first book to the last, Foucault always demonstrated an obsessional historicity, as we can see from these principles of historical analysis. It is not surprising, therefore, that he prioritizes discourse, when history for him consists of the reading of texts. Literature has played a key role in this history, in its transgressive potential, and one carefully illustrated by a chosen canon of madmen and outsiders, from Sade to

---

[31] Foucault, *The Archaeology of Knowledge* (London: Routledge, 1992. First published 1969), 12-13. Subsequent references in text [AK].
[32] Robert Young, *White Mythologies* (London: Routledge, 1990), 79.
[33] Michel Foucault, "Politics and the Study of Discourse" in *Ideology and Consciousness*, 3 (1978. First published 1968).

Artaud. *Madness and Civilization* (1961)[34] could even be read as a literary history. The historicist analysis of discourse takes him into the areas of the "positivities" — as he put it — that dominate a set of discourses, investigating which of these have disappeared, and which have continued to have a long after-life. One of his examples is "immersion" in water as it relates to rites of purification and rebirth in ablution. Thus, water "serves as a universal physiological regulator", and appears in moral as well as medical discourses. Hydrotherapy has a long history, and its forms and modalities, in antiquity, the middle ages, or the eighteenth century, are full of contradictions disguised by the universal belief in its virtues which derive from nothing more nor less than a metaphor (MC, 166-72). Simon During gives the example of "life", a positivity in circulation since the early nineteenth century, and one that orders and shapes quite different discursive practices: "novels like those of D.H. Lawrence; literary criticism like that of F.R. Leavis, as well as biology after Cuvier and Bichat".[35] I would add that they do not just influence art, literature, philosophy, or science, but enter the popular imagination through science-fiction bestsellers, for example. Foucault also called these positivities "operative metaphors" (MC, 162). I shall be looking in some detail at such metaphors in *The Rainbow*.

Another key concept is the *"episteme"* which Foucault defines as the totality of relations between discursive practices. It is the historical *a priori,* a set of constraints on what may be thought and said: "There is, for example, the archaeological description of *sexuality* ... how a discourse of a scientific type was established through the rupture brought about by Freud." Or, in a more ethical direction, how sexuality "is invested not in scientific discourses, but in a system of prohibitions and values" (AK, 193). More controversial is Foucault's assertion that, "In any given period ... there is always only one *episteme* that defines the conditions of possibility of all knowledge".[36] For the period from the late nineteenth century he claims that the dominant *episteme* is anthropology which, "as an analytic of man has certainly played a constituent role in modern thought, since to a large extent we are still not free from it". Anthropology is a discursive formation, at once the science of man and the end of man. However, after Nietzsche, we are no longer able "to think

---

[34] Michel Foucault, *Madness and Civilization:A History of Insanity in the Age of Reason* (London: Routledge, 1992. First published 1961). Subsequent references in text [MC].
[35] Simon During, *Foucault and Literature: Towards a Genealogy of Writing* (London: Routledge, 1992), 98.
[36] Michel Foucault, *The Order of Things: An Archaeology of the Human Sciences* (London: Routledge, 1991. First published 1966). Subsequent references in text [OT].

of our day other than in the void left by man's disappearance". (OT, 340) Foucault's Nietzschean critique of humanism is supported by his theory of discourse: at the moment of man's positioning at the very centre of knowledge he becomes its object. Anthropology will, however, be challenged by ethnology (a lesson learnt from Lévi-Strauss). And, if we turn Foucault's thought back on itself, we can see that the *episteme* that restrains it is none other than psychoanalysis. It is Freud, and Lacan's rereading of Freud, that has made Foucauldian theory possible.[37]

For a Foucauldian reading of Lawrence the notion of sexuality as discourse is enabling. In *The History of Sexuality Volume 1* (1976) Foucault argued that, contrary to popular belief, the Victorian epoch did not repress sex, but instead, as Boyne explains; "witnessed a veritable explosion of sex talk. Underlying this explosion was the creation of the form of sexuality itself".[38] A much more positive way of linking sex as an object of discourse with sex as an ontological experience, however, is captured in the following enigmatic statement, taken from Foucault's homage to Bataille in 1963: "On the day that sexuality began to speak and be spoken, language no longer served as a veil for the infinite; and in the thickness that it acquired on that day, we now experience finitude and being."[39] And later in *The Order of Things* (1966) Foucault reiterates his overriding concern with sex and discourse, describing the age of sexuality beginning after Sade as "desire battering at the limits of representation" (OT, 210). (A formulation that well describes Lawrence's writing the sexual, as I described it through psychoanalytic criticism in the last chapter.) By the time of his inaugural lecture at the Collège de France (1970), published as "The Order of Discourse", his work is turning away from "archaeology" towards the analysis of power. It is here that we find the first explicit attempt to link sexuality and politics. Discourse itself is now power: those who own or use discourse define their objects, and receive institutional support — a well-documented sea change in Foucault after the "Events" of 1968.[40] The discourses that have

---

[37] A claim made by Derrida in "To Do Justice to Freud: The History of Madness in the Age of Psychoanalysis" in *Critical Inquiry*, 20 (Winter 1994). Foucault's concept of the *episteme* is not, however, uncontroversial. Cf. Jameson (1972), op. cit., 193: "one cannot ... reduce history to one form of understanding among others, and then be able to understand the links between these forms historically."
[38] Roy Boyne, *Foucault and Derrida: The Other Side of Reason* (London: Unwin Hyman, 1990), 137.
[39] "A Preface to Transgression" (1963) in D.F. Bouchard ed., *Michel Foucault: Language, Counter-Memory, Practice: Selected Essays and Interviews* (Ithaca, New York: Cornell University Press, 1977), 51.
[40] "The Order of Discourse" in Robert Young ed., *Untying the Text: A Post-Structuralist Reader* (London: Routledge, 1981. First published 1970), 52-3.

sexuality as their object appear right through Foucault's work, from the medical, psychiatric, legal and literary discourses of the early works, to the Christian and ethical discourses of *The History of Sexuality*. In all this, Foucault remains the historicist, only his practice in the later works has shifted to "genealogy", a work much more explicitly Nietzschean.

By *Discipline and Punish* (1975), his study of systems of incarceration and technologies of discipline, he is writing about the power discourses exercise over bodies, a technology of power supported by the State Apparatus. Discourse is linked to subjection.[41] (Pedagogy is one such practice, and I shall discuss it later in a reading of education in *The Rainbow*.) It is here that Foucault first explicitly links power and knowledge: "Power produces knowledge ... power and knowledge directly imply one another." Power-knowledge relations are now the focus of his work: "The history of this *micro-physics* of the punitive power would then be a genealogy of the modern *soul* (DP, 27-29)." By the time Foucault publishes his first book on sexuality, though, power has lost its negative connotations, and is now seen as a productive relation. Influenced by Lacan, as much of his work seems to be, Foucault produces a notion of sexuality as "the will-to-knowledge" (*"la volonté de savoir"*) which, in its ambivalence and complexity, brings politics and psychoanalysis together. Not surprisingly it has been a major influence on sexual politics.

4. A Foucauldian reading of *The Rainbow*

i. The myth of origins
The opening pages of *The Rainbow* are a classic instance of the myth of an origin which then represents both a genealogy and the formation of a discourse. The genealogy is that of the Brangwens; the discourse, a complex redeployment of the Old Testament Genesis story and a Georgic pastoral poem to represent Lawrence's ideal of a pre-industrial Golden Age when man was at one with the natural world. The writing has a "genuine archaic and ritualistic force"[42] because it is "saturated in scripture".[43] The style represents in its paratactic structure the rhythm of the seasons, the work of the men on the land and the succession of the generations, reinforcing a truth that will reappear at key moments in the novel, either thematically or figuratively. The ancient narrative that opens

---

[41] Michel Foucault, *Discipline and Punish: The Birth of the Prison* (London: Penguin, 1986. First published 1975), 23-4. Subsequent references in text [DP].
[42] Kermode, 45.
[43] Hyde, 42.

the modern novel insists on the recurrent patterns of nature and the generations of Brangwens. It also presents a much older, cyclical theory of history whose conservative force will be used to counter that other, modern theory of history as linear, teleological, and progressive. However, the two histories will be linked causally by a third history, and one derived from the Old Testament discourse in these opening pages, namely: apocalyptic history. Once the traditional life is destroyed by the process of industrialization, old values and simple faiths are thrown into doubt, a spiritual degeneration sets in, and the world will have its flood before the rainbow can stand again on the cleansed earth.

Traditionally, the pastoral idyll — strictly a georgic because it extols the virtues of nature and the rural life — argues for an ideal state of harmony in a form that is "mythopoetic".[44] In *The Rainbow*, the mythic will clash with real history, and the poetic will become a more complex expression, so that the simple ideal itself will be put under severe strain on a number of levels as the novel turns modernist. It is the women who will instigate the process of modernity, as they begin to question the settled life of their men. Thus, a gendered opposition, deriving from Lawrence's "Study of Thomas Hardy", will take on the force of an archetypal structure: the women will look for change, the men will resist. In the beginning of the novel the women already face outwards to the world beyond their narrow confines. But it is a magic land shaped by literature and focussed on the squire's lady who is characterized as the living epic that "inspired their lives ... they had their own Odyssey" (R, 12). Although this pattern of opposition between the women and the men has rather shaky foundations for a historical argument because it derives from opposing literary fictions (the female epic or odyssey opposes the male georgic), in a neat reversal of the history of classical literature, Lawrence has the women preparing to go on the spiritual journey while the men stay at home. As the modern world encroaches progressively more on the lives of the Brangwens, this feminist gambit of giving the women the role of keepers of the soul of mankind will take on paradigmatic status.

"Real history" begins in the second part of chapter one ("Around 1840"), when the first coal mine opens and the Industrial Revolution finally reaches the rural heart of England. But Lawrence will keep it on the other side of the canal for most of the book, at a safe distance, only to be observed from the outside on occasional visits, like when Ursula goes to Wiggiston colliery in Yorkshire to pour out all Lawrence's anti-

---

[44] Cf. J.A. Cuddon, *A Dictionary of Literary Terms and Literary Theory* (Oxford: Blackwell, 1991), 366-67, 689-90.

industrial invective at what she sees there. The Brangwen farmers, however, through generations of hard toil, have achieved a certain measure of financial independence. They, like Lawrence, can also remain on the other side of the canal, apart from the modern industrial world. The next three generations, whose growth and maturity and sexual history make up the substance of the novel, will evolve their increasing senses of identity at a tangent to the larger changes of a modernizing world. However, when the railway comes to their valley "the invasion" is complete (R, 13). The town grows, the Brangwens get richer as tradesmen, but Marsh farm, that ideological centre for the rural myth (as Holderness argued), maintains its original remoteness, "beyond all the dim, smoking hill of the town ... just on the safe side of civilization". Working in the fields, they now hear the new rhythm of "the winding engines" on the other side of the embankment. There are colliers, and the "sulpherous smell" on the west wind, which make the farmers conscious of "other activity going on beyond them" (R, 14).

At the beginning of his novel, Lawrence is clearly establishing more than a perspective. History, although amply referenced to real changes in the lives of the people and the topology of the land, is closer to mythology and parable. The myth of origin defines both an attitude to history and the discourse in which it will be represented. Lawrence's history of England will be nothing more or less than ideological, a chronology and a chronicle of the three generations of Brangwens which will enable him to illustrate his anti-industrial thesis. On this point, then, I agree with the gist of Holderness's critique, explained above.

Foucault discusses myths of origins in *The Archaeology of Knowledge* (1969), in his rejection of teleological History. In *The Rainbow*, Lawrence also wants to reject that teleological History of imperial Britain. The novel is a damning critique on a number of levels of the official version of the progress of civilization. In this he is not original, as a general cultural pessimism dominated the period when he was writing, and one that seemed to be confirmed by the outbreak of war. But instead of rejecting any foundations for History, like Foucault as postmodernist does, Lawrence as modernist seeks an alternative foundation: the cyclical genealogy of the Brangwens. Indeed, the recurrent patterns of conflict and struggle between the men and the women is the substance of a personal and family history, even a history of sexuality, which undermines the foundations of the linear traditional history with its ideology of progress by shifting the argument to a different set of principles. By concentrating his attack on the spiritual degeneration of the subject, Lawrence is able to propose a return to older religious values, but based on a sexual consummation of a more profound, instinctive kind. Lawrence's sexual subjects are not, however, immune to Foucault's critique. For, a major contradiction arises when Lawrence wants to insist on the ontological insecurity of the modern self. The latter derives from the critical perspectives on modernity in the emergent discourses of the social sciences and cultural critique of the time, which were based on the concepts of "instrumentality", "rationalization" and "reification".[45] Lawrence actually guarantees the self its security in the archaic gesture of the myth of origins. Moreover, the sophisticated narrative voice represents the progress of the modern self while promoting a return to primitivism. There is, as Brown put it, "an apparent contradiction between the conventional view of Lawrence as promoting a return to primitivism, a kind of mindless blood-intimacy with the universe, and the fact that Lawrence as narrator is highly conscious".[46] Lawrence seems to want it both ways: the unstable self of modernity, and the guarantee of a spiritual renewal. The status of the latter as a necessary fiction is severely undermined by the increasing dominance of the former in the novel.

So much, then, for the notion of history in *The Rainbow*. I shall now turn, in some detail, to the historical archive in the discourses that make up the substance of the novel.

ii. The historical archive 1: the evolutionist discourse
Darwin's theory of evolution had, by the late nineteenth and early twentieth century, established itself in the popular imagination. The general effect had not always been positive. Faith was shaken by the revelation that human beings were not God-given but descended from monkeys. By the end of the century Natural Selection was being metamorphosed into selective breeding (eugenics) to secure the survival of the race. For if the highest form of human development was determined by the imperial powers in the late nineteenth century, then primitivism and savagery were now objects of the official history. Thus the "civilizing mission" to the Dark Continent was legitimized by the Church and by Darwin's science.

The evolutionist discourse appears in *The Rainbow* in two forms. First, references to the British imperial rule in Africa and India are represented in the latter part of the novel by Skrebensky. Second, as a model or pervasive metaphor for the structure and significance of the narrative: Lawrence's attitude is clearly marked by his Brangwen genealogy, an ambivalent evolution at best, which serves to raise serious

---

[45] Cf. David Frisby, *Fragments of Modernity* (Cambridge: Polity Press, 1985).
[46] H.O. Brown, "The Passionate Struggle of Conscious Being: D.H. Lawrence's *The Rainbow*", in David Ellis & Ornella De Zordo eds, *D.H. Lawrence: Critical Assessments, Volume II* (Mountfield: Helm Information Ltd, 1992. First published 1974), 216.

doubts about the stage of civilization reached at the end, on one level, while not neglecting to acknowledge, implicitly, the gains afforded by modern life, on another level. Not that the levels are unconnected. Indeed, they enable the contradictions in the discursive practices ensuing from the metaphor to play an important role in the novel.

The first colonial reference occurs when Ursula begins her relation-ship with Skrebensky. She starts to question his belief in his military duties, and in the point of war. He is blindly idealistic; she adopts a thoroughly materialistic attitude: there is no transcendent point to it, you kill, get killed, and so on. He maintains that you do your job, and there is the point: "it matters whether we settle the Mhadi or not" (R, 288). The passage contains four key signifiers that carry the full weight of the historical reference: "working like a *nigger*"; "the *Mhadi*"; "*Khartoum*"; and "the desert of the *Sahara*". The year is precise: 1885; the event: the death of General Gordon at Khartoum. Skrebensky's is the voice of the official history. The second reference occurs when Will Brangwen is described as being "in a private retreat of his own", oblivious "about the war". Ursula, though, is very concerned, because Skrebensky — the object of her romantic discourse — is out there in South Africa (R, 331). Here, the precise historical reference is to the Boer War (1899-1902). The third, and principal reference, is during Ursula's last year at college, when she receives Skrebensky's letter from Africa after not hearing from him for two years, and not having seen him for six. As a New Woman she has become the focus for Lawrence's iconoclasm. Skrebensky is now a first lieutenant in the Royal Engineers. She has continued to imagine him in romantic terms in order to brighten the "blank grey ashiness of later daytime", still seeing him as the "doorway" to "self-realization and delight for ever" (R, 406). His bright-red officer's tunic will not be enough to meet the expectations of her fantasy version of him. Her profound disappointment will fuel her anger.

This, then, is the narrative context in which Lawrence places his anti-British Imperialist tirade.[47] Ursula imagines Skrebensky in India, "one of the governing class, superimposed upon an old civilization, lord and master of a clumsier civilization than his own". However, this view is complicated by the fact that she also represents Lawrence's anti-democratic beliefs. The British ruling class, at its best, would provide "the better idea of the State". And India did need "the civilization which he himself represented: it did need his roads and bridges, and the

---

[47] This tirade is now believed to have been decisive in the "obscenity" trial in 1915, as it was "bad for morale". Cf. Introduction to the Cambridge University Press edition (1989), xlvi-xlvii. He was also under suspicion for being pro-German, of course.

enlightenment of which he was a part" (R, 411). It is important to appreciate the ironic context in the novel of these statements, because although they correspond in general to Lawrence's views expressed elsewhere, they are given to the representative New Woman to voice (paradoxically, radical and anti-democratic at the same time) who is on the verge of a momentous decision. To preserve her newly won independence, she will not fulfil her traditional destiny, marry Skrebensky and go to India as the officer's wife, even though the idea of leaving England has a strong appeal to her, as it did to Lawrence himself. Thoughts of leaving England, though, offer Lawrence the opportunity to bring together, in Ursula, the colonial-racist and the anti-democratic discourses in one outburst: "I shall be glad to leave England. Everything is so meagre and paltry, it is so unspiritual — I hate democracy .... Only degenerate races are democratic." (R, 427) Nothing less than a "spiritual aristocracy" could lead the way.[48] The key signifiers here are "unspiritual" and "degenerate races". They bring together, towards the end of the novel, the colonialist appropriation of the evolutionist discourse, and Lawrence's critique of modern western civilization in 1915 as a spiritual descent of man. A confusion seems to arise when Ursula goes on to chide Skrebensky for his blind faith in British rule. However, again, we need to see it in the context of their personal-sexual conflict. She accuses him of wanting to go to India to be one of the "somebodies" out there, to compensate for the inadequacies she perceives in him: "It's a mere dodge." This then fuels her attack on him: "What do you govern for, but to make things as dead and mean as they are here!" His imperialist righteousness and superiority are, like him, "old, dead things" (R, 428). He is finally provoked into breaking out of his polite disinterestedness, and the anger that follows arouses him sexually — which is always an important context in Lawrence for such violent arguments.

Now, in order to make the link with the second, and more general use of the evolutionist discourse, we should notice the reference to "darkness" and its figurative-thematic associations: Africa, the Dark Continent, blacks, and hot sensuality — references that belong to the historical archive and the motif-structure of the novel at one and the same time. The "darkness" is a discourse in Foucault's sense, always already a representation of the real in literature (in boys' magazines, popular stories, and serious literature),[49] a well-established colonialist fiction about the white man in Africa. In the key passage in *The Rainbow* (413-

---

[48] Cf. D.H. Lawrence, "Democracy" in *Selected Essays*.
[49] Cf. Robert Burden, *The Critics Debate: Heart of Darkness* (London: Macmillan, 1991), 8-11.

18), Lawrence rewrites Joseph Conrad's *Heart of Darkness* (1902). Skrebensky represents the white man just returned to "civilization" after a tour of the Dark Continent. Most of what he tells his intended, Ursula, is filtered through her reception of it. She reacts exclusively from her romantic side, and is "thrilled" by the quality of his voice (like Marlow is of Kurtz's voice in Conrad's novella), "a voice out of the darkness", as he conveys "something strange and sensual to her". Moreover, what he tells her is exactly what the white woman back in England has been waiting to hear. They, the blacks, "worship ... the darkness ... the fear — something sensual". Here, the historical archive needs no comment today. Its use, however, does. The colonialist-racist (and sexist) fiction of the sensual negro to the home-grown white woman transfers to Skrebensky and is a symptom of her (Ursula's) deep sexual desire: "the hot, fecund darkness ... possessed his blood," and "they walked the darkness beside the massive river" — as if the darkness has now taken on a palpable existence of its own, expanding beyond its status as object of a discourse into the realm of a pervasive symbolism. The sexual potential, though, belongs to the wider implications of the discourse. "African desire" is strange, powerful and fecund: "he seemed like the living darkness upon her, she was in the embrace of the strong darkness". And it is at this point that Conrad's darkness elides into a neo-Romanticism of the Dionysian kind first described by Clarke,[50] symbolized in the paradoxical process of creation-dissolution, and here in Lawrence taking on a primary ontological function. The whole passage is framed by this multi-functional context — at once colonialist, sexual, and ontological — and represented in a poetic discourse of a familiar romanticism: "Dark water flowing in the silence through the big, restless night made her feel wild." Lawrence manages to keep both the Conrad and the Romantic poetry reference in play. Sex brings Ursula and Skrebensky together "as one stream". The images of flowing and darkness bear the full weight of the ontological significance, so that "the light of consciousness gone, then the darkness reigned, and the unutterable satisfaction" (R, 412-414). The darkness is unspeakable in Conrad; and sexual satisfaction is beyond consciousness and rational discourse in Lawrence, and only expressible by the narrator in aesthetic form. The two figures, like the two selves, become one in "the fluid darkness" as, in a canonical Lawrentian moment, "their blood ran together as one stream".

When she returns to rational consciousness, Ursula reacts like Conrad's Marlow back in the "Sepulchral City": "The stupid, artificial,

---

[50] Colin Clarke, *River of Dissolution: D.H. Lawrence and English Romanticism* (London: Routledge, 1969).

exaggerated town" where life is "nothing, just nothing", and the people "only dummies exposed." This is no longer that sensual darkness of a sexualized colonialist discourse, but Conrad's hollowness at the heart of western civilization itself. To reinforce the point, Ursula is reminded of "the Invisible Man, who was a piece of darkness made visible only by his clothes". The reference to the popular H.G.Wells novel (1897) would no more have been lost on Lawrence's contemporaries than the Conrad references. Moreover, the two kinds of darkness — the sensual-creative and the nihilistic — both serve the purpose of a profound social critique prefigured in the statement: "primeval darkness falsified to a social mechanism." (R, 414-15) As Ursula has now experienced the primeval darkness, her newly sensualized self is so real to her that all else is pretence; and, echoing Conrad once more, the real "jungle darkness" is to be found in the modern, urban English world.

The colonialist discourse will reappear on two more occasions. On returning from a trip to Rouen, France, Skrebensky feels that London is like the "Sepulchral City": everything is grey, dead, and full of "spectre-like people." This profoundly affects him. His life seems "spectral", foreshadowing the imminent demise of their love. For without her "the horror of not being possessed him" (R, 423-24). In the context of Lawrence's sexual ontology, Skrebensky's newly acquired fullness of being will be destroyed. But we should not overlook the Conradian "horror" as the key signifier that enables the colonialist fiction to continue to reverberate at various levels in the novel. Skrebensky returns to it a last time when he marries "the Colonel's daughter" within four days of Ursula leaving him, and disembarks for India; he thinks of her (Ursula) in terms that bring Lawrence and Conrad together: "She was the darkness, the challenge, the horror" (R, 447). It is the middle term which belongs firmly to Lawrence, because the highest achievement of fullness of being in consummate marriage is the challenge that Ursula represents for him, and it is one he is not able to meet.

It is always difficult in such a structurally complex novel to hold together in the criticism all the contexts and the recurrent motifs that we perceive in the reading. We ought to notice, for instance, the extent to which the evolutionist discourse comments implicitly on the colonialist archive. They reach the same conclusion, necessarily, in a profound critique of the state of western civilization, a critique derived at least in part from Conrad, but here in Lawrence given a more spiritual-religious emphasis. The myth of origins established at the beginning of the novel, and the narrative logic and the thematic support which it entails, forms the basis of that broader critique of the modern industrial world. In this Foucauldian critique, the "darkness" functions as an operative metaphor in the evolutionist discourse. Darwinian evolution is meant to account for the higher state of civilization that mankind has reached. It is a paradigmatic story of the ascent of man from primitive tribal existence to the more complex states of being and patterns of social relations pertaining in the modern world. Being the product of a specific epoch, it does not evade its "archaeological" analysis which would place it firmly in its nineteenth-century formation. What uses has Lawrence made of it as a model for a historico-narrative pattern that will enable him to give thematic resonance to a genealogical structure?

Perhaps the place to look in the novel for the theoretical debate itself is when Ursula has a discussion with her physics lecturer at college. The latter represents the voice of the new scientific materialism, that empirical scientific attitude which claimed that no spiritual mystery should be attributed to life. For life is no more and no less than a "complexity of physical and chemical activities" already known to science (R, 408). Ursula thinks this proposition through, and — representing Lawrence's view which is argued for on a number of levels — finds she completely disagrees with it. Was she, like electricity, merely an impersonal force? What about will and intention? Life was not limited "to mechanical energy, nor mere purpose of *self-preservation* and *self-assertion*. It was a consummation, a being infinite. Self was oneness with the infinite. To be oneself was a supreme, gleaming triumph of infinity" (R, 409, emphasis added.). The Darwinian reference is countered by a theology of being. However, in the story the Brangwens do preserve themselves well, and do assert themselves progressively more in direct response to the demands of a changing environment. The Brangwen farmers, after centuries of work on the land, are faced with two challenges. The first comes from their women who look outwards towards "another form of life ... in the far-off worlds of cities and governments" (R, 11). They take the initiative to bring the Brangwens into the modern world. The second comes from the process of industrialization (from "Around 1840"). Their hard-won financial independence enables the Brangwens to survive the threat to their agrarian economy posed by the new capitalism. Furthermore, as the town grows, they get richer, presumably as suppliers of essential provisions. But, as the novel is keen to insist, the men and the womenfolk remain for now in their traditional state: "two very separate beings, vitally connected, knowing nothing of each other, yet living in their separate ways from one root" (R, 15). And it is here, in the assertion of an essential vitalism naturally and traditionally connecting the men and the women with themselves and with the land, that Lawrence wants to set up his opposition to the further evolution of mankind towards the sophistications of modernity. In doing this, he reappropriates a much older discourse of the self in order to propose a spiritual counterweight to the various dominant scientific discourses of the late nineteenth, and early twentieth century. For these are not the highest achievements of man's evolution, but instead are symptomatic of his spiritual decline. The rational mind, consciousness, and especially self-consciousness are Lawrence's *bêtes noires*. The vitalistic, unconscious state of being — the Lawrentian ontological ideal — will be more difficult to achieve for later generations as the process of modernity makes greater demands on them.[51] It is precisely the acquiring of greater knowledge, more rational than intuitive, that will precipitate the crisis of the self. The principal question posed by the novel, therefore, is whether the higher state of civilization attained by the twentieth century may be labelled "Progress". Given Lawrence's priority for the spiritual and the intuitive or instinctive relation, the many gains of modernity — the modern improvements in life, and the greater opportunities they afford for men and for women — prefigured in the metaphor of the widening circle (used twice as chapter headings), the circle of the self or being is seen to narrow correspondingly.

It is, though, as if the process of evolution is unstoppable — or even a natural instinct, too. The mothers wish to urge the children towards the "higher form of being" that education would enable (R, 12). And, "the Brangwen wife of the Marsh aspired beyond herself, towards the further life of the finer woman, towards the extended being she revealed, as a traveller in his self-contained manner reveals far-off countries present in himself" (R, 12-13). This metaphor of the traveller after extended being will finally be reinscribed in Ursula. It will be Tom Brangwen, her grandfather, however, who, like Lawrence, will first go to the Grammar School in Nottingham. Although the evolution of his being will only reach a certain stage, it will be significant enough: he will bring foreign (Polish) blood into the Brangwen stock, undermining any myth of racial purity, and bringing the foreign world to the Marsh farm before anyone there takes steps to travel, literally and metaphorically.[52] The narrow existence given credence at the beginning for the spiritual integrity it gives to the self in its "mindless", instinctive relation to the world, will be characterized from now on as a severe restriction on the extension of being; while the price to be paid will be spiritual degeneration. At the very point of its highest stage of evolution, humankind will have discovered its heart of darkness. The greatest achievement of Natural Selection, and the process of civilization is the Great War. This is not an original critique of modernity, but Lawrence gave it his specifically

---

[51] For a discussion of ontology in Lawrence, see Michael Bell, *D.H. Lawrence: Language and Being* (Cambridge: Cambridge University Press, 1991).

[52] Travelling and the ambivalent relation of the traveller to his or her roots are crucial to Lawrence as the biographies and letters confirm.

religious-theological slant, and it is one that we still need to describe. The pervasive metaphor of the organism will be the first step towards that description.

iii. The historical archive 2: the organic discourse

In *The Order of Things* (1966), Foucault described a significant change in natural history in the late eighteenth century which would precipitate the emergence of biology in the nineteenth century. For instead of the principle of external observation that dominated the classical period, the description of internal structure became the aim of taxonomy. Henceforth, beings had an "organic structure", and the characters and functions of plants could be classified by their organic structural differences. Foucault quotes Cuvier from the period: "It is in this way that the method will be natural, since it takes into account the importance of the organs." It is therefore understandable, writes Foucault, "how the notion of life could become indispensable to the ordering of natural beings" (OT, 228). The natural sciences will now look for the deeper underlying causes to explain the surface mutations in organisms. Lamarck further assists the emergence of the era of biology by making the principle of internal organic structure "function for the first time as a method of characterization. .... Organic structure intervenes between the articulating structures and the designating characters — creating between them a profound, interior, and essential space" (OT, 231). Not, though, that vitalism now simply triumphs over mechanism. Rather, in attempts to define the specificity of living beings, the organic structure is prioritized. The dimensions of this discontinuity were explained by Jameson: "Such was indeed the history of the organic model, that concept of the organism as a prototype which with a single spark touched off Romantic philosophy and nineteenth-century scientific thinking."[53]

The primacy of the organic self, and the recurrence of natural figures as ontological guarantee, in works like *The Rainbow*, has not gone unnoticed in Lawrence criticism. Lawrence's relationship to the English Romantic poets is precisely through organicism, described by Clarke as: "the vitalistic virtues — spontaneity, untamed energy, intensity of being, power."[54] Moreover, the metaphor of growth informs the generational structure of the novel, and especially where the three generations of

---

[53] Fredric Jameson, *The Prison-House of Language* (Princeton, New Jersey: Princeton University Press, 1972), vi.
[54] Clarke, 122.

women are concerned.[55] Schwarz has discussed Lawrence's uses of nature imagery to characterize the sex act as a natural act, placing the characters' "urgent sexuality in the context of nature's rhythms".[56] Black writes about the symbolic plant analogies representing "the growing-point of experience".[57] Fjagesund, as I discussed above, points to the organic model as the basis for a cyclical view of history deriving from Romanticism, mythology and ethnology: the generations and the seasons of man are inextricably bound together through the eternally recurrent, key oppositions of birth/death, growth/decay, light/darkness, and so on.[58]

The metaphors of nature go much further than their ostensible function as indirect descriptions of sex. They represent profounder implications in the ontological scheme. One ought to suspect that such pervasive imagery betokens the reappropriation of a Romantic philosophy and its aesthetic. Even while Lawrence's use of nature verges on pantheism, it also provides the metaphor for the structure of the novel: the organic structure. Furthermore, the novel is encircled by nature, so to speak: it opens with the image of man in harmony with the natural world, and closes with the woman's vision of the "new germination". The structure of being — to extend the analogy — grows in complexity in response to the demands of the changing environment. Nature opposes society, the agrarian opposes the industrial, in their vitalist and mechanistic character respectively. The natural goal of life is to be vitally connected, man to woman, the self to its nature. Nature and ontology are bound together. The Lawrentian injunction is: "Be thyself!"

The organic self always precedes self-consciousness. As a young man, Tom Brangwen is "fresh like a plant, rooted in his mother and sister" (R, 20). Lydia Lensky's feeling of helplessness is described "as if crushed between the past and the future, like a flower that comes aboveground to find a great stone lying above it". But then she would wake up one morning "and feel her blood running, feel herself lying open like a flower unsheathed in the sun, insistent and potent with demand" (R, 53-4). The sexual ontology is represented by the organic, natural figures. Thus it is that the natural instincts of men and women are aestheticized. Flower-pollination imagery becomes a recurrent motif. Passion is a sudden flood, sweeping all before it; or a bursting into flame, a destruc-

---

[55] Edward Englebey (1963), "Escape from the Circle of Experience: D.H. Lawrence's *The Rainbow* as a Modern *Bildungsroman*" in Ellis & De Zordo (1992), Volume II, 167.

[56] Schwarz, "Lawrence's Quest in *The Rainbow*", 248.

[57] Michael Black, *D.H. Lawrence: The Early Philosophical Works: A Commentary* (London: Macmillan, 1991), 114.

[58] Fjagesund, 14.

tive-creative Dionysian moment where the self is lost and found and recreates "the world afresh" each time (R, 60). The very spring of the unconscious life — and one that Lawrence strictly opposes to Freud's "mental" unconscious (see the discussion in the previous chapter) — is a fountainhead: "Out of the rock of his form the very fountainhead of life flowed." Anna and Will are described on the morning after their wedding as "both very glowing, like an open flower ... both very quick and alive" (R, 121, 139). "Quick" and "alive" are key signifiers in the Lawrence lexicon. The former is the most sensitive, inmost part of the sentient being. The men, though, have trouble in this novel with the natural process of the fullness of being. Will feels inadequate, limited, unfulfilled. He is aware "of something unformed in his very being, of some buds which were not ripe in him, some folded centres of darkness which would never develop and unfold whilst he was alive in the body" (R, 195). He loses the battle with Anna, gives way to her "little matriarchy", and devotes himself to church buildings, Gothic architecture, and woodcarving. In Lawrence's terms he fails because he does not allow his natural being to grow to maturity. Instead, he gives priority to the mental and aesthetic faculties, and to work.

Nature also represents a plenitude where the organic self may develop, and where sex usually takes place. Tight, poky, interiors have a negative resonance in Lawrence. Simple, colourful, and expansive, nature is used, traditionally, to express states of mind: "She [Ursula] came to school in the morning seeing the hawthorn flowers wet, the little rosy grains swimming in a bowl of dew. The larks quivered their song into the new sunshine, and the country was so glad. It was a violation to plunge into the dust and greyness of the town." (R, 379) Sexually violent states are dramatized expressionistically, as when Ursula responds to the phallic desire of the man as waves or vibrations emanating out of *her* sexual response to him (like the van Gogh field of sunflowers in the hot wind):

> Coming out of the lane along the darkness, with the dark space spreading down to the wind .... So lingering along, they came to a great oak-tree by the path. In all its budding mass it roared to the wind, and its trunk vibrated in every fibre, powerful, indomitable .... And in the roaring circle under the tree .... The man, what was he? — a dark, powerful vibration that encompassed her. (R, 417-18)

Much earlier in the novel we read: "He went out into the wind .... And all the sky was teeming and tearing along, a vast disorder of flying shapes." (R, 48) When Ursula and Skrebensky spend the night out on the Sussex Downs — he only on sufferance, she communing naked with nature and the prehistoric earth-works — the sunrise is one of Lawrence's great van Gogh descriptions: "great waves of yellow flinging into the sky." It is for her, and her alone, the new dawn, where "everything was newly washed into being, in a flood of new, golden creation" (R, 431).[59] The motif of the new dawn of being returns at the end of the novel: "She was the naked, clear kernel thrusting forth the clear, powerful shoot ... striving to take new root .... She was gradually absorbed into growth." And the dream to which this belongs is confirmed by the fresh spring of the real new day (R, 456).

The organic discourse is also represented in animal imagery, and in its most mythological form in Lawrence's totem, the phoenix. Will Brangwen carves a wooden phoenix (R, 108) which then takes on the status of a *leitmotif* in his struggle with Anna. He becomes an eagle, a bird of prey swooping down on her; while her being is represented as the flames that will destroy him, so that he can be recreated from the ashes. Thus the phoenix mythological symbol represents the destructive-creative flame of passion that burns through the very core of being (R, 109). In the recurrent animal imagery, man is the hunter-bird of prey; but woman is the consuming flame. The phoenix *leitmotif* recurs when Tom Brangwen realizes how much the heat of passion has died in his life: "A great deal of ash was in his fire, cold ash" (R 119). In this novel, the young male sexual predator is always consumed by the female fire of passion, never to rise again from the ashes as the reborn phoenix. The animal imagery, however, persists, as if to stress the limits of the phallocentric predatory sexuality in the face of the woman's sexuality. "He came to her fierce and hard, like a hawk striking and taking her .... she was his aim and object, his prey" (R, 151). If he "couldn't be kinder to her, nicer to her," she would cling "fiercely to her known self" (R, 154). Anna, like Ursula, will win the battle of the sexes. Will burns the wooden carving of the large God-like Adam and the small Eve, in response to her disdain of it, in a vain, symbolic gesture to try to salvage his passion: "a new, fragile flame of love came out of the ashes of this last pain" (R, 162). But he can only ever resort to exercising phallic-animal power over her: "as the tiger lying in the darkness" (R, 171) waiting for the kill — and this is her view of him.

Lawrence was fond of describing the sexual tie between men and women in terms of soul-mates. When Tom drowns in the flood at Marsh farm, Lydia knows intuitively that he is dead, and like the she-wolf, her "long, unnatural cry" rings out in the night (R, 230). Similarly, Skreben-

---

[59] For further discussion of Lawrence's Expressionism see Jack F. Stewart, "Expressionism in *The Rainbow*" in *Novel*, 13/ 3 (Spring 1980), 298-315.

sky, in the first love for Ursula, "had to go to her, to follow her call" (R, 174). Later he burns "something like a tiger", in her sexual perception of him (hinting at the thoughts of India on her mind, but also recalling Blake's poem) (R, 411). But, finally, it is the woman's sexuality, perceived by the traditional man, which is both bird-like and witch: "his heart melted in fear from the fierce, beaked, harpy kiss" (R 444).

The Foucauldian reading of the organic discourse in *The Rainbow* has brought out the radical uses that Lawrence makes of a traditional nature imagery to represent the internal structure of the self and its instinctive relation to the other. Additionally, the novel itself is an organism with its structure of the mutations of generations over time. The force of that instinctive relation between the characters is figured in another scientific discourse: electro-magnetism.

iv. The historical archive 3: the operative metaphor of electro-magnetism

In *The Rainbow*, the electric charge, the like and the unlike poles are pervasive scientific metaphors that represent the force of the sexual attraction between man and woman. Passion is "primitive and electric" (R, 47). Will Brangwen finds himself "in an electric state of passion" (R, 108). When he attempts to seduce the young woman in the Nottingham pub he is a phallic power to her passive vulnerability: "The man was the centre of positive force" (R, 212). The scene figuratively represents the woman's tension between attraction and repulsion, but exclusively from the man's phallic, sexist perception: "his whole body electric with a subtle, powerful, reducing force upon her" (R, 214). He draws her nearer to him; she relaxes her resistance; then fights him off again: a rhythm of attraction and repulsion which puts to work the connotations of the figures of the electric charge and the electro-magnetic force-field. About Anna and Will we read: "all was activity and passion, everything moved upon poles of passion." Once they accept their separateness and their difference, they attract each other all the more passionately. After Ursula's first kiss, "she went to bed feeling all warm with electric warmth" (R, 236, 278).

Clearly Lawrence is prepared to make use of scientific metaphors even while rejecting the scientific explanation of life. Ursula speaks for him when she rejects the rational, materialist grounds of modern science, because there the great mysteries of life are reduced to their "physical and chemical activities" (R, 408). The scientific view is represented by her lecturer, Dr Frankstone (a woman): "We don't understand it [life] as we understand electricity, even, but that doesn't warrant our saying it is something special, something different in kind and distinct from everything else in the universe.". For Ursula, as for Lawrence, the essential mysteries were infinite, and the self "was oneness with the infinite". Here, as elsewhere in his work, Lawrence counters the claims of scientific materialism with an idealist assertion deriving from a quasi-religious argument. Ursula does not feel like an impersonal force — like electricity. Yet the phallic power of her desire is described as "a dark, powerful vibration" (R, 418), as if it belongs not to her, nor to the man, but to the space between them. It is a force-field of electro-magnetic attraction; a physical activity belonging to the natural world, already known in its structure and function to the science of Lawrence's day. Later we read that, under the influence of the bright moon, "she vibrated like a jet of electric" (R, 442). Furthermore, when two beings produce the same force or power to dominate the other, they will be forced apart — as the like poles in magnetism. That is, unless the one gives way, and becoming passive is able to submit to the force of the active other. Will and Anna's struggle for supremacy may thus be understood. She wins as he withdraws into a life of passivity. Ursula proves to be too powerful for Skrebensky, and she destroys him. However, the matter is complicated by the male and female principles in Lawrence's theological ontology, and should not be confused with traditional gender distinctions.

Lawrence worked out his dualistic philosophy in the "Study of Thomas Hardy" (1914). It was completed before he wrote the final draft of *The Rainbow*. His theory of being is predicated on the duality of male and female: "every man comprises male and female in his being, the male always struggling for predominance. A woman likewise consists in male, and female, with female predominant. The male exists in doing, the female in being". The perfect, conjugal union of man and woman is therefore complicated by the dual principles of the male and the female within each being, and, crucially, the tendencies for being to suffer an unbalancing of these principles in the relationship with the other. The ultimate goal is consummate marriage which requires for its success "that a man shall know the natural law of his own being, then he shall seek out the law of the female, with which to join himself as complement".[60] Marriage now becomes one of Lawrence's principal concerns.[61]

Once the connections between the Hardy study and the novel are

---

[60] "Study of Thomas Hardy" in *Study of Thomas Hardy and Other Essays* edited by Bruce Steele (Cambridge: Cambridge University Press, 1985. Written 1914, not published until 1936), 94, 127-28.
[61] Schwarz, 242ff: "Lawrence's struggle with his subject (his relationship with Frieda) is a major aspect of *The Rainbow* .... The Anna and Will section corresponds to the passionate struggle that raged between Lawrence and Frieda while he wrote the novel."

made, as Daleski[62] points out, we begin to read *The Rainbow* as "essentially a religious novel about the significance of marriage".[63] But not in the traditional pattern of the English novel, whereby conflicts are resolved by the contrived marriage at the end. For the strenuous demands placed on the main characters by the terms of the Hardy study render the attainment of perfect union in consummate marriage practically impossible. Moreover, the coherence of Lawrence's "theology" is severely undermined by the novel itself. The early reviewers thought it was incoherent in any case. F.R. Leavis admitted that he found it difficult to read, and Bertrand Russell and T.S. Eliot both condemned it as proof that Lawrence was no philosopher.[64] Yet it is clearer now that the "theology" provided *The Rainbow* (and *Women in Love*) with a set of principles that give the novel a certain thematic coherence. The male and female patterning, with its essential oppositions, is pervasive. The men become more impotent as the women become more dominant. In the terms of Lawrence's dualism, therefore, neither man nor woman allows that balance of male and female principles to settle into fullness of being. When Ursula takes positive steps to enter the man's world, she allows the male in her to dominate her being: she becomes ambitious, authoritarian, aggressive. When she lets her female principle make her more feminine to suit Skrebensky's phallic male desire, any semblance of a relationship they may have had is destroyed.

It seems, then, that consummate marriage, like fullness of being, needs a stability of character. True being requires a harmony of principles. But *The Rainbow* continues to undo those propositions from the Hardy study. The force-field of magnetic attraction always leads to a short-circuit. For as the static electricity accumulates to different degrees of intensity at each pole, the force that drives the vibrations of the magnetic field starts to become greater at the positive pole, and the weaker force is drawn to the stronger, and destroyed: "The struggle for consummation was terrible." The moon that controls the tides, controls the moods of the woman. It is a glaring, white force that empowers her to give full expression to the lunacy of her sexuality (which I described in psychoanalytic terms in the previous chapter), destroying the man who, afterwards, is "white and obliterated" (R, 445). She had realized that he was attractive, but "his soul could not contain her in its waves of strength, nor his breast compel her in burning, salty passion" (R, 443).

---

[62] H.M. Daleski, *The Forked Flame: A Study of D.H. Lawrence* (London: Faber & Faber, 1965), 24, and passim.
[63] Kinkead-Weekes, 207.
[64] Source: Introduction to the Cambridge University Press edition.

Metaphors of electro-magnetism now give way to the power of the waves under the force of the moon. Her "strong, dominant voice" seems "metallic" to him (R 444). The signifier: "corrosive" describes this process of destruction in the very first sexual encounter in the moonlight. She tries to understand her sexuality: "Had she been mad: what horrible thing had possessed her? She was filled with that overpowering fear of herself ... that other burning, corrosive self." (R 299) And, significantly, it is a scientific metaphor referring to the chemical process of the corrosion of metal. The moon — the woman's totem — can do that to the hardened soul of man. But, as Middleton Murry was the very first critic to point out, "she is the woman who accepts the man's vision of herself .... She, therefore, becomes a monster".[65]

Lawrence is inventing a new discourse of the sexual relation that would strenuously seek to avoid the Freudian. It is one that Deleuze and Guattari noticed as already post-Freudian, as we saw in the previous chapter — with its metaphors of flows, waves, and vibrations.[66] My discussion in this chapter, working with Foucauldian theory, is attempting to relocate the operative metaphors and the scientific discourses from which they derive in their historical moment.

v. The historical archive 4: the modern episteme
We have seen how the relation between text and history can be formal-ized through the analysis of scientific metaphors and the discourses to which they refer. These discourses have an historically specific forma-tion, and are subject to redeployment in other areas of thought and writing, and in the popular imagination, just as Foucault is reappropriated for literature. In drawing the full consequences of the Foucauldian archaeology, however, I have not just been busy spotting the metaphors in order to characterize the unity or coherence of a style, or a philosophy, or Lawrence's view of life in 1915. Rather what has emerged are certain contradictions. Thus it is that the rejection of the evolutionist discourse, in theory, is contradicted in practice by the Brangwen story itself. The coming of modernity is portrayed not as an evolution to a higher state of civilization but a spiritual degeneration — a not uncommon view in the early twentieth century. Nevertheless, the Brangwens are a clear example of the ability of mankind to adapt to the new circumstances and even prosper. The women get the children educated, thus enabling them to attain a more sophisticated state of being, and a more complex, modern

---

[65] John Middleton Murry, *Son of Woman: The Story of D.H. Lawrence* (London: Jonathan Cape, 1931), 91.
[66] Discussed by Becket (1997). See my discussion in chapter 1 for references.

relation with the world. It is in any case by no means so clear-cut that the original state of being was such a paradise; and certainly not for the women. Why should a more instinctive, primitive existence be any better than its sophisticated modern counterpart? That smacks of romantic idealism. Don't the farmers look to the church tower in an empty sky for support, and aren't they eager for "something unknown"? (R, 9) Lawrence may have espoused such beliefs in his non-fiction writing, but here the myth of primitive origins seems to have a narrative and not a philosophical coherence.

As I argued above, Lawrence is prepared to make use of scientific metaphors even while rejecting the scientific materialist explanation of life. The organic structure of beings was the new way of seeing life biologically. Lawrence wants to hold on to the plausibility of the metaphor for narrative and aesthetic purposes, while criticizing the reduction of being to scientific explanation. Similarly, the metaphors that derive from the discourses of electricity and electro-magnetism are used pervasively to represent the shock of the moment of sexual arousal, or the force of attraction and repulsion in the battle of the sexes. But Lawrence insists, too, on a deeper ontological explanation which requires a more ancient, spiritual discourse. It is worked out in the Hardy study, and is a classic instance of the strategic uses of discourse: in this case, the reappropriation of Biblical and occultist discourses.

Thus, the Foucauldian reading brings out the text's relation to history at the level of discourse. I have not, though, described that text, as traditional stylistics would have done, so as to underline the coherence of the Lawrentian style. On the contrary, discourse analysis has drawn attention to the complex unevenness of the writing, in the sense of a mixture of discourses working at different, and often contradictory levels: the discourses of history and science; but also the aesthetic discourses. The uses of Romanticism and Expressionism are noticeable in the description of emotional states, just as Lawrence's idea of the novel is implicit in his organicism. Because it is also there, in that implicit aesthetics and poetics, that we find the historical archive.

In the previous chapter, I described the figurative, poetic writing that represents sexual feeling or states of being as aesthetic structure. *The Rainbow* wants to combine this with the more traditional, Jamesian poetics of organic form. Thus it is that the novel develops out of the description of a simple form of being, records the degrees of struggle and growth over time, and finally reaches the point of a new germination (giving birth to its sequel, *Women in Love*). The Brangwen genealogy gives it a structure of a familiar kind: the family saga novel, so that Lawrence contains a complex modern writing in the frame of a traditional novel. *The Rainbow* is modernist and realist. At the level of writing there are those moments of Expressionism. At the level of plot there is the inexorable chronology.

Lawrence, then, fits into the epistemological space of the modern period, or what Foucault has called the modern *episteme*, while at the same time using the available discourses to underline the spiritual losses of modernity. Lawrence's relation to modernity can best be understood in his representation of sexuality in *The Rainbow*. To do this, we shall now turn from Foucault's work of the 1960s to that of the 1970s and 1980s — the work on power and knowledge.

vi. Power/knowledge/sexuality
In an interview given by Foucault in September 1983 — very near his tragic and untimely death — he gave a definition of discourse, once again, but in a more straightforward language. It is because "we live in a world in which things have been said," and because "spoken words leave traces, the historical world in which we live" is completely marked with discourses.[67] Lawrence clearly belongs to the formation of the discourse of sexuality.

Sexuality is constructed through a set of representations which have become — as Heath put it — a whole "sexual fix". Indeed, "the much-vaunted *liberation* of sexuality, our triumphant emergence from the *dark ages*, is thus not a liberation but a myth, an ideology, the definition of a new mode of conformity". The new conformity to be sexy and to have multiple orgasms is produced and reproduced in the media. Advertising has commodified sex: it sells products. Popular literature reinforces the stereotype. For Heath, as for Foucault, the formation of this discourse begins with the early sexologists and Freud, and includes Lawrence in its history. *Sons and Lovers* (1913) is credited with the first appearance of "sex-instinct"; *Lady Chatterley's Lover* (1928) provided us with "the sex relation", "the sex warmth", "the sex glamour". Around the same period we see the emergence of "sex-life", and "sex-appeal" (1919); "sexological" (1920); "sexology" (1927); "sexy" (1928); "sexologist" (1929). Sexuality is a modern phenomenon produced in discourses of psychoanalysis, literature, sexology, sociology, and the woman's question.[68] In this precise sense, sexuality is a construct, and Heath traces the history of its formation and its recent reproductions. As I suggest above, Lawrence's sex talk, throughout his works, may seem, on one level, ironic.

---

[67] "An Interview with Michel Foucault" by Charles Ruas, Postscript to Michel Foucault, *Death in the Labyrinth: The World of Raymond Roussel*, 177.
[68] Heath, 2, 9-11.

For he is conventionally understood to be promoting a pre-discursive, intuitive or instinctive level of consciousness, a form of pre-rational primitivism as in the opening pages of *The Rainbow*. This non-self-conscious "blood-intimacy" appears to be contradicted by Lawrence's excesses of sophisticated writing, represented by a highly conscious narrator, and especially in that first scene. When the narrative shifts between the consciousnesses of the main characters, and although they are credited with degrees of intellectual skill that give a plausibility to their represented thoughts, some of their pre-conscious, half-formed thoughts or feelings, especially about sexuality, are represented by the highly conscious narrator through the studied artifices of modern aesthetic form. In this very specific sense, Lawrence also puts sexuality into discourse even while proposing, at least in theory, an ideal of pre-conscious living, spontaneity, and the instinctive sexual relation. It is to the discourses that enable Lawrence to represent sexuality that we now turn.

The discourse of the flesh
What Foucault and Lawrence have in common in their theories of sexuality is their respective quarrel with Christianity. Ironically the one book of Foucault's that would have been most useful here — *The History of Sexuality Volume IV: The Confessions of the Flesh* — is still not published. Traces of its argument, though, exist in the other volumes; indeed, they form an integral part of them. Lawrence's quarrel with Christianity is outlined in the Hardy study, and plays a significant role in *The Rainbow*.

Lawrence rejects the Christian love-ideal of *caritas*, the doctrine of pure altruism. Once subsumed under the moralist discourse of the Victorian church, the deeper mystical sources of life gave way to hypocrisy and cant. Modern love, in its forms of emancipation, is only a function of the will, a kind of automatism, proving that love is cut off from its natural, carnal roots. For Ursula, once again representing Lawrence's view, the quest for a new spirituality has become urgent in view of the new modern sterility. Later, Lawrence would insist on male leadership in *The Plumed Serpent* (1926) to fill the spiritual vacuum left by the failure of Christian love; and at the end of his life he will once more attempt to counter the Christian depreciation of sexuality through church morality by placing a high value on sensuality and tenderness in the conjugal relation between man and woman, in *Lady Chatterley's Lover* (1928). In *The Rainbow*, as I have already noted, there is a return to the old nature mysteries of death and rebirth, here given a new spiritual-sensual form that has to fill that empty space created by the instrumentalities of modern life. Hough explained Lawrence's quarrel with Christianity as follows:

> Catholicism had even preserved some of the old earthly pagan
> consciousness, and through the cycle of the liturgical year had
> kept in touch with the rhythm of the seasons, the essential rhythm
> of man's life on earth. .... However he [Lawrence] may use the
> Christian language, he uses it for a different end. For Christianity
> the life of the flesh receives its sanction and purpose from the life
> of the spirit which is eternal and transcendent. For Lawrence the
> life of the spirit has its justification in enriching and glorifying the
> life of the flesh of which it is in any case an epiphenomenon.[69]

For Clarke, it is difficult to disentangle Lawrence's debt to Christianity
from his debt to English Romanticism. The demonic and Dionysian
elements in Lawrence bring him closest to Dostoevsky.[70]

A classical moment in the representation of Christianity in *The Rainbow* is when the narrative is presented through the consciousness of the
fourteen year old school-girl, Ursula, who has had a thoroughly Christian
education and is steeped in the Bible, the prayer-book and the liturgical
calendar. She has a mind-set — part religion, part romance — dominated
by a mystical quasi-sexual Christ. Passages in the novel become
quotations from the Bible: "the Sons of God saw the daughters of men
that they were fair" (R, 256; Genesis vi. 2-4). The very rhythms of the
Biblical language, seen first in the parable-like style of the opening
passage of the novel, is now Ursula's narrating style. Moreover, the
narrative structure now follows the sequence of her Christian calendar:
the focus of the week is on Sundays; the months on the liturgical year,
Christmas to Easter (R, 259-62), as she tries to live for the epiphanies of
the great mystic events of the Christian faith: "So the children lived the
year of Christianity, the epic of the soul of mankind." Of course, a rhythm
of life that is cyclical and universal is appropriate for a novel in which
generational and historical time are closely linked. But Lawrence
strategically places the perception of that rhythm in Ursula's young
consciousness, in passages of psychological realism, and then shows it to
lead towards a "mechanical action" (R, 261). This is not simply the
author's judgment, but clearly signals Ursula's changing consciousness,
as she begins to question that in which she once found most comfort. The
next chapter takes us into the murky region of her first love. Her religion

---

[69] Graham Hough, *The Dark Sun: A Study of D.H. Lawrence* (London: Duckworth,
1956) 253-4. My section on Lawrence's quarrel with Christianity is essentially a
summary of the appendix in Hough's book.
[70] Clarke, 14.

is now less routine, and more a set of passionate moments of ecstasy: "All the time she walked in a confused heat of religious yearning. She wanted Jesus to love her deliciously, to take her sensuous offering, to give her sensuous response." (R, 267) The spiritual gives way to the physical, and her Jesus to the young, gallant Skrebensky.

The Biblical discourse, in fact, dominates the language of *The Rainbow*. Plausibly so, as Lawrence is true to the place the Bible occupies in the lives of the characters; especially in the small, semi-isolated world they inhabit in late Victorian England. Towards the end of the novel, this discourse is less prominent, because the narrating consciousness is that of the New Woman, and she has clearly rejected her Christian upbringing in favour of a new, broader spiritual rebirth that takes us back beyond Christianity and forward to a new future.

The characters try to make sense of their lives in the terms available to them. Their world is limited to their language: "As he [Tom] walked alone on the land ... and she would be his life" (R, 39). Later: "She was with child." (R, 61) And just before the birth, Lydia only "knew him as the man ... who begot the child in her" (R, 77). Further on we read, "and the Lord took up his abode. And they were glad"; or: "Her [Anna's] father and her mother now met to the span of the heavens, and she, the child, was free to play in the space beneath, between." (R, 91) It now becomes increasingly more difficult to distinguish the Biblical quotation from characters' discourse. Will Brangwen as a young man in the second generation provides another dominant voice of the Scriptures: "[He] worked on his wood-carving .... Verily the passion of his heart lifted the fine bite of steel. He was carving, as he always wanted, the Creation of Eve." (R, 112) Additionally, he represents the Christian occupation *par excellence* — carpentry. The beginning of the chapter, "Anna Victrix" is characterized by his mind-style so that the parable form ensues from the statement: "And he was troubled" (R, 134). However, it is Anna who first sees the rainbow spanning the day, "and she saw the hope and the promise" (R, 181). Christian symbolism reinforces the discourse. There is the flood and the rainbow; and the two Anthonys, although only the one represents the real Saint (Maggie Schofield's brother), while the second (Skrebenksy) turns out to be a false Saint (St Anthony being the founder of Christian monasticism). St Ursula founded the Ursuline Order of teaching. Despite the disillusion of her teaching experience, Ursula's idealism towards the end of the novel is expressed through the Old Testament discourse of apocalypticism and the evangelistic fire and brimstone: "Yea, and no man dared even throw a firebrand into the darkness" (R, 406). And in the end, "the rainbow stood on the earth" (R, 458) and the parable has come full circle, only the parataxis has given way to the complex syntax of a Romantic poetry.

Through the uses of the Biblical discourse Lawrence is also attempting to reconstitute a relationship with Christianity that will be a
revitalization of the spiritual through the sexual. Decisive here is the
recurrence of the verb "to know", and its eliding into the verb "to be".
The Lawrentian sexualized self is an epistemological and ontological
complexity. The first mention of "to know" in its Biblical sense is when
Tom and Lydia first meet. Here, in fact, Lawrence plays on the two
meanings of the verb: "She did not know him" has a double edge
reiterated in: "He was a foreigner, they had nothing to do with each other.
Yet his look disturbed her to knowledge of him." (R, 37; emphasis added)
He senses "some invisible connection with the strange woman," and that
a new other "centre of consciousness" burned within him connecting
them both "like a secret power" (R, 38). Knowing the other takes on a
double insistence in their courtship. Not only the Biblical sense of carnal
knowledge, but also the socio-cultural: she is literally a stranger, the
widow of a Polish aristocratic. The class difference is more a problem for
Lydia. He was not a "gentleman", yet he insisted on coming into her life,
so that "she would have to begin again ... *to find a new being*" (R, 39;
emphasis added). The sex ontology is predominantly an object of the
Christian discourse of the flesh. Sex is evil and sinful, and it is only
sanctioned by Holy Matrimony: "It meant a great deal of difference to
him, marriage .... he knew she was his woman, he knew her essence, that
it was his to possess" (R, 57-8). This patriarchy, legitimized by Christianity, will undergo a severe test in this novel where the women are given
the upper hand. His powerful religious impulses need to come to terms
with the torment of his sex desire and the "carnal contact with woman"
which he first discovered as a young man (R, 21).

Sexuality and religion are brought together in Lawrence in the Biblical discourse of the flesh. However, the language of the Scriptures meets
that of Romantic or Expressionist poetry precisely at the moment when
sex is represented figuratively. In writing about sex in *The Rainbow*
Lawrence refuses the direct naming of the parts. Feelings, passion, and
the sex act are displaced onto the Biblical reference or the aesthetic
figure: [Aesthetic figure] "the shocks rode erect; the rest was open and
prostrate" (R, 113). Or: [Biblical figure] "In himself, he knew her" (R,
121). Here, sexual awareness of the other is intuitive. Further on, in the
early phase of Anna and Will's marriage, we read:

> Always, her husband was to her the unknown to which she was
> delivered up. She was a flower that has been tempted forth into
> blossom, and has no retreat. He has her nakedness in her power ...
> he appeared to her as the dread flame of power ... like the Annun-
> ciation to her .... She was subject to him as to the Angel of Pres-

ence. She waited upon him and heard his will, and trembled in his service. (R, 157-58)

Anna will soon reject his patriarchal stance in the fight for supremacy which she will win. Here, in one instance, we see the full force of Lawrence's representation of sexuality. To do this, he brings three discourses together: first, the Christian, in which sex is both a temptation of the devil, and a carnal knowledge of the other (Woman is the devil-temptress, of course). Second, the aesthetic enfiguration of nature, both a formal source of imagery and the insistence that sex is natural. Third, sex as power, or the will-to-power. Thus in the representation of sexuality Lawrence tries to match quite contradictory discourses. To understand this further, we need now to discuss the third one, sex as the will-to-power, in more detail.

The will-to-power
Lawrence is at pains to insist that sexuality is the most natural thing on earth, if only we can allow it to be so. Foucault maintains that it is a natural given held in check by power. Sexuality is an historical construct (HS1, 107). Thus we can deconstruct Lawrence's sexual essentialism, by attending to the discourses of sexuality which run through the novel and give it its historical substance. Even his insistence on a new spiritualized sexual self relies heavily on a discourse reappropriated from an older Christianity and a neo-Romanticism, itself combined with the late Victorian Gothic revivalism.[71] The Lawrentian universal instinct is deconstructed by the historically specific discourses in which he writes the sexual.

Foucault claims that the incitement to discourse is a "will to knowledge" (*"une volonté de savoir"*) (HS1, 17). Putting sex into discourse, a process that accelerated through the nineteenth, and early twentieth century, was always difficult: "calling sex by its name ... modern prudishness was able to ensure that one did not speak of sex." The more stringent the prohibitions, the more involved and intense the discourse on sex, and also the more indirect. But despite his indirect method of figurative writing, or his essentially religious ethos, Lawrence's writing will still be subject to censorship, so that, perforce, he invents an erotic nature poetry, part Romantic, part religious, an aesthetic discourse of sexuality. However, the Biblical discourse of the flesh and carnal knowledge, despite its reinscription in a liberationist poetics, never quite evades the exercise of power over the body that derives from the

---

[71] Pinkney argues for the centrality of the Gothicism to Lawrence's Modernism.

Christian pastoral and the confession. As Foucault put it in *The Care of the Self*: "In Christianity ... the link between sexual intercourse and marriage will be justified by the fact that the former bears the marks of sin, the Fall, and evil, and that only the latter can give it a legitimacy that still may not exculpate it entirely."[72] Later, this is described as: "a mode of subjection in the form of obedience to a general law" (HS3, 239). Foucault draws a connection between the Catholic Confession and its mirror image in the "scandalous literature" exemplified first in Sade. Lawrence should also belong to this history that begins with the moment sex became a matter for the police (HS1, 24). But Lawrence's critique of the limits of Christianity, while still remaining within its spiritual bounds, turns out to be an ambivalent affair at best. For, like the Christian pastoral which "always presented it [sex] as the disquieting enigma" (HS1, 34), Lawrence rejected, at the same time, the conventional view of "the matrimonial relations as the most intense focus of constraints" (HS1, 37). The critique of conventional marriage is central to *The Rainbow*. The most intense conflict is in the second generation.[73] In the third generation, Ursula rejects marriage altogether, and the extra-marital sex she initiates was a bold step for Lawrence to take in 1915.

Foucault's history of the growing interest in sexuality shows how sex itself became a heuristic principle. Sexuality becomes an ontology, defining individuals. It is in the first instance, though, "constituted as a problem of truth" (HS1, 56). The secrets of the sinner are revealed in the confession; the repressed truth in psychoanalysis. But, for Lawrence, truth would always consist in being true to oneself. The Christian confession has, of course, had a significant influence on literature. The heroic tales of bravery or sainthood have been largely superseded in modern literature by a mode of writing organized "according to the infinite task of extracting from the depths of oneself, in between the words, a truth which the very form of confession holds like a shimmering image" (HS1, 59). The confession became therapy, mediating between the pathological and the normal, so that "sex appeared as an extremely unstable pathological field ... of instincts, tendencies, images, pleasures, and conduct" (HS1, 67). Sex and identity have become irrevocably tied together: "In the space of a few centuries, a certain inclination has led us to direct the question of what we are to sex .... Whenever it is a question of knowing who we are, it is this logic that henceforth serves as our master key." (HS1, 78)

---

[72] *The Care of the Self* (*The History of Sexuality Volume 3*) (London: Penguin, 1990. First published 1984), 183. Subsequent references in text [HS3].
[73] And one based by all accounts on Lawrence's struggle with Frieda. See Schwarz, 442.

In the will-to-knowledge that motivates the discourses of sexuality, a structural relation emerges between power and pleasure so that they "do not cancel or turn back against one another; they seek out, overlap, and reinforce one another. They are linked together by complex mechanisms and devices of excitation and incitement." (HS1, 48) Power is an immanent relation, because domination and resistance seem to define each other, as if the mechanism of power is a strategy without a subject or agent (HS1, 94-97).[74]

Historically, power is related to the will-to-knowledge in a number of ways. Foucault singles out the "pedagogization of children's sex", the "socialization of procreation", the "psychiatrization of perverse pleasure", and the "hysterization of women's bodies". The woman's body was found to be "thoroughly saturated with sexuality" (HS1, 104). Consequently, there emerged new characters in literature: "the nervous woman, the frigid wife, the indifferent mother ... the impotent sadistic, perverse husband, the hysterical or neurasthenic girl." (HS1, 110-11) Sex goes wrong, deviating from the normal. But it is the family, that place where sexuality is formed and where it is most controlled, which was "the germ of all the misfortunes of sex" (HS1, 111). In Lawrence, the moment of hysterization is displaced onto its figurative representation, often in the form of Expressionism. It is not, though, exclusive to woman's sexuality. When Tom Brangwen's passion is roused: "all the sky was teeming and tearing along, a vast disorder of flying shapes and darkness and ragged fumes of light." (R, 48) The "art-speech" itself is hysterized.

Power relations are immanent in sexuality in more complex and subtle ways than the transparent forms of censorship, non-recognition, or prohibition.[75] They are not reducible to one-way modes of domination, nor to repression. The gender issue is only one aspect of the power relation, defined as such by a feminist discourse, including the proto-feminism of *The Rainbow*: "She was left cold by man's stock-breeding lordship over beasts and fishes." (R, 301) For it is also, and more expansively, a complex psychology. Sexual positioning is a dialectic of dominance and subjection, a will-to-power and a willing passivity. The contexts of these sex/power relations need careful understanding in Lawrence's novel.

When Lydia's pregnancy is in its advanced stages, Tom Brangwen is

---

[74] Foucault's theory of power is heavily disputed by political scientists. Cf. Hoy ed., op. cit.
[75] Mark Cousins and Athar Hussain, *Michel Foucault* (London: Macmillan, 1984), 202.

inwardly enraged by her denying him his passion. He develops violent feelings towards her. He "wanted to break her into acknowledgement of him ... smash her into regarding him" (R, 62). He turns to his step-daughter, Anna, for surrogate affection, learning wholesome fatherly affection for the little girl. This gives him the objectivity required to understand the separateness of beings, develop other interests, other centres of living, so that he can "control himself, measure himself" to his wife (R, 79). Lawrence thus represents, in a subtle psychological realism, the character of a recognizable type, the traditional husband, frustrated, restless, who goes down the pub, gets a bit drunk, and becomes aggressive. He manages to contain that violence; whereas his predecessor, Walter Morel in *Sons and Lovers* certainly could not hold back. Although Tom as a young man is no collier, he still suffers a self-consciousness of his want of social graces (R, 86). His violent passion is "relinquished" by the woman, Lydia, on her own initiative. The psychology of sex/power is recognizable here. In the first place, it has an obvious socio-cultural explanation. Lydia is his superior in every way, at once sexually and culturally experienced. He has to come to terms with this fact — a difficult task in his traditionally narrow man's world. He may depend on her utterly for his newly discovered sense of his sexuality, but he has to learn to respect her otherness. In the second place, sexual passion is more often than not aroused by hostile feelings, so that the passion is intense and all-consuming. It is here that carnal knowledge and power are necessarily bound together. Tom has to learn that these moments are never matched by anything else in his daily life; that life otherwise may be dull and unfulfilling. It is a lesson that Will Brangwen also has to learn in the next generation.

It is here, in the story of Will and Anna, that Lawrence begins to focus more sharply on sexual passion as a destructive-creative force that will burn itself through the very core of being. Psychological realism now gives way to the symbolic-mythic, and the aestheticized modes of representation. Will's carving of a wooden phoenix, which the local people do not like at all, takes on symbolic status, as the mythic bird becomes a recurrent *leitmotif*. Like his creation, "Will's loud, vibrating voice ... always sounded strange, re-echoing in the dark places of her [Anna's] being" (R, 109). Then he becomes the symbolic eagle, the bird of prey swooping down on her, while her passionate being represents the flames that will destroy and recreate him, while also heating into a brand that will mark her indelibly. The phoenix, *the* Lawrentian symbol, is complemented by further animal imagery reinforcing the traditional sexist notion that man is the hunter, the bird of prey. However, the context and the implications of the phoenix symbolism take us beyond the sexist discourse, because it is the woman who is the flame that will consume and recreate him (R, 109-11). She is supremely dominant under the golden harvest moon. In the searing light of the moon, the woman always takes complete charge in Lawrence's writing. Her sexuality is at its most threatening. The man becomes a "shadowy figure", eclipsed, "dutifully" going along with her. As Anna bares her breasts to the moon, Will is completely disempowered before the lunacy of the woman's sexuality. In this key passage (R, 114-16), Anna and Will "drift and ebb like a wave" as they gather the harvest, like the rhythms of their Brangwen ancestors working the land, so that her sexuality is implicated with the natural rhythms, just as the harvesting becomes an ebb and flow: "As he came, she drew away, as he drew away, she came." The pattern of work produces a "pulse of steady purpose" for which, here, the connotations are sexual. The pulsating is represented by the recurrent phonemic pattern of the "s" sounds ("the splash of the sheaves") as the lovers are bathed in the silver moonlight. The game of stacking the sheaves she initiates forces him to get faster, until he can finally overtake her and get his kiss, at which point, "the whole rhythm of him beat into the kisses," as the repetitious language becomes an incantation, symptomatic of a rite of passage whose dominant symbol is the flame of the bright moonlight, the woman's power (R, 115). The "long, real kisses ... among the moonlight", creating the image of being surrounded and overwhelmed, metamorphose her into "something new", while "his whole being quivered with surprise, as if from a blow" (R, 116). Now the active-passive poles are reversed: the man is passive, even submissive in the symbolic realm of the woman.[76]

Representing the relations of power at the level of the *leitmotif* carries over into the Tom-Lydia relationship. Now older, Tom realizes how much of that manly battle of their early sex-life has gone, how the hot passion has died out in him: "A great deal of ash was in his fire, cold ash." (R, 119). Having been consumed by the flames of passion, he has waited in vain for his recreation. But the recreative promise of the phoenix mythology will remain unfulfilled. Sex is now rarer if still passionate. So it is, then, that the generations give way to each other, leaving the intense passion of the younger generation in the foreground. In the chapter, "Anna Victrix" Lawrence presents the knowledge-power-sex complex in its most extreme form.

---

[76] Cf: *Genesis 37, 7*: "behold, we are binding sheaves in the field, and, lo, my sheaf arose, and also stood upright; and, behold, your sheaves stood round about, and made obeisance to my sheaf." Joseph's dream is reworked by Lawrence out of the patriarchal into the woman's realm, and made sexual; the discourse, however, is clearly derivative. Source of quote: James T. Boulton, "D.H. Lawrence: His Challenge To Our Scholarship" in Peter Preston ed. (1992), 52.

In their early married life it is significantly Anna who is most at ease with her newly sexualized self. Will is hypersensitive to his own being. The newly discovered passions and yearnings only make him more unstable, "as if the surface of the world had been broken away entire" (R, 139). Admittedly, he feels that she "kept him perfect, in the land of intimate connexion," but it is where he might only be "king for one day in the year". He is on sufferance. The sexual relation has created fear and dread in the man: "shame at his own dependence on her drove him to anger." (R, 141) (And this cannot be financial dependence, as Tom has handed over Anna's shares to him. Cf. R, 119) In their early domestic isolation he has no role, and the "dark storms rose in him" and his "soul only grew blacker" (R, 141). His separate being will be destroyed if he does not find some work to occupy himself, and give him a sense of purposeful identity. The psychological realism of the man's identity crisis belongs in Lawrence to the cognitive, self-conscious level of being. Real passion is a complete forgetting of being, and has nothing to do with psychology in itself. Its representation is always beyond the realism of the mundane, sublimated onto the aesthetic level. The subsequent reflection of consciousness is a return to the psychological realism. Thus Lawrence confirms in the one discourse what had been represented more obliquely, poetically, in the other: "He seemed to lacerate her sensitive femaleness. He seemed to hurt her womb, to take pleasure in torturing her." (R, 142) Or: "She was held by the power of this man who had taken her." As her fear grows, he responds correspondingly to her vulnerability, becoming a bird of prey, eyes glittering "as if with malignant desire" (R, 143). The full complexity of power/knowledge is on display. It is not simply the case that the man exercises power over the vulnerable woman. This is only the case when seen from her perspective at that moment. When we move into his consciousness, the violent reaction to her fears are a complex mixture of deep regret for the pain he has caused, sadistic pleasure, and violent sexual desire, which eventually settles on "compassion for her": "he could not bear to think of her in tears …. He wanted to go to her and pour out his heart's blood to her …. He yearned with passionate desire to offer himself to her utterly." (R, 144) Thus he returns to "an old simplicity", calm again, and "numb with a sort of innocence of love" (R, 145). Once again, the anger and the reconciliation lead to consummate passion beyond the psychological realism of self-consciousness. But, significantly, after his failed attempt to assert his phallic power, the man realizes there could be "only acquiescence and submission" in the "tremulous wonder of consummation". He will need a surrogate passion of his own making for his sense of identity. He will discover in Gothic church architecture the dark, nameless emotion "of all the great mysteries of passion", later to be designated as the architectural form "which always asserted the broken desire of mankind" (R, 220). His life having no "vital importance", it is merely "the margin to the text", as his real being "lay in his dark emotional experience of the Infinite, of the Absolute" (R, 147). His symbolic realm is the great Gothic structure like Bamberg cathedral.

Anna and Will become separate beings *in extremis*. If her soul "and her own self were one and the same to her", his soul and self are disconnected. However, his dark, spiritual conception of himself, almost other-worldly, "fascinates" her — a key signifier particularly attributed to women and implying being enchanted and aroused. But her soul is perplexed by his transfer of passion elsewhere. Her jealous response manifests itself, dark and violent, and is focussed on his wooden carving. He responds to the "chill of her antagonism" by retiring into himself (R, 149). At such moments she feels compelled to become more destructive, and their power struggle leads inexorably to the first explicit sex in the novel, as she caresses him, rousing him with tenderness, so that her phallic man comes to her "fierce and hard, like a hawk striking and taking her" (R, 151). The newly empowered woman, though, responds aggressively; and the battle for supremacy reaches new levels of intensity. The whole sexual relation is now one of a power struggle, and the sex-passion gets correspondingly more violent.

Yet, as I argued above, for Foucault power is not only destructive. This is clearly also the case for Lawrence. In the domestic sphere the fight is conventional. In passion, power and sexuality elide into each other to the extent that the self, becoming unconscious, is obliterated. Lawrence's ideal passion is creative-destructive. Anger and aggression, often born out of deep insecurity or frustration, have a functional necessity in provoking the deepest unconscious desires to break through the superficial manners of the social self. Lawrentian sex is always an intense forgetting, an instinctive act beyond the prohibitions of self-consciousness. It is mindless, often bestial. It forces the self to go back beyond its culture of shame, to discover the instincts or the primal impulses that society and Christianity have put into the discourses of ethics and morality. The power needed to achieve this breakthrough into intuitive understanding of the self was bound to be extreme; the force of the cultural consciousness has the full weight of history and society behind it. The power/sex complex in *The Rainbow* has often been misunderstood, either by being cited out of context, or being read from the perspective of the later "male leadership" phase in Lawrence's work. For we should notice that the daytime self and the passionate self are related causally in the novel. A quarrel entails aroused passion; after passion, the consumed self seeks to reassert its separateness when returning to a conventional state of conscious being. As the passion is all-consuming, the daytime self searches for an equivalent level of being in an all-consuming interest or occupation. Anna has her motherhood and her little matriarchy; Will his passion for church building and Gothic architecture, and later his handicraft which will secure him a teaching career. They will both find ways of coping with their two selves, the one that exists only in so far as it "had relations with another being," and the other "an absolute self" (R, 176). The struggle for power will never be fully resolved: he becomes more and more distant, and she goes through her long "sleep of motherhood", as they fade from prominence in the novel, giving way to the next generation. Here, Lydia's "old brutal story of desire and offering and deep, deep-hidden rage of unsatisfied men against women" (R, 235) will undergo an inversion in her grand-daughter, as the New Woman will be at great pains to satisfy her desire in the man's world.

What begins as a focus for her "sensuous yearning" (R, 267) in the form of the gallant young Skrebensky, and then enters the phase where she lays hold of him "for her dreams," (R, 271) ends up, by degrees of passion — love and hate, submission and aggression — in her striving to exercise her "cold liberty to be herself" (R, 296). When he first attempts to exert power over her she becomes "cold and unmoved as a pillar of salt" (R, 297). The Biblical metaphor presumably insinuates that the defiant woman has blasphemed against the sex of the patriarchy. However, the power relations are more complex than that: "she let him exert all his power over her …. She received all the force of his power. She even wished he might overcome her." His power belongs to her wish-fulfilment; but it is only an interim state of being while she bides her time waiting to emerge into "pure being". From this moment on Ursula is highly conscious of an ontological development. Skrebensky will be the catalyst. Yet, her new self-consciousness is sometimes narcissistic: "For the first time she was in love with a vision of herself" (R, 272). When she gets her first kiss, she opens her lips to him (R, 278). Afterwards (as always in Lawrence) things become more complicated: "it was more difficult to come to him." At sixteen she is mad with desire, but conjugal sex is out of the question. It is all a fantastic romance with the young officer, while her "deepening yearning" leads to a new reserve. We are again in the realm of psychological realism, and Lawrence perceptively describes the young couples' growing desire and innocent frustrations. The relationship attains a maturer stage at the dance (R, 294-300), a change signalled by the switch to the poetic discourse, as they are alone in the bright moonlight. Here the man's conventional phallic power is completely eclipsed. The woman is empowered, and it is a destructive force that she brings to love-making: "his soul was dissolved with agony and annihilation," as she dominates the ritualistic rite of passage — just like her mother before her under the harvest moon. She only returns to the more conventional feminine self — soft and tender — once she has had her victory. Henceforth she will have the upper hand, even when he appears to be in command. Once back in the psychological realism, her feelings are mixed: sometimes unsure of herself, and sorry for hurting him; other times solidly proto-feminist.

Ursula rejects her former understanding. She is now against the authorities of man, patriarchal and theist. Outwardly, in the social world, they are lovers; she receives her ring of troth, pledged in wine before he goes off to war. The event has only a fictional status, belonging as it does to a literary discourse of a recognizable type. And it is soon contradicted by her anti-war sentiments, which she then uses against him. Thus she begins to realize the extent to which his mind-set is not just different, but opposed to hers: "His life lay in the established order of things." (R, 304) Lawrence presents this growing difference without comment, through the dialogue of their arguments and in their separate thoughts. The man represents the conventional male argument about the soldier's duty to serve his country, but the desired effect on her is immediately threatened by the thought that "the male in him was scotched by the knowledge that she was not under his spell or influence". The man and the woman belong to "hostile worlds" that are also the places of their respective desire. It is, of course, a conflict which sets her sexual life unconsciously on fire (R, 309).

Ursula comes progressively into more contact with the discourse of the radical feminism of her day — the Suffragettes, Women and Labour, the Women's Social and Political Union — giving her critical consciousness a political edge. Although the other women who influence her seem more seriously committed to the cause, her sexual conflict with Skrebensky will now be placed in the discourse of a nascent sexual politics. Lawrence will be on the side of the women in this novel.[77] When Skrebensky returns to England, he is but a more mature version of his former self; whereas Ursula has changed profoundly, even though her romantic desire still surfaces from time to time. She will have to recognize the truth that he is not going to be for her "the key, the nucleus to the new world". The power struggle is only about to begin: "they were enemies come together in a truce." He becomes in every respect "alien to her being". And in order to make sense of the paradox that she is still in love with him, she rationalizes what she has so far understood only

---

[77] Lawrence had promised to do his "work for women, better than the suffrage". Letter to Sallie Hopkin, 23 December 1912, reprinted in *The Letters of D.H. Lawrence Volume* 1 (Cambridge: Cambridge University Press, 1979), 490.

intuitively: "a man must inevitably set into this strange separateness, cold otherness of being" (R , 410), itself a recurrent truth argued for in the text on a number of levels. As always, desire is unconscious, dark, animalistic, and unable to speak out: "In his dark, subterranean male soul, he was kneeling before her", even while he asserts his male rights on the conscious level. Her view of him is either a set of external, superficial impressions ("He seemed made up of a set of habitual actions and decisions"), or projections motivated by her sexual desire for that ideal man who would enable her self-fulfilment and self-realization. The problem for both of them is that the two levels are necessarily always separate: "And yet, all must be kept so dark, the consciousness must admit nothing." The characters are trapped in the mannered sophistication of the social life, with its codes of public conduct. His evasiveness and nervous politeness irritates her: "He was always side-tracking ... his own soul." (R, 411) Thus the frustrated attempts to fulfil unconscious desire lead to a severe social critique. Moreover, it is given to the New Woman to expose the "primeval darkness" beneath the veneer of a modern "social mechanism", as she is deeply in touch with that darkness in her self. The ontological imperative — "Be thyself!" — is here, as elsewhere, turned into a pervasive social criticism of the state of England through Ursula's *educatio sexualis*.

Skrebensky remains to the last the representative conventional voice for the stable values of a phallocentric culture: "he had not taken her yet" (R, 417) represents its reductionist sexual relation. The taking of the other presupposes a one-way exercise of power, and it is reinforced by the phallic nature imagery prefigured in the powerful, vibrating trunk of the great oak tree. This phallic reductionism contrasts markedly with the sexual psychology of the love between the two women, Ursula and her teacher Winifred. Swimming naked, touching, and holding, represent a fluid sensuality of caressing bodies (R, 314). Their lesbian relationship is not based on the overt structure of power and submission. Significantly though, it is Ursula who appropriates the male phallic domain in her return to heterosexual love: "She had taken him." The discourse of patriarchy will not be transcended. Her feminism will merely reverse the roles, not replace them. And as if to prove this, her new being is divided, consisting of her everyday self, and "another, stronger self that knew the darkness" (R, 418). Repeating the pattern of the two previous generations, she will be unable to keep her selves apart for long. Once marriage becomes a distinct possibility, her profounder, inner self will rebel violently. She could never be the army officer's wife. This precipitates her supreme moment of defiance, the refusal of marriage, which at a stroke fulfils the logic of the plot and upsets the whole English novel tradition of resolution by marriage. Ironically, Skrebensky and Ursula only play at the roles of husband and wife in a charade of marriage, while they stay at hotels in their "delicious make-belief". Lawrence, however, is quick to insist that beneath the masks they are man and woman, "absolute and beyond all limitation". She is the *Frau Baronin* to his *Herr Baron*, reiterating a dominant class-fantasy first seen in the early Brangwen women, but here reinscribed as the sensuous aristocrats of Romantic literature. Yet, it is only a temporary escape. We are meant to notice the warnings: "He was never aware of the separate being of her." (R, 421) And she begins to identify more completely with her fantasy role. In their role-playing and pre-marital sex we realize how far we have come since the first generation. The woman has attained a greater self-determination. But she seems incapable of learning from the mistakes of her parents or grandparents. In the terms worked out in the Hardy study, the man and the woman are unbalanced and unstable precisely because they have allowed either the male or the female principle, respectively, to take them over. It is only harmonious selves that may achieve consummate marriage. This requires an equilibrium of male and female principles. Indeed, it seems that it is the male principle, prefigured in the phallic sexuality and its corresponding power struggle, that dominates both the man and the woman, and leads inexorably towards the final battle for supremacy. As he feels her growing soul separateness, and hardens his will in response, she "owned his body" (R, 426). These are sure signs in Lawrence that the over-possessive, selfish woman will necessarily require the adjunct of the inadequate man. The changing bias in the balance of power will destroy the relationship. The novel argues on a number of levels — philosophical, political, and social — for the plausibility of this failure.

What stands out most in the text, then, is a destructive female sexuality which is most intensive when symptomatically represented in its moment of lunacy in the glare of the full moon, first during their night out on the Sussex Downs, and finally in the sand dunes. Skrebensky feels he is "a mere attribute of her" — precisely her adjunct, a sort of metonymic subordination to her desire. He clings to his one source of self-assertion, namely his social position. By her final refusal of marriage she denies him that power over her, too, so that "his manhood was cruelly, coldly defaced". (Interestingly, Lawrence reinforces the idea that social positions are no more than books or texts that can be defaced.) He cannot maintain the distance between his two selves, and he breaks down in public (R, 433-36). Ursula will change her mind about the marriage again, but this will be only out of sympathy for him, or desperation because of her pregnancy. This half-hearted decision belongs only to the superficial world of society. The profounder world of her unconscious self is given expression twice more. First, in the climactic destruction of

Skrebensky in the sand dunes; and second, in the nightmarish scene of the stampeding horses. Both are representations of the connections of sexuality with power, and it is to these two episodes that I now turn.

It is tempting to suggest that the sexual assassination of Skrebensky in the bright moonlight is symbolic revenge for the class humiliation of Ursula at the Hall. Once in her lunar element, the veneer of social intercourse is removed to reveal a powerful and elemental female sexuality underneath. She "vibrated like a jet of electricity". The sex is, unsurprisingly, phallic and aggressive. Once again, and for the last time, she plays the dominant role, letting him take her. She, inevitably, remains unfulfilled, even unroused. Her deeper sexual needs are connected with her feeling totally out of place in the society of the Hall: "as if her violent-sensitive nakedness were exposed to the hard, brutal, material impact of the rest of the people." (R, 443) And he belongs precisely there; these are his people. In a perceptive moment she realizes that his "soul could not contain her in its waves of strength, nor his breast compel her in burning, salty passion". Thus, there is a "terrible" struggle for consummation on the beach. It is a fight he is destined to lose. It lasts until his will is broken: "he gave way as if dead ... white and obliterated." (R, 445) The recurrent images of burning, corrosion, or melting signify at the level of the *leitmotif* the object of her attack (his people are hard, brutal, material). The flame of her fiery passion will be strong enough to burn through the protective social covering of his male soul.

Phallic male power makes a final appearance in the symbolic form of the stampeding white horses. They represent a powerful elemental force which threatens to destroy the woman, now vulnerable in her pregnancy, and exposed in the driving rain. It is as if Lawrence wants to give expression, one more time, to an atavistic force that has been hovering around in the unconscious throughout the novel, and by giving it concrete representation allow Ursula to exorcize that phallic power once and for all. As the horses "thundered upon her" her femaleness is fully exposed, and this is given symbolic representation: "her limbs were dissolved, she was dissolved like water. All the hardness and looming power was in the massive body of the horse-group." (R, 453) The female element, water, contrasts with the hardness and massiveness of solid male power. Through the force of will-power, she overcomes her fear and manages to get away, experiencing then an extreme reduction of the self to an unconscious, stone-like passivity, as if petrified by her experience of complete powerlessness before the threat of the collective male forces amassed against her. During the delirium of her illness, and her subsequent miscarriage, with all its symbolic resonance, "she had a dull firmness of being, a sense of permanency". She has to burn the "corrosion of him" in her "till it burned itself out" (R, 455). In doing so she manages to relinquish the phallic male discourse of sexuality, and return to the female element: "she felt like the most fragile of flowers that opens in the end of winter." (R, 457) The world may now be discovered afresh. She has come through, and stands on the threshold of the "new germination" (R, 458). To realize this new dream she will have to wait for Birkin in *Women in Love*, because the female element here is still only one part of the dualism, and therefore only one side of an incomplete being. Moreover, as Smithson has pointed out, the patriarchal structure of modern western civilization represented in *The Rainbow* prevents men *and* women from attaining psychic wholeness. This would be the same in a matriarchy because here too only the one side of the dualist equation is operative. Additionally, it is noticeable that the increasing impotence of the men suggests, implicitly, the failure of the self-fulfilment of the women,[78] despite the power they have learnt to exercise.

The Foucauldian discourse analysis has, thus, drawn out the inherent contradictions in Lawrence's tendency towards a sexual essentialism, not least by insisting that sexuality is an historical construct. The sexualities on display in *The Rainbow* are the objects of a mixture of discursive formations, ancient and modern. The complex psychology of sexual relationships, on the one hand, and the psychoanalytics of desire, on the other, result in a profound representation of power. Foucault's power/knowledge thesis is even more obviously appropriate for reading Lawrence's critique of education in *The Rainbow*.

Discipline and punish
There is a marked coincidence in the terms of reference between Foucault's *Discipline and Punish* (1975) and chapter XIII, "The Man's World" in Lawrence's novel. Foucault's comments on education belong to his general thesis about the power of the modern State apparatus to enforce the process of normalization through the means of surveillance and discipline, themselves more subtle ways of power than outright coercion. The school, like the monastery, the barracks or the prison, has developed regimes of discipline designed to exercise power over the body itself. The institution of the school is an apparatus of the State, which, like any such institution, has an immediate hold over the body. Such power relations, "invest it, mark it, train it, torture it, force it to carry out tasks, to perform ceremonies, to emit signs" (DP, 26). The pupils are subjected to the system by being turned into objects of pedagogic knowledge dictated from above. Supervising, punishing and

---

[78] Isaiah Smithson, "Structuralism as a Method of Literary Criticism" reprinted in Ellis and De Zordo (1992), Volume II, 238.

constraining children to prepare them for citizenship in the disciplinary society is reinforced by the family. These mechanics of power produce docile bodies, useful to the economy and obedient to the political State (DP, 138). The pupils in the Brinsley street elementary school where Ursula works are being prepared for the colliery or the factory. The content of their learning is not important; it is the discipline that counts.

Educational regimes derive from the Christian tradition of the great monastic orders or Jesuit schools. Training for the disciplined life, scholastic or military, requires a detailed timetabling consisting in the "meticulousness of the regulations, the fussiness of the inspections, the supervision of the smallest fragment of life and of the body" (DP, 140). Control over bodies requires a precise distribution of time and space. The basic disciplinary space is cellular in order to guarantee obedience and prevent "dangerous communications" (DP, 143-44). The timetable assures a strict measure of control and guarantee of use: "The *seriation* of successive activities make possible a whole investment of duration by power" (DP, 160). The school becomes a mechanism of learning, a precise instrumentality of power, and especially the primary school because it has the task of disciplining the pupils at an early age by teaching absolute obedience to the authority of the teacher. This is precisely Mr Harby's pedagogy in *The Rainbow*, and one that Ursula will have to learn, against her better judgment, if she is to survive.

Discipline "presupposes a mechanism that coerces by means of observation" (DP, 170). The school building like its prototype, the *école militaire*, should be designed to function as the perfect disciplinary apparatus by enabling constant surveillance which is then "integrated into the teaching relationship" (DP, 175). In *The Rainbow*, the surveillance mechanism is both visual and audible: the small building with its crowded and cramped teaching rooms (60 pupils), separated by glass partitions allows any noisy class to be visibly and audibly observed (noise being the principal symptom of lack of discipline, as any school teacher knows), so that any deviation from teacher-centred rote learning, like group work and more creative pupil participation, as Ursula discovers to her cost, is simply a provocation to be branded a poor teacher. Moreover, admonishing the class or punishing a pupil in front of the class (corporal punishment in Mr Harby's school) will be heard throughout the building, putting fear into the rest of the kids. Conformity is thus enforced: "The normal is established as a principle of coercion in teaching with the introduction of standardized education," (DP, 184) and further supported by the mechanism of the examination which reinforces the formation of a certain type of knowledge bound to "a certain form of the exercise of power" (DP, 187). The power invested in education "produces domains of objects and rituals of truth" (DP, 194).

It is important to emphasize, once again, that Foucault's notion of power is not simply negative. Power is not merely subjection from above. For, as Hoy explains, "the dominated are as much a part of the network of power relations and the particular social matrix as the dominating".[79] While Ursula finally succumbs to the disciplinary regime of the school, punishing the boy, Williams, with a beating, she is herself implicated in a relation of power which has her in its grip. In order to establish authority over the class, she is forced to inflict corporal punishment, against her ideals. But in going too far, she loses her self-discipline, and becomes a mirror-image of the violent children she is supposed to control. In the precise context, Lawrence makes it a personal issue that belongs to Ursula's struggle to assert herself in the man's world. But the terms of that assertion, and the institutional situation in which she is trapped, give her action a context that goes beyond the personal motivation into the discourse of power that is legitimized by the State education system, and represented in the person of Mr Harby. Furthermore, she has not now established a position of equality alongside the men. Although she gains the respect of Harby by becoming like him, Williams' mother, on visiting the school to complain, only addresses Harby in her presence, thus refusing Ursula the recognition she thought she had won. Lawrence unwittingly confirms Foucault's controversial idea that power is strictly without an agent as both the social and institutional relations of power exercise their hold on teacher and pupil alike.

The mother's presence at the school reminds us that the family is "the privileged locus of emergence for the disciplinary question of the normal and the abnormal" (DP, 216). Parents, like teachers, doctors or judges, are the arbiters and guarantors of ubiquitous normality (DP, 303-4). Ursula's own parents, Anna and Will, are the exceptions as far as their younger children are concerned. Indeed, Ursula's ideas about children's free-expression come from her own family, and were part of a serious education debate: "At that time education was in the forefront as a subject of interest. There was talk of new Swedish methods of handwork instruction." (R, 221) Self-expression would be taught through manual dexterity. On Sundays the Brangwen children learn to be quieter and to busy themselves. However, her parents exercise fully their conventional authority over Ursula, putting a stop to her plans to go to college in Kingston-on-Thames. She takes the local teaching post to prove her independence from their authority, but only becomes more subject to its relations of power. The ironic twist is that the corporal punishment which allows her to achieve the status of disciplinarian, putting fear into her

---

[79] In Hoy ed., 134.

class — an action precisely required by the system — also defines her as beyond the pale of normality. As Williams' mother puts it: "it isn't allowed to beat a child like that, I am sure, especially when he's delicate." Punishment is also subject to a certain discipline; it must be measured.

The episodes in the Brinsley street elementary school represent the direct result of educational reform. With the establishment of universal free State education between 1870 and 1891, the school leaving age was raised from 10 in 1880 to 12 in 1899. Those who failed the Standard Five exam had to stay on an extra year, and it is Standard Five where Ursula teaches. Not surprisingly, the particular difficulties she experiences were inevitably a symptom of the overcrowding and the resentment amongst the kids for being forced to stay on at school.[80] However, the narrative context of this episode should not be overlooked. It is narrated through Ursula's consciousness, and, here, two points should be made. First, she represents the idealist, progressive view of education (self-expression), which fails hopelessly in the elementary school.[81] Second, she wants the pupils to love her, when the school ethos is based on fear, as represented by Harby's regime. The school itself symbolizes the system: "The whole place seemed to have a threatening expression, imitating the church's architecture, for the purpose of domineering, like a gesture of vulgar authority ... like an empty prison waiting the return of tramping feet." (R, 343) The metaphor of the prison is reiterated several times, until we get the impression of a familiar Victorian representation of a Dickensian type: "The prison was round her now!" (R, 346) Or: "The prison of the school was reality." She is imprisoned by this microcosm of the man's world with its patriarchal relations. The school is an alien reality to which "she must apply herself" (R, 347).

It is soon evident that the pupils are subjected to a military discipline, too: marching, standing in line, sitting silently in rows. Mr Harby "thrashed and bullied ... like some invincible source of the mechanism he kept all power to himself. And the class owned his power. And in school

---

[80] In "Education and the People" (1920), in *Reflections on the Death of a Porcupine and Other Essays* edited by Michael Herbert (Cambridge: Cambridge University Press, 1988). Lawrence called the elementary school-teacher a "poor devil" whose existence is rendered impossible and undignified by the "system, the parents" (89). This teacher is "that public clown" (94). Forcing kids with no capacity to stay on at school makes them resent it, so that they become cynical and develop a "profound contempt for education" (96).

[81] Ibid., 88. And especially Lawrence's critique of the polarization of the education debate into the idealists versus the materialist — self-expression or vocational training — a debate that is still with us today.

it was power, and power alone that mattered." (R, 350-51) He is an agent of the power only in so far as it is channelled through him, inherent as it is in the schooling system. This relation of power already belongs to the class that Ursula gets. If she tries to replace the relation with one which is more personal and benign, she will cause a breakdown in the tightly linked system of teachers and pupils, surveillance and punishment. Seen through her eyes, of course, it is a personal conflict between Mr Harby and herself, and between the class and herself. It is because of this focus that the institutional critique is often overshadowed by the individual conflicts. When she feels superior because she tolerates the children's spirited behaviour, her colleague's, Mr Blunt's, criticism is brutally pragmatic: if she does not discipline them they will get used to having the upper hand, which will cause insuperable difficulties for her replacement. The indiscipline could even spread through the school and lead to anarchy.

Ursula's progressive views are reinforced in the novel by her exposure, briefly, to vegetarianism, and more extensively to radical feminism. Yet, ironically, it is the feminist, Maggie Schofield, who warns her that the pupils have to be forced to learn anything. And it is at this point that Lawrence presents the views he was later to express in "Education and the People" (1920) — but here, through Ursula, and in a specifically ironic context:

> all the schoolteachers, drudging unwillingly at the graceless task of compelling many children into one disciplined, mechanical set, reducing the whole set to an automatic state of obedience and attention .... The first great task was to reduce sixty children to one state of mind, or being. This state must be produced automatically, through the will of the teacher, and the will of the whole school authority, imposed upon the will of the children. (R, 355-56)

The teachers are the instruments of the will-to-power of pedagogy. Ursula gives voice to its critique in the Lawrentian terms of the belief that the natural instincts of the children will be destroyed by the State education machine. The irony is made explicit in a rare moment of straight authorial comment: "Ursula thought she was going to become the first wise teacher by making the whole business personal, and using no compulsion. She believed utterly in her own personality. So that she was in a very deep mess." (R, 356) She will have to learn to keep order and "inflict knowledge on a class with remarkable efficiency". But she carries on regardless, and Harby starts to persecute her. She fears he will destroy her. Her class was "the weak link in the chain which made up the school" (R, 358). (The terms of reference are military.) He shouts at her class in

her presence, undermining her authority. Power is clearly exercised by
the authoritarian men running the system. The issue is gendered. She
must not admit that she, as a woman, is not tough enough for the
disciplined world of men. Their authority goes right up to the ministers in
the Government who have "supreme control over Education" (R, 362).
Those who infringe the disciplinary code are subject to ritual humiliation,
pupil or teacher.

Ursula does eventually manage to establish order through discipline.
But her growing feminism gives her an alternative discourse, so that the
world of work is "man's convention", and belongs as such to the
reductive instrumentalities that rule the modern world. Although she now
proves to herself that she can function efficiently in the man's world, "she
was not going to be prisoner in the dry, tyrannical man-world" (R, 380-
81). This oppositional stance will help her to reject marriage, that
alternative to teaching for a woman in her day. When she leaves the
school at the end of the summer term, "the irons were struck off, the
sentence was expired," for her and for the children. (R, 392) She even
manages to blind herself to reality one more time by seeing the whole
episode in idealistic terms. She had done her bit "to the fabric man was
building" (R, 394). The irony is not Ursula's but Lawrence's, as the
whole episode is allowed to comment implicitly on her tendency towards
a naive idealism.

If the elementary school is understood as the barracks or prison, the
college to which Ursula now returns is the convent: "There was in it a
reminiscence of the wondrous, cloistral origin of education." She is
momentarily in her medieval wonderland of Gothic architecture, where
"the monks of God held the learning of men and imparted it within the
shadow of religion" (R, 399). The professors are the "priests of knowledge", a fantasy which sustains her during the first year of study,
implicitly reminding us of her namesake, St Ursula (the legendary patron
of educational institutions and founder of the Ursuline Order of teaching
Sisters). On her return for the second year, however, the illusion has
gone, and the religious retreat has become, "a little apprentice-shop
where one was further equipped for making money" (R, 403). Her deep
desire for the mystery of knowledge is significantly undermined when
she admits to the essential materialism of education. (And it is in this
frame of mind that she will meet Skrebensky again after being apart for
six years.)

The levels of incarceration or imprisonment, described by Foucault in
Discipline and Punish, go beyond the institutions of education to infuse
other parts of the modern existence that Lawrence is diagnosing through
the character of Ursula. Her family imprison her in their madhouse of
children running riot, so that there is no escape (except on Sundays) to a

quieter privacy where she can study. The freeing of the children to give vent to their energies reduces Ursula's existence to a greater unfreedom. She is also a captive of her father's authority, a social relation of power in a patriarchal society that extends itself to the school, college, and the prospect of marriage to the army officer. At a general, symbolic level (and one consistent throughout Lawrence) the thematic and structural opposition of closure and plenitude is prefigured in the poky, dingy interiors where families live, and the open spaces of nature where sex takes place, respectively. For Ursula, any code or convention is a form of imprisonment, and when she envisages "the new germination" at the end of the novel, it is a new and necessary life-force because, "they were all in prison, they were all going mad" (R, 458). Moreover, just as Foucault began his study of systems of incarceration with the Ship of Fools and Bedlam, before going on to analyse the formation of hospitalization, imprisonment, and schooling, so Lawrence describes and dramatizes modern society's rationalizations as forms of madness and imprisonment. The natural, instinctive self is trapped in the codes, conventions, and apparatus of its own collective invention. Lawrence's may be a neo-Romantic critique, but its implicit proposition of a "carceral society" seems close in many respects to Foucault's. Lawrence's neo-Romantic idealism may have led him towards his critique of education, but he seems in this, like Dickens before him, to prefigure Foucault's terms of reference.

5. Conclusion: towards an aesthetics of transgression
The strategic uses made of Foucault have enabled a reading of *The Rainbow* as discursive history. The text is no longer predominantly captured by a transparent relation to history — events, people, places, values — nor to History — its writing or record as official teleology; or its relation of hindsight with the present. A Foucauldian approach teaches us that the multi-layered discursive text of Lawrence's novel cannot be finally understood by the multi-styled life of the author alone. Even though the phases of the writing correspond to the changing phases of the life, and the literature responds to the uneven and changing fortunes of the reception — from the extremes of the proto-feminism in *The Rainbow* to the proto-fascism of the male-leadership work of the 1920s; or the Christian-Biblical discourse of the early work, and the Classical-Occultist and ecological discourses after 1915.[82] At best such knowledge

---

[82] "When Lawrence speaks of sex he is also necessarily speaking of what we have come to call ecology, the relationship between people and the natural environment,

of the cultural history of the author offers us a set of radical shifts. Additionally, a Foucauldian reading enables a close-up focus on the discursive structure of Lawrence's writing through which we can ascertain not just the discourses themselves, but the uses made of them.

A general argument running through this study is that Lawrence is most modernist when he challenges conventional realism through aestheticizing strategies. History becomes mythology, and sexual feeling poetry. His novels contain several writing codes, so that he is, by turns, "modernist, counter-modernist, and meta-modernist".[83] What *The Rainbow* does, in its most modernist passages, is to attempt a representation of sexuality that both reaches back to older spiritual truths, and searches for a language that goes beyond the moralistic connotations of the Biblical to some new mode of expression, part Romantic, part Expressionist. Can Lawrence, though, be called a "transgressive" writer? We should proceed with some caution because Foucault's transgressive theory went underground after it was attacked for being idealist, only to re-emerge in ontological guise in the later ethics. The avant-garde according to Foucault is defined as such by its counter-discursive position. It is a crucial vantage point from which, with hindsight, Foucault is able to deconstruct the dominant "positivities" of an epoch. He devised a transgressive canon which was strategically important to his early work on the history on modern rationalism.

Implicit in the notion of discursive transgressivity is Althusser's proposition that art and literature can produce an internal distance to ideology, and therefore that literature has a counter-hegemonic status.[84] Foucault's position is similar to that of his mentor, Althusser.[85] His subversive canon — Sade, Goya, Hölderlin, Nerval, Lautréamont, van Gogh, Nietzsche, Roussel, Artaud — represents "the experience of unreason" (MC, 212) in the ages of Enlightenment and Positivism. Theirs are "barely audible voices" that nevertheless raise the possibility of contesting the dominant *episteme* (MC, 281). Here is one of Foucault's

---

which he called the cosmos or circumambient universe." Keith Sagar, "Lawrence and the Resurrection of Pan" in Peter Preston ed. (1992), 38.

[83] Pinkney, 3.

[84] Louis Althusser, *Lenin and Philosophy and Other Essays* (London: New Left Books, 1971; first published 1968): "art does have a quite particular and specific relationship with ideology." ("A Letter on Art"), 202. And: "that as the specific function of art is to make *visible* (*donner à voir*), by establishing a distance from it, the reality of the existing ideology (of any one of its forms), the work of art *cannot fail to exercise* a directly ideological effect." ("Cremonini, Painter of the Abstract"), 215-16. (Emphases in original). Both essays were first published in 1966.

[85] For details of their friendship and close association that began in the late 1940s, see David Macey, 25, and 196-97.

earliest formulations (1961) of the transgressive theory: "Through Sade and Goya, the western world received the possibility of transcending its reason in violence, and recovering tragic experience beyond the promises of the dialectic." Aesthetic discourse allows thought to escape the trap of rationalism. The work of art compels the world to question itself. Produced by madmen, it transcends madness because it is the mirror-image of reason (MC, 285-288). It is not, though, that art and literature are simply the privileged locus of criticism in *Madness and Civilization*, but rather that for Foucault in the early 1960s the "long story of madness is deeply embedded in the history of literature".[86]

It is a mistake, however, to expect Lawrence to sit comfortably with the experimental writing of Lautréamont or Mallarmé. In fact he spoke out against their kind of aestheticism. About the Italian Futurists Lawrence wrote: "it *isn't* art, but ultra scientific attempts to make diagrams of certain physic or mental states .... It's the most self-conscious, intentional, pseudo-scientific stuff on the face of the earth."[87]. Here, Lawrence is profoundly opposed to the calculated self-consciousness of modern art and modern existence. He is too passionate a writer to be exclusively concerned with purely aesthetic issues. (But as I argue in the following chapters, after 1915 and the difficulties he had with his publishers and his reception, Lawrence's attitude to the formal and aesthetic questions of Modernism will undergo a sea change which has only more recently been noticed.)

For reading *The Rainbow*, we need, therefore, a broader concept of the relationship between the transgressive and the aesthetic. And we need look no further than Foucault's "critical ontology", which Simons describes as "an analysis of the limits of our being, not in the sense of an essential, unchanging being but contingent, plural and transformable ways of being human subjects. Critical ontology is conducted as genealogical analysis of the limits of subjectivity which are to be transgressed".[88] Acts of transgression locate the limits of being, and eroticism and sexuality offer us the greatest opportunity for them. It is something Foucault thought a lot about, both for his writing and for his life. The ontology of sex is also Lawrence's principal concern. As both Foucault and Lawrence showed, transgression is a destabilizing force, undermining conventional foundations for the self. The problem is that the anthropological and psychological discourses of the human (and humanist) sciences have appropriated sexuality and given it a scientific

---

[86] During, 42.
[87] Letter to A.W. McLeod, 2 June 1914 (Lawrence's emphasis).
[88] Jon Simons, *Foucault and the Political* (London: Routledge, 1995), 68-9.

foundation. In order to create an internal distance within the human sciences for his critique, Foucault had to turn to the art, literature and philosophy that has been particularly self-reflective. That notion of a critique from within the post-Enlightenment western tradition also applies to Lawrence's aestheticizing strategies for his ontological enquiry within the tradition of the English novel. In Foucault's later work, privileging a self-referential Modernism is abandoned for an aesthetics of the self deriving from Classical Antiquity.

As Simons points out, the early Foucault's aestheticist posture, which expected the aesthetic realm prefigured in the avant-garde to compensate for everything excluded by all other discourses, was idealist not least because there is no analysis of "the enmeshment of art in power relations".[89] In Lawrence, power relations derive from powerful acts or feelings. In an interview in 1983, Foucault said, "A pleasure must be something incredibly intense …. [Intensity] by its very nature places us beyond the deadening and consoling certainties of conventional life".[90] Here, transgression has become an ethical category, and it is one that we find in Lawrence, too, but for quite different reasons: Lawrence, more spiritual, prioritizing the heterosexual; Foucault, more hedonist, homosexual. A greater difference between them, however, can be seen in the uses they make of the Christian origins of the self. Even though they both go back beyond Christianity for the more ancient sources of the self, Foucault does not propose a return to the pre-modern moralities, and Lawrence does — but with a newer, modern, sexual emphasis. However, as I argue in this study, through the approaches of critical theory, the question of writing (as opposed to ethics) shifts the focus towards a more radically modernist Lawrence than has previously been the case in the dominant reception regimes. This also requires a broader understanding of Modernism — and I shall return to the relation of Lawrence to the problematics of Modernism in the conclusion.

Simon During asks the question, "What would an archaeology of literary studies look like?" He imagines it would have to deal with the relations of power and the self in specific historical formations; and with that specific form of institutional power manifest in the uses made of literature.[91] It would be concerned with the derivation of different literary histories from dominant discursive practices (evolution, biology) that define literature as its object of knowledge. I would add that an archaeology of Lawrence studies would be a cultural history, investigating the

---

[89] Simons, 80.
[90] Cited in Gutting, ed., 22.
[91] During, 116. For a thorough and radical discussion of the uses of literature see Tony Bennett, *Outside Literature* (London: Routledge, 1990).

life, letters, essays and fiction as objects of particular reception regimes whose formation would be historicized. The focus would be on a history of the uses of Lawrence, in which Kermode's Lawrence would be opposed to Leavis's, and so on. What this chapter has tried to do, however, is to use Foucault less for a cultural history of reception (although, as parts of the above have demonstrated, it could never be left out of account), more for the express purpose of a close reading of *The Rainbow* as history.

In the next chapter, I shall be discussing that sea change in Lawrence studies brought about by the belated publication of *Mr Noon* in the 1980s. It has entailed a different approach to the fiction after *The Rainbow* — a Bakhtinian approach.

3

The Carnivalizing Novel: Bakhtinian Readings of *Women in Love*, *The Lost Girl*, and *Mr Noon*

1. Introduction: a Lawrence after Noon?

Since the belated publication of *Mr Noon* in 1984,[1] and the research of the Cambridge University Press editors and biographers, there has been a significant shift in Lawrence studies that hinges on an attitude or mood detected in the letters, and corroborated in *Mr Noon*, that emerges around the time of the completion of *Women in Love* (1917). A more sardonic, self-ironical, cynical mood towards his work, and especially his English reading public seems to have been set in train by the continual difficulties Lawrence experienced after the banning of *The Rainbow* in 1915. Worthen describes the situation as follows:

> *The Rainbow* had been suppressed, his other writings frequently censored or rejected, he and Frieda had been prevented from leaving the country, suspected of spying and finally expelled from Cornwall. They had been frequently impoverished, sometimes homeless, and had been more than once reduced to living on charity .... Lawrence had also been ill; indeed, it is arguable that the poverty and illness of the war years in England accelerated his early death.[2]

Indeed, he despaired of ever having a broad reading public, and preferred to have his novels published by private subscription — as was *Women in Love* in America in 1920.

In such circumstances Lawrence had little to laugh about. However, it was around this time that he turned to comedy,[3] laughing through his

---

[1] All references in text [MN] are to the Penguin edition of the Cambridge D.H. Lawrence (London, 1996).
[2] Introduction to the Cambridge University Press edition (Cambridge, 1984), xxxviii-ix.
[3] Mark Kinkead-Weekes, "Humour in the Letters of D.H. Lawrence" in Paul Eggert and John Worthen eds, *Lawrence and Comedy* (Cambridge: Cambridge University Press, 1996), 183-85.

writing at the public who rejected him, at the English society he had
abandoned, yet also at himself. The biographical and historical formation
of the humorous and self-critical author is then partly the product of a
new direction in Lawrence's writing,[4] corroborated by the new material
available, especially in the Cambridge University Press letters and
biographies, which characterizes a new author-persona; and one that
contradicted the ponderous, humourless scourge of the modern world
first put about by Norman Douglas and T.S. Eliot, and later promoted by
Leavis.[5] And this has now placed criticism in the position of rereading the
fiction from this newer, belated perspective as comic, parodic, and self-
observing writing, even while it continues to propose its serious message.

Are we then to abandon the dominant post-Leavisian history — and
one I have argued for in the two previous chapters — of the progression
in Lawrence towards a serious Modernism because we now read the
earlier fiction with a newer, wholly different retrospect as nascent forms
of comedy and parody realized in the later works? Indeed, a newer
retrospect that sees the decisive turn coming after the trial of *The
Rainbow*? John Worthen tends towards the affirmative: "The great
watershed of Lawrence's writing has, for years, been thought to lie
between *Sons and Lovers* and *The Rainbow* .... [T]he crucial division
may lie instead between *The Rainbow* and Lawrence's subsequent
writing, of which *Women in Love* is perhaps the beginning."[6] However,
the answer really depends on your definition of Modernism. Approaching
it through critical theory opens up Modernism to a broader understanding, as I hope to show in this chapter. For, coincidental with the turn
towards the comic in Lawrence studies has been the attempt, since 1985,
to theorize it through the work of Mikhail Bakhtin. It is the aim of this
chapter to engage with the arguments for this new Lawrence and its
Bakhtinian theorizing.

What began with David Lodge's collection of essays in *After Bakhtin*,[7] reached the point where Lydia Blanchard could confidently declare
that: "The approach taken by Bakhtin, with its emphasis on dialogics,
dramatizes the inadequacy of most other critical theories of the novel for

---

[4] Eggert in ibid., and note 1, 179.
[5] Cf. Worthen, "Drama and Mimicry in Lawrence" in ibid., 24.
[6] Ibid., 42.
[7] David Lodge, *After Bakhtin: Essays in Criticism* (London: Routledge, 1990).
Crucially, the essay on Lawrence and Bakhtin, reprinted in Keith Brown ed.,
Rethinking Lawrence (Buckingham: Open University Press, 1990) was first published
in 1985.

discussing Lawrence."[8] In what follows I shall trace this recent history of Bakhtinian Lawrence criticism, and assess whether Blanchard is justified in her major claim about Lawrence and critical theory; but also whether we can say, as Widdowson has of Lodge, that Lawrence critics have been "drawing opportunistically" on Bakhtinian theory, neutralizing its radical effects by the adventitious, empiricist "testing" of it on the works.[9] In other words, has Lawrence criticism really drawn the full consequences of Bakhtinian theory, and in doing so revised its understanding of the relationship between Lawrence and Modernism?

2. The comic and its Bakhtinian description in recent Lawrence criticism

Bakhtin has appealed to Lodge the novelist as well as Lodge the literary critic. After what he characterizes as "the barren years of Theory" where recourse to the author was the greatest heresy, he discovers a theorist who reinstates the signature of the author as the hidden hand implicit in the narratological architectonics of the text. For Lodge, Bakhtin at last promises a reading of Lawrence more befitting an author whose autobiographical presence in his fiction has apparently been a source of undoing for any ambitious Derridean critic.[10] The author is henceforth the ventriloquist and mimic, performing a "medley of ... voices". After Bakhtin the novel is characterized by a "discursive polyphony".[11]

Large claims have been made for Bakhtin's relevance to Lawrence. His is not only the most appropriate critical approach. Bakhtin and Lawrence also have similar ambitions for the novel. For the latter, it is "the one bright book of life" that can capture the whole "rainbow" of our existence in its vital and vibrant forms.[12] For the former, it is, in Wayne Booth's words, "capable of a kind of justice to the inherent polyphonies

---

[8] Lydia Blanchard, "D.H. Lawrence and his 'Gentle Reader': The Furious Comedy of *Mr Noon*" in Eggert and Worthen eds, (1996), 107.

[9] Peter Widdowson ed., *D.H. Lawrence* (London: Longman, 1992), 12. Significantly, though, Widdowson's collection of critical approaches to Lawrence omits any further reference to Bakhtin even while claiming that Lodge's use of Bakhtin is radical; an omission which is strange given the Left ideology and anti-formalist tendency of the selection, where even the "psychoanalysis" section reprints only Terry Eagleton's Freudian-Marxist critique of *Sons and Lovers*.

[10] Lodge's critique of the "death of the author" is a misrecognition that fudges the issues involved by collapsing the distinctions between structuralism and post-structuralism. See my discussion in the general introduction above.

[11] Lodge, 6, 21.

[12] D.H. Lawrence (1925), "Why the Novel Matters" reprinted in *Phoenix* (London: Heinemann, 1967), 535.

of life". [13] The novel mattered to Lawrence, because as Lodge put it, "of all the forms of human discourse and cognition it was the only one which could embrace the totality of human experience, the whole man alive". [14] Bakhtinian poetics promote a novel that is discursively proliferate, expansively comic in its play of voices and styles, undoing any authoritarian discourse or epic pretensions. Lodge, however, concentrates on one of Bakhtin's key ideas, deriving from his study of Dostoevsky, that true polyphony in the strict sense first argued for in that study stands or falls on whether the relationship between the author's and the characters' discourse is "dialogic". In other words: is this relationship characterized by freely interacting, fully independent voices in Lawrence? For Lodge the answer is a qualified no. The author has a strong presence in works like *Women in Love*. Roger Fowler[15] also hold this view: *Women in Love* is not a "clear example of heteroglossic, or polyvocal" text. Better examples are *Tristram Shandy* or *Ulysses*. Lawrence does not create "a sense of independent consciousness in his central characters". [16] We seem, then, to be off to a bad start.

For Fowler, though, *The Lost Girl*, is an example; for Lodge, it is *Mr Noon*. So perhaps it is simply a matter of the choice of text to substantiate the usefulness of the Bakhtinian approach to Lawrence? Lodge does not give in easily. Indeed, he points out the following Bakhtinian characteristics in *Women in Love*: dialogized, double-voiced speech (speech oriented towards another's speech, or another style, as in parody or stylization) which functions as irony at the level of character. Examples range from the opening scene in the novel, stylizing the upper-class modish speech of the women suffering from a particular kind of modern *ennui*; to Ursula's recourse to a popular romantic language, placing her serious thoughts in a trite context; to the famous reading of Birkin's letter at the café Pompadour by Halliday, where Lawrence directs the laughter in only thin disguise at himself; to that general tendency dominant in the novel for a continual shifting of contexts and perspective, as one character thinks or talks about another, forcefully shifting the text "from one subject position to another"[17] in a kind of

---

[13] Introduction to Mikhail Bakhtin, *Problems of Dostoevsky's Poetics* (Minneapolis and London: University of Minnesota Press, 1984. First published 1929), xxii. Subsequent references in text [PDP].

[14] Lodge, 20 where he refers to Lawrence's claim from "Why the Novel Matters" that the novel "can make the whole man alive tremble".

[15] Roger Fowler, "*The Lost Girl*: Discourse and Focalization", in Brown ed. (1990), 53ff.

[16] Fowler, 53, 56.

[17] Lodge in Brown, 99.

polyfocality, so that nothing remains stable, and ideas (some of which Lawrence is known to support) are dialogized into an ironic and thus destabilizing context. So far so good; Lodge correctly identifies these Bakhtinian patterns. *Only he does not go far enough.* He even stops short of seeing *Women in Love* as an essentially comic, carnivalized novel, even though he claims it is subversive of "orthodox hierarchies", and thus qualifies as "reduced laughter" (in the form of satire and irony) in Bakhtinian theory. For him, the carnivalesque novel is best exemplified in *Mr Noon*.

Fleishman argues that Lodge's use of Bakhtin in his reading of *Women in Love* is limited. The novel is more extensively dialogic than Lodge allows. It is not just a matter of a variety of styles and discourses that contradict each other but a complex dialogic relationship among all the parts of the text, including the author/narrator's framing of the characters' speech or thought, and their reaction to another's speech; but also a more thoroughgoing stylization of everyday "speech genres", from middle-class *argot* to the chic language of decadent *demi-mondaine* metropolitan life (the scenes of Lawrence's best comedy); and the literary parodies about two sisters discussing marriage from Jane Austen to popular romance with which the novel opens, continues to dialogize, and almost mutely ends. Moreover, asks Fleishman, why not describe *Women in Love* as a carnivalesque novel? It is certainly very different from the styles of the previous novels, especially the "pulsating rhythms" of *The Rainbow*. It is a novel of extremes, of hyperbole; it represents the instability of the self in many different guises; it gets the reader to recognize the ironies of misrecognition, as in this carnival of Babel where it seems "everyone is talking at once", Lawrence approaches the conditions of the grotesque realism so favoured by Bakhtin. [18]

But for these critics — Lodge, Fleishman, Fowler — the question still remains: how obtrusive is Lawrence's authorial discourse? As has so often been pointed out, he tends to be doctrinal, and — Fleishman insists — "fundamentalist" (Lawrence insists on cosmic forces in his history of English civilization).[19] Nevertheless, he is still dialogic: of course, we do know when Lawrence is pontificating; but his own authorial and authoritative discourse is also dialogized in the very novel in which it is expressed.

I will return to these Bakhtinian observations in more detail in the main body of this chapter. Bakhtin has been promising Lawrence

---

[18] Avrom Fleishman, "Lawrence and Bakhtin: Where Pluralism Ends and Dialogism Begins" in Brown, 112, 115.
[19] Fleishman, 117.

criticism a lot; the promise needs fulfilling.

A cursory glance at other recent Lawrence criticism reveals a persistent reference to Bakhtin, but hardly any detailed work. Hyde has a chapter headed "Carnivalizing the Midlands" but only two passing references to Bakhtin in text, and one long endnote about the historical context of his theory of the carnival.[20] He does, though, point the way for further work on speech mannerisms and "*skaz*" (representing oral speech or storytelling), and parody; and I shall return to his paper below. Eggert and Worthen allow more space for Bakhtin. In defining Lawrence's humour, Paul Eggert suggests already in the introduction that Bakhtin's theory of laughter "does offer some assistance" — a rather cautious formulation at best. Freud and Bergson are more prominent in this theoretical excursus; while the emphasis on Menippean laughter (i.e. satire) in Bakhtin is left for future studies of Lawrence and comedy. We do, however, get the claim that "Bakhtin's account of the equally disruptive carnivalesque can be illuminatingly applied to Lawrence's novels of the 1920s", because it will demonstrate that neither popularist festive laughter nor the more aloof satire dominate for long in Lawrence: his is a malicious humour creating a kind of compensatory cultural space for itself, feeding off the pressure of his feeling of cultural marginalization at the time. It is a kind of "hysterical laughter", an appropriately enraged response to the state of post-war England, an impulse in his writing that is only now being fully recognized. Eggert calls this new comic stance towards the writing and the reader "anarchoapocalyptic". A new perspective demands a different critical response; and it is one that many of the contributors of Eggert and Worthen clearly recognize. It is a pity then that Bakhtinian theory was not drawn on in other than passing reference. Yet, at least this book offers "a new departure".[21]

John Worthen's essay in the collection does much to establish the new comic Lawrence, whose "malicious humour" draws on an older Dionysian comic sense and one that serves the vitalising purpose of releasing inhibitions. It was a humour that Lawrence's close friends experienced in his private life (the hilarious entertainer and mimic) — an impression that goes against the grain of the consensus of the sex-obsessed bore — and it may be compared with Dickens, the man and the writer: both demonstrated a similar theatricality in work and life, and "enjoyed dramatizing the grotesque". Even central characters like Rupert Birkin and Gilbert Noon are subject to this malicious humour, which ultimately — in their biographical reference — are forms of self-mimicry

---

[20] G.M. Hyde, *D.H. Lawrence* (London: Macmillan, 1990), 123-4.

[21] Eggert and Worthen eds, 7, 12, 14.

and self-parody; a kind of comedy which is not as dominant in the earlier works. As Worthen rightly suggests, [22] Paul Morel in *Sons and Lovers* is never "subjected to parody and ridicule in the way these later characters are". For what we get now in these novels (*Women in Love*, *The Lost Girl* and *Mr Noon*) is a blurring of the boundary between the author and the characters' voices not seen in the earlier work, and one that produces "a series of Bakhtinian 'dialogic' voices" mediating "between the various narrations". The fiction becomes dramatic charade, caricature, and grotesque comedy. Worthen gets closer to Bakhtin here, and I shall deal with these points in more detail below.

Mills takes up Catherine Carswell's description of Lawrence as "the Dickens of the Midlands",[23] selecting passages from *Women in Love* that illustrate Lawrence's "finest humour".[24] Turner goes into the malicious humour and self-mockery as a fitting and not uncommon reaction to the hysteria in post-war England. Lawrence's work of the period exposes "the obsessive idealism and the hysterical patterns of feeling that chain the future to the corpse of the past". The vitality of laughter is the prime antidote, evoking Lawrence's dark gods — Pan, Dionysus — for a comic fiction, which like Bakhtin's carnival "is a matter of the body — not the body abused, as in hysteria, but the body celebrated", freeing "energies and richer social forms".[25]

Lydia Blanchard, as I already noted, calls for a more exclusive application of Bakhtinian critical theory. It promises to undo the misreading of Lawrence's work after *Women in Love*. It takes up the challenge of *Mr Noon*, and the newer comic Lawrence after 1984. Indeed the new perspective reads the letters differently too. In 1917 Lawrence declared: "It is necessary now for me to address a new public," one defined through the new comic, self-parodying, goading pose of the narrator, as Lawrence draws on the established traditions of the English comic novel — Fielding, Sterne, Dickens; and now more like the playful Joyce than would have previously been recognized. Writing is now predominantly parody, and is characterized as a Bakhtinian "heteroglossic" novel: a comic form based on the interanimation of the many voices that make up the literary and the social worlds. In *Mr Noon*, this would include the voice of the "ungentled reader", as well as that of the author's younger, more idealist self — as the narrative takes on the famous earlier leave-taking and elopement of Lawrence and Frieda in lightly disguised form.

---

[22] Eggert and Worthen eds, 30, 35, 39, 41.
[23] Catherine Carswell, *The Savage Pilgrimage: A Narrative of D.H. Lawrence* (Cambridge: Cambridge University Press, 1981. First published 1932), 69.
[24] Eggert and Worthen eds, 60-61.
[25] Ibid., 74-75, 80, 85.

Even his serious ideas are subjected to "a kind of furious comedy".[26] It is
this work, never published in its final form in Lawrence's life time, which
established a new writing characterized by this particular form of
comedy. Its first appearance as a two-thirds completed novel in 1984
clarified this development. Its Shandyian spirit, and the newer perspective it encourages on Lawrence's other writing, invites a Bakhtinian
approach. Blanchard insists on it, even while not engaging with it herself
in any substantive detail.

Paul Eggert in his paper on the Australian novels (*Kangaroo, The Boy
in the Bush*) reiterates the call for more Bakhtin theory in Lawrence
criticism. He reminds us that it has been around since 1985, and the
Cambridge University Press editors' scholarship of the last fifteen years
or so has been providing enough evidence to support claims for the turn
towards the comic in Lawrence; not just the biographical evidence of a
profound shift in mood and attitude on the part of the author, but also
"textual and intertextual traces of those processes"[27] of self-reference and
parody from which criticism might begin to generalize heuristically
through Bakhtin. Indeed, the textual representation of contrary voices
belongs to Bakhtin's notion of "dialogism", and is central to his
insistence on the comic, parodic, and debunking potential of the novel.
Bakhtin demands a closer degree of attention to the internal and external
structures of context — one enabled by the biographical and textual work
of the Cambridge editors, and Eggert has had a significant part in this.[28]
He insists that we should turn to those works of Bakhtin most relevant to
Lawrence, namely the study of Dostoevsky's poetics and the four essays
on the theory of the novel collected in *The Dialogic Imagination*.[29]
Unfortunately, this is only asserted as an endnote, and we are still left
waiting for the meeting of Bakhtin and Lawrence. However, we won't get
it from this otherwise important book on Lawrence and comedy.
Kinkead-Weekes entertains us with humour from the letters, much of it
directed against Lawrence himself and his ongoing quarrels with Frieda.
Bayley concludes the book with a perceptive reading of a scene from
"The Captain's Doll" — a reading which appears also in Brown — and
compares Larkin's humour to that of Lawrence, while also giving us

---

[26] Ibid., 90-91, 104.
[27] Ibid., 136.
[28] For instance, he has edited *Twilight in Italy and Other Essays* (Cambridge:
Cambridge University Press, 1994); and *The Boy in the Bush* (London: Penguin
edition of the Cambridge D.H. Lawrence, 1996).
[29] Mikhail Bakhtin, *The Dialogic Imagination: Four Essays* (Austin: University of
Texas Press, 1981. First published 1975 from work originally done in the 1930s and
1940s). Subsequent references in text [TDI].

Larkin's Lawrence. All these essays concur with Bayley's claim that in the later works, "the aesthete as comedian and creator came to predominate"; and that the aesthete had also to be "the amused or derisive bystander".[30] Moreover, what most of the essays share is the demand for a Bakhtinian approach to Lawrence's comic fiction, even while they do not themselves engage in any detail with that approach. It is the aim of the rest of this chapter to bring Bakhtin and Lawrence more substantively together.

3. Bakhtin's poetics

i. The theory of language
In the introduction to Bakhtin and Medvedev's critique of Russian Formalism we read: "We want to remember Bakhtin because, to know where contemporary literary scholarship is going, it is useful to know where Bakhtin was."[31] In this brief introduction, and in the spirit of this comment, I shall be insisting on the historical contexts of the emergence of Bakhtin's ideas as a complex history of repression in the Soviet Union of the 1920s and 1930s, and the belated reception of a thinker who has been given a high profile in western critical and cultural theory since the late 1960s. We now have access to the complete chronology of Bakhtin's life and work in English, and it is clear just how important he was to the key debates in post-Revolutionary Russia in poetics, but also in philosophy and linguistics.[32] There is no space in a book of this kind to go into sufficient detail to do full justice to Bakhtin. In any case the work has been done well enough already by others. I shall merely draw on some of that work as seems fitting to the task of bringing Bakhtin and Lawrence better together.

In the late 1920s Bakhtin and Medvedev engaged in a thoroughgoing critique of Russian Formalism. It was made possible because the Party declared a period of open debate with Marxism. It was a short-lived tolerance. Bakhtin drew attention to the fact that orthodox Marxism was not able to compete with Formalism in literary scholarship, which it dominated at the time. *The Formalist Method* was intended as a revitalizing of Marxist literary criticism through a critical engagement with the Formalists on their own ground. The book attempts to establish a

---

[30] In Eggert and Worthen eds, 207.
[31] M.M. Bakhtin and P.N. Medvedev, *The Formalist Method in Literary Scholarship* (Cambridge Massachusetts and London: Harvard University Press, 1985. First published 1928), xvi. Subsequent references in text [TFM].
[32] For a useful introduction see Michael Holquist, *Dialogics: Bakhtin and his World* (London: Routledge, 1990).

"sociological poetics", and as well as being an important document of those days, it also establishes some of the principles which will dominate Bakhtin's work. As Wlad Godzich explains in his useful introduction, it takes the "Formalists to task for their excessive avoidance of the social dimension of literary communication" (TFM, x). This is to be done by matching a "structural intertextuality" (TFM, xii) to the "general study of ideologies". Marxism needs convincing of "the essential plurality of the languages of ideology" (TFM, 3), and it needs the sharpness of the Formalist engagement with the text, while principally exposing the reductivism of their constructivist aesthetic which defines the work as a closed unit of devices. While this is a massive gain on the realist view of form as the embellishment of content, the central Formalist tenets of reading as the psychology of perception (defamiliarization), and literary history as the changes in the inner laws of style and form, the work of Shklovski (cf. "Art as Device": "probably the most typical article of early formalism"), Eikhenbaum and others isolated literature from the social forces which shape it, and in so doing they impoverished it. (TFM, 62) Literary texts are not reducible to their formal devices. Devices crucially have "semantic ideological significance" (TFM, 60).

The second major point Bakhtin and Medvedev make is that the Formalist theory of poetic language is idealist. They insist that the Formalists wrongly believed you could differentiate between "poetic language" and "ordinary language" linguistically (TFM, 80). Thus follows the erroneous claim, and one that derives initially from Romantic theory, that literary language is deformed ordinary or practical language, which "led to the incorrect orientation of poetics towards linguistics" (TFM, 85). Some concession here is made to Jakobson's "poetic function of language".[33] Bakhtin and Medvedev's critique derives from a theory of linguistic communication which demonstrates that the idea of a "practical language" is an arbitrary construction only logically necessary for the Formalist theory of poetic language as "making strange". After all, ordinary everyday utterances are in themselves "speech performances" in specific social situations which have all the characteristics of poetic language (metaphor, parody, stylization, etc.) (TFM, 95). Bakhtin will, in fact, later describe such speech performances as "speech genres" in their own right.[34] And this will be put to work later on Lawrence's comic writing. Here, what is crucial is the context and framing of the utterance

---

[33] Jakobson: "Poetry is nothing other than utterance oriented towards expression." Quoted in TFM, 87 — which, we may here speculate, seems close to Bakhtin's later dominant idea that the novel is a self-conscious artefact.

[34] Mikhail Bakhtin (1952-53), "The Problem of Speech Genres" in *Speech Genres and Other Essays* (SG) (Austin: University of Texas Press, 1986).

in a social scenario. Attitudes are communicated by the nuances of intonation, which in turn imply cultural and social values. A chain of responses to the words and attitudes of others conditions the speech genres in use: "The commonness of assumed basic value judgments constitutes the canvas upon which living human speech embroiders the designs of intonation."[35] In this sense, speech is an enactment of the attitudes towards the addressee in a complex psychological relation. The presence of otherness is registered in the inflexions of our speech. We respond; we elicit responses. The speech genre is determined by this interpersonal scenario. Speech genres are relatively stable normative frames which we learn as we acquire our native tongue, and in which we express our individual utterance. There is a huge variety, ranging from the short rejoinder in our daily conversation, the repeating of an absent third party's words reaccentuated for purposes of ridicule, the formal after-dinner speech, the sermon, the impersonation of another's accent or speech mannerism — indeed, reaccentuation through parody or irony is very common and is easily done by slight shifts in nuances of intonation: the effect can be devastating (which after all is the basis of comic mimicry, lampooning, etc.). As we shall see, *Women in Love*, *The Lost Girl* and *Mr Noon* are full of degrees of this kind of comedy. Bakhtin's list extends from the many types of everyday conversation, everyday narration including the very common retelling of someone else's story, to all forms of writing — legal and military documents, academic monographs with their implicit languages and addressees, to literary novels. But is Bakhtin's use of the concept of "genre" so broad and diffuse to be meaningless?

He attempts to answer this question himself by remaining within the general principles of his neo-formalism, pointing out that literature and rhetoric have been studied through genre theory since antiquity, and that his sociological approach to language as interactive utterance would enable the heterogeneity of speech genres to be equally studied from a few common principles: first, that language is best understood not as an abstract system as in Saussure, or as an individual, creative utterance as in Romantic theory, but as living articulation in dynamic interaction. Second, that language is dialogic: utterances take place in a complex situation of addressivity, response, and implicit reference — utterances are implicated with response-eliciting orientation, anticipation, etc. Third, giving types of utterance generic distinction enables stylistic analysis to look closely at the smallest details of addressivity and response within normative sociological frames.

---

[35] Bakhtin cited in Holquist, 61.

For Bakhtin, any poetics should begin with genre. Indeed, genre will become one of the principal components of Bakhtin's poetics. Whereas for the Formalists genre was reduced to "the fortuitous combination of chance devices" (TFM, 135), Bakhtin developed a much broader concept, and one that would play a key role in his Dostoevsky study (which he must have been working on at the time). For Bakhtin, genre was not a narrowly defined literary phenomenon but belonged to consciousness itself: "Human consciousness possesses a series of inner genres for seeing and conceptualizing reality." New genres change our perception of reality. Therefore, a poetics of genre is at the same time a sociology of genre (TFM, 134-35). The Formalist combination of motifs that are always already available, and the combination and distribution of narrative universals is a scientific approach whereby objectivity is "purchased at the price of meaning" (TFM, 146). Moreover, their theory of perception naively presupposes a constant and stable relation between author and reader, and a notion of a fixed and always knowable self (TFM, 152). For the Formalists, literary history is a series of canonizations and sudden changes, a process understood through the psychologistic theory of "automatization-perceptibility" (TFM, 161). But they have no *social* theory of change; it is purely a logical act (TFM, 170). History is a storehouse of generic universals (as the Structuralists too were later to claim). For Bakhtin, on the contrary, criticism has a basic role as "mediator between the social and the general ideological demands of the epoch, on the one hand, and literature, on the other" (TFM, 173).

One further distinction Bakhtin makes in his theory of language is that between primary and secondary speech genres. The former consist of all those simple everyday utterances; the latter the more complex forms of writing like scientific documents or literature. What is interesting for dialogic reading is the interrelation between the primary and the secondary speech genres. A novel, for instance, will "during the process of its formation ... absorb and digest various primary (simple) genres. These primary genres are altered and assume a special character when they enter into complex ones" (SG, 62). In other words, primary genres are reaccented and recontextualized in a literary text while still retaining a degree of their social reference. This process is particularly foregrounded in parody of speech — think of the presentation of Hermione Roddice's speech in *Women in Love* as sing-song intonation: "Expressive intonation is a constitutive marker of the utterance" (SG, 85). Lawrence's writing is full of examples of the foregrounding of speech mannerisms, and even the narrator's discussion of them (a characteristic of *The Lost Girl* in particular), and I shall return to them below. Studying the uses of speech genres in Lawrence's texts should be productive because it promises to be both stylistic and historical at the same time. Fully appreciating the social framing of utterances and the particular inflexions of words is more complex the further back we go in time. Lawrence gives full play to his talent for mimicry in the novels considered in this chapter, which are in many respects satirical of the English upper and middle class speech mannerisms of his day. I shall be looking at this in some detail. Dialogic overtones in these novels are complex because the ironies work at different levels. The framing of intonation in a particular characterological scheme, the social implications that go beyond the novel to a specific historical moment in English class society, and the particular tone that characterizes Lawrence's writing at that time: a cynicism, even bitterness that has been well accounted for by Lawrence's biographers and critics, should be taken into account when attempting a dialogic (Bakhtinian) reading.

In general terms, then, literature, and for Bakhtin the novel in particular, will define its peculiar nature by the manner in which it includes such diversity of speech in dialogic interaction. Literature needs a sociological poetics, and language needs a social theory of the utterance. The most extensive version of this theory of language will appear later in "Discourse in the Novel".[36]

Bakhtin's theory of language, then, goes beyond Formalism and Saussurean linguistics. Describing the state of linguistics in 1929, Bakhtin identifies the two dominant and opposed trends as "individualistic subjectivism" and "abstract objectivism" (TFM, 26). The latter, represented by Saussure and his followers, defines language as an internal system of rules, where the relationship between signs within the closed system of language is conventional and normative. Like Formalist poetics, Saussurean linguistics promotes the idea of universals. For example, the inner logic of the closed system of language derives from a universal grammar (TFM, 30). Bakhtinian theory questions the premise that an individual utterance derives from a fixed inert system of possibilities. The utterance acquires new meaning in use in particular social and historical contexts. The sign is always adaptable. Thus: not system and form, but context of utterance, because "*any true understanding is dialogic in nature*" (TFM, 35; Bakhtin's emphasis), and the analysis of language should concern itself rather with the problem of "the interrelationship between meaning and evaluation" at the level of "expressive intonation", "specific evaluative accent", and "evaluative orientation" (TFM, 36). Thus, we understand the historical process of language, its generation of meanings and functions within particular social groups and institutions (TFM, 37). Bakhtin will develop his social

---

[36] Bakhtin, "Discourse in the Novel" in TDI.

theory of utterance and discourse throughout his work. It will play a significant part in this chapter in my reading of the three Lawrence novels.

We should keep in mind these early general principles, with their emphasis on the social and the dialogic in poetics and in linguistics. For they are also basic to understanding the more central work on Dostoevsky and the polyphonic novel, Rabelais and the carnivalesque, as well as the theory of the "novelistic" as a heteroglossic and parodic writing from which the concept of the hybrid comes in an expanded theory of genre.

ii. The polyphonic novel

Problems of Dostoevsky's Poetics (1929), while ostensibly evaluating the importance of Dostoevsky for the modern novel, argues for a theory of the novel which has been recognized as relevant to Lawrence's works from *Women in Love* onwards. For Bakhtin, and for Lawrence, the novel is the only form of writing capable of doing justice to the complex interaction and interanimation of the discourses and voices, the languages of the social world. As Wayne Booth puts it, "novelists can maintain a kind of choral vitality, the very words conveying two or more speaking voices" (PDP, xxii). Bakhtin's world is in permanent dialogue. The key questions a Bakhtinian reading always asks the text are: Who is speaking? In what circumstances? With what levels of authority? Who is being addressed? Who is responding? To be a Bakhtinian reader you need "to recognize the major voices embedded in [dialogue]" (Emerson, Introduction to PDP, xxxvii) — a reading response requiring a sensitivity to the details of history.

For Bakhtin, Dostoevsky's great contribution to the development of the novel was his invention of "polyphony", a term deriving from music and used by Bakhtin as analogy for: "*A plurality of independent and unmerged voices and consciousnesses ... each with its own world*" which are combined in a dialogic relation. It is the angle at which discourses or words are placed, in the dialogic interaction of this plurality of voices, which is important. Utterances are implicit responses, oriented towards other utterances, eliciting further responses or answers. In Dostoevsky, it is precisely here in these "microdialogues" where "a conflict of voices takes place" (PDP, 69; emphasis in original). The characters' discourse and the author's discourse are also unmerged: "In no way, then, can a character's discourse ... serve as a vehicle for the author's own ideological position" (PDP, 7). And it is this rather stark claim that has always been seen as the sticking point for reading *Women in Love* strictly as a polyphonic novel, as the readings by Lodge, Fleishman, and Fowler demonstrate.

Now, we need first to understand Bakhtin's development of this point carefully; and second, even if we take the point literally and see Lawrence as an obtrusive author, we should not stop using Bakhtin — the authority of narrative discourse is only one point in a greater array of points as we shall see below. In any case, Bakhtin insists that it would be absurd to maintain that the author has no conscious presence in his work. He or she is always implicit in what Bakhtin designates as the "architectonics" of the novel, the hidden hand responsible for the overall design (PDP, 67-68). Furthermore, we should not confuse the author's monologic ideas in essays or letters with what happens to those ideas once they enter the novel, where they are subject to the dialogic process. This goes for Dostoevsky (PDP, 91-92) and Lawrence.[37]

The broader linguistic and philosophical implications of Bakhtin's multi-voiced, multi-perspectived novel are the new orientation towards otherness (the alterity of the utterance, and the unfixed self/self-for-the-other, respectively); and the "profoundly *pluralistic*" world, represented and promoted in Dostoevsky (PDP, 26). Indeed, his texts are characterized by a kind of simultaneity of interrelationships in which internal contradictions force a character "to converse with his own double" in what Bakhtin calls internal dialogics. In this "sociology of consciousness", a character lives "on the borders of someone else's thoughts, someone else's consciousness" (PDP, 32). It is interaction and interdependence represented in a play of voices whose embryonic tradition includes Rabelais, Shakespeare, and Cervantes. (PDP, 33) Such literature represents the process of self-awareness of the principal characters, so that the field of vision is transferred from the author to them. Thus the author's monologic view is decentered, and the dialogic world becomes creatively indeterminate in texts dominated by persons on the threshold of momentous decisions or crises, and unpredeterminable turning points. (PDP, 61) This sounds like a description of *Women in Love* and its modernist representation of the old stable ego in crisis. I shall return to it below.

Bakhtin next takes up once again his work on the poetics of genre. He contrasts his favoured novelistic tradition of the comic novel with the more serious literary forms.[38] His main claim is that seriocomic genres are by definition dialogic as they challenge the fixed and stable universe of the serious, monologic forms. (PDP, 106-7) It is here that Bakhtin first designates a "carnivalized literature" with its parodic, multi-generic mix,

---

[37] As Lawrence wrote in 1923: "Never trust the artist. Trust the tale", *Studies in Classic American Literature* (London: Penguin, 1977), 8.
[38] See also Bakhtin's later essay, "Epic and the Novel" in TDI.

whose tradition goes back to Rabelais and medieval folklore. It will become the principal and dominant condition of the novelistic (*romanost*). The novel develops as a kind of anti-genre, incorporating in hybrid form a whole array of genres and sub-genres. The carnivalizing tendency, with its mocking of authority and its reversal of social hierarchies, enters literature as the undermining of epic pretensions and generic truth in Cervantes (1547-1616). Its ritual laughter becomes the reduced laughter of parody and satire, especially in the comic tradition of the English novel in the eighteenth century — in Fielding, Smollett and Sterne. It is characterized by a liberating humour, and is hostile to any conclusiveness and any overarching seriousness and dogmatism. (PDP, 161) It is a tradition which now includes Lawrence's comic novel, *Mr Noon*. A typical description of such a novel is the following by Bakhtin of Dostoevsky's *Crime and Punishment* (1886):

> Everything in this novel — the fates of the people, their experiences and ideas — is pushed to its boundaries, everything is prepared, as it were, to pass over into its opposite, ... everything is taken to the extreme, to its outermost limit. There is nothing in the novel that could become stabilized .... Everything is shown in a moment of unfinalized transition. (PDP, 167)

This could also be a description of *Women in Love*.[39] Everything is on the border of its opposite — as love is to hate, tragedy to comedy, the self to the other, so that complete fullness of being is not found in the self alone. (PDP, 169-177)

Bakhtin's own polemic in the Dostoevsky study, as well as most of his work, resurfaces in his discussion on the nature of language. It begins with his first definition of "discourse" as "language in its concrete living totality", which requires for its analysis a kind of metalinguistics (PDP, 181), and one which will not simply look for styles of language, dialects, sociolects, and so on. For, "what matters is the *dialogic angle* at which these styles and dialects are juxtaposed or counterpoised in the work" (PDP, 182). Bakhtin reiterates here his theory that language is a living social phenomenon where every individual utterance has its author, and is oriented towards the other. For Bakhtin, the focus of his work in this area is *"double-voiced discourse"*, itself an inevitable outcome of dialogic interaction, and manifest in literature in the forms of parody, stylization, dialogue (in form of rejoinders), and *skaz* (the representation of oral speech or oral narrative). The common characteristic here is the twofold

---

[39] As Lodge claims, 61.

orientation of discourse, "both towards the referential object of speech, as in ordinary discourse, and towards *another's discourse*, towards *someone else's speech*" (PDP, 185, Bakhtin's emphasis). Wilful stylization is using another's discourse "precisely as other" (PDP, 191). The same goes for parody and irony. Everyday speech is always "full of other people's words" (PDP 193-195). Literary discourse, and the novel in particular, is an extreme version of this process which may be characterized as "internal polemic" at the level of style. For Bakhtin, stylistics "in the narrow sense" is not equipped to deal with this, the most dialogic of discourse functions.[40] Such multi-contextual dialogic writing, "employing on the plane of a single work discourses of various types, with all their expressive capacities intact, without reducing them to a common denominator", is the most fundamental feature of novelistic prose. Therefore, a Bakhtinian stylistics is equipped to deal with this "eternally mobile, ... fickle medium of dialogic interaction" (PDP, 202). It is also an historical stylistics investigating the different discourses and their relations in different epochs.

Dostoevsky's writing is the model for the novelistic variety of discourses, double-voiced and internally dialogized. The words in the text are doubly oriented, intonationally subtle, refracted at angles, anticipating, responding, addressing, parodying, ridiculing, quoting, stylizing, to varying degrees and purposes. Awareness of this multi-dimensionality of internal dialogics enables the critic to appreciate the hidden polemics of the work. This requires careful historical research. Such polyphonic writing also "novelizes" other genres. That is, in reworking established patterns of writing and consciousness, past forms may be perceived in their generic limits for the first time. (PDP, 271) Thus we could argue that *Women in Love* novelizes *Middlemarch*, or even *Sons and Lovers*; *The Lost Girl* novelizes Arnold Bennett's *Anna of the Five Towns*; and *Mr Noon* novelizes Lawrence's travel writing and his earlier self of 1912; and all three dialogize the reception of Lawrence's work as a hitherto exclusively serious project. The Bakhtinian approach to Lawrence's "hidden polemic" should be productive.

iii. Grotesque realism and the carnivalesque
The Rabelais study[41] makes extensive historical links between the

---

[40] This belongs to Bakhtin's polemic in the 1920s, but today stylistics is a broader discipline. See Roger Fowler, *Linguistic Criticism* (Oxford and New York: Oxford University Press, 1986).

[41] Mikhail Bakhtin, *Rabelais and his World* (Bloomington: Indiana University Press, 1984. First published 1965, from work done in the 1930s). Subsequent references in text [RW].

novelistic and the carnivalesque. As is now well known, this history of folk carnival and laughter has its own hidden polemic, allowing the repressions of Church and State in the Renaissance and the seventeenth century in France to speak to those of Bakhtin's own time in Stalin's Russia.[42] In this spirit, giving priority to the tradition of grotesque realism may be seen as a polemic against Socialist Realism (RW, xvii). This may also account for the tendency to idealize folk culture and its traditions. Rabelais is the last representative of that basic folk culture in literature, with its humour of the marketplace, which would later, in the Classical Age (the seventeenth century) and the Enlightenment (the eighteenth century), be consigned to the lower orders of the vulgar and be denied the name of Literature.

Grotesque realism is the closest literature gets to that folk culture of the carnival. Coarse banquet scenes, buffoonery, ridicule and degrading laughter; the grotesque body in all its forms: the work of Rabelais, Boccaccio, Shakespeare, and Cervantes are representative. The grotesque image of the body is central to the carnival tradition of the Middle Ages with its festive spectacles: "in the feast of the fool, in charivari and carnival, in the popular side show of Corpus Christi, in the *diableries* of the mystery plays, the *soties*, and the farces" (RW, 27). Such "ugliness" was anathema to the Renaissance and Classical "aesthetics of the beautiful" (RW, 29). And this accounts for Rabelais' belated reception in the late nineteenth, and early twentieth century. What is important here for our purposes is that, although we still see remnants of the folk tradition in the *Commedia dell'arte*, Molière, Voltaire, and Swift, with their emphasis on the grotesque body itself, the critique is transformed into the more studied literary forms of satire and parody, as in Sterne's *Tristram Shandy* (1767), even while the traces of the older tradition are still there. The Gothic novel and German Romanticism, reacting against the cold rationalism of the Enlightenment, transformed the laughter of carnival into the more abstract modes of irony or sarcasm. This new "reduced laughter" lost its regenerative force (RW, 38), only to be revived in modernist form in Jarry, Brecht, and others (RW, 46).

The realist tradition of the novel was profoundly influenced by grotesque realism and its carnival origins in Rabelais, Cervantes, and Shakespeare. Dickens, for instance, may be clearly placed in this tradition (RW, 52). We can see just how useful Bakhtin's history of laughter is for reading the comic scenes in *Women in Love, The Lost Girl* and *Mr Noon*: "The essence of the grotesque is precisely to present a contradictory and double-faced fullness of life" (RW, 62), and this for regenerative

---

[42] For further details see Holquist, Prologue: xiv ff.

purposes. Even if we do not laugh as Rabelais and his contemporaries did, appreciating the origins of the comic tradition gives us an historical context in which to approach the comic phase of Lawrence's writing. It is one which certainly takes us back to the formation of that comic tradition in the eighteenth century. The coarsening of manners of the travelling players in *The Lost Girl*, for instance, is a locus for the grotesque undermining of bourgeois refinement.

In this chapter, then, the "carnivalized novel" should be understood in Bakhtin's particular sense, as argued for in the Rabelais and in the Dostoevsky studies. Carnivalizing and novelizing belong to one and the same impulse; one which critics have begun to detect in Lawrence emerging around the time of *Women in Love*. Before we return to Lawrence, though, I shall complete this brief explanation of Bakhtinian theory by looking at his most extensive work on the theory of the novel: the four essays collected in *The Dialogic Imagination* (TDI).

iv. The theory of the novel: an historical poetics

It cannot be emphasized enough that in Bakhtin the theory of the novel is inseparable from the theory of language. The latter gives priority to the utterance and this leads to a rethinking of the categories of style and genre. As Holquist reminds us (TDI, Introduction xxi), Bakhtin had already argued in his work on Dostoevsky that the novel could represent the essential alterity of language in the nuances of addressivity and orientation, doing justice to the social and historical dynamics of heteroglossia and the dialogics of communication. The novel, then, is discursively inclusive, and generically expansive. Indeed, it is not a genre in the traditional sense, like epic or tragedy. It was for a long time not even considered one of the serious genres of Literature because of its impure hybrid form. For Bakhtin this has proved to be its strength: "The novel parodies other genres (precisely in their role as genres); it exposes the conventionality of their forms and their language; it squeezes out some genres and incorporates others into its peculiar structure, reformulating and reaccentuating them" (TDI, 5). One of Bakhtin's favourite examples is Cervantes *Don Quixote* (1615) because it novelizes the epic and chivalric romance genres, undermining their serious pretensions. The process of novelization in the comic tradition liberates the novel from the epic or romance genres by dialogising the structures of their conventions (TDI, 34-39). To substantiate these claims, Bakhtin traces the prehistory of novelistic discourse in conjunction with its status in literary scholarship. It is only in the late nineteenth, and early twentieth century that the serious stylistic and morphological study of the novel begins.[43] In the Bakhtinian approach, the novel cannot be described in terms of a single, unitary language (as in "the language of the novel", or "the author's style") rather it acknowledges its "*system* of languages that mutually and ideologically interanimate each other" (TDI, 47). The author, for his part, may not be found "at any one of the novel's language levels: he is to be found at the centre of organization where all levels intersect" (TDI, 49). It is here that Bakhtin's theory of the novel (and novelization) informs his critical methodology. If his ideal is an immense novel which is "multi-generic, multi-styled, mercilessly critical, soberly mocking, reflecting in all its fullness the heteroglossia and multiple voices of a given culture, people and epoch" (TDI, 60), then it follows that a Bakhtinian stylistics of the novel would take account of:

> a diversity of social speech types (sometimes even diversity of languages) and a diversity of individual voices, artistically organized ... [stratified] into social dialects, characteristic group behaviour, professional jargons, generic languages, languages of generations and age groups [etc.] .... The novel orchestrates all its themes ... and ideas depicted and expressed in it by means of the social diversity of speech types ... authorial speech, the speeches of narrators, inserted genres, the speech of characters are merely those fundamental compositional unities with whose help heteroglossia can enter the novel; each of them permits a multiplicity of social voices and a wide variety of their links and interrelationships (always more or less dialogized). (TDI, 262)

Understanding the particular inflexions of intonation, and the impulse and object of a parody or a stylization requires a detailed historical knowledge; a knowledge that in the case of Lawrence has been emerging over the last fifteen years or more. Once recognized as such, Lawrence's comic writing of this period belongs to the hybrid genre of the English comic tradition that Bakhtin describes as a form "for appropriating and organizing heteroglossia" (TDI, 302).[44] As Bakhtin shows in his analysis of Dickens *Little Dorrit*, there is a play through parody and stylization on a whole variety of languages — oratorical and epic, property law, Biblical — and the belief systems they represent, enabling Dickens to expose common opinion for its greed and hypocrisy, and institutional

---

[43] One thinks immediately of Propp's *Morphology of the Russian Folktale* (1928); but also the early Lukács of the *Theory of the Novel* (1920).

[44] As Lydia Blanchard has argued in her paper in Eggert and Worthen, 90.

authority for its cant; never allowing the boundary between the narrator's and all the other discourses to be other than ambiguous, while flexibly stylizing these incorporated languages. Similarly, incorporated genres bring their own "verbal and semantic forms for assimilating various aspects of reality" (TDI, 321). The novel as hybrid genre has a syncretic function, bringing all these speech and literary genres together in a dialogic relation. It decentres the monologic authority of any incorporated genre. In doing this, it demythologizes any unitary theory of language and any absolute form of thought, including the dominant ideology (TDI, 366-67). (Here, once again, Bakhtin's own hidden polemic resurfaces.)

A Bakhtinian historical poetics enables both a level of a generality and the kind of textual detail necessary for a dialogic reading. Form is always already historical, and the novel is essentially intertextual. [45] As Bakhtin puts it, "every age re-accentuates in its own way the works of its most immediate past". This goes for the intertextual, parodic novel of his comic tradition, as well as for the critical receptions of literary scholarship. "Thanks to the intentional potential in them, such works have proved capable of uncovering in each era and against ever new dialogising backgrounds ever newer aspects of meaning" (TDI, 421). What we have here is also an apt description both of the latest shift in Lawrence criticism towards the comic, and the internal dialogics of the novels themselves. In the rest of this chapter, I will attempt, in some detail, to put Bakhtin to work on Lawrence's comic writing.

---

[45] Bakhtin gives the example of the "chronotope" — a temporal and spatial reference in the one image that reveals the dominant concepts of time and space in an epoch. Chronotopes are the "organizing centres for the fundamental narrative events of the novel", concretizing time. Some principal examples are: the "meeting", and the "road" in the "adventure time" of the Ancient Greek romance of ordeal; the "path of life" with its moments of metamorphosis in the early Christian "Lives of the Saints", later adapted in the "criminal trial" in Dostoevsky; the "public square" in the ancient biographical novel, a place for the oratorical revelation; and the chronotope of the "family-clan-soil" in Ancient Roman memoirs; or the "space of parlors and salons" in the novels of Stendhal and Balzac (TDI, 206), and the "provincial town" in Flaubert; the "threshold" or "crisis and break in life" in Dostoevsky (TDI, 248). The next question is always: What are the transformations effected by the later processes of novelization on these chronotopes? Herewith we see Bakhtin's theory of the narrative device which goes beyond the limits of Formalism by insisting on a cultural-historical explanation. For further discussion see Holquist, 88, 110-111.

4. Dialogics and speech genres in *Women in Love, The Lost Girl,* and *Mr Noon*

i. Introduction

In the arguments of Lodge, Fleishman, and Fowler over the relevance of Bakhtin to Lawrence, which I discussed above, the Bakhtinian approach is restricted to the question of whether any of Lawrence's fiction can be truly classified as polyphonic, in the precise Bakhtinian sense derived from his reading of Dostoevsky. Fowler applies a more technical stylistics and narrative analysis to *The Lost Girl*, and I shall return to his important paper below. Their various arguments raise a number of key points about Lawrence's relationship to his characters — his tendency to be heavy-handed, using his characters to preach through. This has been commented on many times, although in these three examples more thoroughly and technically. It is my contention that limiting Bakhtinian reading to the theory and practice of the polyphonic novel — itself a highly prescriptive theory, and one that Bakhtin distanced himself from in his best work of the 1930s[46] — has caused a paralysis in Bakhtinian approaches to Lawrence.

It was Fleishman who first called for a more all-inclusive approach to textual dialogics in Lawrence, one which would include analysis of heteroglossia in the stylization of everyday speech genres, the literary and self-parodies, the presence of carnivalesque features in the grotesque realism and hyperbole in novels which upset any stable notions of identity and any authorial doctrine. However, he still sees the doctrinal authorial discourse as a problem, even while it is being dialogized in ironical contexts, for any Bakhtinian approach to Lawrence. But no one would question the claim that Lawrence is no Dostoevsky, in Bakhtin's description. Therefore I suggest we start looking with Bakhtin's eyes at what is there in the text, and bracket off the question of polyphony.

To attempt a broader understanding of dialogics in Lawrence's writing, I shall therefore base my readings on Bakhtinian stylistics as understood by his notions of "speech genres", the comic novel as "*romanost*", and the features of the carnivalesque, as defined above, which appear in *Women in Love, The Lost Girl,* and *Mr Noon*.

ii. The satirical world of *Women in Love*

Women in Love[47] is a difficult novel for Lawrence scholars to write about

---

[46] See "Discourse in the Novel" in TDI where Bakhtin is more interested in the "polyglossic" text.
[47] All references in text [WL] are to the Penguin edition of the Cambridge D.H. Lawrence (London, 1995).

because, no sooner had the author established a modernist writing in which he could represent his sexual ontology and his "work for women"[48] in *The Rainbow*, than he seemed to want to place everything under erasure. Clearly much of *Women in Love* is a polemical questioning of everything that had gone before, and a search for a new direction. In Bakhtinian terms, it dialogizes Lawrence's most monologic thoughts, while remaining a philosophical novel. The doubts about the direction of his writing are expressed in many places and in many ways, as we shall see. The following words attributed to Birkin sum up the mood: "One Hamletizes, and it seems a lie .... I hate myself serious." And: "he was irritated and weary of having a telling way of putting things." (WL, 187-89)

If *Women in Love* is a seriocomic novel, then it is the relationship between the serious and the comic that is important; and this is where Bakhtin is helpful. The tendency to send up anyone who takes himself or herself too seriously, anyone superior or in authority, or even the epic or philosophical pretensions of high literature, characterizes Bakhtin's comic novel tradition with its roots in the medieval carnival and *charivari* (as I described above). However, although in the period of his writing that includes *Women in Love*, *The Lost Girl*, and *Mr Noon*, Lawrence belongs more and more to the tradition of Swift, Sterne, Fielding, and Dickens, that does not mean that his writing is no longer serious; the best comedy always has a serious, disquieting message.

The wedding which the sisters witness in the first chapter of *Women in Love* is a highly comic, Fieldingesque description, mocking the solemn pretensions of such occasions, full of social embarrassment and vitality. The scene acts as a relief from the soul searching that we have just been reading. It is a carnival scene causing havoc; and by implication it is in dialogue with the opening discussion about the prospect of marriage (a parody of the mannered Jane Austen novel about two sisters, as Fleishman pointed out — see above) which Ursula casually yet ironically remarks would be "the end of experience" (WL, 7) — ironically, because the young couple's joy will be short lived, and because Ursula will get married. But also the ironies around the key question of marriage will be kept in circulation in the text, so that the recurrent question will keep the dialogue going, but the question will remain open.[49]

---

[48] Letter to Sallie Hopkin, 23 December 1912.

[49] See the brief history of the Criches for a view of the older generation with Gerald's mother a destroyed woman, WL, chapter XVII; Gudrun mocking Birkin/Lawrence's notion of "*ultimate* marriage", WL, 289-91; Birkin and Gerald in "Marriage or Not" for a man's view, WL, 350-53; which is followed by the episode at the market with the chair which represents a more materialist and class-bound view of marriage; and

"The Water Party" is another moment of high comedy in the tradition of social satire and comedy of manners. It is also the moment that gets the two central relationships started, has Gudrun do her Isadora Duncan dance while accompanied by Ursula singing a popular song, and in the company of a herd of cattle (a scene that Lawrence will parody in *Mr Noon*). And as Birkin is giving his famous Lawrentian lecture on the theme of the "river of dissolution", they are interrupted by high melodrama and tragic death, so that the drowning of the newly-weds becomes a metaphor for the prospects of the two couples. What begins as comedy ends in tragedy. Moreover, what is significant for a Bakhtinian reading of this chapter is that the juxtaposition of each event or scene is not just part of a seamless narrative sequence but creates a dialogic commentary implicitly, which leaves the serious challenged by the comic in a process of perpetual destabilization.

Many ironies are produced by the access the reader has to the inner thoughts of the characters, and by the use of the central characters as focalizers, through whose eyes and mind-sets (even if they are often close to that of the author) we see things. One example towards the end of the novel is when Gudrun thinks about how stable Gerald is while she is disintegrating in an agony of cynicism. This recalls Gerald's mind-set in "The Industrial Magnate" chapter earlier. The irony of misrecognition is perceived only by the reader.

There are, then, many levels and instances of dialogics in *Women in Love*. However, what I wish to concentrate on in my Bakhtinian approach are the instances of the stylization of speech genres.

Intonation is central to any Bakhtinian stylistics, and there is no better place to begin than the opening scene in the novel (as Fleishman suggested — see above). Notice the italics for emphasis, drawing attention to the affected intonation and high-register speech in a context of boredom: " ... 'don't you *really want* to get married?' .... 'You don't think one needs the *experience* of having been married?' .... 'Of course,' she said, 'there's *that* to consider' ..." (WL, 7). The italics are the author's directions to the reader about how to pronounce these spoken words. The speech genre (in this case middle-class modish speech of the New Woman under the strain of *ennui* in the provincial working-class town) is being stylized, and therefore, although the intonation is addressed in the first instance to the other sister — marking a shared set of social and cultural values — another level of irony is addressed to the

the final scene where doubts are cast on the success of heterosexual marriage — an ending that makes more sense now that the suppressed Prologue with its homosexual theme is widely available, reprinted as an appendix to the Penguin edition of the Cambridge D.H. Lawrence.

reader. The two sisters discuss the prospect of marriage, itself a common enough beginning for an English novel, in a pastiche and mannered speech which serves to send up the whole scenario. Moreover, as we know from Lawrence,[50] this kind of talk is trite and superficial — consummate marriage was sacred to him. While the two sisters understand themselves as social superiors in the provincial world of Beldover, in the Lawrentian metaphysic the superficial world of social intercourse is what must be transcended. There are many places in the text where the deeper, inner world is set against the outer social world. Stylistically, this is usually marked by the conjunction, "And yet" (e.g. WL, 16).

From the outset, then, Lawrence is drawing attention to styles of speech through mimicry and parody; and the speech parody is addressed to the reader. Indeed, all three novels discussed in this chapter are characterized by degrees of address to the reader about the characters' speech mannerisms. Lawrence had by now gone much further than the representation of the unstable ego of the character by adding to it the unstable relationship with the reader. As we shall see, by the time Lawrence writes *Mr Noon* that relationship had almost collapsed into insulting the reader. Here, in *Women in Love,* Lawrence is already concerned that the reader gets the stylization and therefore the satirical purpose. Ursula seems unrecognizable after the grand symbolic gesture of the feminization of the earth that ends *The Rainbow.* Gudrun, in her representation of the New Woman — an artistic, freethinking person of the modern metropolitan world — is not only made to speak in the rather chic, fashionable manner of the day, but is always described in some detail as flamboyantly and garishly dressed as if to challenge the dull provinciality of her home town, or the Victorian novel itself. Indeed, the three modern women are often described in flamboyant costume. Angela Carter[51] called *Women in Love* "Lawrence's most exuberantly clothed novel ... Gudrun's emerald green stockings ... become almost a symbol of her contrariness". Carter wonders whether Lawrence is not obsessed with female clothing (a fetishistic, closet transvestite!). "Stockings, stockings, stockings everywhere. Hermione Roddice sports coral-coloured ones, Ursula canary ones. Defiant, brilliant, emphatic stockings." What is Lawrence's game, she asks, with this mocking "sartorial eccentricity"? My answer would be that it is neither an attack on women's sexuality, alienating them safely under layers of bright clothing; nor, more

---

[50] Fowler rightly insists that there is a recognizable Lawrentian discourse with its codes and values reinforced by the uses of Lawrence in education.

[51] Angela Carter, "Lorenzo the Closet-Queen" reprinted in *Nothing Sacred: Selected Essays* (London: Virago, 1992), 208-10.

fancifully, is it proof that Lawrence "enjoys being a girl"(!).[52] It is a carnivalizing gesture, first in the "ash-grey coffin" (*The Lost Girl,* 347)[53] of provincial England where it was "chic to be perfectly ordinary" (WL, 457); and second, in Switzerland, where Gudrun's notoriety for her stockings becomes more explicitly symbolic of the new, modernist space she has entered in the company of the bohemian artist Loerke, while she is more desperate than ever to resist, through art and the grotesque carnival of the *demi-mondaine,* the dull mechanistic existence of modern life. In an implicit reference to Mark Gertler's painting *Merry-Go-Round* (1916), Lawrence has Loerke, the modernist artist, recommend riding the carousel all day instead of searching for life's ulterior motive. And in the novel's moment of greatest cynicism, Loerke is given to comment: "Women and love, there's no greater tedium." (WL, 458) This is a sentiment taken further by a defiant Gudrun: "Nothing is so boring as the phallus, so inherently stupid and stupidly conceited" (WL, 463). Here Gudrun, in a supremely anti-phallocentric moment, predates Kate Millett, as if Lawrence had also had enough — at least for the time being — as he kills off the inadequate man (Gerald) and sends the rebellious modern woman off to the German Bohemia he so detested, with the homosexual modernist artist he so despised.

We need to return to the whole question of cynicism displacing idealism later in this chapter. For the tone of these novels from the period 1916-1921, as many critics have noted, signals degrees of disillusion which are being played out in the parodic, self-parodic, and carnivalizing strategies of Lawrence's writing.

Lawrence's opening gambit, then, is significant in setting the tone of the text's satiric purpose. Indeed, the sham of social graces and pseudo-artistic and intellectual talk is an important part of the polemic in *Women in Love.* None more so than in the presence of Hermione, the representative upper-class socialite who is persistently sent up in her manner of speech: "in her slow, odd, singing fashion, that sounded almost as if she were poking fun" (WL, 37). Her speech is "almost rhapsodic", and clearly marked by highly attitudinized intonations: "Hermione resumed, in a sing-song casual voice" (WL, 40). Lawrence is very precise about the speech genre, the intonation, and its mode of addressivity: her relationship to the addressee in text is always one of mocking superiority (carried off well by Eleanor Bron in Ken Russell's film). But it is framed in the author's satirical purpose that runs right through the novel. Moreover, it

---

[52] Linda Ruth Williams would disagree. See: *Sex in the Head: Visions of Femininity and Film in D.H. Lawrence* (Hemel Hempstead: Harvester Wheatsheaf, 1993).
[53] All references in text [TLG] are to the Penguin edition of the Cambridge D.H. Lawrence (London, 1996).

is a purpose that is meant to be shared with the reader, and endorsed by the other characters — especially Birkin who publicly castigates her.

In this novel, speech may have a narrow social and class range, but it is dialogized by a complex contextualization. First, there are the dynamics of the scenario of the utterances within the story; second, the larger parodic play with the addressed reader; third, the implicit relationship of social banter with the other metaphysical discourses represented by the inner thoughts of the characters — their deeper, inner fears and anxieties to which the reader is party. It is thus significant that Hermione is introduced as both socially and culturally superior and at the same time tortured by her own inner vulnerability (WL, 16). Lawrence mocks her characteristic speech even when presenting her thoughts: "He [Rupert Birkin] would be there, surely he would see how beautiful her dress was, surely he would see how she had made herself beautiful for him. He would understand, surely he would understand ... surely, at last." (WL, 17) Here the repetition of "surely" articulates the characteristic pitch of her voice, and at the same time is made ironic by the dialogic context it can be placed in with the profound inner uncertainty which tortures her, and compounded by the impression of superiority she attempts to communicate to the other characters.

Lawrence's writing from *Women in Love* onwards is characterized by this kind of stylization of speech genres, and more especially by those that mock the English ruling aristocracy or the smart set of modernist, metropolitan English culture. Indeed, you can imagine that "upstart" Lawrence from humble origins enjoying giving his aristocratic patrons their come-uppance, turning his skills as mimic which they so enjoyed on many a soirée at Garsington back on them.[54] And it is certainly focused on Hermione, modelled in large part on the aristocratic socialite, who is introduced as a representative of her class through Ursula's thoughts: "Her father was a Derbyshire Baronet of the old school, she was a woman of the new school, full of intellectuality, and heavy, nerve-worn with consciousness. She was passionately interested in reform, her soul was given up to the public cause." (WL, 15-16) Ursula is given two significantly contrasting speech genres here. We recognize instantly the author's discourse about too much intellect and "nerve-worn conscious-ness". It contrasts markedly with the long-drawn stress on the word "passionately" in the following sentence, which foregrounds Lawrence's satirical intent to mock at every opportunity "the slack aristocracy that keeps touch with the arts" (WL, 16). (In *Lady Chatterley's Lover*

---

[54] For further details see Mark Kinkead-Weekes, *D.H. Lawrence: Triumph To Exile, 1912-1922* (Cambridge: Cambridge University Press, 1996).

Lawrence returns once again to the satire of upper-class speech and attitudes — and I discuss this in chapter 6.) What is also interesting here for the Bakhtinian reading is that instead of polyphony we have what might be called a polyfocality, whereby the main characters are framed by each other's singular views, which are always then double-voiced (in dialogic relation to another view), so that we get the whole picture piecemeal, as readers being party to the characters' inner thoughts about themselves as well as about each other. Thus a relativity of focalizations[55] dramatizes textually the provisionality of selves and others.

Lawrence always overplays his hand by framing Hermione's speech with mocking precision: "She asked, musingly, with expressionless indecision"; "with strange assumption of authority"; "domineering and cold"; "saying with a laconic indifference" etc. (WL, 28-30), so that attitudes and values are expressed not only in what she has to say and in the way she addresses her words to others, and in the responses to them (either elicited or in reaction), but significantly in the way Lawrence carefully frames her speech ironically for the reader. Indeed, the serious discussions (in an Oxford debating society genre) about political philosophy, education, and the arts are framed in comic-satirical scenes. As has often been pointed out, Lawrence's own self-cynical attitude is noticed in the framing of his own "pollyanalytics"[56] in such scenes, while at the same time these set pieces keep in play social and psychological forces between the fictional protagonists. While Birkin/Lawrence's overdetermined ponderousness is being ridiculed by the other characters following Hermione's lead, Lawrence strikes back for the damaged man: "The laugh of the shrill, triumphant woman sounded from Hermione, jeering at him as if he were a neuter"; "She said, with slow, cold, cunning mockery", taking her exit with a theatrical "Goo-oodbye" (WL, 43).

The critique of Hermione that emerges through speech stylization and the dynamics of interaction in set pieces on the social level is corroborated by her self-understanding presented in chapter one (WL, 16). But just in case we wanted to use this perpetual undermining of the New Woman to attack Lawrence for his misogyny, the sisters are often the textual source of views on Hermione, and Ursula is used to question Birkin's generalizations about women. Moreover, an important dialogic frame in *Women in Love* is encapsulated in the notion that when Birkin is pontificating the author's deeply felt beliefs, lecturing the women, they

---

[55] I shall return to the problem of focalization below, where I challenge Fowler's reading.
[56] For Lawrence's self-deprecating description of his "pseudo-philosophy" see Foreword, *Fantasia of the Unconscious and Psychoanalysis and the Unconscious* (London: Penguin, 1971). First published 1922, 15.

are either silently hostile or appear not to be listening. "There was a silence in the room. Both women [Ursula and Hermione] were hostile and resentful. He sounded as if he were addressing a meeting." (WL, 44) Hermione ignores him, while Ursula watches him and notices his physical attractiveness. Hermione interrupts his flow with a request for tea, but only addresses Ursula as if in solidarity. Birkin stops abruptly, and walks out. Ursula is left in emotional turmoil. (WL, 45) The interpersonal dynamics of this scene are complex. These dynamics are played out on the level of intonation and addressivity, as an ongoing mockery of the authorial discourse in the mouth of the principal male character has an ambivalent effect: the "pollyanalytics" are being undermined even while they get to the heart of Hermione's identity crisis and Ursula's emotional turmoil. Birkin has a profound effect on both women by speaking his mind, a brutal honesty which goes against the grain of upper and middle class English reticence and understatement. Hermione's predictable reaction is to snub him. His is to walk away. The triangular tensions, in a kind of power struggle played out in speech, are sharpened by the reader's knowledge of the concealed deep wishes of the women characters, especially those of Hermione. In this sense, the scene is very dialogic. It is also one of many examples in the fiction of this period where it becomes increasingly more difficult to describe clearly Lawrence's attitude to his characters. Bakhtin is useful here because he expects a novel to be an interweaving of dialogue and the dialogic, a multivoiced text full of contradictory ideas in differing registers, fitting for the unstable world it attempts to represent. If you add to that the author's doubts and anxieties that underpin the writing then you appreciate the complexities of *Women in Love*. For this mode of dialogic writing is characteristic of it, and sets it apart from *The Rainbow*. It seems to have more affinities with *The Lost Girl* and *Mr Noon*.

The satirical writing established in these early pages is best exemplified in the four key scenarios: "Creme de Menthe", "Breadalby", "Café Pompadour", and the hotel in the Swiss Alps. I want now to look at these in more detail. In "Creme de Menthe", as in the other set pieces, Lawrence is sending up a situation he must have known only too well, and despised — a chic piece of play-acting, full of cynicism and boredom, with a darker current waiting just below the surface. The comedy derives principally from the lisp he gives the character nick-named "the Pussum". She asks Gerald in a moment spiced with sexual implication: "Were you ever vewry much afwraid of the savages?" (WL, 66). The narrator has already described exactly how we should read her speech mannerisms: "lisping with a slightly babyish pronunciation which was at once affected and true to her character. Her voice was dull and toneless." (WL, 63) Now we know how to read her voice, we are set up to take the side of the others (the men) who indulge in ritual group mockery of her. The play of sympathies, however, is more complex largely because, in characteristic Lawrentian fashion, the scene is focalized through Gerald — in other words, we arrive with him and get an outsider's view that renders the scene more absurd. It also becomes highly sexist, as Gerald is aroused by her affecting vulnerability and submissiveness. But the comedy is still dominantly one of language: "'Wupert!'" the Pussum cries; and the Russian is aptly named Maxim Libidnikov, as Lawrence seems tempted to turn comedy of manners into music-hall farce.

"Breadalby" also plays on the speech mannerisms of Hermione, once again placing serious thoughts in a highly comic frame. We might ask whether this mode of writing effectively undermines the ideas, or leaves them largely intact at the cost of further ridiculing Hermione and what she represents. She continues to sing her words while having "her little scene" (WL, 83). Intonational comedy is rampant: "'Roo-o-opert'" (WL, 88) she cries, flamboyantly swishing about in her extravagant oriental costume (WL, 91) as she tries to humiliate Birkin by reducing his refusal to come out and play to a little boy's sulking. But the humiliation backfires, as always. The whole scene is highly comic, with its mock German from the young *Fräulein*, its Russian ballet improvisation, its charade that rehearses the real drama to come (as in the play within the play in *Hamlet*). There is mock-stichomythic exchange (WL, 99), and a highly comic swimming scene. The women are well educated and up on the talk of the day, and of course thoroughly modern as they join the men in smoking cigarettes or pipes. But the narrator cannot resist commenting, just in case the visual and verbal comedy was not enough, that they were "spattering with half-intellectual, deliberate talk" (WL, 84).

The dialogics are complex. Serious ideas are framed in social and verbal comedy; biographical and literary references are explicit and implicit (although hardly concealed); and the mockery of the speech of overacting protagonists is so obviously addressed to the Lawrentian reader used to set pieces on modern identity that we are in danger of overlooking the focalizing strategy of seeing it all through the eyes of the sisters, Ursula and Gudrun: "Gudrun, mocking and objective, watched and registered everything." (WL, 87) Partiality is attributed in the first instance to them. It is of course a guise for Lawrence's own bitter commentary on English upper-class society. Nevertheless, the framing device enables a complex interplay of perspectives as the satirical female gaze textualizes a mocking portrait of the aristocracy at play: "'Aren't they terrifying? Aren't they really terrifying?' said Gudrun. 'Don't they look saurian? They are just like great lizards.'" (WL, 101) The grotesque swimming scene carnivalizes the highest of English civilization, turning them into images of the bestial and the primeval. Gerald, by contrast, is a happy Dionysus in this exhibition of the purely physical — recalling the chapter "Diver" when his exhibitionism was first the subject of the female gaze. Indeed, the dialogics work in this way too; as actions and speech repeat previous ones, now in a different context and for a different purpose. The sisters too will not be spared the ironies, as their superior attitude to their "betters" is compounded by their striving to get above their lowly provincial origins. They will walk away from what English society can offer them, but where will it leave them? The answer is left open by Lawrence.

Beneath the thin veneer of social play is a destructive frustration that gradually wells up, culminating in Hermione's attack on Birkin, and his purgatorial cleansing of society and the destructive modern woman by nature, in the firs and ferns (WL, 106-7). Moreover, it is in this kind of detail — "this tensed atmosphere of strained wills" (WL, 299) — that the whole destructive ethos of the novel is kept in play. This is most famously the case in chapter XXVIII: "Gudrun in the Pompadour".

Focalized through Gudrun,[57] the scenario brings together all the destructive cynicism that has been circulating amongst the characters, and results in Birkin's "pollyanalytics" winning through as at least better than modern cynicism. Gudrun attacks fashionable, chic metropolitan culture for its "ugly mocking persistence" (WL, 381), the "laughter, and lower voices and mockery" (WL, 382) aimed at the letter that contains Birkin/Lawrence's metaphysic. Lawrence's talents for mimicry are on full display as the tipsy party listen to Halliday reading "in the sing-song, slow, distinct voice of a clergyman reading the Scriptures" (WL, 383) what are recognizably Lawrence's own most serious metaphysical thoughts: "uniting the dark and the light ... the Flux of Corruption", etc; adding more hilarity as the Pussum interjects, "'Oh, he was always talking about Corwuption.'" This is one of the best examples in Lawrence of what Bakhtin called "double-voiced speech", where one discourse is framed in another, and thus given a new sense or significance. We also have a supreme moment of carnival, where drunken revelry and grotesque mimicry ridicule the pretensions of the utterly serious, yet where the laughter circulating amongst the Halliday party is not curative nor ultimately a creative release but is rather bitter and destructive. Indeed, Lawrence is at pains to turn the laughter back on the cynics, and this he does through the device of Gudrun's anger — which is Law- rence's anger thinly disguised: it "made the blood mount in her head"

---

[57] Modeled on Katherine Mansfield acting in a similar manner on Lawrence's behalf at the Café Royale.

(WL, 384); and also through the detailed description of her fashionable attire as she walks with deliberate poise and dignity out of the café with the letter to a chorus of booing:

> dressed in blackish-green and silver, her hat was brilliant green, like the sheen on an insect, but the brim was soft dark green, a falling edge with fine silver, her coat was dark green, lustrous, with a high collar of grey fur, and great fur cuffs, the edge of her dress showed silver and black velvet, her stockings and shoes were silver grey. She moved with slow, fashionable indifference to the door. The porter opened obsequiously for her, and, at a nod, hurried to the edge of the pavement and whistled for a taxi. (WL, 385)

By dwelling on Gudrun's flamboyant dress and her dignified gait, Lawrence textualizes an extreme gesture of defiance. Gudrun, like Lawrence, walks away from more than metropolitan society; she abandons England altogether in search of a new spiritual home. Once on the continent she can proclaim, in better spirits, and as several Lawrence characters do: "One could never feel like this in England, for the simple reason that the damper is *never* lifted off one, there. It is quite impossible to really let go, in England, of that I am assured." (WL, 397; Lawrence's emphasis)

However, as you might expect from a novel characterized by polyfocality, things will get funnier before they get tragically serious in a shifting of narration between the author's discourse and those of the two sisters, as the caricatured Herr Professor introduces the participants of the evening's entertainment causing different degrees of bowing. And while Gudrun gazes spellbound at the artist-figure, Loerke, Ursula it is who first bursts into spontaneous laughter before affecting the others. Here, it is a laughter of release that goes beyond the immediate situation of petty embarrassment and tension to encompass much that has gone before. Furthermore, Lawrence insists that the foreigners (Germans and Swiss-Germans) make Ursula "feel fine and infallible" (WL, 407) in the "*Fasching*" spirit which Lawrence knew well — which is remarkable for a novel written by an Englishman during the war with Imperial Germany. Indeed, Lawrence's pro-German sympathies surface in this section, but are complicated (even self-ironical) by being concentrated on Loerke, the Dresden hunger-artist. Gudrun's attraction to him is seen as perverse, especially in Gerald's eyes: Loerke is presented as a grotesque figure of the carnival, where all things are inverted including the object of Gudrun's gaze — once attracted to the worldly, physical woman's man (Gerald), but now to the mischievous, homosexual, gnome-like Loki.

While Ursula gives the text a gaiety and abandon fitting the Baccha-
nalian evening, Gudrun fuels Gerald's increasing disintegration by
resorting to the very mockery she so indignantly rejected in England.
And all the motifs that Gudrun attached to the sex object Gerald in the
opening pages of the novel — the lone arctic wolf-figure and its
reverberating connotations — recur here just as he is about to fulfil his
symbolic destiny. The attentive reader will pick up these dialogic signals,
as the mythic symbolism returns with a vengeance. Moreover, the
contrast between the metaphysical inner speech of the main characters
and the speech as dialogue in the carnival hilarity becomes a black
comedy. Gudrun may openly mock Gerald by flirting with Loerke in
front of him, but inwardly she is tormented by her own "terrible
cynicism" where everything is "turned to irony" (WL, 418). The total
despair that we are a party to in Hermione earlier now reappears in
Gudrun. Two of the New Women are seen ultimately to fail because they
are too intelligent and self-aware. The third one, Ursula, succeeds only by
submitting herself more to the man. All the gains for women at the end of
The Rainbow now seem to count for nothing.

The scene is full of grotesque contrasts: Loerke and Gerald, the comic
and the serious, life and death, the brightly coloured dress — Gudrun in
"scarlet and royal blue" (!) — and the darkness inside. The contemporary
art debate is now framed by decadence, mocking laughter and carnival, in
a grotesque merry-go-round of whirling dancing and wildly contradictory
views. In such unstable circumstances the key proto-Freudian question is
posed: "What *do* women want, at bottom?" (WL, 428) — and this
alongside Loerke's strident claims for the autonomy of art, which
Lawrence places in ironical dialogue with his own well-know organic
synthesis of art and life. A damning indictment of the whole Modernism
debate is brought about by making Gudrun, the English artist and New
Woman, and Loerke, the decadent advocate of Art for Art's Sake,[58]
kindred spirits (even soul mates, at least in Gudrun's fantasy). In this
scene we have one of the most puzzling statements of Lawrence's
problematic relationship to Modernism.

"Women and love — there is no greater tedium." (WL, 458) Loerke's
comment could so easily be Lawrence's, as his writing begins to turn
inward against his own metaphysic, as though after all the failures with
the English reading public and the censor he was beginning the move
towards self-parody that will culminate in *Mr Noon*. The changes in his
work will not just consist of the turn against women which feminist
criticism was quick to seize upon — although it is of course already

---

[58] With a sidelong glance at Roger Fry, Clive Bell and the Bloomsbury group.

evident in *Women in Love*. The change will consist, first, of the turn
against the serious, literary modern novel towards popular fiction (*The
Lost Girl*), and second the turn against the reader (*Mr Noon*).

iii. *The Lost Girl*: parody, carnival, and popular fiction

In many respects, *The Lost Girl* is a record of the lost author. Lawrence,
who had given up hope of ever finding an English reading public, was
now living in self-imposed exile in Sicily, trying to reinvent himself as an
American writer,[59] and generally taking stock of his life and writing. He
could not simply finish "The Insurrection of Miss Houghton" — the
earlier version of the first part of the novel abandoned before the war —
because it belonged to the creative period before *The Rainbow* and the
idealism and optimism of his younger self. The only option left to
Lawrence, it seems, was to rework the old material from his current
position. This enabled a fictional reassessment of that position. The
novel, therefore, poses the question about Lawrence's doubts about his
writing, about what it might mean to write an English novel in 1920. The
doubts that first began to emerge in *Women in Love* now take on a more
overtly comic and parodic form, which in Bakhtinian terms means that
Lawrence carnivalizes the English novel tradition as such, and his own
particular kind of writing that had become recognizable as "Lawrentian".

He set out deliberately to write popular fiction, and the result is a self-
conscious, parodistic text, which nevertheless managed to win the James
Tait Black Memorial Prize.[60] (It would also be his first novel published
since the banning of *The Rainbow* in 1915.) His models for English
popular fiction were Dickens and Arnold Bennett. Lawrence had read
Anna of the Five Towns (1902) in 1912 while staying at the Villa di
Gargnano. It is not insignificant perhaps that, when reworking the story
first begun 1912 of a young woman's revolt in provincial Woodhouse
(Eastwood), he has her run away to Italy. Bennett's novel must have left a
strong impression on him, as the letter to Arthur McLeod at the time
records. Lawrence had been away from England for five months,

> and scarcely seen a word of English in print ... but today ... to read
> almost my own dialect makes me feel quite ill. I hate England and
> its hopelessness. I hate Bennett's resignation. Tragedy ought really
> to be a great kick at misery. But *Anna of the Five Towns* seems
> like an acceptance — so does all the modern stuff since Flaubert. I
> hate it. I want to wash again quick, wash off England, the oldness

---

[59] Kinkead-Weekes, note 72, 853.
[60] Ibid., 700.

and grubbiness and despair.[61]

In rewriting the earlier manuscript in his post-*Women in Love* frame of mind, Lawrence will continue to use the cultural and spiritual displacement of leaving England as a narrative device. In this respect *The Lost Girl* and *Mr Noon* have a similar structure. The story begins in the provincial Midlands of Lawrence's early life, and ends in Italy. But if Bennett's Midlands is Lawrence's model now, and if we take the letter to McLeod seriously, then Lawrence will want to get beyond Bennett's naturalism and its bleak world. As we shall see, *The Lost Girl* turns that naturalism on its head in a sometimes hilarious carnivalization.

Catherine Carswell called Lawrence "the Dickens of the Midlands":

Nobody who ever heard him describe the scenes and persons of his boyhood, or watched him recreate with uncanny mimicry the talk, the movements and the eccentricities of the men and women among whom he grew up, can doubt but that Lawrence, if he had liked, might have been a new kind of Dickens of the Midlands.[62]

It was F.R. Leavis who first noticed the affinities between *The Lost Girl* and Dickens.[63] There is a Dickensian mix of literary genres in the one story: gritty detail in the realism of dull urban life; the threat of poverty and destitution; the fallen woman; vaudeville caricature; and a lively, familiar narrative voice talking directly to the reader from the first page. This is Lawrence: "Here we are then: a vast substratum of colliers .... Such the complicated social-system of a small industrial town in the Midlands of England, in the year of grace 1920. But let us go back a little. Such it was in the last calm year of plenty, 1913." (TLG, 1) This is Dickens: "It was the best of times, it was the worst of times .... There was a king ... on the throne of England .... It was the year of our Lord one thousand seven hundred and seventy-five."[64] Or: "The scene was a plain, bare, monotonous vault of a classroom .... A very regular feature on the face of the country, Stone Lodge was." And Coketown "as a town of red brick, or of brick that would have been red if the smoke and ashes had allowed it".[65] Indeed, *Hard Times* is set in a Victorian mill town in industrial Lancashire, a place of drab brick terraced houses, factories, and

---

[61] 4 October 1912.

[62] Carswell, 64.

[63] F.R. Leavis, *D.H. Lawrence: Novelist* (London: Penguin, 1985. First published 1955), 34.

[64] *A Tale of Two Cities* (London: Penguin, 1985. First published 1859), 35.

[65] *Hard Times* (London: Penguin, 1974. First published 1854), 47, 54, 65.

the dreadful school ruled over by Gradgrind's Utilitarianism. Nothing could serve Lawrence as a better model for the beginning of *The Lost Girl*. For into the hard-working and lacklustre world of James Houghton, where one scheme after the next for making his family fortune fails, comes the rebellious daughter, Alvina. It is through her that Lawrence can break out of Victorianism, bring colour to its greyness, meet its taboos head on. He does this through her connections with the travelling play-actors and their Red Indian fantasy world.[66]

Lawrence takes stock of the possibilities of writing the English novel in 1920 by going back beyond his own beginnings to the tradition of realism. It may seem strange for him to do this after categorically stating that after *Sons and Lovers* he would not write again in the manner of the dramatic realism promoted by the *English Review*.[67] However, we should notice that the Flaubertian model for such writing (represented in Lawrence's day by Arnold Bennett) is here, in the part of the novel set in England, being challenged by an older comic tradition represented by Dickens. Thus the answer to the question why Lawrence should want to go back to Dickens, or the home-life scenes of *Sons and Lovers*, or Arnold Bennett's Midlands is contained in that letter to McLeod quoted above. As Hyde puts it: "The initial motivation for writing *The Lost Girl* is thus not to imitate Bennett, whom Lawrence had a low opinion of, but to compose a riposte, and cock a snook at England."[68] Lawrence is reviving his pre-war feelings, but of course spiced by his newer feelings of rejection and being lost. In his search for a direction for his writing he produces a novel that is a kind of patchwork of the stories and writing styles of others, including those of his former self. Much of the final part, for instance, derives from his travel writing collected in *Twilight in Italy* (1916). The story of the woman who emancipates herself is now given a new twist, and one that records the change indicated already in *Women in Love* in his attitude towards women: her struggle for independence ends in her willing submission to the phallic man.

The naturalism of Arnold Bennett and the Victorianism of his Midlands are carnivalized in two distinctive ways. First, literally by the central role given the vaudeville players, a group of diverse foreigners whose presence threatens the staid life of the English small-town community. They also represent the decline of the music hall, which at the time was being displaced by the cinema as the new form of popular

---

[66] An idea he may well have got from Dickens, and one that irritated Leavis: cf. Leavis, 34. For a Bakhtinian reading of the comic play of discourses in Dickens, see TDI, 303-08.

[67] Cf. letter to Arthur McLeod, 23 April 1913, in *Letters II*, 132.

[68] Hyde, 77.

entertainment.[69] Second, the deliberate foregrounding of speech genres which the lively Dickensian narrator comments on — a Bakhtinian comic mode of narration we have already seen in *Women in Love*. Lawrence thus deconstructs the objective narration of Bennett's naturalism by constantly drawing attention to the artifices of fiction-making in the story's self-conscious inclusion of the idiosyncrasies of speech, including the "*skaz* illusion". This he does, in Hyde's words, "by means of a gesturing, self-dramatizing narrator who, like a music-hall entertainer, enacts the disconcerting switches of code that frustrate and disorientate passive readerly expectations".[70] While Lawrence, like Dickens before him, bears witness in his writing to the heteroglossia of the social world, he also appeals to the reader as music-hall audience; that is, not the passive reader of Bennett's naturalism, a consumer of the overdetermined text, but rather the active participant in the entertainment — a music-hall audience by definition.

Charades, cross-dressing, playing at Red Indians, as well as the comic distortions of English (Madame is given to speak quite a lot in her polyglot tongue); the folktale element and the mock-Apache ritual, and more seriously the coupling and marriage of Alvina and Ciccio, are degrees of transgression that work on a number of levels. First, the child-like play of the acting-troupe seems to compensate for the lack of joy in Alvina's own childhood. Second, the adult world of moral realism and its dour variety, naturalism, is transgressed by play, ritual and charade. Third, rigid social conventions are undermined by Alvina's transgressive behaviour (and Lawrence gives lots of space in the story to her family history, the community and the constraints of their world to make the undermining of it effective, even plausible in a post-Victorian, Freudian way). Fourth, gender transgression in transvestism. Fifth, and perhaps most significant of all, the manner in which the lost girl loses herself. Her loss of virginity has provoked strong reaction. Kinkead-Weekes comments: "The loss of Alvina's virginity is potentially the most repulsive scene he had ever written .... [T]he episode itself is very close to rape."[71] However, Carol Siegel suggests a quite different reading, rightly insisting that the comic and serious are kept in play by such transgressive acts.[72] It may, of course appear overdetermined on Lawrence's part — like the insistence on anal sex.[73] (I shall return to

---

[69] On Lawrence's negative attitude to the cinema see L.R. Williams (1993).

[70] Cf. Hyde, 81, where he refers to the work of Eikhenbaum.

[71] Kinkead-Weekes, 575.

[72] Introduction to the Penguin edition of the Cambridge D.H. Lawrence.

[73] For a critique of anal sex in Lawrence see David Holbrook (1988), "Sons and Mothers: D.H. Lawrence and *Mr Noon*" in David Ellis and Ornella De Zordo eds,

Lawrence's changing sexual theory and its feminist critique in the following chapters.) The need to get beyond the stifling constraints of conformity on a number of levels required, it seems, extreme measures.

Bearing in mind these senses of transgression, *The Lost Girl* is what Hyde has called a "strong reading of Bennett" in Harold Bloom's sense of a wilful misrecognition of a literary forebear, or poetic Father, in order to displace him.[74] Lawrence, who seems to have lost his own distinctive voice, textualizes a heterogeny of other voices. These include primary and secondary speech genres in Bakhtin's sense — everyday speech varieties and literary discourses, respectively.

Critics have been alert to the literary parodies. I have already mentioned Bennett and Dickens. The following have also been noted: George Moore's *A Mummer's Wife* (1885), which influenced Bennett's *Anna of the Five Towns*, so that Lawrence is reworking plot structures that have clear literary antecedence (perversely, perhaps in the work of Flaubert, especially *Madame Bovary*, whose influence on the naturalism of the English writers was encouraged by the *English Review* aesthetic which Lawrence had categorically rejected);[75] Blake, with his diagnosis of a sterile, dead England, and a plea for an acceptance of one's physical sexuality. Also from Blake Lawrence could have got the idea of "The Little Girl Lost", and the idea of losing the self in love as a dangerous and unknown territory, so that self-fulfilment has a price.[76] The story of Alvina and Ciccio, as Kinkead-Weekes claims, "may have been suggested by Mackenzie's *Sylvia Scarlett* whose heroine joined a troupe of actors, and about whom Frieda was reading admiringly". The Natcha-Kee-Tawara is a parody of Fenimore Cooper — which is not implausible as Lawrence had been working on what would become *Studies in Classic American Literature* (1923), and he had started to see himself as an American writer, or at least writing predominantly for the American reader. Indeed, as L.D. Clark argues, the quest narrative is a predominant form in American writing,[77] and Alvina's quest for soul-fulfilment takes

---

D.H. Lawrence: Critical Assessments Volume III (Mountfield: Helm Information Ltd, 1992).

[74] Hyde, 80. Harold Bloom, *The Anxiety of Influence: A Theory of Poetry* (New York and London: Oxford University Press, 1973).

[75] For further discussion see Christopher Heywood, "D.H. Lawrence's *The Lost Girl* and its Antecedents by George Moore and Arnold Bennett", *English Studies*, 47 (1966).

[76] Gary Wiener, "Lawrence's 'Little Lost Girl'", *D.H. Lawrence Review*, 19/3, (1987). Also Jeffrey Meyers ed., *Lawrence and Tradition* (London: The Athlone Press, 1985), a collection of papers showing Lawrence's affinities in general with Blake, Carlyle, Ruskin, George Eliot, Hardy, Whitman, and Nietzsche.

[77] Kinkead-Weekes, 573, 74.

on perverse twists. For Hyde the American reference suggests Crève-
coeur, with the name Natcha-Kee-Tawara "perhaps echoing Chateaubri-
and's *Les Natchez*".[78] Simpson notices that "the very first page of the
novel makes reference to Gissing's *The Odd Woman* (1893), which
Lawrence read in 1910" — a popular sociological problem novel, where
characters attempt to get beyond the conditions of their oppression. There
is something about the jaunty tone of *The Lost Girl* which recalls the H.G.
Wells of *Ann Veronica* (1909), representing "a kind of parody of the tone
adopted by writers like Wells", while Forster's *Where Angels Fear to
Tread* (1905), the story of an English widow marrying an Italian of
inferior social standing, may also have been an influence. In any case, as
Simpson points out, the existence of a large proportion of unmarried
women, especially after the war, was a potential market for such stories.
Lawrence had been interested in the "woman question novel", which *The
Rainbow* develops out of *Sons and Lovers*. Alvina's revolt partly belongs
to this genre, but here modified by a "healthy vulgarity" which triumphs
over "an outdated, false refinement".[79]

However, what should concern us here is not just the spotting of
literary cross-references and possible sources for the story, but the use
made of them in Lawrence's text. If parody, then the source should be
turned on its head, turned in fact into comedy. Lawrence, in using this
novel as retrospect on the English novel tradition and his novel writing, is
carnivalizing the sources of characters, plots and stories in his own quest
for a new voice, a new start. Yet where does Lawrence end up? Apparently rejecting the forms of fiction for travel writing. Derived from his
pre-war writing collected in *Twilight in Italy* (1916), the last pages of the
novel describe what Simpson calls "the primitive but breathtakingly
beautiful landscape"[80] in the Abruzzi mountains where Ciccio takes
Alvina, and where she literally fulfils her destiny as the lost girl.

Thus Lawrence completes his fictional retrospective in a form he will
try out again in *Sea and Sardinia* (1923), while his quest for a direction in
his fiction writing will undergo one more perverse twist in the unfinished
Mr Noon. Before turning to this novel, I want to look in a bit more
technical detail at the polyvocal style of *The Lost Girl* and its Bakhtinian
explanation. There is no better place to begin than with Roger Fowler's
paper, "*The Lost Girl*: discourse and focalization",[81] not least because it
challenges the Bakhtinian reading.

---

[78] Hyde, 82.
[79] Hilary Simpson in Peter Widdowson ed., *D.H. Lawrence* (London: Longman, 1992), 97-99.
[80] Simpson, 100.
[81] Fowler, in Brown (1990).

Fowler also points out that the styles of the beginning and end of the novel are different, the former deriving from the text's 1912 origin with its Dickensian and Bennettian parody, the latter from the newer 1920's Lawrence. And that the text is characterized by an unusually "complex stylistic intertextuality" in which Alvina's perception of sex is expressed in the metaphysical language of *Women in Love*; the Italy section re-uses the travel writing; and Bennett's Midlands and naturalism appear side by side with the grotesque realism of Dickens' circus people from *Hard Times*. It is dialogic, then, in its literary references, because like any discourse there is an orientation towards an addressee — here the implied English reader of 1920. This level of address is taken a step further when the narrator is given to comment on and interpret the characters' speech mannerisms:

> For Miss Pinegar was not vulgarly insinuating. On the contrary, the things she said were rather clumsy and downright. It was only that she seemed to weigh what she said, secretly, before she said it …. She seemed to slide her speeches unnoticed into one's ears, so that one accepted them without the slightest challenge. That was just her manner of approach. (TLG, 12)

Or: "And her [Alvina's] voice had a curious bronze-like resonance that acted straight on the nerves of her hearers." (TLG, 23) And: "There was an odd clang, like a taunt, in her [Alvina's] voice." (TLG, 28)[82] In Bakhtinian terms, there is a constant insistence on the speech genre in specific interactional and communicative contexts. We are constantly being told how to read the manner and voice of speech, to pin down the precise attitude and social position of the speaker and the response elicited. Although Fowler does not go on to make the link, it could be suggested that this aspect of Lawrence's style is also a location of the Arnold Bennett parody. Precise and copious social detail is the hallmark of naturalism, and the narrator's over-insistence is un-Lawrentian.

Fowler's principal claim, however, is that, notwithstanding the diversity of registers and speech styles, point of view is singular. A stylistic heteroglossia is not matched by ideological plurality. The characters are not given views independent from those of the author. We always know when it is Lawrence speaking, because we are educated Lawrence readers; the metaphysical language, the sexual theories and the developing misogyny — when Alvina is given such speech, predominantly in the form of inner monologue, we Lawrence readers instinctively recognize

---

[82] Examples cited by Fowler.

the authorial discourse. Fowler uses a more technical approach to demonstrate what has been said many times about Lawrence: that he has a tendency to be heavy-handed with his characters in order to make his point. In order to understand this more technically, Fowler insists, first, that we should differentiate between the narrator and the implied author. Second, we should look closely at Lawrence's use of characters as focalizers. The narrator's discourse is clearly the location for much of the parody; at times the Dickensian persona chatting to the reader, indulging in proverbial generalizations like the omniscient narrator of the nineteenth-century realist novel, as in the following examples: "But let us retreat to the early eighties, when Alvina was a baby: or even further back, to the palmy days of James Houghton". "For let class-jealousy be what it may, a woman hates to see another woman left stately on the shelf" (TLG, 2) — here a particularly early twentieth-century preoccupation, as we saw above. And in case you had not got it: "No French marquis in a Dickens novel could have been more elegant and raffiné and heartless." (TLG, 4) At other times, he is the Bennett of *Anna of the Five Towns*. Fowler chooses the following passage:

> Alvina looked at the room. There was a wooden settle in front of the hearth, stretching its back to the room. There was a little table under the square, recessed window, on whose sloping ledge were newspapers, scattered letters, nails and a hammer ... and a litter of faggots, cane, vine-twigs, bare maize-hubs, oak-twigs filling the corner by the hearth. (TLG, 310)

This level of detail contrasts markedly with the more symbolic-metaphysical writing which is Lawrence's stock-in-trade:

> In February, as the days opened, the first almond trees flowered among grey olives, in warm, level corners between the hills .... The sun was on them for the moment, and they were opened flat, great five-pointed lilac stars, with burning centres, burning with a strange lavender flame, as she had seen some metal burn lilac-flamed in the laboratory of the hospital at Islington .... And she felt like going down on her knees and bending her forehead to the earth. (TLG, 332)

Here we recognize that the description has a deeper purpose as the character is associated symbolically with the perceived natural world. However, I would go further than Fowler on this point. For when Lawrence is writing in his usual Lawrentian manner, even the narrator drops the Dickens or Bennett guise and becomes more recognizable:

But Alvina was looking at Ciccio at that moment. He had turned with the rest, looking inquiringly at the car. And his quick eyes, the whites of which showed so white against his duskiness, the yellow pupils so non-human, met hers with a quick flash of recognition. His mouth began to curl in a smile of greeting .... It was as if he did not want to see her looking at him. (TLG, 272)

The narrator in this passage continues his role of commenting on the interpersonal dynamics which underpin silences as well as speech. But here there is a recognizably Lawrentian discourse that goes beyond the objective detail of Bennett's naturalism and Dickens's social comedy. It is as if the device of the narrator, which could give Lawrence a distance to his text, now gives way to the author's earlier voice which he thought he had lost. Indeed, just as Alvina has to lose herself in order to find herself again, so the lost author plays with the narrative masks and the speech and discourses of others (including that other which was his earlier self) so as to emerge in the end in an authorial discourse which once again resembles his own voice.

As the passage quoted above also demonstrates, Fowler is right to insist that focalization is problematic in Lawrence. Alvina more than any other character is given a focalizing role. It is through her eyes that we see. But Fowler's main point is that we do not see through her mind as a consciousness independent of the author's. Here, once again, a Bakhtinian reading will be stuck in that impasse of the relationship between the author and his characters which Lodge and Fleishman were the first to insist disarms claims for Lawrence's novels being truly polyphonic (in the precise sense of Bakhtin's reading of Dostoevsky). To what extent, though, is Fowler right about focalization in *The Lost Girl*?

In Genette's concept, focalization[83] describes the importance of the position from which things are seen. Indeed, focalization had from the outset the connotation of the precise camera-angle in which things are perceived. The classic examples that are always mentioned in this discussion are the beginnings of Dickens' *Great Expectations* (1860-61) and Joyce's *A Portrait of the Artist as a Young Man* (1916), when we see though the eyes of the narrator's boyhood self. To save confusion, focalization has usually meant perception attributed to a particular character, and not a narrator — although it is extremely complex when it comes to "free indirect discourse". Sometimes, as in *Women in Love*,

---

[83] Gérard Genette, *Narrative Discourse* (Ithaca: Cornell University Press, 1980. First published 1972).

there are several character-focalizers, although Gudrun is used more than the others. Toolan tries to circumvent the confusions of this slippery concept by suggesting we call such a narrational device, "orientation", thus avoiding "point of view". But Fowler seems to mean "point of view" when he discusses focalization in Lawrence. He collapses the distinction between who sees and who speaks. Alvina's thoughts and perceptions may carry the weight of the Lawrentian metaphysic resulting first in her insurrection and then her submission and exile, but they are positioned through her focalizing role in precise contexts in the story. They undergo change, they are subject to the force of otherness. But, most important of all, they are subject to dialogics. Even when the perceptual and psychological are at the service of the author's ideology, as it always is in Lawrence, that ideology is dialogized by its complex representation in a heteroglossic text. We are alerted to this process in *Women in Love*: when Birkin speaks the author's philosophy, the dialogics of its textualization render the ideas at least in part as "pollyanalytics". In any case, if as Fowler suggests we are all competent Lawrentians now, we do not need any ideological orientation towards the author's metaphysic. If we are competent Bakhtinians, however, we can see the more complex dialogic orientation of Lawrence's writing at the moment he is trying to reassure himself of its direction.[84] It is not that focalization is unimportant in Lawrence; but, like the question of polyphony, it is not in itself a sufficient reason for rejecting Bakhtin. Elsewhere in his paper, Fowler clearly shows the appropriateness of the Bakhtinian approach, locating the text's heteroglossia in its several varieties of styles, languages, and dialects. What Fowler does not do is look at the dialogic contexts of speech, especially in those focalized through Alvina. In order to demonstrate how this works, I want to end this section with an example of heteroglossia placed in its dialogic contexts. I have chosen a passage from the funeral scene:

> Poor Alvina, this was the only day in her life when she was the centre of public attention. For once, every eye was upon her, every mind was thinking about her. Poor Alvina! said every member of the Woodhouse "middle class": Poor Alvina Houghton, said every collier's wife. Poor thing, left alone — and hardly a penny to bless herself with. Lucky if she's not left with a pile of debts .... Perhaps she'll take up that nursing. She never made much of that, did

---

[84] For further discussion of the complexities of focalization, see Michael Toolan, *Narrative: A Critical Linguistic Introduction* (London: Routledge, 1988), chapter 3.4. For a fuller discussion of Fowler's position see Fowler, chapter 9.

she …. Pity some nice young man doesn't turn up and marry her.
… They say the grave was made for the both of them …. Look,
there's room for Alvina's name underneath. — Sh! (TLG, 186-87)

The passage represents the speech genres and the dialect of local gossip.
The narrator locates speech in social class. The text is dominated mostly
by the speech mannerisms of the colliers' wives and their addressees.
Interestingly for any discussion of focalization, the passage switches
away from Alvina as focalizer: now she is being looked at — but also she
is aware of being looked at. And their opinions are certainly not being
endorsed by the author, although they are common enough, and although
they are no doubt motivated by his own experiences as a young man. We
are, momentarily, reminded of the wage-collecting scene in *Sons and
Lovers* when the young Paul Morel has to go among the colliers and their
wives and is made a fool of (focalized through his paranoiac over-
reaction — which I discussed in chapter 1). It is not, though, the
heteroglossia alone which makes this passage significant, nor the comedy
in the mimicry, but that it is dialogically framed in the narrative by, on
the one hand, the scene that precedes it — the ritual play on Apache
ceremony (and its Fennimore Cooper reference) and the renaming of
Alvina as Allaye; and, on the other hand, it is followed by Alvina's brutal
and loveless loss of virginity. Conventional values are subject to a severe
irony.

Thus Bakhtin offers us a greater potential for textual and narrative
analysis than either his concept of polyphony, or Genette's concept of
focalization alone. In the next section, I shall put Bakhtin to work on
Lawrence's most hyperbolic writing of the period, *Mr Noon*.

iv. *Mr Noon*: Lawrence's carnival

In many respects *Mr Noon* is the mirror image, or dark side of *The Lost
Girl*. While the latter remains comic popular fiction, and tries out
different narrative voices and different modes of address to the reader, *Mr
Noon* positively assaults the reader. What is worse, the reader becomes
distinctly gendered: Lawrence's most dangerous reader, the "sterner sex",
is female — as if he knew what the future would hold in store for him.

Mr Noon is the product of the continuing crisis in the writing life of
the author. At the time of writing, 1920-21, Lawrence was so unsettled
that he was writing several texts by turns, never completing any one
before breaking off to do a bit more on another. Just after finishing *The
Lost Girl* he had started on *Mr Noon*, in the same spirit — indeed Hyde

has suggested that the first part of *Mr Noon* derives from unused material from *The Lost Girl*.[85] Both texts use the Woodhouse setting, and Alvina Houghton makes a brief appearance in *Mr Noon*, sitting among the altos in the choir (MN, 45). Lawrence was revising *Studies in Classic American Literature* that summer; by October he was correcting proofs of *Women in Love* and *The Lost Girl*, writing another chapter of the history textbook *Movements in European History*, continuing to write poems, and working on *Aaron's Rod*.[86] And it seems to have been the trouble he was having with the latter text that motivated or caused him to begin *Mr Noon* — which must have come easier, at least to start with, as it was a continuation of the kind of comic writing in *The Lost Girl*. He also interrupted his writing to travel to Sardinia, and on his return wrote *Sea and Sardinia*, before continuing with his different fictional projects. All three fictional texts — *The Lost Girl*, *Mr Noon*, and *Aaron's Rod* — treat autobiography in one way or another. The crisis in the writing was, it seems, also a crisis in the life.[87]

Mr Noon reflects, in its content and in its writing, the unsettled spirit of its author. Its comedy is tinged with something close to bitterness; and the comedy is not always maintained — which may, of course, be excused because what we have is only a first draft, and Lawrence would have rewritten the whole manuscript, making it thematically consistent and organically better structured had he decided to finish the novel for publication. He did not, breaking off the story in mid-sentence, and making no reference to it again after 1922. The consensus view now is that not only had Lawrence found a direction for his writing by then which took him a long way from thoughts about his pre-war life, but also the revelations in *Mr Noon* about Frieda's infidelity on their honeymoon made him decide for self-censorship. Indeed, the two reasons may well be associated, as Holbrook explains: "Lawrence was seriously compromised by the circumstances of his own marriage," and by the influence that the sexual liberationist theories and practice of Otto Gross had on Frieda. *Mr Noon* records the challenge of Gross to Lawrence's own sexual theory of consummate marriage, and the new direction which he was to take after *Noon* may well have been a reaction: Gross's matriarchal sexual role for women, showing the way to change society through sexual freedom by giving themselves freely to the needs of men without moral scruple, will be displaced by Lawrence's call for male leadership

---

[85] Hyde, 87.

[86] Source of information: Introduction to the Cambridge University Press edition of *Mr Noon*, edited by Lindeth Vasey (Cambridge, 1984), xxi-xxii.

[87] Kinkead-Weekes, 627.

and woman's utter submission.[88] (And this is discussed in some detail in the next chapter.)

The anger directed against a narrow-minded public at home, which began to surface after the banning of *The Rainbow*, now becomes explicit invective. It is directed at the reader, and is the most striking feature of the novel. The playful, Fieldingesque asides to the reader are sometimes gentle and at other times bitter as the reader, or the critic, is verbally abused. The narrator's sudden changes of mood appear to be the author's, for here Lawrence has abandoned the device of character-focalization altogether and gone for omniscience. And as the source of the story (or rather stories — Gilbert and Emmie; Gilbert and Johanna) derives from the pre-war life of the author, its narrative fictional presentation is only thinly disguised autobiography. The voice of the author certainly adds to this impression.

As we saw in the previous section, Lawrence was trying out different voices in his fiction. His own emerged in those passages of Lawrentian metaphysical description. Here, in *Mr Noon*, he is still in his comic-parodic mode, but the voice cannot disguise itself always in literary artifice. Sometimes Lawrence seems unable to contain his anger:

> No, gentle reader, please don't interrupt, I'm *not* going to open the door of Johanna's room, not until Mr Noon opens it himself. I've been caught that way before. I have opened the door for you, and the moment you gave your first squeal in rushed the private detective you had kept in the background .... So don't interrupt. Am *I* writing this book, or are you? (MN, 137; Lawrence's emphasis)

And, earlier, at the beginning of chapter XIV, Lawrence speaks directly about the critic "in the *Observer* of December 1920", and "How a *Times* critic dropped on me for using the word *toney!*" (MN, 118). These are references to reviews of *The Lost Girl* which, of course, had angered him.

When the narrative shifts between several authorial voices, they each create a different authorial persona. Another way of putting it is, in Peter Preston's words: "The persona of the author that emerges from the narrative is by turns facetious, ironical, defensive, aggressive, slangy, earnest and exhortatory."[89] Lawrence was sensitive to criticism, especially

---

[88] Holbrook in Ellis and De Zordo, 224. For further bibliographical information on Lawrence's connections with Germany and German thought and literature see *Lawrence and Germany: A Bibliography*, complied by Michael Weithmann and Regina Hoffmann, with an introduction by Robert Burden (Passau: University of Passau Library, 1995).

[89] Preston, "Lawrence and *Mr Noon*", in Ellis and De Zordo (1992), vol. III, 202.

after the notoriety he achieved as a banned author. He tended to respond in a heavy-handed and sarcastic manner — a response done in the voice, so to speak, of the Lawrence-persona of that reputation. In his struggle to find a voice in 1920, Lawrence tries out several. But in the end the frustration shows through: "I'm writing this book myself." (MN, 137) Although it does seem that he is writing it *for* himself, no longer confident of his addressee (having only just had his first novel published since the banning of *The Rainbow*). Moreover, with *Mr Noon* more than any other novel, Lawrence struggles to find a form for his fictional autobiography. It is a more sardonic continuation of the style and structure of *The Lost Girl*, with its first part in England, and its second part in Europe; with its extended metaphor of the journey of self-discovery. Both novels are a kind of rite of passage to Italy; and satire, comedy and parody are common to both novels. Lawrence is still taking stock, still working out through the writing the direction his work should take.

The Bakhtinian approach should be quite appropriate for such writing that is "subversive of its theme".[90] It was Lydia Blanchard's reading of *Mr Noon* that provoked her to declare that: "The approach taken by Bakhtin, with its emphasis on dialogics, dramatizes the inadequacy of most other critical theories of the novel for discussing Lawrence."[91] Indeed, *Mr Noon* is a carnival of parodies and self-parodies, of intertextualities and the stylization of speech genres in a text characterized by a "furious comedy". Mark Kinkead-Weekes describes its comedy as follows:

> Lawrence experiments with Fielding's comic epic, which creates not only the distancing of comedy but also a teasing relation between showman-author and "gentle reader". All the comic-epic devices are present: perverse anti-climax, inflated apostrophe, "heroic" sports, battles with monsters or villains and the learned survey of a tract of knowledge (i.e. "spooning"); but the eighteenth-century genre always had a more serious purpose also, behind the fun, and used the comic distance and the constant invention by the "author", to bring that out. In Fielding moreover, the relationship of the reader with a teasing "author" is also part of another level of irony, in which readers may find themselves suddenly in the dock instead of on the bench. This certainly happens in *Mr Noon*, in which moreover the "author" never quite manages Fielding's win-

---

[90] Michael Black (1988), "Gilbert Noon, D.H. Lawrence and the Gentle Reader" in ibid., 248.
[91] Eggert and Worthen, 107.

ning geniality. Something of the irritation of 1920, as well as the
alienation from England, gets into the tone even of the first part,
much more in the second, and the irony is increasingly subversive,
moving towards contempt. *Caveat lector* ["let the reader beware"].[92]

The opening scenes at the Goddards are a parody of the English novel
of manners, with a particularly modern flavour. They are Fabian
socialists by inclination, but are trapped in a bourgeois marriage, made
the more evident by their boredom on a typical Sunday at home. The
satire is spiced, of course, with personal reminiscences on the part of
Lawrence. Noon is loosely based on George Neville, the Goddards on
Willie and Sallie Hopkin; Johanna is Frieda, and most interesting of all
the author as a young man becomes a character in his own fiction as
Gilbert Noon in Part II.[93] The fate of the Goddards is meant to await
every couple after the excitement and dangers of "spooning". It is from
an English provincial life that offers no real hope or challenge that
Gilbert Noon has to get away; just as Alvina had to, and the two couples
in *Women in Love*. In fact, provincialism is a dominant target in
Lawrence's writing generally. However, here it is more bitter, and will
give more credence and significance to Gilbert's process of becoming
"unEnglished" (MN, 107) once he finds himself in what is described as
the natural plenitude of Alpine Germany.

The journey, a geographical and spiritual displacement, is full of
intertextual resonances to Lawrence's other writing — fictional and
autobiographical. As the quotation above from Kinkead-Weekes
suggests, comedy is a serious business. Lawrence poses the question once
again about the English provincial life in 1912 that seemed to offer him
no future, but from the perspective of 1920 at another moment of crisis in
his writing life. Yet he is able to get a certain distance or objectivity at
times through the device of literary parody. That is to say, Lawrence
writes his best comedy when writing about 1912, both in the satire on
provincial English middle-class life in Part I, and the more comic
moments of the episodes in Germany in Part II, drawn from memory and
in a dialogic relation to his earlier travel writing. When he is writing
about matters closest to his 1920 situation — the continuing problems of
his relationship to the English reading public, the critics and the public
libraries — his objectivity disappears, and he speaks his anger and
frustration in his own voice. His best lyrical writing is enabled by

---

[92] Kinkead-Weekes, 615.
[93] See Introduction to *Mr Noon* (1984), xi.

nostalgia for his younger self in love, at the moment of his elopement with Frieda Weekley, the professor's wife.

Scandal, of course, had attached itself to Lawrence's name from 1912.[94] Remembering those days must have been easily motivated by his 1920s self. The scandal of his schoolteacher friend losing his job for getting a woman pregnant; and the scandal of his eloping with Professor Weekley's wife are "the germ of the whole novel".[95] In Germany, Johanna's family are scandalized not just because she has a lover but because he insists on her divorcing her husband, thus making the whole thing public. In a sense, Lawrence takes that level of shock and outrage that is endemic to public morality and social convention and turns it inward, back onto the form of the novel itself. In Bakhtinian terms, Lawrence novelizes the scandal, making it the scandal of the novel. There are a number of key moments in the text which illustrate this best.

The Goddards bourgeois marriage frames the spooning, as if the latter can only end in the former, sooner or later. The English novel of manners gives way to the eighteenth century comic mode, with its aggressive and playful stance towards the reader, sometimes in the guise of Sterne with its Shandyesque implausibilities (as in Noon's potency: sex three times in fifteen minutes); sometimes in the guise of Fielding with its pseudo-moral generalizations or its mock philosophical digression. For instance, on spooning: "Since the spoon is one of the essential mysteries of modern love" (MN, 22), which is also turned against both the upper-class reader and "the whole English race" in parody discourse where Lawrence sends up the pious seriousness of chivalric love (Grail-stories), while turning literary scholar in insisting that "the seducer and the innocent maid" who were always invaluable to fiction have now faded into mere spooners. The whole thing has become so nice, the coarseness of sex has been hidden away by "so much reciprocal old-beaniness!" Here the discourse slips into a more recognizably upper-class speech, and the eighteenth-century discourse gives way to its twentieth-century equivalent. The passage (MN, 21) is a chaotic display of literary and social languages, a heteroglossic jumble of speech genres from middle-class slang to proverbs, literary quotation in French (Molière), everyday Italian, and classical reference (common to the comic tradition, of course). There is intertextual cross-reference to one of the central themes in *The Lost Girl*: the attack on false refinement through the vulgarity of the travelling players, and Alvina's preference for them. There is the first direct address

---

[94] And continuing with the 1960s trial of *Lady Chatterley's Lover*, and the post-Millett feminist attack.
[95] Black in Ellis and De Zordo (1992), 246.

to the reader as a potential adversary. Moreover, when the text returns to the spooners in question, Lawrence cannot resist sending himself up:

> A little shudder ran through her, and she seemed to leap nearer to him, and then to melt in a new fusion. Slowly, slowly she was fusing once more, deeper and deeper, enveloping him all the while with her arms as if she were some iridescent sphere of flame half-enclosing him: a sort of Watts picture.
>
> A deep pulse beat, a pulse of expectation. She was waiting, waiting for him to kiss her. Ah, how she waited for it! Only that. Only let him kiss her ears, and it was a consummation.
> (MN, 21-2)

The language of metaphysical gestures is recognizably Lawrentian. But here, in the spirit of the comic tradition, the high Lawrentian register is in the service of a mock-elevation of the trivial and banal; in Lawrence, a kiss on the ear is hardly a consummation! The scene is also described as an allegorical tableau: "a Watts picture" — the sort of picture of which the middle classes would have reproductions.[96] Lawrence overplays his hand, as so often in this novel: "We have risen to great heights, dear reader, and sunk to great depths. Yet we have hardly fathomed the heights and depths of the spoon in the Co-op entry." (MN, 23) The whole effect is deflationary, as in the best mock-heroic writing of the comic tradition.

Lawrence's self-parodies focus also on his inclination to repetition. As he wrote in the Foreword to the American edition of *Women in Love* (which must have still been fresh in his mind when writing *Mr Noon*):

> In point of style, fault is often found with the continual, slightly modified repetition. The only answer is that it is natural to the author: and that every natural crisis in emotion or passion or understanding comes from this pulsing, frictional to-and-fro, which works up to culmination.[97]

So, when we read in *Mr Noon*: "glancing over the lurid Sunday paper,

---

[96] George Frederick Watts (1817-1904), the English painter, was more publicly known for his portraits of nobility, but was enormously popular in his lifetime for his moral and allegorical pieces, monochrome reproductions of which would have been hung in the homes of the late Victorian middle classes. One such composition was *Love Triumphant*. Source: Magnus Magnusson ed., *Chambers Biographical Dictionary*, (Edinburgh, 5th ed, 1990).

[97] Reprinted in the Penguin edition of the Cambridge D.H. Lawrence of *Mr Noon* (1996), Appendix I.

whilst the women made pies .... whilst the saucepans bubbled ... whilst the meat sizzled in the oven, and his father came and went, fidgetty, and drank a glass of beer between-whiles" (MN, 35), the repetition is used for less metaphysical or sexual purpose, as Lawrence continues his diatribe about the boredom of the English Sunday. The parody is marked by the verbal play on "whilst" in the expression "between-whiles".

In Part II there are moments when the self-parody reaches levels of comedy never seen before in Lawrence: "Johanna meanwhile watched the same sunk flame flapping and fighting for life, fighting, sipping, sipping avidly at the spent wax", where the over-alliteration begins to alert us to a devious intent, and one which is confirmed by the deflationary, ironic statement which ends the paragraph: "So there she knelt with luxurious tears in her eyes. I say luxurious. For after all it wasn't her candle, it was only the cavalry captain's. And he was no longer indispensable". And then followed by the aside to the reader: "So, gentle reader, before you light your next candle to the Virgin, make up your mind which emotion you're going to get out of it." (MN, 156) Lawrence, thinly disguised in the persona of the omniscient, cynical narrator, is most bitter at times about the expressions of love between "Johanna of the golden fleece, and poor dear shorn lamb of a Gilbert" (MN, 157). Self-parody is most obvious in the following passage:

> Dawn at the window. A big, white, horrible, intensifying blotch on the darkness. Dawn at the window. Dawn at the window. Seething, seething — he could almost hear it! — seething with a pale, maleficent, leprous sound. But dawn! Dawn at the window. Could he make out the window frame? Could he distinguish the centre-bar? Light seething like some fatal steam on the black solidity of the darkness: seething and seething its way in, like a disease. (MN, 203)

The mock-horror and melodrama deflate the stock-in-trade metaphysical discourse, while the repetitions ("dawn at the window") are denied significance because they are not modified in a structure of recurrent motifs as in much of Lawrence's best writing. They are merely repetitions for their own sake.

Lawrence also parodies scenes from his other novels. Chapter IV. "Aphrodite and the Cow" may have originated in a real incident,[98] but what is dialogic about it is the comic send-up of the nightmarish scene of Ursula and the phallic stallions in the last chapter of *The Rainbow*. We

---

[98] Introduction to MN and note 303.

are also reminded of Gudrun's Expressionist dance in front of the Highland cattle, while Ursula looks on in fear (WL, 167-68). But the scene is internally dialogic too. Gilbert Noon and Patty Goddard are both humiliated after their serious discussion about the New Woman, the vote for women, and the question of modern marriage. The narrator takes the side of the sexist man, as Patty is accused of retreating to the safe "theoretic platform ... of Woman" (MN, 39) as he tries to call her bluff. The cow's arrival on the scene is a kind of *dea ex machina* of high comedy as Patty scrambles away and Gilbert plays the gallant toreador (MN, 42). The man has a lot of fun, but the older woman loses all her composure — a comic deflation of Lawrence's target, the New Woman, as the serious ideas are dialogized by the comic incident.

Another intertextual moment is Johanna's verbal tirade against the sons of mothers, with their mother-love — and here we are back on the terrain of *Sons and Lovers*: "They're all Hamlets, obsessed by their mothers ... mother-love. It is the most awful self-swallowing thing." (MN, 124) In a calculated irony, Lawrence has Johanna, the Frieda-figure, attack him. Nothing is sacred in this novel; not even the author's own most important ideas. And Lawrence gets the central female character to speak for his 1920's self, and one that had come a long way personally and thematically since 1912. Later, the whole case against the sons of mothers is summed up by Johanna's sister in a stylization of German-English: "Oh yea, all Englishmen are Hamlets, they are so self-conscious over their feelings, and they are therefore so false .... these men with their tragical man-hysterics!" (MN, 196)

Not all the intertextual references are comic. Some of the travel writing from 1912, and the poetry are pure nostalgia for the man who was once in love. These are the most lyrical passages (cf. MN, 184: "Hennef was a station ... ").[99] Sometimes the poetry is simply written into the description: "Beautiful bridled creatures of fire and darkness, sun and smoke" (MN, 187). In these lyrical passages the Bavarian gentian becomes a focus for the memory, "gentian-flowered", a metaphor for the man in love on the Alpine walking tour in 1912; just as the crucifix in the mountains, signifying a terrible, strange "medieval Catholicism" (MN, 249), comes direct from the travel-writing and the poetry of those days.[100]

Lawrence, of course, does not keep it up. As a friend joins them — modelled on David Garnett — so the biting satire displaces the lyricism: "an ardent youth of Fabian parents, who had been given a rare good time

---

[99] See the poem "*Bei Hennef*" (1912); discussed in note, 320.
[100] Cf. *Look! We have Come Through!* (1917). Also *Twilight in Italy and Other Essays* (1916).

all his life, and who expected the jolly game to continue." (MN, 255) The skill of the mimic is once again on display, as the stylization of the precise speech mannerisms of the young Englishman signal a return to the comic mode. This continues in the mocking of the crucifixes as Stanley, in the spirit of British music-hall humour, turns *INRI* into the song about "Inry the eighth"! (MN, 258) And the music-hall song is matched by those scenes of farce: the spooners discovered by the father (MN, 30-33); the Hogarth-like description of the choir (MN, 47-49); and the bedroom-farce, as Johanna's sister arrives unexpectedly, with its implicit reference to Feydeau (MN, 153-54).[101] There is also the Rabelaisian moment at the May fair, with its carnival grotesque caricatures, yet given its Lawrentian twist of the "old blood-association" (MN, 158). The idealization of an ancient Germanism will give way to the lighter gaiety of Italy later (until they discover the toilets! — cf. MN, 287). Indeed, the pattern of idealization followed by disappointment in Part II is another way of understanding the radical instability of the text.

These at least are some of the obvious comic and parodic scenes. However, what is still the most foregrounded device for destabilizing the text is the address to the reader. In fact, this is the place where Bakhtinian stylistics is most useful. For while we were able to get some way towards a sociological poetics in analysing the dialogic relationships of the speech genres in *Women in Love* and to a certain extent in *The Lost Girl*, here in *Mr Noon* considerations of addressivity, intonation and attitude should be focused on the different genres of narrator-address to the reader. It is sometimes comic (as in Fielding or Sterne); sometimes serious (as in the realists, George Eliot or Charlotte Brontë); sometimes even sentimental ("gentle reader"), although usually with lightly concealed malice. And there are those furious tirades against the reader: "But why the devil should I always *gentle-reader* you ... you sniffling mongrel bitch of a reader" (MN, 204-5; Lawrence's emphasis) — in a passage which predates Reader Response theory in a list of reader types to make the Konstanz School wince; but which is nevertheless — and joking aside — a serious gendering of the most detested of readers. Lawrence has finally brought his two obsessions together in the one persona: his turn against the reader and against women now becomes an assault on the female reader. Lawrence has reached the point in this novel where he wants to have power over the reader, to control the way she reads; and yet where the whole instability of the text works implicitly against it. The fixing of

---

[101] Georges Feydeau (1862-1921): popular French dramatist in the late nineteenth and early twentieth century of "bedroom farces" where bourgeois couples are surprised in compromising situations of adultery, with lots of hiding under beds and in cupboards — a more recent British version would be the Brian Rix stage farce.

authorial meaning in a monologic creed is challenged by the play of meaning and reference, as if Lawrence is saying: "Do not look in my novel for the old stable meaning of the text." Moreover, the assault of the male author on the female reader in 1920 is always a threat to the love-ethic that Lawrence is attempting at times to recapture in the nostalgia for the man in love in 1912.

In its belated publication, *Mr Noon* may have ushered in a period of reappraisal of Lawrence as a comic writer, so that we now look for the evidence in the other works retrospectively, accompanied by Bakhtin. But *Mr Noon* also — and significantly — marks the place where Lawrence works out a solution to his crisis; where he abandons many of his ideals first developed between 1912 and 1915: the revolt of women; consummate passion and the belief in sacred marriage; and also the great English novel with its lyrical and metaphysical writing. (He will revert to the novella form for his best writing in the 1920s, until he tries once more to write the English novel with *Lady Chatterley's Lover*.) Perhaps it was not only the crisis in his personal life which made him decide not to finish *Mr Noon*. For what we have in this text is Lawrence's carnival — a holiday from his serious writing project in which the author may permit himself to dress up in the sometimes grotesque masks of other author-personas, play the mimic on the page, dance with the style of the others, and indulge in the therapy of laughter. The novel probably had more point in its writing, that is the act of Lawrence writing it, than in its reading — and maybe he could not imagine it being read.

5. Conclusion

Bakhtin has enabled a more detailed, studied reading of Lawrence's comic writing. What has emerged most strikingly from the application of a Bakhtinian stylistics is the recognition of a satirical play on speech mannerisms, located in specific class and narrative contexts. Lawrence insists on the precise intonation of speech, the addressivity, and then the way in which the words and speech of characters are appropriated by others for purposes of mockery and ridicule, in a society that has resorted to cynicism. Indeed, cynicism is the style of interaction between the most modern selves, and is in fact a last resort for the self-conscious, over-intellectualized modern self. *Women in Love* is in many respects an indictment of cynicism.

But what also emerges in the Bakhtinian reading is the extent to which Lawrence turns that cynicism back onto himself, as philosopher and as writer. We now know, thanks to the work of the Cambridge University Press editors, much more about the contexts of Lawrence's writing. Dialogics is not just a matter of the contexts internal to the fiction — the stylistic and narrative frames for speech and action. It may also enable us to focus in significant detail on the historical and biographical frames which place the fiction in dialogue with its wider contexts. This is not to resort to an older, transparent relation between the life and works of the author. It is, rather, to go some way towards an appreciation of the complex, ironic relationships between the different modes and styles in which Lawrence, at a specific period of his writing-life, attempted to overcome a crisis, to find a direction. As I hope to have shown, the three novels discussed in this chapter record that self-questioning in their formal instability and in their stylistic play. A Bakhtinian critical approach seems most productive to the Lawrence of this period. Moreover, it draws attention to a different kind of Modernism to that of *The Rainbow*, thus challenging the monolithic understanding of Lawrence's relation to Modernism in the critical reception. I will discuss this further in the next chapter.

We may, though, legitimately ask whether Lawrence could ever really break away completely from the metaphysical and lyrical style that marked his best writing. Lawrence returns to writing more serious philosophical fiction in *Aaron's Rod*; yet the newer comic, parodic mode will never completely disappear, so that the more doctrinaire fiction of the 1920s will be framed in such disruptive strategies, as we shall see in the following two chapters.

Both *The Lost Girl* and *Mr Noon* were conscious attempts at popular serio-comic fiction, written rapidly, not worked on in the usual manner; and of course *Mr Noon* was abandoned as a two-thirds completed first draft. He wrote *The Lost Girl* in just eight weeks,[102] the revising of *Women in Love* for his American publisher fresh in mind. As I have been arguing, *The Lost Girl* is a kind of stocktaking in an attempt to find a new direction that would get more public recognition, and money. It seems, then, that it was these two novels which enabled Lawrence to work out a new direction for his writing. A Bakhtinian reading has brought out the detailed connections between Lawrence and comedy. However, the "male leadership" fiction, and *Lady Chatterley's Lover* require different approaches — as we shall see in the next three chapters.

---

[102] Kinkead-Weekes, 573.

4

Deconstructing Masculinity 1: The Crisis of Post-War Masculinity and the Modernism of *Aaron's Rod*

1. Introduction

In the next two chapters, I shall discuss Lawrence's "leadership" novels in the light of theories of masculinity. The consensus view that Lawrence promoted masculine supremacy in phallocentric and phallocratic fictions has been variously challenged in recent criticism by claiming that it is precisely here, in these novels of the 1920s, that Lawrence was at his most experimental, his most modernist. The masculinist doctrine undergoes degrees of deconstruction in fiction characterized by Lawrence as "thought-adventure".[1] The ideas expressed categorically in the essays are tested out in the fiction. However, there is a tendency now to go further than the author's own view by reading the adventure of thought as an adventure of writing, in which the theories of masculinity are promoted in texts which in their play of linguistic and representational codes implicitly question fixed meaning and grand narratives. In this and the following chapter, I shall argue that a deconstructive approach enables us to draw out the characterological and textual instabilities which function to undermine the doctrinaire assertions of male leadership. What is now becoming clearer in Lawrence studies today is that the post-war cultural crisis was also a crisis of the novel.

Yet nobody would deny that Lawrence turned more explicitly against women after the First World War. The essays, fiction, and letters from about 1918 are filled with what has often been called an "hysterical masculinity". What is now becoming clearer, though, is the extent to which the misogyny and the phallocratic beliefs of the post-war period are, first, emergent already in the earlier fiction, albeit in less strident form; and second, are not only Lawrence's personal philosophy but also part of a general post-war reaction against the extent of female emancipation; and third, they are represented in fictional texts characterized by degrees of formal instability. Lawrence's ongoing quest is not just philosophically utopic, and predominantly reactionary; it is also a formal

---

[1] *Kangaroo* (London: Penguin edition of the Cambridge D.H. Lawrence, 1997), 279.

enquiry into the future of the novel.[2]

In what follows, I shall discuss Lawrence's ideas for a "new masculinity" which emerged from the non-fiction writing in the 1920s, and then briefly place those ideas in the context of some of the major propositions from masculinity theory. This will be followed by a résumé of the general discussion on masculinities that has been taking place in recent Lawrence criticism. Then I will look in some detail at the three novels — *Aaron's Rod* in this chapter, *Kangaroo* and *The Plumed Serpent* in the next. Following the principle, consistent throughout this study, that Lawrence's writing only makes sense in the detail, I will look at the effects of dissemination and play, the textual instabilities which enable us to deconstruct the gender oppositions that attempt to establish a new masculine essentialism.

2. Lawrence's "new masculinity", masculinity theory and Modernism

McCracken, in a review of Balbert,[3] makes the general point that modern feminism "has challenged the way much of what was new in the 1920s has been institutionalized in post-war culture and social institutions". He then goes on to ask: "However, as debates have inevitably revolved around representations of femininity, might it not be time to reassess the historical changes in masculinity?" And in the light of Balbert's study (which is concerned about "feminist misreading"): "Could it be that Lawrence has been badly treated by today's feminists?" It is not the focus of my polemic to argue that feminism is wrong about Lawrence. There is not in any case a monolithic feminist theory. There are different feminisms with their own history and internal disputes. Lawrence, the man and the works, has been subject to one form of feminist critique or another throughout the history of reception. (I shall return to the feminist reception of Lawrence in chapter 6.) Like any strong ideological reading, the persona of the author or the texts of his writing become the exclusive object of criticism. In this precise sense, argued for since at least the mid-1960s in critical theory, all readings are to some extent partial truths or misreadings — including the ones in this study.

Masculinity theory begins by acknowledging its relationship to femi-

---

[2] In the essays "Surgery for the Novel — Or a Bomb" ("The Future of the Novel"); (1923) "Morality and the Novel", "The Novel", "The Novel and the Feelings", "Why the Novel Matters" (all written in 1925), Lawrence theorizes what he has learnt from experiments in his fiction-writing.
[3] Scott McCracken, "Blinded by Intense Revelation: Peter Balbert, *D.H. Lawrence and the Phallic Imagination: Essays on Sexual Identity and Feminist Misreading*" (London: Macmillan, 1989), in *Times Higher Education Supplement*, 11 May 1990.

nist theory. This is true in recent theory as it is in the debates of the early twentieth century in what is now designated as the broader area of gender studies. In the early period, the First World War is a watershed: traditional gender positions had been questioned in late Victorian and Edwardian England in favour of an emancipatory women's movement for which the war would be decisive in securing rights and more self-determination for women in politics, society, and sexuality. Women would henceforth be able to move out of the domestic sphere into the world of work.[4] It was not so much the efforts of the Suffragettes that secured these changes, as the necessities of war. Women did not make it to the trenches — it was still the male prerogative to die for King and Country. But they did help make the weapons of destruction in the munitions factories, just as they produced the food by working on the land. The transformation in roles reinscribed a gender coding in an uneven way. Traditional masculine codes of heroism and patriotism were still kept in place by the propaganda machine even while the feminine codes that supported such male heroism were being questioned. When the men who survived returned home after the war the restructured New Woman would only exacerbate a masculinity already confused by shell shock and a general disillusionment. What would it mean to be a man after 1918?

Lawrence, like many writers of his generation, registered these shifts in gender coding. Indeed, he was particularly sensitive to them because his main concern was the changing relationship between men and women. Before 1915, he supported wholeheartedly the "feminization" of the culture. After 1915, he began to propose a "new masculinity", a reassertion of degrees of patriarchy which by the end of the war took on more strident tones. The dates are crucial for an historical understanding of Lawrence because they coincide with dramatic shifts in the writing. After the banning of *The Rainbow* in 1915, and the "nightmare" of the war years (the basis of the chapter of that title in *Kangaroo*, which will be discussed in the next chapter), Lawrence's final version of what became *Women in Love* is in many respects the place where the problems of the new gender crisis were being worked out in fictional form. The effects on the style and narrative of the writing of this period (1917-1922) were discussed in the previous chapter, and theorized through Bakhtin. Lawrence is an interesting case for gender studies because, as Simpson pointed out, his writing career "spanned one of the most crucial periods in women's history", with its intense period of radical feminism up to 1914, and the anti-feminist reaction after 1918.

---

[4] For working-class women, though, only recently.

Simpson's study is exemplary not least because it goes beyond the sometimes narrow biographical interest of Lawrence studies by insisting on a broader historicist approach: "Lawrence's post-war paranoia was not merely personal, but shared with many men of his generation."[5] Furthermore, the sea change in sexual ideology was the more total in inverse proportion to the utter belief in the New Woman before the war, when Lawrence made the three most quoted categorical statements: "I shall do my work for women, better than the suffrage." "[*The Rainbow* is about] woman becoming individual, self-responsible, taking her own initiative." "[Men should] draw nearer to women, expose themselves to them, and be altered by them."[6] The early Lawrence spent a lot of time in the company of radical women; and, the extent to which his modern women friends and lovers were also his literary collaborators is now much clearer.[7] After the war, Lawrence registers that general reaction to feminism which took the form of a firm belief that the changes had gone too far. Women had become too idealistic, too wilful. They had succumbed to the general malaise of modernity in losing their "natural feminine instinct" through mechanical adherence to the latest chic behaviour. In terms of sexual politics, as recent feminist theory has so often argued, Lawrence is representative of the masculinist reaction of his day, striving to reassert itself at a time of post-war disillusionment and dislocation.

A good example of the new masculine anxiety is recalled by Lawrence in his late essay, "The Real Thing" (1929)[8]: "Perhaps the greatest revolution of modern times is the emancipation of women .... The fight was deeply bitter, and, it seems to me, it is won. It is even going beyond, and becoming a tyranny of women." (P, 196) The sexual revolution has gone too far. Men have become submissive to the demands of women. Men have lost faith in themselves. But this is not instinctive; it is willed, and therefore false. It began in worshipping and glorifying women (a cultural convention reinforced by literature and now by the new cinema). It has ended up in a period (the 1920s) "of the collapse of instinctive life-

---

[5] Hilary Simpson, *D.H. Lawrence and Feminism* (London: Croom Helm, 1982), 15.
[6] Letters to Sallie Hopkin 23 December 1912, Edward Garnett 22 April 1914, Arthur McLeod 2 June 1914, respectively. Cited in Simpson, 16.
[7] Cf. Simpson's last chapter. The collaboration was not changed by the war. *The Boy in the Bush* (1924) was a reworking of Mollie Skinner's text; and Lawrence had plans to write a novel with Mabel Dodge Luhan called "The Wilful Woman" (1922), a fragment of which is extant.
[8] Reprinted in *Phoenix: The Posthumous Papers of D.H. Lawrence* (London: Heinemann, 1936). All page references for this and other essays which appear in *Phoenix* are to this edition, and will be indicated in text [P].

assurance in men", so that sex has become "a great weapon and divider". The new freedom for women has led to a greater unfreedom. So man's old self needs to die and be reborn into a new instinctive masculinity, which, as the fiction of the 1920s shows, is in fact a very old, forgotten instinct. The "real thing" is to "feel right" by being "in touch with the vivid life of the cosmos" (P, 202).

This essay then, can be taken as a summary of Lawrence's most consistent principle: the instinctive is the natural, and any attempt to change instinct by thought is an aberration. The problem is that feminist thought, from its beginnings, has been arguing that the instinctive and the natural are cultural constructions. Lawrence's own rhetoric of the instinctual is no exception. It is a very specific cultural coding. For instance, he writes that modern woman is "always tense and strung-up" with "less peace, less of that lovely womanly peace that flows like a river, less of the lovely, flower-like repose of a happy woman" (P, 197).

Lawrence was not always so poetically sentimental. In 1918 he wrote in more categorical and programmatic terms to Katherine Mansfield:

> I do think a woman must yield some sort of precedence to a man, and he must take this precedence. I do think that men must go ahead absolutely in front of their women, without turning round to ask for permission or approval from their women. Consequently the women must follow as it were unquestioning.[9]

It is here, as Simpson rightly argued, that Lawrence's belief in the return to male superiority is first expressed. In the same year, 1918, he is writing the essays, "Education of the People", soon to be followed by "Democracy"(1919);[10] and, in 1921 *Fantasia of the Unconscious*, where he formulates in stark terms his critique of the ideals of liberal democracy, especially equality (seeing it as unnatural, and an attempt at the kind of mechanical process of standardization in modern industry and mass society), and the traditional role of motherhood in the upbringing of children which he accuses of destroying the child by "emotional and psychic provocation" (P, 621). Maternal love is now a specific target, driven no doubt by Lawrence's own case as represented in *Sons and Lovers*. The "deadly idealism" of idolizing the mother-child relationship has lead to "the grovelling degeneracy of Mariolatry!" Thus children should be removed from their mothers at the earliest age before any damage can be done. The denunciation of the *Magna Mater* was already

---

[9] 5 December 1918.
[10] Both not published until 1936.

evident in *Women in Love*. Lawrence continues to insist that women have this tendency to smother or dominate men as boys. They are "devouring mothers". These post-war essays are, in Simpson's words, "a violent and often sadistic attack on democracy and liberal idealism, in the ranting style that now begins to characterize Lawrence's writing".[11] It is with this attitude and in this tone that Lawrence insists on a new masculinity which will abolish the kinds of gender relatedness sought in *The Rainbow* and *Women in Love*. Henceforth there will be a return to the hierarchical order of Patriarchy, but not simply in the senses analysed by Millett in sexual politics. Lawrence's Patriarchy will be based on more ancient models close to the Old Testament Church Fathers, or a pre-Columbian "natural aristocracy", as Lawrence understood it. It would not be the last time in the twentieth century that, in the general chaos of post-war dislocation, masculinist mythic solutions will be found for the problems of political realities.

However, Lawrence was not exclusively anti-women. In his essay, "On Being a Man" (1923) he warns women to beware of the sons of women: "And oh women, beware the mother's boy!"[12] Such statements are more usual in the fiction — like in *Mr Noon* where Johanna complains about those mothers' darlings, "all Hamlets, obsessed by their mothers, and we're supposed to be all Ophelias, and go and drown ourselves" (MN, 124). But, of course, it is not a general denunciation of men, but of that type destroyed by the "devouring mother". Moreover, it is in this essay that Lawrence reiterates a general feeling that the war ruined manhood: "These are the heroes of the Great War. They went and fought like heroes, truly, to prove their manhood". But they did this from a wrong idea of manhood. Like "heroic automata", they understood themselves within the given masculine codes of heroism, unquestioningly believing they were making the world safe for democracy. They "never faced the strange war-passions that came up in themselves". They believed the world would be the same again. For Lawrence, the opportunity for a new world has been missed:

> Out of the strange passion that arose in men during the war, there should have risen the germ of a new idea, and the nucleus of a new way of feeling. Out of the strange revulsions of the days of horror, there should have resulted a fierce revision of existing val-ues ... and the fierce repudiation of false values should have rip-

---

[11] Simpson, 93.
[12] "On Being a Man" (1923) reprinted in *Reflections On the Death of a Porcupine and Other Essays* (1925), edited by Michael Herbert (Cambridge: Cambridge University Press, 1988), 216.

ened the seed of a whole new way of experience, the clue to a whole new era.[13]

This statement is crucial to the thematics of the post-war fiction with its quest for a new masculinity for a new spiritual age. Post-war man is disillusioned, disoriented, and deracinated. T.S. Eliot's "hollow man" wanders in the waste-land of post-war England. Lawrence will take himself and his fictional protagonists abroad in search of alternative cultural models of man. He will also experiment, at least in the fiction, with notions of political and spiritual leadership. By 1925 he will be able to declare that: "The reign of love is passing, and the reign of power is coming again."[14] But we should be clear about what Lawrence means by "power". He differentiates between "will" and "power". The Nietzschean "will-to-power", as Lawrence understands it, is just "bullying" — like the force imposed by the fascist dictator on the masses which Lawrence had witnessed in Italy, and which is emergent in *Aaron's Rod*. And this would be the same in principle for any dictatorial political leader where power is the imposition of an ideology through the will of the one charismatic person. As we shall see later in this and the following chapter, Lawrence works through the problems of power and leadership in *Aaron's Rod*, *Kangaroo* and *The Plumed Serpent*.

Power is beyond the egotistical will, it "comes to us ... from beyond". It cannot be grasped through "willing and intellectualizing", it is "self-generated". It comes from living, which consists in "doing what you really, vitally want to do: what the *life* in you wants to do, not what your ego imagines you want to do." But usually we cannot know this very easily. Somebody, presumably somebody who has "understood" this natural vitalistic inner power to live to the full, has to lead others towards feeling "the power of life" in themselves. Lawrence's theory of power derives from the idea of the charismatic leader common in political theories of the time[15] combined with the notion of a "natural aristocracy" of prophetic artists or writers, like himself, who would lead the people by example into an era of cultural regeneration. The political version of this is played out in *Kangaroo*, an Australian staging of the political theatre of 1920s Europe. The process of a cultural regeneration through spiritual

---

[13] "On Being a Man", 219, 221.
[14] "Blessed are the Powerful" in *Reflections on the Death of a Porcupine*, 321-23.
[15] For the sources of Lawrence's political ideas, see Rick Rylance, "Lawrence's Politics" in Keith Brown ed., *Rethinking Lawrence* (Buckingham: Open University Press, 1990); Peter Fjagesund, *The Apocalyptic World of D.H. Lawrence* (London and Oslo: Norwegian University Press, 1991); Anne Fernihough, *D.H. Lawrence: Aesthetics and Ideology* (Oxford: Clarendon Press, 1993).

Radicalizing Lawrence

revivalism is dramatized in *The Plumed Serpent*.

The theory of a natural, inner power (whose source is the Lawrentian "creative unconscious") is used by Lawrence to argue against the ideals of equality or equal opportunity so central to modern democracy: "In living life, we are all born with different powers, and different degrees of power: some higher, some lower." Power can be destructive and creative. But in Lawrence's sense, argued for in the essays, true power is always instinctive; and, by implication, when responsibly used is creative: it always "puts something new into the world"; it "calls love into being". [16] Lawrence's essay is an appeal in the form of a sermon on the mount: "Blessed are the … ". Furthermore, if the "reign of love" was the era of women (New Woman, devouring mother, *Magna Mater*), then the "powerful" who will regenerate the culture in the new "reign of power" are exclusively men. What Lawrence means by "love" here is the modern, self-conscious variety for which the new wilful women or domineering mothers have been responsible. In *Fantasia of the Unconscious* (1922) he blames the whole post-war cultural crisis on living "from the head" instead of "from the spontaneous centres" of the self. His solution to the crisis is quite explicit:

> We can't go on as we are. Poor, nerve-worn creatures, fretting our lives away and hating to die because we have never lived. The secret is to commit into the hands of the sacred few the responsibility which now lies like torture on the mass. Let the few leaders be increasingly responsible for the whole. [17]

In order to make it absolutely clear that these "few" are men, Lawrence resorts to a conservative theory of sexual difference, simplifying the work on male and female principles of the "Study of Thomas Hardy" (1914), along the lines: women are naturally passive, men active; women belong in the domestic sphere, men in the public sphere; women live by feeling, men by a sense of purpose; man is the great adventurer with the passion of collective purpose, etc. Lawrence's new masculinity is based on old gender stereotypes. Women are to blame for the discontents of civilization because they became more active in politics, in the job market, but worst of all in sex. [18]

The newer sex education and modern birth control, as Simpson explains, made women generally more aware of their bodies as a site of

---

[16] "Blessed are the Powerful", 327.
[17] *Fantasia of the Unconscious and Psychoanalysis and the Unconscious* (London: Penguin, 1971), 83, 88.
[18] *Fantasia*, 97, 102-3, 109-10.

pleasure. Modern sex was now for its own sake, not just for procreation. Women had more control over their sexuality. And we should remember that Lawrence was still challenging Victorian prudery and championing the New Woman in *The Rainbow*. Indeed, his whole writing life was devoted to that challenge, at least as it persisted in the forms of public censorship and hypocrisy. The new frankness about sex is part of the importance of Lawrence as a writer and as a force for cultural change. Therefore, it is even more important to understand the contexts, personal and general, for his post-war reactionary theories of gender difference. For even to the bitter end he was arguing against the work of such important campaigners for better sex education for women as Marie Stopes. In *Pornography and Obscenity* (1929), he wrote that, though "to be wise and scientific ... like Dr. Marie Stopes is better than to be utterly hypocritical, like the grey ones", her work is "idealist" and kills "dynamic sex altogether", leaving "only the scientific and deliberate mechanism" (P, 182). As Simpson points out, in the post-war reconstruction, feminism was reformist, progressivist and oriented towards health-care and welfare.[19] By the 1920s Stopes was advocating a more stringent birth-control in the form of artificial insemination to maintain the health of the nation. As we now know, proposing a welfare politics of eugenics became the dark side of health-care — racial purity had already been long in discussion, and would form the corner-stone of fascist thought. On this point Lawrence and Stopes were in agreement. It is in the fiction of the 1920s, contemporary with these discussions, that Lawrence takes the woman's question and the reaction to it in the form of the new masculinity on a series of "thought-adventures". What makes these works still interesting is the way they both assert and deconstruct the new masculinist doctrine.

At worst, the Lawrence after 1918 wants a woman who has learnt to "hold her tongue", accept her "pure femaleness", and have all that modern self-consciousness beaten out of her by her man, to make her yield "to her own real unconscious self ... make her yield once more to the male leadership".[20] Not unsurprisingly, the new masculinity will require a return to a submissive femininity — a male fantasy that deliberately works against the grain of the new feminism in the 1920s, and one that has been the target of feminist criticism ever since. The new masculinity will urge a phallocentricity ranging from the fertility and law-giving rituals of more ancient social formations in *The Plumed Serpent*, to the most explicit celebration of the sexual potency of man in

---

[19] Simpson, 101.

[20] *Fantasia*, 137, 188, 191.

Lady Chatterley's Lover. Women in the fiction will be expected to become the worshippers at the temple of the new phallus. Fortunately, Lawrence's women characters are not as one-dimensional as the doctrine demands, so that the "thought-adventures" of the 1920s discover different degrees of uncertainty in the doctrine which lead to the saving compromises and open-endedness of the fiction.

Middleton explains how men began to reflect on themselves as a gender, asking themselves and each other what it meant to be a man, after feminism had done a lot of work raising consciousness about gender difference. Men turned their gaze inward, and began questioning culturally-constructed images of masculinity, the process from boyhood to manhood, manliness, and their position of power, social expectations and conventional responsibilities. The danger in such self-reflexivity is that men might succumb to fantasies of "self-aggrandizement".[21] Literary Modernism was very preoccupied with the issues of masculine subjectivity, and in a more self-conscious way than popular culture at the time. Lawrence belongs to this moment in the early history of twentieth-century masculinity. For him, as for others of his generation, the "relation between subjectivity and power" was — as it still is — "difficult to articulate". Man only became consciously gendered once patriarchy was questioned as the dominant mode of socio-cultural formation. Rethinking "existing concepts of gender and identity in terms of the relations between society, reason and emotion" enables a theorizing of masculinity as a preliminary to cultural change.

The First World War was a focus for the crisis in masculinity. Traditional codes of heroism and cowardice, patriotism and sacrifice, violence and pacifism could no longer be taken for granted. On the Western Front the new war machine was a transpersonal instrument of mass destruction. At home the force of changing social and cultural values was partly the result of the women's movement. State propaganda was no longer going unquestioned. As Middleton puts it: "There are better ways to negotiate relations with other men than annihilating them and hoping that one's own vulnerability will triumph."[22]

Modernist writing represented a subjectivity at odds with itself. Sometimes the male case was meant to carry universal weight. Sometimes gender difference was explicit even when generalized as ontology.

---

[21] Peter Middleton, *The Inward Gaze: Masculinity and Subjectivity in Modern Culture* (London: Routledge, 1992), 9.
[22] Middleton, 10, 12-13, 42.

The Rainbow has often been analysed in these philosophical terms.[23] Middleton makes a case for this novel as "a text permeated with the same philosophical speculation out of which post-structuralism emerged". What he means by this is that *The Rainbow* represents a kind of late nineteenth-century Hegelianism which tries to relate the history of consciousness to the movements of history itself in a process of increasing enlightenment onto a higher plane of being; in short, the process of modernity itself. This history of consciousness is a gendered history, as the men characters struggle to form "an inward gaze", while the women characters from the outset cope better with the pressures of modern subjectivity. The portrait of Will Brangwen "is one of the first important analyses of modern masculine sexuality in English writing". [24] Traditional codes of manliness, virility and patriarchy are increasingly under threat in the novel from, in Lawrence's words, "woman becoming individual, self-responsible, taking her own initiative".[25] Anna's fight with and victory over Will, and Ursula's destruction of Skrebensky, just as Gudrun's battle for supremacy with Gerald in *Women in Love*, are all key instances of modern masculinities succumbing to the new, independent-minded woman. But the men are supposed to learn about their emotions and their sexuality from the women. Yet it seems that the men will not change that easily because the old masculine codes are deeply ingrained, and the pressures to be a man are sometimes overwhelming. Will, the craftsman, devotes himself to Gothic church art; Skrebensky, the army officer, marries the colonel's daughter and is posted to India; Gerald, the captain of industry, commits suicide. The more successfully "feminized" man, Birkin, already shows signs of the emergent new masculinity. First, he feels the need for a close relationship with a man — although the precise form that should take is left teasingly ambiguous — and he thus foreshadows the relationships between Lilly and Aaron, Cooley and Somers, and Ramon and Cipriano in the three 1920s novels. And, second, he reacts violently to the power of a woman's love, which he wants to destroy forever because it is so wilful and insistent. Birkin wants to get beyond the "messiness" of sex, into a more impersonal relationship; and in this he prefigures Aaron Sissons walking out of his marriage and trying to live without sex altogether.

    Middleton reminds us of Freud's work at the time of the First World War, analysing so much male violence and masculine death drives under

---

[23] Cf. Michael Bell, *D.H. Lawrence: Language and Being* (Cambridge: Cambridge University Press, 1991); Anne Fernihough (1993); Fiona Becket, *D.H. Lawrence: The Thinker as Poet* (London: Macmillan, 1997).

[24] Middleton, 68, 75.

[25] Letter to Edward Garnett 22 April 1914.

"the contemporary pressures to be a real man". The "rat man" case history is exemplary: "the rattiness of the patient is masculine violence"[26] which it becomes the aim of psychoanalysis to trap, if not to cure.[27] More significant for the development of boys is Freud's "*fort-da*" game which masculinity theory would reread as an example of training in good manliness: the little boy suppresses the tears for his absent mother by mastering the situation himself. Furthermore: "The "*fort-da*" game has the war as its subtext; war in which fathers leave sons behind ..., war which threatens little boys ... a threat they learn to master in play".[28] Boys learn early to control their emotions, to be tougher, and to play out their aggressivity in object relations. Emotional development may be impoverished by the conventional manliness instilled in boys. Male intimacy outside gay groups is a problem. It is one that first emerges in Lawrence's fiction in the Gerald-Birkin relationship: they only get close to intimate physical contact by staging a wrestling contest, albeit naked. In *Aaron's Rod*, Lilly massages Aaron's sick body, in a bolder moment of homoeroticism on Lawrence's part. Yet the role model is that of mothering the sick boy. Indeed, in that novel where the men try to go it alone without women, domesticity has only female models, and it is described as such in text as the men take it in turns to be mother.

It seems, then, that conventionally there have been only two kinds of close physical relationship for men to others: violence and sex. Men are highly competitive, derive their belief in supremacy from the dominant ideologies in patriarchal society, understand women as sexual objects or as threat, and are only just beginning to understand the importance of their own emotional conflicts thanks to the "men's movement". Historically, however, we are now more aware than ever of the lack of discussion about men's sexuality, "as opposed to the objects of their desire".[29] Lawrence has an interesting gloss on this history by having women characters as voyeurs admire male bodies. Linda Ruth Williams has rethought Lawrence through such gender terms, derived from recent film theory, about the psychology and politics of the male gaze.[30] The two

---

[26] Middleton, 84-85, 88.
[27] Psychoanalysis is a male institution whose reputation was founded on the analysis of female hysteria, yet had serious difficulties understanding female sexuality. It must have felt it had a better chance with male sexuality not least because its own theories originated in Freud's self-analysis. For masculinity theory, the problem here would be that Freud and his relationship to his own father was the model for a psychoanalytic theory of masculinity.
[28] Middleton, 91.
[29] Middleton, 126.
[30] Linda Ruth Williams, *Sex in the Head: Visions of Femininity and Film in D.H. Lawrence* (Hemel Hempstead: Harvester Wheatsheaf, 1993).

usual ways of explaining this are, first, [31] that Lawrence was a "closet-queen", implying a latent homosexuality — a claim made first by Murry;[32] or, second, that having women admire healthy male bodies is both a masculinist wish-fulfilment fantasy, and the deep (and sad) dream of an ill man. All these explanations are partially true.

What is clear is that concepts of masculinity are historically as well as culturally specific. Lawrence's writing in the period of Modernism coincides with key discussions on sexuality and gender difference in Freudian psychoanalysis, the sexual theories of Edward Carpenter and Havelock Ellis,[33] Marie Stopes' *Married Love* (1916), as well as the assault on Victorian taboos and prudery in literature.[34] Carpenter promoted a more open recognition of homosexuality, which in itself enabled the sexuality of women to emerge as a phenomenon and a discourse in its own right. Gender difference drew attention to the sexuality of men, but the discussion has taken long to emerge. Indeed, men developed a consciousness of their gender and sexuality because of the First World War, as the general transvaluation of values affected masculinity too. Lawrence's work clearly belongs to this discussion and the crisis in masculinity from which it came.

Lawrence's search for a new language to express feelings and sexuality, however, contrasted markedly with mainstream Modernism. T.S. Eliot founded a whole theory of literature on ways of containing emotions in an acceptably aesthetic form. If emotional outburst, like female sexuality, is dangerous then the "objective correlative" would textualize it in such a way that the reader or spectator could experience it impersonally — at a safe, aesthetic distance. Lawrence, of course, rejected Eliot's neo-classicism for expressive theories first developed by the Romantics. His representations of moments of emotional crisis are closer to the Symbolists, and sometimes to the Expressionists which both belong to the Romantic tradition of individual inner expressivity (as I argued in chapters 1 and 2). Lawrence's writing is by definition a locus for the expression of emotion, masculine or feminine, against the grain of

---

[31] Angela Carter, "Lorenzo the Closet-Queen" in *Nothing Sacred* (London: Virago, 1982).

[32] John Middleton Murry, *Son of Woman* (London: Jonathan Cape, 1931): "Lawrence's hatred of women" (43); "His loathing of women only grew with the years" (45); Lawrence's was "a hypersensitive masculinity" (73), and "it was inevitable that Lawrence should turn towards the possibility of a relation with a man." (119).

[33] Edward Carpenter, *Civilization, its Cause and Cure* (1889); Henry Havelock Ellis, *Studies in the Psychology of Sex, 7 volumes* (1897-1928, revised edition, 1936).

[34] For a well-informed study see Sally Ledger, *The New Woman: Fiction and Feminism at the Fin de Siècle* (Manchester: Manchester University Press, 1997).

the conventional gender designation of the emotional sphere as exclusively female. In *The Rainbow*, as Middleton shows, the principal male characters struggle to express their feelings, and need the female characters to help them do this. The public sphere is the place where men are least expected to be emotional, except in collective pride, or anger at injustice (the football match, of course, is the arena for collective male emotion). Emotions may thus be understood socially. They can be trans-individual articulations of grief or joy, anger or pride.

The novels of the "male leadership" period of Lawrence's writing career engage fully in the crisis of masculinity in the post-war world, telling stories of men questioning their lives with women, their sexuality, their sexual difference, in fiction where Lawrence tries to imagine masculinist alternatives to the cultural crisis. After they fail to go it alone, male characters tend to be involved in collective alternatives for men only — a political group planning to reassert itself on the public stage; or a religious movement planning a return to a more authoritarian ritual order.

These fictions are themselves stories men invent and tell each other. They are stories of quest, travel, adventure, leadership. They allow men to imagine a superior place for themselves at a time of crisis in masculinity. Moreover, they are ancient, traditional masculine narratives. As Ben Knights has argued, masculinity is more than gender difference, or male encoding; it is at the same time a way of telling stories.[35] Lawrence draws attention to narrative as a gendered construct. I will discuss later the effect of the gendered reader, positioned in narrative texts in ways that often frame the masculine story in irony. Lawrence thus problematizes the obvious claim that these "leadership novels" are nothing more than male fantasies against women by giving women a debunking role in a world of idealist men, or by positioning them as focalizers with mixed feelings about male supremacy. Ever since the banning of *The Rainbow* Lawrence had difficulty imagining a readership. The problem of reading and decoding (especially a foreign culture in the fiction and travel-writing of the 1920s) was addressed in his writing. At its worst, the reader is abused — as in *Mr Noon* where the reader is clearly female (as I argued in the previous chapter). At best, the narrative is focalized through a western woman, like Kate Leslie in *The Plumed Serpent* who tries to understand the contradictions of Mexico. The one novel where the woman's viewpoint is marginalized is *Aaron's Rod*. Aaron Sissons' attempt to live without women is represented at the narrative level by his

---

[35] Ben Knights, *Writing Masculinities: Male Narratives in Twentieth-Century Fiction* (London: Macmillan, 1999).

exclusive masculinist reading of the situation, often objectively and without moral scruples as he abandons his wife and children on Christmas Eve for an itinerant existence as a flute-player. Women readers find this difficult to accept, albeit brutally honest. *Aaron's Rod*, as masculine story certainly appeals to men more than women readers, a solidarity already represented in the degrees of male bonding in the text. However, as we shall see, we can read the text against itself by repositioning what is marginal, and allowing the women's voices in the text to undermine any doctrinal certainty.

Masculinity theory is more than a record of the images of men in literature and culture; it is about the gendering of representation itself. Moreover, as modernist writing turns back on itself and becomes self-questioning, so the masculine and the feminine are deconstructed by the texts that attempt to represent them. I approach Lawrence's fiction of the 1920s as examples of this process of self-questioning, in order to assess the extent of his critical stance towards the new masculinity which he promotes aggressively at the same time in his essays. A serious methodological point that arises from this approach is that we should be wary of reading the fiction exclusively through the essays. It might be more useful to read the essays from the critical perspectives of the fiction, and in the process find the grounds for an effective challenge to the early feminist attack, which begins with Murry's character assassination of Lawrence and reaches its high point with Millett. Although, as I hope to show in chapter 6, feminist criticism does not end there. It has had its own internal disputes out of which less reductionist appoaches have emerged. To quote Ben Knights once again:

> To set about re-writing male narratives was to risk rendering the whole subject unstable, so Lawrence's later programme was not simply a performance of a script supplied by his own neuroses, but a response to problems he had himself courageously opened up.[36]

In Lawrence's fiction, gender becomes mobile as the characters move out of the traditional feminine and masculine spheres of self-definition, and travel in search of new identity. The rooted Brangwen existence of the opening of *The Rainbow* will give way to deracination for which the restless women are initially responsible. Aaron Sissons, Rawdon Lilly, Lovatt Somers, and Kate Leslie — all as part-selves of a travelling author — are representations of the new mobile self in the writing of the 1920s.

---

[36] Knights, 84.

The first three characters are in flight from the feminized world of post-war England in search of a new masculinity. Kate is in flight from herself in a story which attempts to reverse the historical process of modernity and the feminization of culture. However, by imagining in *The Plumed Serpent* the consequences of a return to a pre-Columbian patriarchy, and filtering the story through the critical views of a modern woman, Lawrence draws attention to the constructedness of what is otherwise passed off as ur-instinctual. The female protagonist creates enough doubt through a modern disarming irony, to make the ground infirm on which the new patriarchal grand narrative is founded. In Lawrence's fiction, gender difference was being destabilized in a narrative Modernism that now requires careful understanding. The representation of masculinity and femininity in these novels undermines the reductionism of subsequent ideologically-narrow criticism. It seems now, from a post-structuralist perspective, that the fiction is characterized by an undecidability.

3. Masculinity in Lawrence criticism
Linda Ruth Williams has drawn attention to the fact that it is only recently that criticism has started investigating Lawrence's relationship to masculinity.[37] Whereas the representation of women was the focus of the Lawrence criticism of the 1970s and 1980s — the decades dominated by feminism — the 1990s has seen a shift in interest towards Lawrence's representation of men and male fantasies. This is certainly the case in Williams (1993, 1997), Middleton (1992), and Knights (1999).[38] Williams' claim is not strictly true however because, as all these studies demonstrate, masculinity is a focus that was emergent already during the decades of feminist criticism, and indeed derives from it. The seminal study that most subsequent ones rely on is Simpson (1982). As I argued above, she is exemplary in demonstrating the importance of an historicist approach which sees the shifts in Lawrence's *oeuvre* in conjunction with broader historical shifts in reactions to the women's movement in the early twentieth century. As Simpson puts it: "One of Lawrence's foremost concerns in the later work is to extend the range of what is commonly understood as masculinity ... to represent the full complexity of maleness."[39]

I think a more accurate account of gender difference and sexual

---

[37] Linda Ruth Williams, *D.H. Lawrence* (Plymouth: Northcote House Publishers, 1997), especially chapter 3.
[38] Although these last two only write about Lawrence in general books on masculinity, literature and culture.
[39] Simpson, 128.

politics in Lawrence studies would need to go back to Murry to trace the origins of a whole mythology of Lawrence as a "repressed homosexual" and "hater of women". Challenged by Carswell, but "confirmed" by Frieda, the polarization of views about the man has tended to influence the reading of the works in a reductive way. Those who engage in speculations about the man tend to go back even further to the memoirs of the women in Lawrence's life, like Jessie Chambers, for confirmation of his attitudes to gender, even in the early years.[40] A more recent version of this is Ruderman who focuses on Lawrence's "obsessional fixation with the Mother, and his fictional and real attempts to overcome it". She argues that Lawrence did not turn against women only in the 1920s, and that the "leadership novels" demonstrate a continuity, because in them there is evidence of "unresolved pre-oedipal conflicts" in the advocacy of male superiority, an assertion of masculinity against the figures of the "devouring mother" and the "superior, arrogant females".[41] Indeed, "one can trace a direct path from *The Lost Girl*, which depicts the invidious role of the *Magna Mater*, to *The Plumed Serpent*, which restores the *Pater Magnus* to his rightful throne."[42] The smothering and destructive mother-figure in *Sons and Lovers* is challenged by the male "dark god" of the later novels. But the question still remains: can a man have the love of a woman which is not of the destructive mother-love type? Carlotta in *The Plumed Serpent*, and Mrs Bolton in *Lady Chatterley's Lover* are examples in the later fiction. Ruderman reminds us of Lawrence's comment, when discussing Hawthorne in the earlier version of *Studies in Classic American Literature* (1923), "when woman is the leader or dominant in the sex relationship, and in the human progress, then the activity of mankind is an activity of disintegration and undoing". Ruderman rejects the commonly held view that this attitude to women is abandoned in *Lady Chatterley's Lover*. Connie submits to the sexually superior male, Mellors, and is purged of her modern woman self: "an undertone of misogyny exists ... undercutting the prophet's message". Being broadly part of the feminist reception of Lawrence, then, this critical approach has its origins in the early polemic about Lawrence's diatribe against domineering modern women.[43]

Balbert belongs to the anti-feminist camp, redeploying the hysteria of

---

[40] "E.T." (Jessie Chambers), *D.H. Lawrence: A Personal Record*; John Worthen, *D.H. Lawrence: The Early Years* (Cambridge: Cambridge University Press, 1991).
[41] Judith Ruderman, *D.H. Lawrence and the Devouring Mother: The Search for a Patriarchal Ideal of Leadership* (Durham, N.C.: Duke University Press, 1984), 6-7, 14.
[42] Ruderman, 36.
[43] Ruderman, 131, 164.

Lawrence's own post-war reaction to women. Bell, in an otherwise excellent study of the ontological questions in the fiction, simply writes off feminism as having no serious bearing on Lawrence studies. In an earlier paper, Blanchard[44] challenges the Millett-influenced feminist attack, claiming that Lawrence was not advocating male dominance in the fiction, but examining why women and men dominate one another, and the consequences when they do. Spilka[45] describes the transformation from the earlier fiction where wilful men are broken by stronger women who are the emotional leaders, to the later fiction where wilful women are made to submit to the new male phallic leaders. The novella, "The Fox" is for him the turning point. Dix[46] has a less helpful defence of Lawrence. She believes Lawrence was right about women, especially in *The Rainbow*, and that the leadership phase was only a digression. Ellis argues that many of the basic ideas are there from the start in Lawrence, only they receive different emphases at different times. In the 1920s, however, Lawrence had become "fundamentally conservative on women's issues".[47]

Fjagesund is a useful background source for Lawrence's political ideas, especially what he learnt from contemporary German and Italian Right Wing political thought. Crucial here, for example, is the masculine utopianism of the "*Männerbund*" with its call for a charismatic leader, and for the exclusion of women. In "Education of the People" (1918) Lawrence wrote: "And between men let there be a new, spontaneous relationship, a new fidelity …. in these womenless regions …. Let there be again the old passion of deathless friendship between man and man." (P, 665) These thoughts are put to the test in the novels of the 1920s. Fernihough also engages with the ideological coordinates of Lawrence's thought, his organicism and his relationship to fascism; but to Freud as well, and to Heidegger's philosophy of being — in common with Bell and Becket.[48]

The problem with this critical reception is a general absence of any thoroughgoing discussion of the deconstructive strategies at play in the fiction. However, there have been signs recently of a change in approach. I shall investigate in some detail in this chapter and the next, how each of

---

[44] Lydia Blanchard, "Love and Power: A Reconsideration of Sexual Politics in D.H. Lawrence", *Modern Fiction Studies*, 12 (1975), 431-443.
[45] Mark Spilka, "On Lawrence's Hostility to Wilful Women: The Chatterley Solution" in Anne Smith ed., *Lawrence and Women* (London: Vision Press, 1978).
[46] Carol Dix, *D.H. Lawrence and Women* (London: Macmillan, 1980).
[47] David Ellis, *D.H. Lawrence: Dying Game 1922-1930* (Cambridge: Cambridge University Press, 1998), 430.
[48] Anne Fernihough (1993), Michael Bell (1991), Fiona Becket (1997).

the three novels might be better read by drawing out the contradictions and the instabilities of writing. Thus I might effectively challenge the consensus whose readings of the works as doctrinaire seemed to have been so settled that the novels could be relegated to the status of minor fiction or digression.

4 *Aaron's Rod*: the deconstruction of gender coding

i. Critical reception

Aaron's Rod (1922)[49] is the exemplary story of early post-war masculinity. However, like the other "leadership novels" it has had a mixed reception. Tristram[50] has suggested that it is "more satisfying" than a novel like *Women in Love* because the central protagonist walks out of a marriage in a symptomatic defiance of the Lawrentian structure of male-female polarization and, refusing the gender codes of the traditional novel, undergoes a struggle with his single self against the pressures of the wider social world. At a time when the novel had already received a poor press, Murry also found it more than satisfying. Indeed, he felt it was Lawrence's best novel as it confirmed the truth of the ideas in the *Fantasia*. "Satisfying" appears to be an ethical judgment: Lawrence was being "honest" about himself. For Murry all the rest of the *oeuvre* was a tissue of lies covering up the author's repressed homosexuality and his hatred of women. I would add that, since the belated publication of the suppressed Prologue to *Women in Love*, speculations about the author's sexual orientation have gone beyond prejudice, and as Lawrence himself commented that *Aaron* was the last of a trilogy of "serious English novels" which included *The Rainbow* and *Women in Love*,[51] it would not be implausible to read *Aaron* as a working through of Birkin's belief that he wants a man friend. Indeed, the novel concentrates almost exclusively on the idea of men trying to live without women; although same-sex love is not explicitly treated. The whole homosexual question is left undecided — despite Murry's claims.

Kermode reads *Aaron* as the first expression of the male-leadership principle, of Lawrence as the prophet of cultural degeneration. It is thus a truly post-war fiction: "The world is like a shell-shocked soldier."[52] Aaron, the new man, refuses to worship a woman, and needs to submit

---

[49] All references in text [AR] are to the Penguin edition of the Cambridge D.H. Lawrence (London, 1995).
[50] Tristram, "Eros and Death: Lawrence, Freud and Women" in Anne Smith (1978).
[51] *The Letters of D.H. Lawrence, Volume IV*, compiled and edited by George J. Zytaruk and James T. Boulton (Cambridge: Cambridge University Press, 1987), 92-3.
[52] Frank Kermode, *Lawrence* (Glasgow: Fontana, 1973), 78.

himself to the influence of a charismatic man to give a new and
meaningful direction to his life. His flute-playing is a solace and also "an
emblem of male creativity". The new message is that men should keep to
themselves and not give themselves away to women. Kermode diagnoses
a hardening of the metaphysic. Whereas *The Rainbow* is seen now as
proposing a false optimism, and *Women in Love* a false apocalypse,
Aaron's Rod more forcefully expresses the gender crisis as the location of
cultural degeneration in terms of "male potency and separateness, the
distrust of love because women and mothers could control and own it,
requiring male surrender". You could not fault this description. The only
problem with Kermode's reading is that he insists the ideas are expressed
"with complete indifference to the form of the novel".[53] As we shall see
shortly, it is a view that has recently been challenged.

Pinkney reads the novel as a particular kind of Lawrentian allegory,
tending towards reworking the Moses/Aaron story, but which is spoilt by
its "dreary metaphysical tirades" in a narrative that threatens to collapse
into nihilism. It is the structure of the "male pseudo-couple" (Aaron and
Lilly) that keeps it going. The sense of modern vacuity reinforces the
general bleakness of a historical crisis. The problem of sexual relations
can be seen as "a code for the study of an entire new culture", although
taking the diagnosis seriously is made difficult by the very "absurdity" of
the "equations of female sexuality and male disaster".[54]

Fjagesund goes further than Kermode in finding the novel ultimately
disappointing. Bell, by taking *The Rainbow* as the measure of the
Lawrentian novel, reads *Aaron's Rod* as the first of the texts that takes
apart the "elements comprising the classic Lawrencean novel",[55] a
process begun in *Women in Love*. Dix[56] sees the phase begun with
Aaron's Rod as a digression on the theme of manliness before Lawrence
returns to his main project with *Lady Chatterley's Lover*. F.R. Leavis
declared that *Aaron's Rod* was "full of life and interest", but along with
Kangaroo and *The Plumed Serpent* were "very much open to criticism as
novels and works of art". Leavis does concede that they are "exploratory
and experimental", but refuses to elaborate, the silence judging them as
beneath serious consideration.

Not all criticism has been so condemning. There has also been a
serious consideration of the writing itself, the generic and narrative
issues, so that it has been raised from minor status or digression to a

[53] Kermode, 80-81.
[54] Tony Pinkney, *D.H. Lawrence* (Hemel Hempstead: Harvester Wheatsheaf, 1990),
111.
[55] Bell, 145.
[56] Dix (1980).

further example of that modernist experiment begun in *Women in Love* and carried on through *The Lost Girl* and *Mr Noon*, which was discussed in the previous chapter. Barr[57] began the reassessment with a direct critique of Kermode whose judgment of the formlessness of *Aaron's Rod* may now be understood as deriving from false expectations. It has indeed been quite common in Lawrence criticism to judge one novel in the terms of another in the Lawrence canon. Early critics found the work after *Sons and Lovers* disappointing or incomprehensible. They felt Lawrence's strengths lay in those home-life scenes derived from his working-class experience. Indeed, some condemned the second part of that novel as incoherent. Its coherence was, of course, based on different formal and philosophical premises. For the early critics, the idea of the novel was narrowly defined by the new realism of the *English Review* (edited by Ford Maddox Hueffer) and the influential editor Edward Garnett. Once *The Rainbow* and *Women in Love* had begun to get their reception, after the Second World War, critics made these novels central to Lawrence's achievement as the consensus became more sympathetic to Modernism. More recently, a greater openness to reading, encouraged by the plurality of critical approaches, and in particular by the post-structuralist notion of the text, has lead to a re-reading of novels like *Aaron's Rod*, *Kangaroo*, and *The Plumed Serpent* as a search for new modes of writing the crisis in gender. This work has been assisted by the details that have emerged, in the volumes of the Cambridge biography and the letters, about Lawrence's travelling in the 1920s — not just as physical journeys, but as the quest for new locations of writing, and the mapping of new territories for cultural and individual regeneration.

Aaron's Rod should now be read as a sequel to *Women in Love*, and which, in its generic destabilization, belongs to that phase of self-conscious burlesquing best exemplified in *Mr Noon* (as I argued in the previous chapter). Continuing in the satiric vein, Lawrence appropriately turns to the *picaresque* genre in *Aaron's Rod*. Barr first drew attention to the genre shift, enabling a re-reading of what previous critics had understood as formlessness or chaos, or what Eagleton called "the radical rupturing and diffusion of literary form".[58] Once the *picaresque* form is recognized, the reader has different expectations. It is the genre that best represents the chaotic and debilitated post-war Europe, as the *picaro* travels abroad and is subject to chance encounters, enabling a satirical panorama of absurdities (seen especially in the social gatherings of the

---

[57] William R. Barr (1976), "*Aaron's Rod* as D.H. Lawrence's *Picaresque* Novel", in David Ellis & Ornella De Zordo, *D.H. Lawrence: Critical Assessments Volume II* (Mountfield: Helm Information Ltd., 1992).
[58] Terry Eagleton, *Criticism and Ideology* (London: Verso, 1976), 160.

expatriate community in Italy). In Barr's words:

> The social apparatus of this chaotic world is unstable; held to-
> gether by make-up, alcohol, shreds of manners, and cant, it erupts
> repeatedly in violence .... Some episodes are connected only ar-
> bitrarily by the resurrected clichés of nineteenth-century popular
> fiction. "Our story ... ". (Barr, 452)

In this reading, the chaos of the novel is not its fault but a defining
characteristic of the genre it parodies. Aaron is detached and mobile
enough to act as the objective satiric perspective; while, in a modern
variation of the *picaresque* tradition, he is often at the mercy of the
generosity of those who are the focus of the satire — as Lawrence
himself was for so many years. Aaron's desire to remain an outsider is
compounded by his need for charity, and by his sexual desires (despite
his avowed intention to do without women and sex altogether). The
inescapability of the social and the sexual as necessities continually
undermine the new philosophy of "going it alone". We are faced with
Aaron's failure on a number of levels, yet we do not identify with him
because of the presence of a detached, self-observing narrator who "calls
attention to the novel-as-fiction", (Barr, 456) just as much as the
picaresque form underlines the precariousness of the new masculinity.
Through this approach we can see that Lawrence is exploring new modes
of writing, and just as Aaron's new understanding of himself is representative of the need for mobility in gender codes, so the novel requires a
new mobility in literary codes.

Baker[59] focuses on the significance of the stylistic device of distancing which reinforces Aaron's attempts to withdraw more from the world.
It is a "stubborn withdrawal" that represents Aaron's "misanthropic
resistance to all commitment or responsibility", and which is a single
case of the greater "malaise infecting an entire society". The effect of
distancing draws attention to Aaron as outsider, and even in the love-
making scene with the Marchesa we are given to imagine Aaron
watching himself, as if at one remove. Earlier in the novel he returns
home to see the family he has abandoned. This he does from the outside
(through the window), thus making it difficult for the reader to engage in
the conventional sympathy with the central protagonist, through a kind of
proto-Brechtian alienation-effect. And the narrator, through detachment
and playfulness, creates an internal distance in the text from the serious

---

[59] Paul G. Baker, "Profile of an Anti-Hero: Aaron Sissons Reconsidered", reprinted in
Ellis and De Zordo (1992), Volume II.

Lawrentian ideas that are circulating within it. Baker concludes that *Aaron* created Lawrence's "bleakest portrait of the deracinated individual's uncertain struggle for self-possession amidst a world of fragments".[60]

Worthen, drawing on the newer textual research in which he has had a leading role, has shown that the novel's fragmentary or directionless sense was largely the result of the cuts made by the first editors. Lawrence had become less tolerant about editorial interference, as the tone of *Mr Noon* makes clear. In *Aaron* he wrote much more explicitly about sex for the first time. Yet these were the passages removed by the editor, and not reinstated until the publication in 1988 of the full unexpurgated text. Since then it has become clearer that Lawrence was trying to show the power women can have over men through sex. In trying to live without women, Aaron realizes he has to do without sex; but he cannot. The result is "intensely misogynistic", and one which hovers on the edge of implausibility and unacceptability because it challenges traditional family values as well as gender codes. However, the extant text before 1988 gave the impression of a vagueness and a lack of direction which critics blamed more on the author than his central protagonist. The passages of explicit sex that were cut were, as we can now see, absolutely central: "Aaron's particular state of awareness of women's power as a potential threat to him makes it important that his sexual relationships with them be explored in whatever detail is necessary".[61] It is, of course, an exclusively masculinist view of sex; and a particularly cool and detached one too. In fact, *Aaron* represents the direction of Lawrence's post-war thinking about sex and gender, a thinking that has come a long way from the insistence on consummate marriage explored in the "Study of Thomas Hardy" and *The Rainbow*. Moreover, by displacing marriage from its central position in the English novel, Lawrence is extending his enquiry into the future of the novel into broader generic considerations.

For Hyde, *Aaron* — as a sequel to *The Lost Girl* and *Mr Noon* — is "not just Midlands domesticity that must be outwitted, but the power of the female as such". He rightly links the gender problematic to the problematics of writing:

> Linking fantasies of male self-sufficiency with new kinds of writerly freedom from narrative "Law", Lawrence has produced ... a heady synthesis of satirical fiction and the contingencies of

---

[60] Baker, 459, 466.
[61] John Worthen, *D.H. Lawrence* (London: Arnold, 1991), 71.

travelogue, infusing the whole so deeply with fear and suspicion of women that in places it starts to look like the sort of "gay" novel that *Women in Love* ... might have become. [62]

The satire, the mockery and the distancing effects in the narrative are symptoms of a depressive view of the state of things. However, any "totalizing vision" or "authoritative statement" is postponed, despite the "fierce polemic" (Hyde, 95). The subtleties and ironies undercut the claims for male power. I shall look at this in more detail shortly.

Virginia Hyde[63] explains how the allegorical sub-structure derives from Biblical analogies, so that the spiritual quest for the new Patriarchy should be understood in the context of the Old Testament lawgivers. This quest goes beyond the coincidences and satire of the *picaresque* into an adamic fable of transformation and rebirth. But we might add that Aaron hardly succeeds in a quest which begins only instinctually, and needs Lilly to lead him in the right direction. He does not though remain committed to Lilly, his new male leader. Leadership, in any case, is off to a poor start framed as it is in the ironies and textual instabilities of the novel.

Steven Vine reminds us that the novel's formal and thematic problematics reflect its own long process of coming into being (written over several years, off and on, from November 1917 until May 1921), in the generic instability and in Aaron's ontological quest. [64] It is, therefore, a truly post-war fiction reflecting the collapse of a culture and its grand narratives. Its "subversive energies" have largely gone unnoticed in the history of reception, I would insist, because the dominant critical assumptions and values — some of which still persist today — have disarmed the reading of the text.

ii. *Aaron's Rod*

The opening of the novel is a kind of overture; and the music analogy will recur throughout the text as a *leitmotif*, sometimes for the flute-playing as an ethical gesture, sometimes as a commentary on modern music, and other times as a symbol for rebirth as, Pan-like, Aaron imagines a future where he will "blossom" again, or when he assists the "flowering" of the Marchesa. Once in Italy, the action hovers on the edge of the *opera buffa* with its plot of the adulterous wife, the younger music

---

[62] G.M. Hyde, *D.H. Lawrence* (London: Macmillan, 1990), 92.

[63] Virginia Hyde, "*Aaron's Rod*: D.H. Lawrence's Revisionist Typology", reprinted in Ellis and De Zordo (1992), Volume II.

[64] In a useful introduction to the Penguin (1995) edition of the Cambridge D.H. Lawrence, xvii.

teacher, and the cuckolded husband; and, as Hyde points out, "punctuated by comic opera fantasies of the Italian peasants rising and dispossessing them (the ruling élite) of their splendid home".[65] In a masculinist story which tries to insist that men should break away from women and sex once and for all, the erotic is never far from the aesthetic.

The opening movement, then, rehearses the motifs that will recur and develop in the text, in what is a rewriting of the classic Lawrentian novel. We are back in the familiar Midlands location, but Lawrence makes it strange. The domestic scene reminds us of the home-life scenes in the mining community that patrician, early critics valued so much. But, through Aaron, we are presented with a perspective which represents the new post-war masculinity — detached, and disillusioned. The two daughters are aggressive and selfish, the wife nagging. She disparages the political activity of men (Aaron is the local secretary of the Miners Union). The war is over but nothing has changed — a recurrent theme represented by the war-destroyed men, the wilful women, the expatriates who behave as if nothing has happened, and the threat of further hostilities as, in Italy, the Left and the Right square up to each other in the street. Aaron, however, has changed. At least, his perspective, characterized as it is by the refusal of "the unspeakably familiar" (AR, 11), is symptomatic of a post-war depression with the state of things. His therapy is flute playing. In the quiet moments alone with his simple music he can "find himself" (AR, 8). He produces the delicate sound of a much older music from the sixteenth century; and one that will always save him for a moment from the warring thoughts on his mind. Moreover, much will depend on his psychology: the new masculinity is at first a negative state of mind; and the novel will struggle to turn it even into a negative dialectic. The next stage of the journey will have to wait for the masculine politics of *Kangaroo*. What is implied by the distanced and critical narrative perspective is made explicit: "He never went with the stream, but made a side current of his own." (AR, 14)

The rejection of the love of the family is a prelude to the general turn against women. Aaron is repulsed by the "neurasthenic" excitement which translates into the "desperate and savage" hostility of the last-minute Christmas shoppers (AR, 15). Once in the company of men, in the Royal Oak, Aaron's views are sharpened: "Bah! The love game! A wave of revulsion lifted him" (AR, 23). His depression turns to an anger directed at mankind in general, and the false goodwill and materialism at a time of scarcity. But there will be no political solution yet. The Hindu doctor is given to utter a different philosophy which goes beyond politics

---

[65] G.M. Hyde, 95.

and culture to a more "elemental difference", and one which would call into existence "individual responsibility" (AR, 24). But Lawrence's protagonist is not ready to listen to the "dark god" in him. He will require another teacher to lead him into the era of male power — which for Lawrence meant the empowerment of the individual man to live from his spontaneous centres.

The new, self-aware woman has become dominant. The psychically-damaged post-war man has to find himself again. He can only do this alone. This is the story of *Aaron*, and it is a man's story. Indeed, the dominant male perspective is reinforced at the narrative level with Aaron as focalizer. As Knights has argued, we need to look more closely at the way stories are gendered even in their narrative structures.[66] Lawrence's "thought-adventure" follows the premises of his diagnosis of the state of post-war culture, and his call for a new masculinity. Aaron abandons wife and children without moral scruples. In London he has an affair with a New Woman and claims his illness is a direct result of his giving himself completely to her. He is mothered back to health — his body is massaged back to life by a man, in an implicitly homoerotic moment; and he is convinced for a while that the future is with his new male friend, Lilly. In Italy, sex with the Marchesa is the last straw as it takes away too much of himself. The other men he meets engage in discussion about the state of things, and the need to learn to be alone and be responsible for your self, as women have shown that they cannot help anymore because they only want to dominate their men, or smother them in love.

The male version of the story of motherly, female love is countered at another level by the *picaresque* and the quest. They are both male narratives, which although characterized by the structure of the journey derive from quite different literary traditions — the first being comic-satirical, the second serious with its modern version of a psychological exploration into the self. Both share the structure of travelling to the unknown, and of chance encounters. The *picaro*, however, is often a victim of circumstances in his quasi-aimless wanderings; the quester has a clearly defined goal, and has to prove his manliness by achieving that goal. The *picaresque* originated as an anti-Chivalric, debunking genre, deconstructing the codes of heroism and honour. Lawrence reworks these contradictory sub-genres in pastiche form. They are brought into play to displace the realism with which the text opens. The closure in marriage which attempts to resolve the contradictions of so many nineteenth-century novels is thus rejected from the beginning; and on this level — generic and thematic at the same time — Lawrence sends out signals to

---

[66] Knights (1999).

the attentive reader, warning her that *Aaron* may be more than simply a diatribe on sexual politics.

Other subgenres come and go in the text. There are passages of travel-writing (more prominent in Lawrence in the 1920s, and a male prerogative). Then there is the popular novel of adultery and its comic opera variety, with the implication that it appeals to women, like its romance variety of the handsome young stranger who rejuvenates the older woman. There are passages of the comic fiction in the English tradition first parodied in *Mr Noon*, with a narrator interrupting the story with meta-narrative asides, and with the satire and burlesquing mimicry which Lawrence could do so well (as described in the previous chapter). And there is the *"Zivilisationskritik"* of chapter XIII with its German title (*"Wie es Ihnen Gefällt"*), encouraging us to think of Shakespeare (*As You Like It*), as the comic play of masks frames the serious discussion of the state of civilization. Also, there is the melodrama and sensation of popular political drama with its scenes of violent confrontation and an anarchist's bomb exploding in a café. And the other male stories of war, now in its modern variety of horror instead of heroism, and told obsessively by the veteran, the war-affected Captain Herbertson, to the other men.

Aaron is a text of gendered stories; and the masculine stories are given precedence over the feminine ones. It is also, though, a text about readers and reading. As we have already seen, it is Aaron's reading of the domestic and local situation that dominates the opening of the novel. It would be very different if the story was exclusively told from the wife's point of view. Aaron is also a decoder of other social classes and cultures. We see the traditional codes of Christmas through his estranging, anti-idealist reading. After he has left his family, we watch his wife doing her housework through him, outside secretly watching. At the opera, we get Aaron's view of the unreality of other people. He has to learn to read the world through Jim who wants to drink with the men alone, and "damn the women" (AR, 55). Or, at other moments in the text, we look at the world through Lilly's ideology (transposing the material from Lawrence's essays) which is summed up in the prohibition: "don't fling yourself all loose into a woman's lap ... Learn to be by yourself" (AR, 81) — which seems to coincide with Aaron's simple wish "to be left alone" (AR, 68). Yet, not only does he fail to be left alone, he also later rejects Lilly as mentor but without a viable alternative except travelling further afield. Aaron's reading sometimes turns out to be misreading. We enter the expatriate society through Aaron, reading it through a distancing satire; and we have to decode the strange, unexpected events of the "*XX Settembre*" public holiday through his bewildered eyes. But even though dominant, Aaron's readings are not exclusive. For instance, when he is ill we see him through Lilly.

The principal discussion about the state of the culture is predominantly carried on between the men. They are not necessarily reliable, being war-weary and women-weary. They are the new hysterics, as if they have lost their manliness through the war and taken on all the symptoms of women first analysed by Breuer and Freud.[67] Jim eats bread in excess to calm his stomach nerves, wants only to be with men, and can be unpredictably violent — he punches Lilly in the stomach, apparently because he believes that violence leads to connection (a notion learnt in the war, and a symptom of his solipsism). Despite fearing and despising women he spends his time "philandering and weeping" (AR, 74) while he waits for the next cataclysm. It is Lilly who detects in Jim "the sort of maudlin deliberateness which goes with hysterics" (AR, 83). His case may be an example of shell shock. But Aaron's is more puzzling. His own reasons for walking away from his family responsibilities — to lose himself, to be able to breathe better, not to be forced to care when it is not genuine, to get away from the stifling love of a woman, and simply to be left alone — are symptoms of his depression. His state is meant to be caused by "the violence of the nightmare released now into the general air" (AR, 5). In other words, his condition represents the general state of post-war culture.

Lawrence's critique of a disillusioned manhood is part of the general discontent prefigured in the worsening industrial relations in the coal-mining region of the Midlands. The miners want the pits nationalized to guarantee investment, wages and job security. Feelings are running high. However, talk about the current issues is positioned in the higher-class view of a woman, Josephine Ford, who romanticizes the pit (AR, 30), and is excited about the prospect of bloody revolution (AR, 60). Here the other women join in what is presented as silly, chic, idle talk by bored women. It is left to Robert, the young army officer to offer a more cautious view: "don't you think we've had enough of that sort of thing in the war?" The whole scene, just like the one at the opera house before it, is a relocating of the "Breadalby" talk from *Women in Love* into the post-war world. But as the text so often insists, nothing has changed; although this truth now applies exclusively to the women. Josephine seems to be an amalgam of Hermione and Gudrun from the earlier novel. She is Gudrun when she wilfully seduces and nearly destroys Aaron. However, at these moments, the narrator and the protagonist collude in masculinist fictions about women which are hardly disinterested.

Aaron needs Lilly's protection from Josephine. Fearing women is the

---

[67] Joseph Breuer and Sigmund Freud, *Studies in Hysteria* (1895).

next stage for a masculinity overwhelmed by mother-love. Sex with women can now make you ill! As Aaron explains to Lilly: "It's my own fault, for giving in to her. If I'd kept myself back, my liver would not have broken inside me, and I shouldn't have been sick." (AR, 90) Such talk when taken outside the context of Lawrence's *Fantasia* is, of course, absurd. There Lawrence complains of "this infernal self-conscious Madonna starving our living guts and bullying us to death with her love". And as "the first seat of our primal consciousness is the solar plexus, the great nerve centre situated behind the stomach", [68] men have to learn to live from the spontaneous centre only and not allow themselves to be coerced against their better instincts. Even marriage, cynically labelled an *"Egoisme à Deux"* (AR, 100) by Lilly ("a self-conscious egotistical state"), requires the partners "to be separated sometimes", as Lilly is from his wife.[69] But, we should of course notice that Aaron's reading of his illness can be taken as a misreading within the historical realism of the story. There was a globally virulent influenza epidemic in the immediate post-war period.[70] These new Lawrentian men are unreliable storytellers. Aaron's physical weakness translates into a moribund spirit: "his bowels won't work" (AR, 95), which in the discourse of *Fantasia* means that the primal centre of his instinctual self is dying. Lilly has to "rub the life into him" (AR, 96-8).

Aaron's manliness restored, the two men can indulge their sexism: women are too full of their own importance; once she has got her children, a woman is "a bitch in a manger"; "men have got to stand up to the fact that manhood is more than childhood — and then force women to admit it"; "[t]he man's spirit has gone out of the world"; "marriage needs readjusting"; men have got to stand together against female "self-conceit"; etc. (AR, 100-1). The two men will travel abroad in the hope of changing things and themselves; although Aaron is less idealistic. The principal question is: can a man be alone (implying without a woman)? Josephine thinks not; and neither does Aaron. He sticks to Lilly for the time being, like the *Blutbruder* Birkin wanted Gerald to be. But it has the desired effect, as Aaron's rod is symbolically "putting forth again" (AR, 108).

Another war-affected, hysterical man is Captain Herbertson. He is a

---

[68] *Fantasia of the Unconscious*, 34, 143.

[69] Like Lawrence, who had gone to Italy without Frieda. Lilly's wife, like Frieda, travels to her relatives quite independently.

[70] Just over 150,000 died in England alone. Lawrence caught influenza, and was very ill. He always had a psychosomatic explanation, though. Cf. Kinkead-Weekes, *D.H. Lawrence: Triumph To Exile 1912-1922* (Cambridge: Cambridge University Press, 1996), 496-97.

focus for the anti-war rhetoric. He has had too many bad experiences; he needs to talk about them, but who should he turn to? Certainly not the women; he can only talk to men, as he does obsessively. But the talking is not a cure. His soul won't recover (AR, 114). Herbertson is another *"homme-récit"* (a storytelling man), a source of masculinist stories: about the gruesome horrors of war; about the manly codes of behaviour in the regiment of Guards where men just do not show their feelings; about the attitude towards the Germans who were "too methodical" and, apparently, so easily fooled. He, the nerve-worn veteran, has bad dreams, and is a text-book case for Freud. Indeed, psychoanalysis is busy with post-war men, as later Lilly is said to be "in Munich, being psychoanalysed" (AR, 194). The war was an impersonal machine, "a vast obscene mechanism", a nightmare where the "mass-psyche" overcomes the individual with a kind of "mob-sleep" so that he "becomes completely base and obscene" (AR, 119). This anti-war diatribe raises the question: what is a real man? Or: what is manliness? Heroism and patriotism have been destroyed once and for all for the war veteran; but not for the women. Lawrence has Aaron's wife accuse him, in his last visit home, of being "unmanly and cowardly", for not facing up to his family responsibilities (AR, 125). In this she hints at her own story of the abandoned wife, fated to be a single mother at a time of hardship. Aaron's response, though, is abstract and distancing as he describes the quality of her voice: "The strange, liquid sound of her appeal seemed to him like the swaying of a serpent which mesmerizes the fated, fluttering, helpless bird" (AR, 127). The higher cultural register of the symbolic connotations privilege his side of the argument. Her position is reduced to the mundane, while he is able to resist yielding "mastery to the woman" by relocating his position in the aesthetic realm — not for the first time, though. When he is in fear of Josephine's seduction, the text reinscribes the feeling in an expressionist description: "it all seemed so sinister, this dark bristling heart of London. Wind boomed and tore like waves ripping a shingle beach" (AR, 70). Also as she weeps her feminine tears, he distances himself through violent images. Here, gender difference is inscribed in the text's stylistic shifts.

After the play of masks and the social satire aimed at the expatriates at the villa of Sir William and Lady Franks, the ground is prepared for the direct transcription of Lawrence's post-war doctrine on the "wilful woman" versus the "natural man": women have always thought themselves the centre of creation in their maternal instinct; men have worshipped the female ideal of the *Magna Mater*; they have gone wrong because they believed in "this great ignominious dogma of the sacred priority of women"; women instinctively seek men's yielding to their "all-beneficent love", which is the basis of the woman's idea of marriage.

Herewith, the old idea of Lawrentian marriage argued for in *The Rainbow*, with its fight, its passion, and its final compromise; or Birkin's "star-equilibrium" in *Women in Love*, is abandoned. Now the emphasis is on the overbearing woman's will to possess and destroy the man. This had already emerged as a potential danger in the previous fiction, but here it is the whole situation. However, Aaron is determined not to yield to the woman's demand for worship. He will go it alone (AR, 159). He had already learnt not to give all of himself to his wife, but to withhold "the central core of himself" (AR, 160). "Isolate self-responsibility" is the new male principle: "His intrinsic and central aloneness was the very centre of his being" (AR, 162). It will be a difficult principle to maintain.

The discussion about the new masculinity broadens into a general cultural critique about modern identity, about the masks people wear in public, and their inauthentic behaviour, and paradoxically, about the modern *idée fixe*: self-glorification through self-confession — that more common form of giving yourself away. However, the anti-woman rhetoric is never far away. The ideal of the "*ewiges Weib*" (Eternal Woman) is another construction passing itself off as human nature (AR, 165). Such ideals have lead to modern sensationalism and degeneration. We need to return to the natural, organic, instinctual self. How that is to be achieved is not clear from this novel. These thoughts are framed in the comic satire of the gathering at Sir William's, and registered at a distance by Aaron. They are followed by the street-riot scenes, which is also filtered through Aaron's estranging witness. Then there is the chance meeting with the two gay expatriate Englishmen, Angus and Francis, who represent the "feminized" man, the homosexual alternative of men without women that the Aaron-Lilly relationship will not become. And the incident in the train deflates any idealism Aaron may have felt about the Italians as "open and casual" compared to the English who are "tight and gripped" (AR, 199). The women, though, will continue to need their idealism. Lady Franks disapproves of Aaron's "cold and unmanly and inhuman" way of looking at things (AR, 147). The Marchesa is incensed by men's talk of their need to stand up to the "terrible" modern woman (AR, 240-47).

By the end of the novel, we have not come much further in the discussion of the new masculinity. The same ideas are reiterated and reinforced, but in differing contexts which make their inconclusiveness telling. After sex with the Marchesa where, as Worthen has explained (see previous section), the reassertion of masculinity is carried out as an assertion of power within the sex act, it is as if a chapter in the life of man is closed. Henceforth, men commit themselves only to each other, living without sex. This turns out to be another false solution, because despite the general critique of idealism as feminine, this masculine assertion of autonomy is idealist too, and the novel is necessarily open-ended and inconclusive. The only event that punctuates the incessant masculine talk is the bomb explosion in the café — itself another masculinist story of anarchy and violence. It is also a brutal reminder of the real history made by men.

Aaron, though, remains the idealist, dreaming a futurist vision. At first it is of an England, part Midlands part Cornwall, with an organized communal existence. Then in a lake-city in Mexico which he journeys to in a boat he sees the vision of an idol. Aaron refuses to interpret his dream; but, enigmatic as it is, we can detect the idea of the future as a journey towards a new social formation which is also a return to older ritual. It is not clear whether this is a utopia or a dystopia. But it does look forward to the travel to other continents that Aaron plans, as did Lawrence, and the latter's visit to Mexico and his writing of *The Plumed Serpent*. But the future looks suspiciously like a fascist State, which answers the question Lilly poses to Aaron: "Do you want love, or to be obeyed?" The era of love is over. We need a new male leadership which will teach men to acknowledge their inner instinctual power as the source of life and creativity. Aaron should not give up just because his flute has been broken. But he is not so certain anymore about Lilly/Lawrence's new masculinity. His journey, like the author's, is not finished.

If this were all the novel is about, then it is a direct transcription of the doctrine from the essays. But the text is not so consistently transparent. It offers us degrees of deconstruction at different levels. We should look to the margins of the text to decentre the masculinist ideology. How exclusive is the male perspective? How absolute are the dominant anti-feminist ideas? How certain is the Lawrence of the essays of the ground on which his new masculinity is built? Can we trust the tale? There are two points of entry into a deconstructive reading of *Aaron*. First, the marginalized role and speech of the women characters which casts a shadow of doubt over all the masculinist assertions. And, second, the meta-narrative intrusions of the narrator which undermine the authority and reliability of the male stories. The truth of the text may well be in its margins.

For an ideology to remain coherent, it can tolerate no contradiction. Contradictory voices are marginalized. The workings of ideology are made visible once inscribed in textual form. In order for a novel to maintain the coherence of the ideology it represents, it has to maintain a determinate silence on what might threaten to tell a different story.[71]

---

[71] This is the classic Althusserian argument best exemplified by Pierre Macherey in *A Theory of Literary Production* (London: Routledge, 1979. First published 1965).

Aaron's Rod is a *locus classicus* for the representation of an ideology — the new masculinity. However, it is questioned from outside that ideology by the critical voice of the feminine speaking from the margins of the text. Rereading the text through feminist theory which is already in the text demonstrates that the authority of the masculinist ideology is based on its exclusivity and its marginalization of the feminine. Feminist criticism has made this clear for a number of years now. What is interesting about *Aaron* is that it already prepares the ground for the feminist critic through the women characters in the novel. Whilst the masculine ideology of Lawrence's post-war essays remains internally coherent and can only be accepted or rejected by the reader as a matter of belief, the novel with its play of narrative perspective already offers the reader the possibility of rejecting the dominant ideas it is trying to promote. In this respect the fiction demonstrates the limits of the ideas in the essays.

Aaron's wife is only seen from his view, in both sense as focalized and as ideology, except once when on his last visit home she has it out with him, accusing him of not being a man (with all its traditional connotations). Most significant, though, is when she says: "You ran away from me, without telling me what you've got against me." (AR, 125) He can only reply that he went because he had had enough. Her conventional way of seeing things breaks the monopoly the man has on the truth. And as the reader is kept at a distance from Aaron as focalizing agent, it is not difficult for Lottie's marginalized view to win our sympathy, coupled as it is with more conventional sympathies for her and the children's plight. The new masculinity seems rather shaky as an ideology. It is not Lot's wife who will be turned into a pillar of salt, as the chapter title leads us to expect, and neither will Aaron although, in a reversal of the biblical story, it is he who looks back one last time.

Josephine Ford, the representative modern, metropolitan woman-artist, comes off well in contrast to the more easily excited, nervous Julia. It is Josephine who is given the privileged role of focalizer at the opera through which we get biting satire of the sham representation of Verdi's Egypt. Lawrence marks her exceptionality by giving her "some aboriginal American in her blood" despite her self-conscious arrogance (AR 46-48). She is close to the Lawrentian polemic against modern society (usually attributed to the male characters) when she is given to think, in a proto-feminist moment, "she was mortally afraid of society, and its fixed institutions". She takes the initiative, inviting Aaron to dinner, gets him to talk about himself, and finds him inwardly indifferent to her, if not to everything (AR, 65). She takes the lead, sexually, seducing him in spite of his avowed refusal of women and love. Her view of him and her behaviour establish a level of plausibility which undermines his version later that sex with her was the direct cause of his illness (we do not get the sex described). And this, even though we can read between the lines, as competent Lawrentians, that she has become "masculinized" because she takes the active role, and therefore represents the greatest threat to the new, vulnerable male. There is also the suggestion that men want to avoid women because they are frightened of them. Later, Lilly reports her as having said, "men are simply afraid to be alone" (AR, 107). Josephine is the second female character whose voice has refused to remain marginalized, although after this she plays no more part in the story.

Lady Franks is the strongest figure of traditional feminine idealism. She is satirized for her belief in her work of reform, and the "restoring of woman to her natural throne" (AR, 147). She disapproves of Aaron's attitude to life, even though he can impress her with his music. Again, we get a critical perspective, albeit from a representative type mostly at the receiving end of the masculinist attack. She reads him from her own firm ideological position.

The Marchesa is also a critical voice incensed by the general misogynistic attitude of the young men (AR, 236ff). Although she is seduced by Aaron's music, as he revives her singing and her sexuality with his phallic flute, it is she who scripts his role in her *opera buffa*, despite the sex-scenes being told from his privileged focalization. His earnest and deliberate dominance of her[72] is undermined by her easy acceptance of his explanation that he cannot continue the affair because he is still attached to his wife. His lie is clear to us; but it matters less to her because the rules of the affair are what count. Her casualness is a symptom of her experience in the game of adultery with a younger man. This genre (with its implications of comic opera) offers the reader a completely different perspective in its value as light entertainment to that of Aaron's masculine seriousness. Indeed, we are shown by an older, wiser woman that he takes himself far too seriously. We are again made suspicious of his motives for giving up the affair. Furthermore, just as he turns her into the object of his desire, fetishizing her body in part-objects (like the foot-fetishism of Hanold in Freud's reading of the *Gradiva*), so she for her part uses him as her "fetish", a magic, phallic implement for her pleasure (AR, 250, 272-73). Although it is Aaron who becomes aware of this, and thus it could be read as yet another male fantasy, it seems plausible that it is the woman's view because of the way she sets up the affair and uses the younger man, with the utmost discretion.

These women's voices speak, each in their own way, from the mar-

---

[72] Now clear through the reinstated passages — see the comments on Worthen above.

gins, and give us a vantage point from which to read the masculinist ideology against itself. From now on, it is not so easy to accept masculinity as a return to natural instinct, given its constructedness as a force to counter the perceived dominance of the New Woman. Moreover, motives for the male attitudes towards women are in their contexts suspicious. Personal fears or war-affected weariness are often talked up into a frenzy of misogyny and idealist solutions, as they are in Lawrence's essays. Yet in the novel they seem to lead nowhere, except further away. Travel is the only remedy offered for the crisis of masculinity. The assumptions on which the masculinist ideology relies for its authority are questioned by what the women say and do in the text. These assumptions are also in doubt because of Aaron's inability or unwillingness to commit himself to Lilly as the new leader. However, the decisive point is that the reversal of an opposition is no guarantee of a fundamental change. For Derrida all oppositions are violent hierarchies, the first term being in the position of power.[73] If for Lawrence the wilful woman was dominant in the post-war culture, then reversing the hierarchy gives power back to the men, but the situation is still one of power and subjugation. We need to go one step further and, by understanding the assumptions on which the binary of male-female relies, displace the power struggle by changing the terms of the social formation. How you do this is another matter. This does not invalidate the method of deconstruction. Lawrence offers his most definite solution in *The Plumed Serpent*. But it is utopic and phallocratic.

We need not take everything away from *Aaron's Rod*, however. For the role of the narrator, as distinct from the focalizing agents, is a destabilizing one. Like the narrating persona of *Mr Noon*, only less anarchic, the narrator of *Aaron* breaks the flow of the story with meta-narrative comments: "Our story will not yet see the daylight"; "Our story continues by night"; "Behold our hero" (AR, 39, 45, 131). And in doing this, a different relationship is established with the reader: a pact at a meta-narrative level demanding a satirical attitude to the fiction from the reader. We are thus at several removes from the dominant masculinist views of Aaron: first, through his distancing and estranging perspective; second, through the further distance created by the marginalized women's voices; third, through the doubts Aaron has about Lilly and the idea of being able to go it alone; and, last, through the self-conscious narrator. None of this will mitigate the force of the misogyny for those readers who, seeking to prove a case against Lawrence, will be offended. The question to ask, though, is why Lawrence writes a novel characterized by

---

[73] Cf. Jacques Derrida, *Positions* (3 interviews) (London: Athlone Press, 1981. First published 1972).

degrees of play and instability which undermines the authority of ideas he firmly believed in at the time? Did he want to pre-empt the attack from his women readers? Should we really trust the tale?

There are two other intrusions from the narrator which have more significance. The first is when he discusses how he has to represent Aaron's self-understanding in a way that Aaron could not. What is "risen to half consciousness" in the character, is made explicit by the narrator in the form of commentary; but one that is also meta-commentary. Aaron thinks deeper thoughts in music, while the narrator has to translate them into words. And here the narrator with the comic persona of the English tradition (dominant in *Mr Noon*) turns modernist too: "If I, as word-user, must translate his deep conscious vibrations into finite words, that is my own business. I do but make a translation of the man. He would speak in music. I speak with words." (AR, 163-164) Aaron is not as articulate with words as the narrator; and the "gentle reader" should not "grumble" at this fact, but merely decide whether the thoughts attributed to Aaron are plausible. The second is just an aside, but a telling one. When Aaron has written a letter to Sir William which contains the gist of Lawrence's current philosophy, the narrator comments: "When a man writes a letter to himself, it is a pity to post it to somebody else. Perhaps the same is true of a book." (AR, 264) If Lawrence felt in the early 1920s that writing was like sending a letter to yourself, then we are reminded that it must have been difficult for him to imagine a reader because of the difficulties he had getting his books published after the banning of *The Rainbow*. Moreover, this might account for the presence of characters as readers in his fiction since *Women in Love*, and the extreme frustration shown by his now infamous assault on the female reader in *Mr Noon*.

Now this is all a much more serious matter than just playful meta-narrative markers about the story's progress. It goes to the heart of the representationalist crisis of Modernism. And here, music is important both as Aaron's private language and solace, and as the focus for discussion about Modernism in the text. Aaron's flute-playing, like Lawrence's writing, is a source of income (meagre as it is) to support his travelling (and to send money to his wife). It gets him invited (as did Lawrence's writing) to the villas of the wealthy aristocrats who sponsor the arts. In such surroundings music is played, but also discussed. Aaron wants to return to the more ancient simple music of the flute (Pan-like) — a much older language of cultural regeneration; and away from the bombast of grand opera. Earlier, Josephine Ford is given the role of lambasting the performance of Verdi's *Aida*. As Hyde rightly puts it, Stravinsky is promoted over Beethoven "since the former does not fasten you down to depths ... (but) an art of surfaces".[74] (cf. AR, 46, 136, 167-168). One thinks immediately of the "Rites of Spring" (1913) or Debussy's "*Après-Midi d'un Faun*" (1894) as representative of the modernist return to simpler folk melodies to counter the orchestral overstatement of nineteenth-century Romanticism typified by Wagner and culminating with Mahler. Lawrence seems a long way from the Wagnerian movements and Nordic mythologies of *Women in Love*. Aaron also prefers the Italian Baroque: "some Pergolesi and the Scarlatti he liked, and some Corelli. He preferred frail, sensitive, abstract music, with not much feeling in it, but a certain limpidity and purity" (AR, 210). Music is feminized as against the now rejected, masculine Wagner or Verdi grand opera, or the Beethoven symphony. But the masculine music will return in its more "primitive" forms in *The Plumed Serpent* with its Indian drum-beat and dance, and the ritual chanting of the *Quetzalcoatl* hymns. Here, in *Aaron*, though, and like Stravinsky's music, the flute's one simple tune will be a lone vibration in a whole medley of textual pastiche. Strangely though, the flute will also be a potent symbol of a revived virility, as Aaron reawakens the Marchesa, musically and sexually. Aaron's flute is transformed into the Pan-pipe. It is also a natural, organic object — like Lawrentian art — sometimes blossoming and flowering, sometimes withering. It has to carry a lot of symbolic weight. In the end it is destroyed by the anarchist's bomb, and without his flute Aaron is directionless, even though Lilly thinks it will "grow again" (AR, 285). Yet, as Kinkead-Weekes has suggested, "Aaron's rod of divine power ... has shown little sign of budding like the one in the Bible".[75]

Music as the purest of the aesthetic forms is redefined, in its older organic and cosmic connection, against the modernist theorists of artistic autonomy and "significant form".[76] More generally, the great music theatre of grand narratives is deconstructed in the several ways described above. If *Aaron's Rod* is an expression of the new masculinity at the same time as its questioning, *Kangaroo* and *The Plumed Serpent* are also texts with deconstructive effects even while being Lawrence's most explicitly political and masculinist fictions. It is with these two texts that the next chapter is concerned.

---

[74] G.M. Hyde, 95.

[75] Kinkead-Weekes, 648.

[76] Bell, *Art* (1914); Roger Fry, "A New Theory of Art" in *The Nation*, 7 March 1914. For further discussion, see Fernihough, chapters 4 and 5.

5

Deconstructing Masculinity 2: Male Bonding, Mythic Resolution and Textual Instabilities in *Kangaroo* and *The Plumed Serpent*

1. *Kangaroo*: male bonding and textual fragmentation

i. Critical reception

There have been two dominant schools of thought about *Kangaroo* (1923).[1] From the first reception it was considered to be a failure as a novel. Because it was written in only six weeks during Lawrence's short stay in Australia, critics had generally assumed that the novel remained an unfinished draft. Its fragmentariness and apparent lack of cohesion, its shifts in style, its overall absence of coherence were judged as evidence that what was published was chaotic, poorly written didacticism. This view has recently been challenged. This second school has two versions. The first version runs on the lines that as we now know that Lawrence revised the text in his usual thorough manner, and that as he was working on his essays on the importance and the future of the novel,[2] his fiction of the 1920s should be read as part of that general consideration of novelistic form. Therefore the text is not chaotic and incoherent but experimental, and should be read through a different paradigm of coherence. The second version of this new critical school agrees in principle with the first, but goes beyond Lawrence for its description of the novel. It reads the text from the vantage of postmodernism and post-structuralist criticism, drawing out the manner in which the destabilizing of conventional representationalist writing is part of a broader questioning of grand narratives. It is this reading that I shall develop in the next section.

Murry was the first to declare *Kangaroo* "a chaotic book". He blames its incoherence on the psychology of the author — as he does consistently in his study of Lawrence. Millett relocates Murry's reading in her

---

[1] All references in text [K] are to the Penguin edition of the Cambridge D.H. Lawrence (London, 1997).

[2] Cf. "Surgery for the Novel — Or a Bomb" ("The Future of the Novel") (1923); "Morality and the Novel"; "Why the Novel Matters", and the other essays on the novel from 1925.

sexual politics, where political realities become exclusively masculine realities — wish-fulfilling fantasies to compensate for Lawrence's "failures as a man". Here, Lawrence is read through the arch-antifeminism of Norman Mailer, and his (Lawrence's) misogyny is confirmed by reading the fiction as transcriptions of the essays. The novel has "a raffish tone, a vulgarity and cheapness of effect which make it the Lawrence novel that commands least critical respect".[3] Draper,[4] although recognizing that this was not a traditional kind of novel, also accused it of blatant didacticism. The novel fails because there is no conviction behind the assertions about the state of England, or Australia. Mood-swings are unsettling, and the character, Kangaroo, is implausible as a revolutionary leader.

For Kermode, *Kangaroo* is interesting as "a surprisingly naked self-portrait, a record of fact and uncensored fantasy not elsewhere to be found".[5] However, it is not a good book, as it was not carefully revised. This is now known to be untrue, as creative textual revision and even the three endings for the different editions confirm.[6] We should, of course, acknowledge that the kind of Lawrence we now read is influenced by the publication of *Mr Noon* (1984) and the work of the Cambridge University Press editors and biographers — none of which was available to Kermode in 1973. He reads the novel as autobiography, as a confusion of the author's current opinions and fantasies about himself as leader of men, coloured by the post-war mood. Despite its passions, the novel is "careless" with narrative, and therefore in places it is "perhaps the worst writing in the whole canon".[7] Eagleton insists that like *Aaron's Rod*, *Kangaroo* is "signally incapable of evolving a narrative, ripped between fragmentary plot, spiritual autobiography and febrile didacticism".[8] Ellis claims that the disjunctive narrative and the experimental features that Lawrence claimed put him in the Joycean camp are only "superficially" modernist. For the text is characterized by an "uncomfortably playful and suspicious mood", and "the sudden flurry of self-conscious gestures ... are also meant to protect it from criticism".[9] Lawrence is still trying to

[3] Kate Millett, *Sexual Politics* (London: Virago, 1969), 282.
[4] R.P. Draper (1959), "Authority and the Individual: A Study of D.H. Lawrence's *Kangaroo*", reprinted in David Ellis and Ornella De Zordo eds, *D.H. Lawrence: Critical Assessments, Volume II* (Mountfield: Helm Information Ltd., 1992)
[5] Frank Kermode, *Lawrence* (Glasgow: Fontana, 1973), 99.
[6] Cf. Appendix II to the Penguin (1997) edition of the Cambridge D.H. Lawrence.
[7] Kermode, 103.
[8] Terry Eagleton (1976). Reprinted in Peter Widdowson ed., *D.H. Lawrence* (London: Longman, 1992), 34.
[9] David Ellis, *D.H. Lawrence: Dying Game 1922-1930* (Cambridge: Cambridge University Press, 1998), 40.

tell a story, but the transitions are casually handled; and there is little effort on Lawrence's part to distinguish Somers from himself. That is to say, for Ellis it is poorly written autobiography, even when partly redeemed by the descriptions of the Australian landscape.

It was Worthen who first challenged this critical consensus, setting in train a new interest in the novel. As he explains, the belief that it is carelessly written because Lawrence had lost interest in it, as a symptom of his growing misanthropy, is no longer tenable. He worked hard at the revision, and the essays on the novel that date from this period confirm that Lawrence had not lost interest in his art.[10] *Kangaroo* is not a travelogue with some journalism and philosophy added for good measure. It is a fictional version of "The Future of the Novel" and "Why the Novel Matters". It is a challenge to the reader of the conventional novel, and also of the kind of self-absorbed modernist writing represented, for Lawrence, by Dorothy Richardson's writing with its minutely detailed enquiry into identity. Lawrence's novel is both comic and serious; experimental in ways that now seem appropriate to the representational crisis of Modernism. The scruples of the English novel, popular or modernist, are replaced by a fragmentariness that describes better Somers' experience of cultural dislocation and alienation. What is strange about the reception of this novel written in 1922 is that, while objections were raised to digression being central to its narrative, and to its apparent lack of a cohesive and coherent storyline, no one has said the same about *Ulysses* (1922).[11] Lawrence himself made the comparison, insisting that Joyce's writing was too deliberately schematic ("mental") as opposed to his own more spontaneous ("organic") writing.[12] For Lawrence, *Kangaroo* went further than *Ulysses* in experiment. And, as he put it in "Morality and the Novel" (1925), any "really new novel" would "always provoke resistance".[13] Yet Lawrence is rarely considered an experimental writer, even today; despite the reviewer in the *Times Literary Supplement* in 1923 who saw its experimental side. Worthen rightly suggests that we now need to look at the novel as a "thought-adventure" concerned with the question of the novel itself as an expression of the experience of modernity. I would add that, of course, Lawrence had been asking this question since *Sons and Lovers*; only

---

[10] John Worthen, *D.H. Lawrence and the Idea of the Novel* (London: Macmillan, 1979); extract revised and reprinted in Ellis and De Zordo (1992), Volume II, 492.

[11] Worthen, 496.

[12] Cf. *The Letters of D.H. Lawrence, Volume IV*, compiled and edited by George J. Zytaruk and James T. Boulton (Cambridge: Cambridge University Press, 1987), 255, 264, 271, 275.

[13] Cited in Worthen (1979) in Ellis and De Zordo (1992), 497.

differently, as he and the world changed. The conditions for the novel after the war were rather different from those before 1914. As we saw in the previous chapters, the question about the form of the novel is tied in with the writer's shifting expressive demands. A contradictory and unsettling experience in search of a new certainty, on the part of Somers, is fully captured by the representational experiments of the text.

There is much to admire in this new reading. However, Worthen does rely too exclusively on Lawrence's own understanding of his writing. Moreover, the argument is finally confusing in claiming that "Lawrence is writing a continually honest novel rather than a continually successful one"[14] — as if it does not after all demand new criteria for "success" (implying that we still judge the novel from a clear idea of coherence, which the foregoing approach seemed to be refuting). In a later reading, Worthen recuperates the novel into a conventional scheme more explicitly: "The novel's journey to Australia takes on the status of a mythic journey away from the European past, and away from the old world's obsession with marriage and sex".[15] It is a good point to make that, given Lawrence's reputation, this novel is unusual for the absence in it of sex. But if you want to promote the novel as experimental, you should look in more detail at the radical shifts in genre rather than seek to explain it in terms of one of its genres.

Humma also rejects the view that *Kangaroo* is chaotic and fragmentary; though he does not believe that Worthen's claim that the novel is self-consciously experimental will "sway many sceptics".[16] We should, instead, understand the novel as symbolist. The Australian bush is an "objective correlative" for the dark inner world, aboriginal and suppressed by a fragile civilization perched on a narrow coastline. It is Lawrence's "Moby Dick", resonating with symbolism so that action and meaning are organically indivisible. Humma cancels the fragmentariness by rereading the novel as organically unified by its symbolism. Admittedly the symbolism in those descriptions of the Australian landscape has a significant resonance in the text's play of meaning. But, I would ask, what about all the other stylistic and generic shifts in the text? Humma's paper is a singular example of misreading by resorting to an Eliotian aesthetic: unity is brought about by the "objective correlative". The novel is doubly modernist: in T.S. Eliot's neo-classical sense of textual unity; and in Yeats' sense of "symbolist poetry". It seems that the critical consensus has been wrong to accuse the novel of fragmentariness,

---

[14] Ibid., 499.
[15] Worthen, 83.
[16] John B. Humma (1986), "Of Bits, Beasts, and Bush: The Interior Wilderness in D.H. Lawrence's *Kangaroo*" reprinted in Ellis & De Zordo (1992), Volume II, 507.

because it is unified — and not because it has been judged by a false notion of coherence. Humma evidently still works from within the same notion of coherence ("organic unity") as those whose criticism he rejects. In order to maintain his position he has to erase all trace of fragmentariness by unifying the novel through its symbolic resonance.

A more appropriate use of T.S. Eliot is in the whole modernist, post-catastrophe scenario of 1920s waste-land culture. As Hyde has argued, the bits and collages represent well the cultural reality; just as the talk of extreme political solutions, and their rejection in the name of an aestheticized landscape capture the mood of the times when politics and aesthetics were closer than ever in trying to hold things together.[17] However, there is an aspect of continuity with Lawrence's other works in that *Kangaroo* is also "an anguished fable of modern marriage". As in much of Lawrence's later fiction, focalization is mobile enough to deconstruct the absolute categories of political ideologies through an "abrasive satire and an insistent dialogism, though the Fascist notion of a final 'solution' continues to exercise a powerful appeal". [18] In the spirit of an unfixed idea of the novel, Lawrence promotes an ideological open-endedness (before he has one more go at his "final solution" in *The Plumed Serpent*).

Pinkney argues that the novel's Modernism is an example of Eliot's vision of the "Unreal City", strewn with the rubbish of modern life, squalid with the effects of the "massification" of culture, but with none of the redeeming high-cultural traces nor the cultural memory of an organic society when sensibility had not yet dissociated.[19] Pinkney explains some of the textual instability as a result of its hovering "constantly on the borders of some fundamental generic shift from novel to dystopia" which "disconcerts us even further by seeming to metamorphose, at odd moments, into utopia".[20] But why is this disconcerting? Is it because, like Worthen, Pinkney has a traditional idea of the well-made novel? He does share with the critics in the other school the revulsion with the one-dimensional harshness of the later Lawrence's social thinking. But who would support such ideas today in any case? The best readings of the fiction have always been those that are able to accept the ironies that frame the ideas, and therefore allow the novels to remain readable. This

---

[17] G.M. Hyde, *D.H. Lawrence* (London: Macmillan, 1990), cf. note 16, 125 on the "Brecht-Lukàcs debate".

[18] Hyde, 97-99, 125, note 16.

[19] I would add that the Australian bush is presented as a non-Eurocentric memory of the aboriginal culture, and may therefore count as post-colonial *avant la lettre*.

[20] Tony Pinkney, *D.H. Lawrence* (Hemel Hempstead: Harvester Wheatsheaf, 1990), 114-15.

notwithstanding, Pinkney's reading of the Modernism of *Kangaroo* provides us with an important historical context. He draws attention to the critique of the new mass culture in two ways. First, there is a dispersal of class divisions through mass democratization which leads to a new classification into the haves and the have-nots, but without the old class loyalties and communities as a location of identities (Australia being at an advanced stage with its reduction of social organization to friendly neighbours and "mates"). Second, there is the new phenomenon of mass communication in the form of the boulevard press, like the Sidney *Bulletin* or, in England, the infamous *John Bull*. The latter was always particularly aggressive towards Lawrence (and Somers), performing a kind of hegemonic function in its monopoly of the nationalist truth, and standing for the popularist ideology that Lawrence labels "Bottomleyism", after the newspaper's owner. The fear of mass culture was endemic in Modernism, and Lawrence is representative.[21] The novel draws attention to the way the process of "massification" destroys individual desire as everything is "induced in us by fashion, advertising, the market", and "revolutionary politics is a matter of mere velleity and caprice". What keeps things going in the narrative is the "male pseudo-couple" (as it does for Pinkney in *Aaron's Rod*). But now they are being dragged "out of ontology and back to history" so that the text is thoroughly "wrecked", collapsing into doctrine and "pages of indulgent landscape painting". Furthermore, this is a degeneration of Lawrence's art for those who take *The Rainbow* as its *locus classicus*. The novel becomes increasingly a dialogue directly with the reader, and Pinkney draws the suggestive conclusion that, in yet another genre shift, it almost "turns into a treatise on reader-response and reception-theory".[22]

Daly[23] stands out amongst those in the second school by insisting on a reading from a postmodern and post-structuralist perspective. This is groundbreaking, and I shall be developing some of his ideas below. He begins by associating his reading with those who have recently been trying to rescue *Kangaroo* by "recuperating its seemingly formal excesses as 'experimental'. But is what was experimental then, experimental now?"[24] It is attractive to postmodern readers in the first instance because it bears out Lyotard's claim that grand narratives have become

---

[21] Lawrence also had cause, as we can see in the dreadfully slanderous reviews of his works in *John Bull*. His critique of the trend towards mass culture is no doubt what was attractive to F.R. Leavis.

[22] Pinkney, 119, 122.

[23] Macdonald Daly, Introduction to the Penguin (1997) edition of the Cambridge D.H. Lawrence.

[24] Daly, xiii.

discredited. Lawrence is now a proto-postmodernist. He always believed he would get a favourable reception one day, and that day seems to have arrived.[25]

I have already indicated that criticism has been approaching *Kangaroo* (and presumable all the novels since the second part of *Sons and Lovers*) through the wrong criteria. Those in what I have called the first school have based their notion of coherence on an old idea of verisimilitude deriving from the conventional well-made novel, as Daly also argues. But as other critics have noted too, the text shifts between voices, languages and generic codes. The earliest critics were generally the most misled. Yet Lawrence had warned us back in 1914 in that famous letter to Garnett how not to read his novel (then referring to what would become *The Rainbow*). Moreover, he was constantly committed to formal innovation. Lawrence's writing does not fit the Jamesian (or even less the Flaubertian) model; and criticism that starts from the wrong premiss misreads Lawrence — which has been the case throughout the history of Lawrence's reception. This is not only a case of getting Lawrence wrong; it is, as Daly rightly argues, also symptomatic of "the insularity of English literary aesthetics".[26] My reason for writing this book in the first place is to break out of that "insularity" in Lawrence studies.

The next important point Daly makes is that *Kangaroo* pre-empts those misreadings: the reader is invited to reflect through Somers and Harriett on the process of decoding a new culture. They certainly have problems doing this because it reads from the start like Eastwood, and the bush like those Italian landscapes in *Twilight in Italy* (1916). The meta-fictional asides go further than Modernism, yet do not quite match up to their postmodern equivalent.[27] Moreover, the novel is not just "thinly disguised autobiography", as many critics have insisted, but also unashamedly draws attention to this fact. However, Daly insists, passages of proto-postmodernist meta-narrative do not make the novel "pure textuality". It is also about the nightmare of history and the struggle to come to terms with it. Somers seems to be suffering from "post-traumatic memory", as well as a massive legitimation crisis as the great ideals and belief-systems have been discredited by the war. Especially suspect now

---

[25] J-F. Lyotard, *The Postmodern Condition: A Report on Knowledge* (Minneapolis: University of Minnesota Press, 1984. First published 1979).

[26] Daly, xviii.

[27] For Daly a prime example of postmodern metafiction is John Fowles (1969) *The French Lieutenant's Woman*. That Lawrence is somewhere beyond Modernism but not quite postmodernist is true; but I would add that Lawrence is partly also in the comic tradition of the Sternean narrator in the eighteenth century, as he showed most ostentatiously in *Mr Noon*.

are the grand narratives of "Emancipation" and the "Nation State". Yet Somers travels in search of a new grand narrative which can replace the ideals of Christian love (*caritas*) and consummate marriage which Lawrence had once intensely promoted. We should of course add that the legitimation crisis is one the Lawrentian novel is experiencing from within.

I would certainly endorse the idea that we are now in a position to do justice to modernist fiction because of the greater sophistication enabled by the revolution in critical theory. In Lawrence studies, feminist criticism has been a lone voice in rereading Lawrence (and sometimes in an ideologically reductive way, as I shall argue in the next chapter). It is good to see newer post-structuralist approaches to Lawrence, even belatedly, like Daly's introduction to the new Penguin edition of "The Cambridge D.H. Lawrence". In what follows, I shall continue the work of the previous chapter on *Aaron's Rod* by reading *Kangaroo* as a deconstruction of the new masculinity and its politics.

ii. *Kangaroo*

If, as Hyde suggests, *Kangaroo* is autobiography, the story having "something of the air of a celebrity tour"[28] — recording impressions of Australia before continuing the world tour through the south seas via New Zealand and on to America — then what is the significance of the fictionalizing process? The travelogue was becoming Lawrence's preferred genre, alongside the essays he called his "pollyanalytics". If you read the Lawrence of the early 1920s in the spirit of the double attitude implicit in his term "pollyanalytics" — a self-deprecation for a philosophizing seriously intended — then you get close to the spirit of the fiction. The search for a direction in the writing, which I discussed in chapter 3, is also now a journey to, and quest for new locations of writing; a quest for new models for cultural regeneration. In this, the fictionalizing process in the form of an internal enquiry into the future of the novel is symptomatic of the general enquiry into the future of the culture. The fictional process enables a more telling "thought-adventure" than the other genres of writing — autobiography, essay and travel-writing.

Lawrence firmly believed the novel could "make the whole man alive tremble" (P, 535). It communicates more than any other kind of writing, including the autobiography, because it alone can capture in its "tremulations" the writerly self:

---

[28] Hyde, 97.

Me, man alive, I am a curious assembly of incongruous parts. My yea! of today is oddly different from my yea! of yesterday. My tears of tomorrow will have nothing to do with my tears of a year ago. (P, 536)

The autobiography and the thoughts from the travel-writing and the essays are reinscribed in fictions which take them on an adventure. I shall argue in what follows that Lawrence's "thought-adventure" should also be understood as an adventure of writing. As he put it: "only in the novel are *all* things given full play" (P, 538, Lawrence's emphasis). Moreover, even while he still wants to believe that, "out of the full play of all things emerges the only thing that is anything, the wholeness of man, the wholeness of woman", the novel, *Kangaroo*, tells a different story: for as it deconstructs the old certainties — married love, cultural identity, political ideologies, colonial hegemony, and the well-made novel — the old stable ego of the author is dispersed into the fictional bits and fragments, the histories and ironies he has created. The only solace will be once again the natural landscape and his reconstruction of it as consolation for everything that is missing in the culture.

It is well understood today that the novels that follow each other in the Lawrence canon are part of a work-in-progress. The inconclusiveness of one novel is taken further and worked out in the next novel, only in the end to have posed new unanswered questions, which will then be taken on in the next novel. This process describes well the relationship of *Aaron's Rod*, *Kangaroo*, and *The Plumed Serpent*. The question of male leadership was posed and worked through in *Aaron*, its assumptions deconstructed. It seemed that the new era of power and masculinist revival was a necessary fiction. It was not clear what form it would take, nor whether Aaron could commit himself to it. His needs and doubts are clarified more in *Kangaroo* in the character of Somers.

We arrive in Australia with Somers and his wife, Harriett.[29] It is Somers who is in the privileged position of focalizer. His difficulties reading Australia rehearse the reader's own, inscribing cultural difference as one of several destabilizing forces that give the text an appeal to the reader today which, as I argued in the previous chapter, a large part of the critical reception was unable to perceive. The post-war Europe that Somers and Harriett have left behind is "finished", "played out" — a continuation of the cultural analysis in *Aaron*. However, we do not encounter Australia first through Somers' eyes. Lawrence gets us to look

---

[29] Somers and Harriett are the closest portraits of the post-war Lawrence and Frieda we have, and ones which can be compared to the pre-war portraits in *Mr Noon*.

at Somers and Harriett through local eyes, reminding us who the strangers are in this country, and how suspiciously they are received: "They looked different from other people .... the strange, foreign-looking little man with the beard .... A comical-looking bloke! Perhaps a Bolshy." (K, 7) From the outset, Australia appears like another version of England, replaying the same ritual prejudices they (and the Lawrences) experienced in Cornwall during the war — as we find out later in "The Nightmare" chapter. It is soon made clear, though, that these Australians are themselves foreigners. For once Somers encounters the bush for the first time he senses the "horrid thing", a "presence" that was "biding its time with a terrible ageless watchfulness, waiting for a far-off end, watching the myriad intruding white men" (K, 14-15). Here, in a melodramatic writing that also recalls Conrad's *Heart of Darkness* (1902), Lawrence is post-colonialist *avant la lettre*.

It is the shifts in perspective and register, but also in genre, that draw attention to a level of understanding which goes beyond the transparent representation of ideas. Once the intuited horror of the bush is rationalized by Somers as a force waiting for the end of the white man's intrusion, the text switches into its meta-narrative mode and frames the description in a light irony about the poet (Somers, but implicitly Lawrence as well) needing "to feel something, at night under such a moon" (K, 15). And we are then sent back to review the deeper thoughts Somers has of annihilating the locals as a symptom of his frustrations at being badly treated on arrival — thus switching the perspective of those opening pages. We understand difference in terms of a much greater personal fear of otherness, rather than as a result of the group pressures of a loose affiliation of local men making casual yet xenophobic remarks. However, the first two impressions will reverberate through the text: that the locals may not be the force for change to a new culture of male leadership; and that the bush will become the focus for a Lawrentian cosmic force that will, symbolically, dwarf the grand narratives of the new masculinity, once Somers comes to terms with it. The aboriginal culture represented by the bush will be a marginal presence, yet it is also a rhetorical force that will decentre the grand designs of politics. This rhetoric extends to the coastline which takes on an increasingly therapeutic function for Somers, as the machinations of political groups and the characters on whose charisma they rely for their success begin to collapse into bar-room brawls. The Australian land and seascapes have to carry the full utopian weight.

However, we do not have to rely on the symbolic presence of the cosmos to obtain a critical perspective on the ambitions and ideals of the men. Harriett's is a debunking voice, and one less marginalized than the female voices of *Aaron*. The men cannot so easily exclude her even when their bonding demands it. Jack Calcott, who introduces Somers to Kangaroo and the Diggers, imagines a place for her in the new Australia after the Right Wing revolution: "A woman like that ought to stop in a new country like this and breed sons for us" (K, 339). It is a role for women that Nazi Germany will promote, and one that reminds us of the debates at the time about countering the decay of the culture through eugenics. In the context of the fiction, though, the idea is discredited because in the end the political movement is in disarray with Kangaroo dying; and because Somers, like Aaron before him, finally cannot commit himself to the leader or fulfil the expectations he has of him, and this for personal and not ideological reasons. Harriett is in any case "too well-bred" for Australia (K, 17). She belongs to the old "aristocratic principle of Europe" (K, 21), which disqualifies her from the general democratizing tendency of the new country at the social level, while making her ancestry the ideal model for the leaders of the new political class. She thus represents one of the many paradoxes in the novel. Australians, for instance, are presented by Lawrence as "uncouth" (K, 20), as "barbarians ... with their aggressive familiarity" (K, 21). Whereas in Europe order is maintained by the class "instinct of authority" which derives from "a caste distinction" between "the proletariat and the ruling classes", in Australia class had gone and with it authority and leadership; which at first appeals to Somers even though he is disoriented by it. He first thinks of it as the English Midlands with its lack of reserve between neighbours (here no ideal community for one who remembers how repressive that can be). He will soon discover that the absence of strong leadership has become an issue. Yet, in a different mood, Australia is a relief from the old European tension and at the same time a terrifying freedom for Somers, because the "great sense of vacant spaces" is absent of "any inner meaning". The people have "no inner life, no high command, no interest in anything, finally" (K, 27).

Somers' responses, his changing and inconsistent attitudes and passions (a truly Lawrentian new man), are not Harriett's. She is to some extent above it all, and would be content to live on a farm.[30] It is this detached view of things that makes plausible her critical voice which regularly throws a spanner in the works of male ideals. In response to Somers' declaring that he had an important job to do for mankind with his fellow-men, she tries to warn him not to get involved because he will be profoundly disappointed again (a clear reference to Lawrence's failed

---

[30] A fantasy that speaks to the "Rananim" project which Lawrence and Frieda would soon be able to try out at the Kiowa Ranch near Taos in New Mexico, for better or for worse.

attempts to set up "Rananim"). She says: "men are too foolish for me to understand them" (K, 69). Her wisdom prevails; yet he will travel on after Australia, still in search of his ideal role as prophet-leader of the cultural regeneration. He is "always so extreme", she warns Jack (K, 78) — which, of course, Jack is pleased to hear. Through him, Somers hopes to achieve his ambition to become a leader of men. But he reluctantly has to accept the ruling of the Diggers, common to the ideal of the "*Männerbund*", that women have to be excluded from real politics, even Harriett (K, 94).[31] It is an irony that only works if you have read *Sea and Sardinia* (1921) that Jack wants the male leader to be like the "queen bee". Somers/Lawrence laughs at the metaphor, as well he might: the "Q. B." was Lawrence's nickname for Frieda. Her alter-ego calls the whole business of him wanting to work alone with men a "bit of little boy's silly showing off" (K, 95).[32] She refuses to be excluded so easily from his life, and the novel moves in and out of the classic Lawrentian genre of the drama of modern marriage, even in its comic, *Noon*-like burlesque in the chapter: "Harriett and Lovatt at Sea in Marriage". As Hyde has rightly claimed *Kangaroo* is "an anguished fable of modern marriage" as well as being a political novel.[33]

The feminist case against Lawrence's leadership fiction is already made by Harriett. She understands Somers' need for male bonding, even through politics (which he will reject later), is a repudiation of her. His flirtation with the idea of an active and leading public role is seen by her, and through her by us, as a compensation for all that has gone wrong in their relationship.[34] Somers attempts to answer her challenge by claiming that his involvement with the Diggers is not strictly for the politics, but "a new life-form". She is rightly suspicious of his involvement, because he had always despised politics (K, 98). And she continues to argue away at the shibboleths of 1920s Lawrence creed, always resorting to the personal to undermine the political, which is very effective in a novel when truths about persons are revealed through the psychology of characters whose unstable egos are on display. Harriett has an important part to play in

---

[31] Cf. Fjagesund (1991), and Fernihough (1993) — a point of contention in feminist criticism that Lawrence turned against women in a vengeful way only makes sense when read historically as a general as well as a personal reaction against women's liberation in the 1920s, as I argued in the previous chapter with reference to Simpson (1982).
[32] Which I can only guess closely mimics Frieda's speech mannerism.
[33] Hyde, 97.
[34] The new biographical knowledge we have makes it quite clear that Lawrence was working out his own marital problems in writing these novels, just like he was at a much earlier stage in *The Rainbow*, and more ironically in *Mr Noon*. See Kinkead-Weekes (1996), and Ellis (1998).

directly exposing Somers' inconsistencies, and thus she has a greater function as the critical (female) voice which undermines the positive statements of the new masculine ideology. Somers explains his/Lawrence's theory of power: "somebody must have power, so those should have it who don't want it selfishly, and who have some natural gift for it, and some reverence for the sacredness of it" (K, 100). She responds with derision, and claims that power for Jack and his like cannot be sacred because he is just a sentimentalist — which is very perceptive; but more significantly she is repeating Somers' words back to him. In other words, she always has to remind him of his inconsistencies, especially when he gets carried away with his "pollyanalytics".

The greatest danger for Harriett is that Somers could become Kangaroo, or rather the type of man Ben Cooley represents, who, in his own words, is "wedded" to his ideals, and is conceited enough to wonder whether "*any* woman" could stand him (K, 119). Jack Calcott is also no role model, although Somers can see what is attractive about the "manly man" with his "lovely wife" by his side. Somers admires the unproblematic woman in Victoria Calcott: "she had none of the European woman's desire to make a conquest of him, none of that feminine rapacity which is so hateful in the old world" (K, 33). This masculinist perspective is a continuation of the argument in *Aaron*, and a further point in the psychological explanation of the Somers' marriage problems. It also cleverly gives a different perspective on Harriett and her belief that her husband cannot do without her (K, 288), that she is a mother to him, and that "no man was beyond woman" (K, 96). It is a perspective that is reinforced by Kangaroo when he accuses her of being afraid she will lose the monopoly over her husband if he joins the Diggers (K, 123).[35] There is of course some truth in all of this. But what is important is that by shifting perspectives between the characters the truths become relative and dependent on the context of their utterance — a strategy already put to good use in Lawrence's best fiction.

Harriett's letter to Kangaroo adds another textual genre, and a more cynical register which upsets the seriousness of the men's idealism. She begins: "Dear Kaiser Kangaroo, Being only a poor domestic female ...." Nevertheless, he takes the letter as legally binding her to the "gift of Lovatt", while she continues to warn her husband: "I think he's rather foolish." (K, 124) Her attitude fuels his misanthropy, which resurges with increasing frequency and is the main reason for his doubts about political idealism turning into revolutionary change. Harriett's greatest

---

[35] As far as marriage is concerned, Lawrence is taking further the questions posed at the end of *Women in Love*.

tirade comes near the centre of the book and casts a greater shadow over the men's idealism:

> What is all their revolution bosh to me! There have been revolu-
> tions enough, in my opinion, and each one more foolish than the
> last. And this will be the most foolish of the lot. — And what have
> *you* got to do with revolutions, you petty and conceited creature?
> You and revolutions! You're not big enough, not grateful enough
> to do anything real. I give you my energy and my life, and you
> want to put me aside as if I was a charwoman. (K 162)

In a clearly autobiographical passage, Harriett/Frieda is determined to keep the "vital connection" with Somers/Lawrence. She represents Lawrence's pre-war theory of consummate marriage, combined with the newer insistence on the difference between "a vitally active man" and "that worst of male vices, the vice of abstraction and mechanization" (K, 164), which she is given to think is typical of conceited men. This, of course, is Lawrence speaking: going it alone without any vital organic connection through "the root of marriage ... with God, with wife, with mankind"; insisting on exclusively male activity, Somers "had ruptured the root flow". Male bonding through political ideals is already being condemned as willed and mechanical, not natural and instinctual.

It is, therefore, important to notice that Lawrence endorses Harriett's critique at the point when it represents one of his most consistent beliefs. He does this stylistically by replacing her quasi-Germanized English with what are recognizably Lawrentian statements of creed quoted directly from the essays, before switching back to the language and register of her mind-style, and alternating it with Somers' (K, 163-5). This stylistic shift is telling, because all those who think Lawrence is endorsing the proto-fascist politics in the novel should read the text more carefully. Lawrence manages to blur the distinction between the political ideologies. Both Left and Right want a fairer deal for "native" Australians, which means white supremacy, anti-immigration, and anti-Semitism. Both political groups rely for their authority on the charisma of the leader. Yet in the Socialist camp, Struthers is accused of corruption by secretly having shares in Nestlé; and in the Nationalist camp, Cooley is portrayed in greater detail as a kind of homosexual bully who wants rule by love yet is not averse to having people killed if necessary (as he warns Somers). Indeed, the political ideologies are less convincing (they are after all the standard positions of Left and Right transposed from the ideological theatre of 1920s Europe), than the psychologies of the characters who represent them. Thus it is that Lawrence undermines the authority of ideology by the unstable egos of the characters. Political solutions are only personal obsessions with deep psychological motives. This is especially the case with Somers, and his relationships to Jack and Cooley, which are symptoms of his ongoing crisis of marriage to Harriett. The desire for a male friend reworks the ending of *Women in Love* into a greater need for recognition through his becoming the writer-prophet of the masculine revival. The instabilities in character and the questionable motives behind beliefs and actions are part of a recurrent interrogation of the assumptions behind the turn towards male leadership. Harriett's is the voice that reinforces this level of criticism.

At the point of Lawrence's greatest intrusion in the text, there is a genre shift into journalism, taking the title of the chapter, "Volcanic Evidence", literally, with newspaper discussion on the threat of volcanic activity in Australia — a textual fragment disrupting the flow of the narrative, yet serving also to reiterate nature's own instability which could undermine more effectively the ambitions of man. Somers offers a different gloss on the instability of mother earth as analogy for the explosive potential of a man who happens to have "a devil in his belly!" (K, 168) As he argues, "some men have to be bombs" (K, 165). They will create havoc because they have a deep need to express their frustration — which again gives the personal priority over the political. However, nature is a force to be reckoned with, as stars, tides and volcanoes implicitly frame the puny and hollow efforts of men to reassert themselves against the industrial mechanism, against women, and against the cosmos (K, 168).

The next genre shift follows immediately: chapter IX "Harriett and Lovatt at Sea in Marriage", where the whole crisis is reinscribed in the parody of an eighteenth century comic discourse on marriage (similar to the discourse on "Spooning" in *Mr Noon*). The writing indulges in the play of the semantic associations of "all at sea" and "adrift", in a proto-deconstructive play on the figure of marriage as a bark with the woman now as the captain, "in her grand capacity of motherhood and attendant wifehood" (K, 170). The register is highly literary, the tone cynical, and the style drifts from Fieldingesque moralizing discourse and instruction manual for young couples, to Sternean burlesque and biblical parable. Here the writing is a textual mirror of the story, and a highly stylized comic summary. Lawrence writes comic fiction even while working out his new ideas. *Kangaroo* has become an adventure in writing, so that the future of the culture now seems to be bound up with the future of the novel.

The text continues to shift genre and register, style and attitude, signalling sometimes explicitly, sometimes symbolically that the old grand narratives of man's invention and the forms of their expression are discredited. The only possibility left lies with nature in the form of the "ancient land .... [t]he dark world before conscious responsibility was born" (K, 178). For Somers, the Australian landscape overwhelms any attempt "to be an alert conscious man". He can only "drift into a sort of obscurity", as the ancient spirit of the land forces him into a kind of "torpor" of semi-consciousness and indifference — a return to the Lawrentian ideal organic state of the Brangwen men at the start of *The Rainbow*, where men, as he puts it in *Kangaroo*, "didn't have emotions and personal consciousness, but were shadowy like trees, and on the whole silent, with numb brains and slow limbs and a great indifference" (K, 179). We know this is serious Lawrentian doctrine. However, in context, Somers has an ambivalent attitude to the forceful presence of the ancient land. On the one hand, he has an urge towards idealism, wishing to establish a new masculinist order. Yet, at the same time, he is not unaware of the absurdity of men's efforts in the sphere of politics, as they rely too much for their success on individuals who are, after all, not gods. The land is at times solace, at other times threat. But are its secrets only an imagined force that prevents any positive action? Somers at times sounds like Lawrence preaching a return to a kind of primitive state where man was at one, organically, with the cosmos. At other times, nature reminds him that he does not belong in Australia, reinforcing his sense of isolation, so that he cannot wait to leave. But will he ever find what he wants, even assuming he knows what he wants? Towards the end of the novel, Jaz says what others have said about Lawrence: "seems to me you just go round the world looking for things you're not going to give in to" (K, 348). Harriett sees the problem in personal terms: "He's always breaking his heart over something — anything except me. To me he's a nether millstone". She is cynical to the end about his metaphysical pretensions. "Metaphysical! .... You'd think to hear him he was nothing but a tea-pot brewing metaphysical tea." (K, 349)

Things start to look worse for the great new metaphysics of masculinity when Somers develops a critical attitude towards Kangaroo. The latter begins to look like a prototype of today's televangelist: all charisma, yet managing to make love sound "like a threat" (K, 136), and being a very poor listener. When Somers tries to explain his/Lawrence's position on the need now to go beyond love, "Kangaroo looked at him for once overbearingly, and with a sort of contempt" (K, 134). He cannot take the criticism that his kind of love is willed — in other words it is a destructive will-to-power because it is not instinctive. Kangaroo responds with anger (K, 135). And it is here that he is portrayed as a homosexual bully, and is disqualified for projecting the wrong kind of leadership; not instinctive and natural, but willed and "mental" — attributes that always carry the most negative connotations in Lawrence. Therefore, the whole male-leadership project is not rejected *per se*, but rather Australia is not the location for the ideal community which will lead the culture out of decadence. Lawrence will have to look elsewhere; in fact he will have one last attempt — in the Mexico of *The Plumed Serpent*. But the project may well be as impossible as the forms of literature that should express it. The only answer to the unstable text will be mythology, which like ideology enables the degree of closure required by blind faith.

We may also be justified in asking whether we are even allowed to take the political ideas in the novel seriously. Here is Jack's utopia: "We shall be just cosy and Australian, with a boss like a fat father who gets up first thing in the morning, and locks up at night before you go to bed" (K, 187). Is this the basis for a revolutionary politics? It looks as if the future will be another version of Eastwood home-life, where the closed community will not tolerate difference (a metaphor for a greater intolerance at the national level). Moreover, Kangaroo is the perfect leader for this future, as Somers tells him: "you're such a Kangaroo, wanting to carry mankind in your belly-pouch cosy, with its head and long ears peeping out" (K, 210). Political realities are reduced to domestic realities, as if the games of power will be acted out precisely there where the woman has reigned. This cosy utopia is, of course, a very old idea of patriarchy — the Father of the Nation. It is one that the dictators of the twentieth century, Stalin, Hitler, and Mao, will get their mass propaganda machine to sell to the people.

The grand narrative of the Nation State, though, is discredited in the long, autobiographical chapter, "The Nightmare". Here in a major genre shift, a memory triggered off by the violence threatened by Kangaroo works through the events during the war which changed Somers for ever. As is well known, the story is that of Lawrence and Frieda, harassed by the authorities, expelled from Cornwall on suspicion of spying, and culminating in Lawrence/Somers suffering physical humiliation at the hands of Army medics in the recruitment centre in Derby. The chapter thematically illustrates the idea of bullying (thus being continuous with the Kangaroo episode), and extends to a trenchant critique of the state of English democracy which the war has changed into rule by mass hysteria. Pinkney has rightly drawn attention to the way Lawrence illustrates with unprecedented accuracy Gramsci's concept of "hegemony", "grasping how deeply a dominant ideology seeps into the fibres of lived experi-ence".[36] In the novel, the ideology is "Bottomleyism", named after the owner of *John Bull*, a particularly jingoistic popular newspaper. We are given a clear idea of the extent to which the newspaper would go to attack any difference, to "break the independent soul in any man who

---

[36] Pinkney, 117.

would not hunt with the criminal mob", as Somers puts it in *Kangaroo* (K, 212). Moreover, "Bottomleyism" is the State ideology of the "*John Bull* Government of '16, '17, '18" (K, 214). They tried to abolish his difference by shaving off his beard — a personal Lawrentian symbol for difference which takes on greater resonance in the text in its associations as code for radicalism and threat: Harriett first mistakes Jack for a Socialist "because he had a beard and wore a little green house-jacket" (K, 19). And, by extension, the bush is the menace to new Australia. Harriett/Frieda is not spared the harassment, threatened as she is with internment because she is a foreigner, her fears clarifying her deep resistance: "in her soul she hated the fixed society with its barrenness and its barren laws .... all the black animosity of authority was encompassing her" (K, 240). Moreover, this committed sense of difference brings her closer to Somers than the rest of the novel allows, and confirms her superiority as a more stable character who has the strength of conviction to see through Somers' flirtation with reactionary politics.

The old, "liberal" England is ruined by the war (K, 206). But Lawrence's England is its Literature.[37] Shakespeare's "wistful autumn" or "Hardy's woodland" (K, 257), or Adam Bede country in a snowy winter (K, 258): literature, like the isolated countryside, is solace. Now that the writing of the new, dominant mass media has destroyed the soul of the culture, England has become "expressionless". Yet not quite. Lawrence will give it the expression of literature, implicitly aligning himself with the great tradition, but also with the exiles of Modernism. Leaving on the boat from Harwich he sees "snow on the downs like a shroud" so that England appears "like a grey, dreary-grey coffin sinking in the sea behind" (K, 258). Thus England becomes nothing but its literature, a kind of Gray's "Elegy"; but also a reminder of the other leave-takings in Lawrence's fiction (in *The Lost Girl*, or *Women in Love*). Somers/Lawrence may feel "broken off from the England he belonged to". But he will still be tied to it by literature.

What the chapter illustrates is summed up at the end: "the fear of the base and malignant power of the mob-like authorities ..., the dread, almost the horror, of democratic society, the mob." (K, 259) This goes for Australia, too, by analogy. The great Nation State, however, is not the only discredited grand narrative: "For the idea, or ideal of Love, Self-sacrifice, Humanity united in love, in brotherhood, in peace — all this is dead." (K, 264) Yet, we cannot live without ideals. This is Somers' dilemma. The Whitmanesque comradeship of the Diggers is attractive at

---

[37] As it is in the late essay, "Nottingham and the Mining Countryside", (1929). See P, 135.

first, but it is finally rejected, just as it was by Lawrence in the final version of *Studies in Classic American Literature*.[38] Somers' solution, and the only one Lawrence proposes for the cultural and political crisis, is that man must learn to listen to his own soul, to "turn to the old dark gods" (K, 265). It is not possible to do this in Australia, nor in *Kangaroo*. But it signals the point where the novel ends its "thought-adventure", and demands the next leave-taking, in the continuing quest for a location where the new man can be in touch with his dark god, and imagine a way of leading the culture out of its crisis. This will be the "thought-adventure" of *The Plumed Serpent*.

Yet, as I suggested already, *Kangaroo* is also an adventure of writing. Lawrence may insist on his ties with English literature, but his relationship to it in *Kangaroo* is critical. The next genre shift in the novel, chapter XIV: "Bits", with its quotations of local trivia and gossip from the Sydney *Bulletin*, is symptomatic of a greater fragmentation of the codes, registers and unities of the old English novel. The metonymies of realism are further dispersed into their synecdoches, as textual bits break loose from the unifying whole and become part-objects of the real whose meaningful connections are left to the reader, as in collage. Thus the textual process carries a level of meaning semiotically, about the way we make sense by imposing coherence on what are essentially fragments of perception. The formal experiment comments on the "thought-adventure" as the men attempt to impose order and meaning through their new grand narrative of male leadership. The unbinding of conventional textual cohesion deconstructs the male bonding it represents.

Lawrence goes even further, however. The narrator intrudes at a meta-narrative level, addressing the reader directly, in the spirit of *Mr Noon*, and with Joyce's *Ulysses* in mind: "Now a novel is supposed to be ... "; "We insist that a novel is ... a thought-adventure, if it is to be anything at all complete" (K, 279). Yet, if the new genre of "thought-

---

[38] Lawrence's belief in the male comradeship promoted by Whitman is contained in the first version of *Studies in Classic American Literature*, written between August 1917 and September 1918. It was not published at first, but later completely revised in a different register — racy, colloquial, intended for the American market — between November and December 1922. Lawrence's pro-Whitman stance of 1918 became his anti-Whitman stance of 1922. The first draft of *Kangaroo* was written during June and July 1922. It was revised during October 1922 and in early 1923. Therefore it would be plausible for Somers to be pro-Whitman at first. But just as he rejects the matiness of the Diggers, so Lawrence rejects Whitman's ideal of male comradeship. The writing of the novel *Kangaroo* seems to have got Lawrence to change his mind about Whitman. A useful source for dates of writing, revision, and publication is Paul Poplawski, *The Works of D.H. Lawrence: A Chronological Checklist* (Nottingham: D.H. Lawrence Society, 1995).

adventure" is supposed to give the novel its sense of completeness, its cohesion and unity, then the text's own deconstructive strategies indicate that this is an impossible demand. Somers speaks the author's truth when he is given to think: "The bulk of mankind haven't got any central selves ... They're all bits." (K 280) This "gramophone of a novel" replays in such passages the thoughts of the author. In other passages, the narrator's address to the reader is more aggressive: "I hope, dear reader, you like plenty of conversation in the novel." And later, more cynical as well: "Chapter follows chapter, and nothing doing .... If you don't like the novel, don't read it." The cynicism easily elides into jokey word-play when the expression "queen bee" becomes: "Beatitudes, beatitudes. Bee attitudes or any other attitudes" (K, 282-284), in a Joycean moment where the mood of a self-cynical, world-weary writer (continuous with the attitudes communicated at the meta-narrative level in the abandoned *Mr Noon*) undermines the assertions of the new masculinity.

It seems that the cultural regeneration will be first and foremost a regeneration of writing. The future of the world is bound up with the future of the novel. The deconstruction of the conventional English novel is cognate with the discreditation of the old grand narratives. The old textual unities, like the old fixed ideals are rejected for new kinds of relationships; ones that challenge the automatism of response, communicating messages through new "vibrations", new "flows" (K, 299-303). Thus the "old life-mysteries" and "difference" will gain a "new recognition". However, it is a difference which does not go as far as Derrida's "*différance*" which wants to unfix meanings to let them remain in the play of undecidability.[39] In Lawrence, the old values and coded meanings are de-automatized (a modernist process by definition) so that they can be relocated in their forgotten truth, deep within the instinctual, creative self. However, the textual experiment in writing deconstructs all certainties and essentialisms, and we are left waiting for the resolution of contradictions. *The Plumed Serpent*, will make one last attempt, and it is to this novel that we now turn.

2. *The Plumed Serpent*: from satire to mythic resolution

i. Critical reception
The reception of *The Plumed Serpent* is also polarized between outright rejection and high praise. The appraisal stands or falls, once again, on whether you read the text as destabilizing the doctrine it promotes

---

[39] For further discussion see Jacques Derrida, *Margins of Philosophy* (Hemel Hempstead: Harvester Wheatsheaf, 1982. First published 1972).

through generic and stylistic shifts; or whether you read the work only as doctrinaire and rather dubious sexual politics. Careful reading of the context of ideas in the fiction is, as ever, crucial. Not, though, to rescue Lawrence from his own worst moments of misogyny, but to appreciate the art which emerges even then, and which ultimately expresses senses of uncertainty absent from the essays. This is the principal claim of this, and the previous chapter; and it is one that is being endorsed by deconstruction which, by definition, teases out the contradictions in fictional texts which the critical consensus has read in ideologically transparent and unified ways. *The Plumed Serpent*, like any of Lawrence's novels, is reduced to the sexual ideology the text is in part questioning if the complexities of the representational problematics are left out of account. Such reductionism blames the novel itself for the faults of the characters.[40]

Walker[41] also claims the novel has been largely misunderstood because the approach was so often based on false criteria. As we saw in the previous section, a notion of coherence deriving from traditional realism and the "well-made novel" leads to all sorts of difficulties when reading a text characterized by shifting modes of writing: beginning as parody tourist guide and "the 'classic' American tale on the open road", the text shifts between realism and myth, satire and symbolism, ritual drama and melodramatic action, travelogue and sermonizing — to name but the most prominent. Therefore, to apply the assumptions of plausibility germane to the realist element alone to the rest of the text is misleading. However, Walker suggests that the formal instability can be explained by the fact that Lawrence had trouble responding to Mexico because of its "bewildering contradictions" and the author's own "inner divisions". [42] Now, it seems to me, it is one thing to suggest that Kate Leslie has difficulties reading Mexico, but quite another to suggest the same about Lawrence from the evidence in the novel alone. She is the focalizer, and we rely on her views and perspectives from the early prejudices and ignorances, to her changing, expanded and more competent reading of the foreign culture later. The novel may well be a fictional record of Lawrence's struggle with Mexico, but we only know that from the letters and essays, from the memoirs and the biographies. Knowing this about the author does not necessarily help us to read the novel better. All Lawrence's novels are in certain senses autobiographical; but not straight autobiography.

---

[40] Cf. Pinkney, 148.
[41] Ronald G. Walker, Introduction to the Penguin edition of *The Plumed Serpent* (London, 1985). All references in text [TPS] are to this edition.
[42] Walker, 24, 30-31.

Walker's point about Lawrence's "inner divisions" reminds us of Murry's book. Here we have the classic case of misreading the fiction through the biography (or worse, through Murry's own personal view of the author he "knew"). As I pointed out in the previous chapter, Murry felt that *Aaron* and the *Fantasia* were the best things Lawrence had written because in them the author was being honest about himself. In everything else his fictions were compensation fantasies for his "inward divisions". Thus, for instance, in *The Plumed Serpent* Cipriano is a wish-fulfilling version of the author, a version of masculinity that would never be realized in life. Fiction, therefore, gives a sense of wholeness to the divided self of the author. The only problem with this, Murry's principal claim, is that the fiction is not the old stable text of Murry's aesthetic. If he could have read the fiction with an open mind, and different critical assumptions, he might have produced a quite different reading. If anything, the instabilities of the text reflect those of the author — but it would be difficult to prove. The text reflects far more tangible instabilities: those of the characters, the volcanic land, the revolutionary politics, the assertions of indigenous revivalism, the new male leadership, the sexual politics.

Carswell was quick to counter Murry's reading. For her, *The Plumed Serpent* was "the most ambitious and the most impressive novel of our generation". It is the product of Lawrence's "savage pilgrimage", and "far from showing 'disintegration' it creates".[43] As she would understand far better than Murry, it was a record of Lawrence's "pilgrimage" to find any vestige "from the pre-white, pre-Christian era".[44] Even though Carswell's is a biographical study too, her comments on the fiction are sympathetic and intelligent.

Only a few years after Carswell, Tindall published his groundbreaking study of what he called, against the critical consensus, "by far his best novel".[45] Although not many would share this enthusiasm, what is important about Tindall's reading is that it is not a biographical study, for once, but rather a detailed analysis of the mythic references and their sources. At a time when interest in Lawrence had waned, a new impetus was given to study the work instead of just the author, looking in detail at the structures which give the text a greater significance as modernist writing than had hitherto been the case. This put *The Plumed Serpent* in the same general camp as other modernist texts, like those of W.B. Yeats

[43] Catherine Carswell, *The Savage Pilgrimage: A Narrative of D.H. Lawrence* (Cambridge: Cambridge University Press, 1981. First published 1932), 183.
[44] Ibid., 177.
[45] William York Tindall (1939), "Savage Wisdom: D.H. Lawrence's *The Plumed Serpent*" reprinted in Ellis and De Zordo (1992), Volume III, 3.

and T.S. Eliot whose writing derived many of its images and references from the new interest in ancient myth, ritual, and the occult. Tindall draws attention to Lawrence's return to primitivism in antediluvian fiction, and traces the possible sources for the myth and ritual, and the Mexican revivalism. The recovery of Atlantis is central to the wish to regenerate the culture. Ramón is given a modified version of what derived from Madame Blatavky's *Secret Doctrine*. Kate is sympathetic to ancient myth because of her Irish-Celtic origins. The primitive wisdom is re-enacted through cultic rituals and ceremony to recover its truth in the forgotten meanings of the ancient symbols. The novel also shows an interest in "metempsychosis", with "several references to the cyclical developments of races and to reincarnation" exemplified in the *Quetzalcoatl* cult. True to his times, though, Tindall finds that this cult is Lawrence's "objective correlative".[46] Today we would be more interested in T.S. Eliot's use of myth in *The Waste Land* than his aesthetic theory.

A more structuralist version of myth criticism is found in Cowan. The symbolic structures are divided into their essential oppositions in a thematic reading of the formal representation of Lawrence's dualism. For example, the organic and the instinctual is opposed to the machine and surface sensation of the dissolute modern world; indigenous Mexican revivalism is opposed to modern western European modes of being; "dark consciousness" is opposed to "white consciousness"; the ancient pagan religion to the Catholic church; creativity to sterility. The symbolic structures derive from the central opposition between dark and white — and I would add that all the associations with the former have a positive and creative value in Lawrence's iconography. The problem with this reading is that Cowan wants "the reconciliation of opposites", so that "the realistic and the metaphorical modes of the novel" would cohere better. The novel is thus a failure despite the "brilliance of Lawrence's symbolic conception".[47] Once again an older notion of coherence leads to misreading. It would be more to the point to notice that the shift in genre from realism to myth cancels all paradoxes and contradictions. Furthermore, what is interesting about Lawrence's essential oppositions is that generally they reverse the conventional structures of Eurocentric, colonialist thought in a post-colonialist rereading *avant la lettre*. I shall return to these points later.

Vickery is able to say, by the early 1970s, that the "impact of myth and ritual on Lawrence's poetry and fiction is generally well-known". He

---

[46] Tindall, 7.
[47] James C. Cowan (1970), "The Symbolic Structure of *The Plumed Serpent*" reprinted in Ellis and De Zordo (1992),Volume III, 23-4.

goes further in this paper, however, by claiming that Frazer's *Golden Bough* provides *The Plumed Serpent* with "organizing principles for the novel's characters, themes, and controlling rhythms".[48] The sacred drama of song and dance as means of spiritual renewal is meant to convert the reader; while the ritual action is writ large as a structural principle for Kate's slow process of conversion. Although Lawrence is eclectic in his uses of primitive rites — even combining them with biblical creationism, the story of Christ's "Second Coming", and the chapel hymns of his youth — the overall impression of ritualistic acts that lead physically to spiritual awakening dramatizes the interaction of the human and the mythical. Thus *The Plumed Serpent* begins in the modern urban wasteland, and the world reflects Kate's personal crisis. Then she goes back to the simple life of the country peasant, to be alone, and is helped by the newly resurrected god to undergo a rite of passage towards a newer womanhood. The structure of the novel is "this protracted struggle to renounce the old and familiar and to accept the new and alien that constitutes Kate's rites of transition". When the newly revived gods tell their propaedeutic stories, they are, like the old legends, casting spells too. Kate is fascinated (bewitched) by Ramón and Cipriano; and sex, like death, is enshrined in ritual ceremony, as it is in the primitive myths described by Frazer and others. But Kate has to keep the myth and the reality separate. Her equivocations bring irony and myth into a strange "collocation". Perhaps, Vickery suggests, these doubts might also derive from Frazer, "from *The Golden Bough*'s own ambivalences about myth and religious ritual — on the one hand, studying it in detail and on the other, subtly decrying it as outmoded forms of superstitious thought".[49]

What the readings of myth and ritual reveal, besides the useful information on important sources during the modernist period, is that the text does not signify by myth alone. There are other, contradictory genres — realism is usually mentioned (but there are many more, as Walker discusses — see above). Yet what mediates between them is the psychology of character. Kate may need the new experience and the attentions of Cipriano for other than religious reasons. The equivocation is a symptom of her instability (her mid-life crisis). Ramón's utter belief in his key role in the *Quetzalcoatl* revival is in part at least a symptom of his marriage crisis. (Somers in *Kangaroo* does not have the option of becoming a god; he cannot even become a leader.) Once Carlota is dead, Ramón can take a more doting, submissive wife to suit his god-like

---

[48] John B. Vickery (1972), *"The Plumed Serpent* and the Reviving God" reprinted in Ellis and De Zordo (1992), Volume III, 28, 30.
[49] Vickery, 33, 45, 49.

ambitions. Kate, however, will never quite be able to go beyond her European scepticism, so she can only accept the terms of her marriage to Cipriano as just better than turning into a frustrated old woman — a typical western, "feminine" story.

Nevertheless, the turn away from biography to source criticism has introduced a critical rigour to Lawrence studies, a welcomed attention to textual detail. The more biographical or ideological approaches (and they have dominated the reception of Lawrence's works) have been largely responsible for what Doherty has called "confused and confusing readings". Moreover, even though there have been major shifts in readings over the years, "these interpretations have lacked any substantial basis in the text itself, more often reflecting ideological shifts in attitudes towards the male/female relationship".[50] One example is the reaction to the phallocentric sexual doctrine when, towards the end of the novel, Cipriano denies Kate orgasm, and she appears to accept it. For readers today this is especially implausible. But as Linda Ruth Williams, and before her Hilary Simpson point out, the distinction which Lawrence makes between clitoral and vaginal orgasm is one already made by Freud in 1905,[51] and it is important today to understand the place of such theories in the modern history of female sexuality, in its mythologies and Lawrence's reinforcement of them. Doherty approaches the whole controversy differently. He demonstrates in some detail how the sex scene could be read as an example of a quite different sexual theory, one deriving from yogic or Tantric yogic practice, whereby both partners are passive, and sex is "a method of ego transcendence". Orgasm is withheld by the man too, so that the sexual drive is maintained as a force of transcendental awareness. The Tantric ethos brings the partners into closer unison with the cosmos through the continual play without end of "a motionless sexual union".[52] For Doherty, the two sexual scenes are examples of an eastern practice which displaces western sexual theory. Passivity and submission in the western sense are beside the point. Kate is transformed as she learns that her former sexual modality is inferior to the new non-orgasmic paradigm. The opposition of these sexual modalities is given figurative value in the text as the movement of the waves breaking on the shore is contrasted to the continuous circulation of

---

[50] Gerald Doherty (1985), "The Throes of Aphrodite: The Sexual Dimension in D.H. Lawrence's *The Plumed Serpent*" reprinted in Ellis and De Zordo (1992), Volume III, 51.
[51] Freud, *Three Essays on the Theory of Sexuality* (1905).
[52] Doherty, 55, 56.

water in the fountain.[53] Ritualized sex is practiced in another symbolic form: in the drumming and dancing which enacts the pulsing of blood and the life force of the cosmos.

Such a reading puts a different gloss on the feminist attack on Lawrence. Whether you accept it or not — and I think it certainly contains some truth — it does illustrate the way partial readings produce a different text as their object. When Doherty's paper ends with the claim to have "offered a reading which is coherent and unified",[54] we can only agree that, as with any reading deriving from a unified theory or ideology, the approach reads its own coherence into the fictional text. However, as Picharde[55] reminds us, the text of *The Plumed Serpent* is constructed not just by a series of oppositions but contradictions, evoked by the unstable Mexican landscape. Appearances are subverted, statements are questioned as soon as they are expressed — which is all very unstable ground for single, unified meaning. In other words, there is a perpetual dissemination without fixed meaning, as even the new masculinist ideology is on slippery ground. The case may be exaggerated, but it offers at least a partial truth — and one we shall return to. Picharde though, misses the way in which myth or allegory fixes meaning, by definition, even if the constructions are arbitrary. Yet he also illustrates the way a strong reading appears to rewrite the text it reads.

From these differing perspectives, we can see then, the force of critical approaches which may well lead us to appreciate just how labile the text itself is. Conflicting readings seem to be a combination of ideological exclusivity and textual undecidability.

F.R. Leavis found *The Plumed Serpent* boring and unreadable, "the least complex of all his novels". He does not see the point of using Kate as the principal "dramatized consciousness" (as she is not even Frieda!).[56] Kermode thought it inferior to the work of the great period because there is a spurious religious rhetoric and posturing which he finds unacceptable. Both the racial and the sexual problems are "troublesome", and the denial of the woman's orgasm will seem to many extremely chauvinistic, even while the point of it is unclear. Kate may be sceptical, but not effectively enough. For Kermode, Kate has to atone for the sexual

---

[53] I would add that we should remember that for Lawrence the fountainhead, or wellhead is the figure of the creative unconscious.

[54] Doherty, 60, 61.

[55] Jean-Paul Picharde (1988), "A World To Save" reprinted in Ellis and De Zordo (1992), Volume III.

[56] F.R. Leavis, *D.H. Lawrence: Novelist* (London: Penguin, 1985. First published 1955), 77, 78.

demands of the New Woman which have ruined the culture.[57]

The feminist reading that begins with de Beauvoir takes up Murry's attack on Lawrence's attitude to women and makes it the cornerstone of a sexual politics which will be developed further by Millett. Male supremacy is raised to a religion, the new virile man becomes a god for the newly submissive women to worship. Most of the feminist anger is reserved for the suggestion that Kate willingly complies with the renunciation of her sexual autonomy. For de Beauvoir it is "dreadful nonsense";[58] for Millett, Kate is "a female impersonator" who, like all Lawrence's heroines, has to learn her female part, to be exemplary for all women.[59] As many have said since, this reading is the object of an agenda which would spare no male writer on female sexuality. The limits of its approach are seen in its lack of history and contextualization, even while its truths cannot be overlooked. Subsequent feminist criticism has been less partial, because more sophisticated as criticism. I shall return to the history of the feminist reception of Lawrence in the next chapter. For now, let de Beauvoir and Millett exemplify yet another strong reading from an ideologically coherent position which will come unstuck once the proposed unity of the text is seen to be produced by the critical approach rather than by the text itself. Such a claim is substantiated by the proliferation of so many opposed readings, and not by fetishizing the text itself as autonomous object. The problem for the critical reception of *The Plumed Serpent* is well put by Rylance when discussing the difficulty of simply maintaining that the text promotes a particular political ideology: "Emphasizing its ideological line perhaps obscures its specificity as a literary text, i.e., the degree to which it is a self-interrogating work, exploring the limits of its own argument even as it advances it".[60] Even when the degree of self-interrogation is less effective than in *Kangaroo*, the point is still valid.

Hyde stresses the positive attempt to go beyond the critique of the culture of the previous two novels, and, even when the theatre of politics becomes operatic, scenes are "a collage of fragments of nonconformist hymns, Victorian medievalism, newspaper 'bits', Hollywood romances, and Nietzsche's *Zarathustra*, among other things". Whatever the moral confusion the politics may bring with it, Lawrence's pre-Columbian religious revival is never far from Christian values. [61] In other words, it

---

[57] Kermode, 77, 107.

[58] Simone de Beauvoir, *The Second Sex* (London: Vintage, 1997. First published 1949), 253.

[59] Millett, 284-86.

[60] Rick Rylance, "Lawrence's Politics" in Brown (1990), 170.

[61] Hyde, 100-102.

may be anti-clericist, but it is not fundamentally anti-Christian. In this, the novel is closer to *Lady Chatterley* than *Kangaroo*. Indeed, *The Plumed Serpent* foreshadows the diagnosis of "the tragic age" as "the radical confusion of power and authority in a dying culture". Kate prefigures Connie Chatterley, as she too needs a kind of spiritual renewal after the "death" of her husband, and the disillusion with her culture. Sex will be the "sacrament", and a new masculinity will be the "priest".[62] Ritual is carried over from one novel to the next, albeit less explicit in *Lady Chatterley* and more part of a mythic substratum. Hyde explains what others have said before, that Lawrence's insistence on ritual and myth was not unusual to his generation — the generation of Freud, Frazer, and T.S. Eliot. As Lawrence demonstrates in *The Plumed Serpent*, dramatic ritual is a way of physically possessing one's experience, of renewing one's life. The whole modernist concern with myth and ritual is a symptom of the cultural crisis.

For Worthen, the novel goes to the roots of religious, social and sexual experience. It is an ambitious work that attempts to imagine an alternative model for the world, like science fiction does.[63] It is unusual in using Kate as "narrative centre" because she is the kind of woman who would have always opposed the new masculinity. However, she is made to undergo an experience of otherness which transforms her. Her life is radically challenged by the new man.[64] This is doctrinaire. Yet despite the mythic enforcement of the doctrine, "there is always a more ordinary Kate". Worthen though does not believe that her protests carry much weight as they are "regularly subject to the controlling narrative ... in order for it to point out how wrong she is". But as far as sex goes, it is implausible that Kate would simply give up her "own way of achieving sexual satisfaction". Lawrence turns "sexual experience into something exemplary", as he so often does. The novel is thus too "assertive and confusing".[65] Worthen is close to the feminist critique described above, but with a more studied textual reading.

Pinkney notices how the text dramatizes the processes of decoding, as characters double for readers of new cultures and old mythologies. Indeed, *The Plumed Serpent* is "a formidably self-conscious work, preoccupied almost to the point of obsession with questions about the

---

[62] I would add that the male supremacy is toned down in *Lady Chatterley*, and given negative connotations because it is the property of Sir Clifford and his cronies. Also, Connie revives Mellors as much as he is the phallic source of her renewal.
[63] Why science fiction, when it looks to the past for that model?
[64] Worthen, *D.H. Lawrence* (London: Arnold, 1991), 91.
[65] Worthen, 92, 95, 98-9.

nature of reading, writing and meaning".[66] Kate is the principal reader, of course. Not only does she have a lot of time on her hands to read, but in the wider sense it is her efforts at decoding the difference she comes across in Mexico that we read. Reading practices are central to the novel's politics. Kate's high cultural reading is contrasted to the collective readings of the *Quetzalcoatl* revivalists. As she becomes a more competent reader of that cult and its myths, so she moves out of the privacy of her reading space (her room) into the servants' quarters for her first encounter with communal reading. As for writers, "the socialists are writing their great script; Teresa's father, with his rich library of Mexicana, had spent a lifetime working on a history of the State of Jalisco; Owen Rhys, Garcia and Don Ramón are all poets" — and the latter writes the hymns. Mexico is a struggle between different histories; and even the landscapes and skyscapes struggle "to articulate themselves as text". The struggle over the meaning of Mexico is carried on in Ramón's removal of the icons and symbols from the Christian church to replace them with those of the indigenous revivalists. It is hardly a naive novel when it reflects on its own literary project. In this it is modernist. Moreover, as Pinkney explains, it is modernist in its encounter with the modern city, "that new matrix of social experience" like Joyce's Dublin, T.S. Eliot's London, or Dos Passos' New York, and Alfred Döblin's Berlin. This contrasts markedly with the provinces of the nineteenth-century novels of George Eliot or Hardy which were so central to the Nottingham of Lawrence's early fiction.[67] *The Plumed Serpent* is thus not naively doctrinaire; it is a reflection on both first wave Modernism, as in Conrad's *Heart of Darkness* where the fiction of going native is part of a deep-seated critique of western civilization; and second wave Modernism, where social contradictions are given the purely formal resolution of myth as in Joyce and T.S. Eliot.

Pinkney's is a useful corrective to narrowly ideological readings. It ties in well with the work on Modernism and myth begun by Tindall. However it is tellingly silent on the question of sexual politics. Linda Ruth Williams is a corrective to Pinkney. She insist that Lawrence is also always a Romantic.[68] His insistence is on the "dark unseeing"; and this is Lawrence's "darkest novel".[69] Yet, paradoxically, the novel is obsessed with seeing. Moreover, it is a dark, primitive masculinity which women-

---

[66] Pinkney, 148.

[67] Pinkney, 151-52.

[68] As he is throughout his work. What Williams does not mention is that relationship to Romanticism discussed in Colin Clarke, *The River of Dissolution: D.H. Lawrence and English Romanticism* (London: Routledge, 1969).

[69] Linda Ruth Williams (1993), 36-37, 129.

voyeurs are given to idolize. Lawrence reverses the gendered gaze, from a masculine perspective which subjects women to the object of male desire, to a feminine vision of men. For Williams, the strategy does not mitigate the sexism, because Lawrence gets his women characters to confirm his masculine essentialism. This is tried out in novels like *Women in Love* as Gudrun watches Gerald, where what is presented as the object of her sexualized gaze is really nothing more nor less than a male fantasy about being watched. Even the landscape is gendered with its "phallic cacti and sperm-like water". As Williams puts it in a later study, "Masculinity as spectacle is thus writ large in Lawrence's corpus".[70]

Bell, while ignoring the sexual politics altogether, sees *The Plumed Serpent* as an attempt "to recover a holistic narrative vision by rhetorical force" which reads like "unwitting self-parody". Its assertions about pre-conscious existence are doctrinal, and not subtly evolved through the narrative like they are in *The Rainbow*. The narrative language is "highly self-conscious and explicit", making it hard to take the doctrine seriously. Part of the problem is that Lawrence is responding to the doubts about his readership (and ones I discussed in chapter 3). His fiction since *Mr Noon* has dramatized the problem through a series of reader-surrogates. Now because Bell takes *The Rainbow* as the classic Lawrentian novel, the norm so-to-speak of his writing, he insists that *The Plumed Serpent* is still faithful to realism, yet shifts genres between travelogue and novel as he fragments the "delicate organicism of the Lawrentian novel".[71] As the contract with the reader broke down, Lawrence's own organic novel (as in *The Rainbow*) started to come apart in the 1920s. What is unusual about this argument is that Bell refuses to see Lawrence as moving into the general stream of modernist experiment from *Women in Love*, as others are now tending to argue. As I have suggested in this study, there is a crisis in Lawrence's writing which, as Bell (and others) rightly explain, is a reaction to the banning of *The Rainbow* in 1915, and the difficulty of getting published subsequently. And that Lawrence, as usual, turned the crisis in his writing life into the subject of his writing. He does not, though, just dismantle his writing norms of 1915. As many have said before, he was always experimenting with the form of the novel; it is just that in the 1920s, as I have been arguing in this chapter and the previous two, he discovers that the best expression of his frustrations is comic-parodic fiction. Even when he tries to put his latest doctrine through the

---

[70] Linda Ruth Williams (1997), 99.
[71] Michael Bell, *D.H. Lawrence: Language and Being* (Cambridge: Cambridge University Press, 1991), 165-168, 195, 201.

"thought-adventure" of his new novel, he tests it out in an adventure of writing.

ii. *The Plumed Serpent*

Just as *Aaron's Rod* is Lawrence's Italian novel, and *Kangaroo* his Australian novel, *The Plumed Serpent* is his American novel. The Italy of the first novel is its peasants. In their simple life, they remind Lawrence of the ancient peoples before the sophistications of modernity. The Australia of the second novel is the bush, the aboriginal land which keeps the white invasion pinned to the coastal areas. The America of *The Plumed Serpent* is the pre-Columbian civilizations, the Aztec, Maya and Incas. The Indians of New Mexico and Mexico are their descendents. In 1920 Lawrence wrote, in "America, Listen To Your Own": "America must turn again to catch the spirit of her dark aboriginal continent." Americans must "catch the pulse" of the "life-mysteries" of the time before the Pilgrim Fathers and before Cortés and Columbus. "It means a surpassing of the old European life-form ... a departure from the old European morality, ethic ... even a departure from the old range of emotions and sensibilities" (P, 90-91). In "Indians and an Englishman" (1923) he insists that this does not mean a complete return to primitivism, but only a recognition of ancient ancestry, and to "stand on the fire edge of their firelight ... neither denied nor accepted" (P, 99). In what follows, we shall not lose sight of this last statement when Lawrence revives the cult of *Quetzalcoatl*, the "plumed serpent". The spirit of place is the goal of the journey; and that spirit is aboriginal. In its traces Lawrence finds his solace from the instrumentalities of modernity. In his American novel, he sends Kate Leslie on the journey (his journey) into the heart of Mexico — which in "Au Revoir, U.S.A." (1923) he calls the "solar plexus of North America" (P, 105). It will be an exasperating experience, as modern Mexico is a "paleface overlay" of North American material values and the Spanish church, while the remnants of the great pyramids and temples threaten with a blind malevolence, reminding you that the "white superimposition" is temporary, and the old-gods in the form of "snake-blooded birds" always have their fangs ready to bite (P, 106).

The western experience of Mexico will turn out to be a complex process of decoding for Kate Leslie, as representative white European, but also as woman. Through her we will get an anti-colonialist reading, which, as Ellis rightly suggests,[72] should appeal to post-colonial thinking today. As others have noted (see critical reception above), Kate is the principal reader-in-the-text, and she attains a level of cultural competence

---

[72] Ellis, 219.

in her reading of Mexico and its ancient cults so that her disinterestedness gives way to a lack of distance. She becomes so involved in the culture, or rather the cult, that she will need all her resources of western common sense to resist the invitation to stay. She is, however, made to undergo a rite of passage which coincides with her own emotional needs, and this will complicate her decision. The rite of passage will also be a masculinist wish-fulfilling fantasy of reconstructing the wilful woman into a submissive wife, justified through a mythology of the male "dark mysteries", and supported by a combination of Frazerian anthropology and indigenous revivalism. The central question is: how far is the assertion of the "ancient phallic mysteries" endorsed and sustained as the basis of the new masculinity and the abolition of the modern woman? Are the recurrent critical perspectives, the protesting voice of the woman and the instabilities of the writing, sufficient to deconstruct the masculinist fiction?

In one respect *The Plumed Serpent* is a traditional novel. The central protagonist is also the focalizer, and we follow her impressions of the foreign culture, and how the experiences she undergoes change her. In the two previous novels the central characters are changed at the beginning, and the novel records their struggles to come to terms with themselves. But in this novel there is a process of development in the character which gives the novel a traditional narrative structure. Much of the critical reception has rightly deplored that development as a return to the dark ages of patriarchy.

Kate Leslie, like Aaron Sissons and Somers, is also going through a personal crisis, and we are mostly limited to her self-understanding. There are, though, shifts in focus to an outside view of her, quite characteristic of Lawrence at his best, like when Ramón (TPS, 94) or Cipriano (TPS, 242) challenge her modern, western view; or when Teresa is given to think of her as "one of those women of the outside world, who make a very splendid show, but who are not so sure of the real secret of womanhood, and the innermost power" (TPS, 446). Kate is, of course, aware of what others think of her; she is, after all a highly self-conscious woman. Although she is supposed to learn to lapse out of modern consciousness into a mindless, submissive femininity, she can only achieve this state temporarily. For a brief moment she experiences what it means to be a pagan goddess, to be "saluted by the real fire in men's eyes, not by their lips" (TPS, 357). Then she is in a state beyond speech, an impersonal condition where "she wanted to be addressed in the third person". In the ritual wedding, she is the passive agent, and once submissive she kisses the feet of her man-god, and is ritually baptized in the rain, bathed in warm, oily water, and clothed in ritual costume. After the ceremony, she is described sitting in her rocking chair, thoughtless, waiting (TPS, 365-68). Her new trance-like passivity is broken by Carlota's hysterical outburst in the de-sacralized church. The incident returns Kate to her modern self, and she attends to the dying woman. Her critical insight into male supremacy is a feminist gloss on her own passive submission: why should women relieve men "of the responsibility of their manhood"? Why should men define women's rights? However, the conclusion she draws is the author's: "Perhaps after all life would conquer again, and men would be men, so that women could be women. Till men are men indeed, women have no hope to be women." (TPS, 384-385)

However one may object to the sexism of individual statements, the contexts are important. There is a pattern illustrated by the above extracts which is unsettling. Kate is first critical, then she acquiesces, then she is critical again. It is the psychology of the central protagonist which lends a certain plausibility to the textual instabilities. Even at the end of the novel, she is still an agent of undecidability. Yet the process of her increasing submission partly undermines the credibility of her resistance. Hers may be a feminist voice, but it is not so steadfast as Harriett's in *Kangaroo*.

The transformations at the level of character are matched by shifts in genre. As the "thought-adventure" takes the modern woman on a journey back to patriarchy, so the adventure of writing takes us on a literary guided tour. We are at the bull-fight, we are introduced to the customs of modern Mexico, the city and, later, village life, the gap between rich and poor, the food and the climate, the mountains and the lakes. We travel south and experience the poor transport system and the bad roads. We are warned constantly about the volatile political situation, so that nowhere is safe. The Spanish Church is repressive, indigenous revivalism and revolutions are an integral part of the history, corruption and chaos is everywhere; indeed, Mexican society is threatening to explode at any minute, just like the volcanic earth itself. Everywhere, the land and the people are marked by traces of the pre-Columbian history: in the archaeological sites, and the remnants of the Aztec Temples. The tourist industry version is contrasted to the ones in the books Kate reads, and the mythology of *Quetzalcoatl* revived by Ramón and Cipriano. In relating all this, the text shifts between the genres of the tourist guide and the travelogue, modern history and archaeology, political journalism and sociology, satire and melodrama, ritual and romanticism, realism and mythology. The changes in writing reflect the mood swings and transformations of the central protagonist. There is, for instance, less satire and more mythology in proportion to Kate's growing cultural understanding. Her sympathy for the genuinely indigenous culture is established in the early chapters where satire on life in the modern city interchanges with parody of the tourist guidebook, and offset by the more serious guidance given by Mrs Norris, the archaeologist. She it is who first draws attention to an older history silently present in the walls of old buildings, with their layers or traces going back to the *Conquistadors*; and the garden with its "Aztec cypresses", and the "dead silence" of the "lava rock" beneath (TPS, 64). It is as if the foreign woman scientist, living alone in a house "like a museum", is the keeper of the real culture. It is an irony that, in a novel generally noted for the revivalists being an exclusively male group, the English ambassador's widow is the initial source of Kate's knowledge of the indigenous past, and her introduction to Ramón. Mrs Norris is described as "a lonely daughter of culture, with a strong mind and a dense will, she had browsed all her life on the hard stones of archaeological remains". Yet she stands out of the mass of people as one of the few individuals who could play "her social game" and remain aloof, "and all alone" (TPS, 65). Lawrence makes her an ambivalent character: "strong mind and dense will" are negative connotations in Lawrence; yet she is truly independent and self-sufficient. In narrative terms, though, she is only a catalyst; and once she has fulfilled her function she will take no more part.

The satire is largely confined to the early scenes, beginning at the bullfight, which is described through Kate's eyes in a series of grotesque caricatures reflecting her disgust and fear. The stadium is a place of "mob authority" and jeering crowds. The incident when the fat Mexican sits down "plumb between Owen's knees", and will not move despite protestations (TPS, 44), is the kind of threatening situation we saw in the train in Italy in *Aaron's Rod*. Here, the cynical narrator interjects an address to the reader.[73] Kate, like the other westerners, reacts with cultural arrogance: "'Insolence!' said Kate loudly. 'Insolence!'" (TPS, 45) Moreover, and despite the tone of the intrusive narrator, the incident adds to the general threat of violence and Kate's growing paranoia. The stadium becomes a microcosm for a greater social unrest. She is too sensitive to sit through the gory show in the arena (an attitude that will harden later), and runs out in a fit of hysteria. In this condition, in the rain and confusion, she meets Cipriano, the general, who, gallantly, "rescues" her. The writing elides into melodrama and romance for a brief moment. However, the dark-eyed stranger does not attract the distraught western woman; she finds his "glassy darkness so wearying" (TPS, 54). Kate has a long way to go before she can see him the way he wants to be seen. Mexico is still under western eyes.

---

[73] And one we are accustomed to in the writing of the 1920s. But in this novel such comic asides will not last.

The text returns to the satirical mode at Mrs Norris' tea-party. Social gatherings of expatriates are classic locations for satire, as we saw at the villa of Sir William and Lady Franks in *Aaron's Rod*. Here, though, Lawrence goes much further in his caricature of arrogant and reactionary North Americans who despise the natives. When, later, Kate is shown the political frescoes on the walls of the university patio, Lawrence uses the chance to criticize them as too deliberate (like "socialist realism") and not "the spontaneous answer of the blood" (TPS, 84). Kate is given to comment that "these caricatures are too intentional" (TPS, 85).[74] But as Walker claims, the revolutionary artist's concern with the modern suppression of the indigenous culture and the need for its revival roughly parallels Lawrence's own scheme in the novel.[75] Equally as significant, I would suggest, is that one of the frescoes is called "Reactionary Forces" by José Clemente Orozco.[76] Moreover, it seems to me that Lawrence is satirizing those reactionary forces at Mrs Norris' tea-party.

Here, the American, Judge Burlap represents the worst form of cultural arrogance: "They (Mexicans) don't like honesty and decency and cleanliness .... What they call liberty here is just freedom to commit crime." (TPS, 70). He is acerbic, intolerant, and expects the other foreigners to agree with him. Yet Burlap's opinions are only extreme versions of Kate's: when she is in one of her paranoiac moods, she feels oppressed by Mexico; the black eyes of the local men are empty, showing "no real I. Their middle is a raging black hole" (TPS, 72). However, Don Ramón is there to challenge her Eurocentricism. He accuses her of not yet seeing Mexicans as real people (TPS, 73). She has not yet learnt to read them other than as an object of her emotional state, therefore she can only resort to western stereotypes. She will learn to read better, but will never completely lose her own cultural identity, never be totally convinced that she really belongs in Mexico. For now: "Used to all kinds of society, she watched people as one reads the pages of a novel, with a certain disinterested amusement." (TPS, 74) Through her, we are being taught how to read. The key phrase is: "with a certain disinterested amusement." This defines the reader of satire, a post-Enlightenment persona for whom reading is amusement, and literature is the novel of manners where society is limited to "polite society". Nothing could be further from Lawrentian reader-response theory than "disinterestedness".

Lawrence uses the opportunities afforded by such social gatherings

---

[74] And this draws attention to the paradox in the modernist attraction to primitivism: a conscious pursuit of lack of consciousness. I am indebted to my colleague Ben Knights for pointing this out.

[75] Walker, notes, 487.

[76] Cf. the reproduction in Ellis, plate 21.

for his anti-American invective: North America represents an advanced stage in the cultural degeneration, hegemonically spreading its materialist values throughout Mexico. Americanization is the greatest danger for Mexico, breaking the blood-tie with the pre-Columbian culture. It is the second wave of colonialization after Cortés. The signs of both "invasions" are in the Spanish Church and the American factory, respectively (TPS, 113). Once bound to the machine, which is to say, the modern spirit itself, the native Indian soul is lost. It is a spirit symbolized by the car, the "real insanity of America" (TPS, 146-50). As young Henry puts it: "Bolshevism only smashes your house or your business or your skull, but Americanism smashes your soul." (TPS, 76) However, modern Mexico seems incapable of doing anything about it. Kate comes to the conclusion that the Mexicans, "are a people without the energy of *getting on*, how could they fail to be hopelessly exploited" (TPS, 183), as indeed they have for centuries.[77] It is a general inertia that seems to prevent them from changing things. Kate notices how her servants just continue to sleep on the cold floor with only one blanket, always miserable, but never doing anything effective about it. Such thoughts lead Kate towards a theory of racial superiority. The white races have dominated the dark races; but the white man, for all his words, is "hollow with misgiving about his own supremacy". Once he shows any signs of weakness, "the dark races will at once attack him, to pull him down into the old gulfs" (TPS, 182). This is Kate in one of her paranoiac moods, reiterating the old fear that the dark races are what the white races once were before they became "civilized". Kate will become conscious of this colonialist mentality in clear-sighted moments when she will first reverse the racial opposition, and then deconstruct it by abolishing otherness altogether, removing the threat of yet another violent hierarchy in agreeing to play her part in the revival of the *Quetzalcoatl* cult. Moreover, the text's shifting genres from post-colonialist critique to myth effectively cancels all contradictions. The "backward races" (TPS, 183) will be given back their indigenous culture, which the text values from the outset as superior by challenging the dominant Eurocentric ideology.

Racial difference, however, is confused with sexuality: "these dark-faced silent men ... were columns of dark blood". The white Americans were "bloodless, acidulous ... with their nasty whiteness ... !" (TPS, 79) These are Kate's thoughts in reaction to the Burlaps. Yet, much later, in her feminist frame of mind, she resists Teresa's phallicism: "He (Ramón)

---

[77] Interestingly, Lawrence emphasizes the very expression his mother would have used, as if to recall the best authority he knew on how to "get on" in life. See John Worthen, *D.H. Lawrence: The Early Years 1885-1912* (Cambridge: Cambridge University Press, 1991).

is a man, a column of blood. I am a woman, and a valley of blood." (TPS, 448) But then a short while later she accepts this explanation of sexual difference (TPS, 454), as part of the general drift towards becoming the submissive woman to the new masculinity. Moreover, the signifier: "blood", like the signifier: "dark", disseminates ambivalently through the text.[78] Connotations of sexual potency and virility, but also violence (when the blood is roused to hatred, blood will be shed), racial purity, and class or caste as social and tribal superiority percolate through the text. Kate comes from the European aristocracy and has Irish-Celtic blood. The "dark eyes" are traces of the proud and potent aboriginal blood of the native Indian. Ramón and Cipriano are western educated, but of native Mexican origin. "Dark eyes" are associated with an instinctual passion and violence. Yet these connotations have their specific contexts in the psychology of Kate's changing moods. She learns to read them more positively, and sexually, as her fears are relinquished. The text, though, oscillates between the conflicting meanings, so that the signifier: "blood" never settles on the one signified for long. Its connotations reverberate in the atmosphere, as the spirit of the place is "mysterious and menacing" with the threat of bloodshed (rumours of bandits frighten Kate as she travels south). The local villagers at times represent a "primitive darkness", the men "a heavy, blood-eyed resentment" (TPS, 169). It seems the pre-Christian "dark mysteries" are only found in dangerous places, "full of scorpions" (TPS, 139). Kate has to get beyond her Christian fears of an atavistic hell to make her divided self whole again through the last great mystery left, and the one degraded most in the modern world, namely sex (yet later she will deny that sex has any

---

[78] "Dissemination" in its common usage means the spreading of information. Derrida uses the term to signify the process of a play of meaning by calling on the many semantic connotations of "play": more play, meaning a freer movement (of a rope); bring or call something into play, meaning causing it to have an influence; the state of play (in a game); as well as a play on words (pun, or language game), etc. Thus the signifier: "play" does not have a single, fixed signified, but a series of shifting connotations depending on usage and context. Lawrence's writing is often characterized by what I have called an "aesthetic structure", which consists of a pattern of recurrent signifiers which shift their connotations in different contexts, but keep all the implications in play. Thus the best writing is characterized by a structure of recurrent motifs. This is the case in *Sons and Lovers*, *The Rainbow*, and *Women in Love*; but also to a certain extent in *The Plumed Serpent* (cf. 87, 103, 106). This "aesthetic structure" may be described by Derrida's "dissemination". It is still a spreading of information, but at a semiotic level, where the signifiers themselves are multi-referential as opposed to transparent signs with single meaning. Derridean "dissemination" deconstructs fixed meaning at the semiotic level. Cf. Jacques Derrida, *Dissemination* (Chicago: Chicago University Press, 1981. First published 1972).

importance at all). Once settled in her house in the country, the water of the lake is "sperm-like" (TPS, 127), and the "jarring, exasperating reality had melted away, a soft world of potency stood in its place, the velvety dark flux from the earth" (TPS, 143). Here, potency is associated with the signifier: "dark" as a natural cosmic process. Her moods will still fluctuate, but through Ramón she will understand the force of the "dark sun" (TPS, 157), and the potential for rebirth.

All these fluctuations of mood are registered in the genre shifts, like the romantic lake serene in the Mexican morning, or the expressionism of an elemental force in a black mood, or in response to the man's phallic power: "She could see again the skies go dark, and the phallic mystery rearing itself like a whirling dark cloud." (TPS, 346) Or the scenes of squalor in a critique of poverty and slum life with its sociological discourse. Then there is the melodrama and suspense as, alone in the dark night, Kate fears the primitive man as intruder, and her fear is given a psychological plausibility. Then the text shifts back into the essayistic mode of a rationalizing discourse: "No! ... [W]e must go back to pick up old threads. We must take up the old, broken impulse that will connect us with the mystery of the cosmos again, now we are at the end of our tether." That mystery is represented by the dance and the drum, that "old savage form of expression" (TPS, 172), which beats the rhythm of the pulsing blood, the life force; while the "slow round dance, with the ancient rhythm of the feet on the earth" belonged to "aboriginal America" (TPS, 297). And yet, in another change of mood, Kate as superior western woman questions whether mixed-race marriages work (TPS, 307).[79] She believes in equal partnership, reiterating Lawrence's theory of oneness in separation, developed through *The Rainbow* and *Women in Love*. It will be her most difficult act of cultural transcoding to accept the new theory of submission to the man. Cipriano will demand nothing more nor less than her total acquiescence. He will lead on his horse, she will follow on her donkey "like a peasant woman" (TPS, 360). She still wants a modern marriage, and is determined not to submit; but it seems less likely as she becomes more like Teresa, and at the end of the novel she is reduced to an older model of femininity, where men are valued for keeping sex "powerful and sacred"; and she weeps her tears of submissive dependency. The final words of the text, however, are ambivalent: "'You won't let me go!'" (TPS, 482) means either: "you won't allow me to go" (back to England and her family. He had already threatened to use his rights as husband); or it means: "please don't let me go".

---

[79] It has often been assumed that this is a reference to Mabel Dodge's marriage to Tony Luhan. Cf. Ellis, 132-33.

The problem with the association of the "dark races" with sexual potency is that it gets close to the orientalist stereotype of the profligate and virile black man, the "noble savage", or the Sheik with his Harem, and the masculine sexual fantasy of the aristocratic white woman being seduced by the black man. She resorts to such stereotyping herself: "Kate watched his (Cipriano's) deep, strong Indian chest .... How dark he was, and how primitively physical, beautiful." (TPS, 239)[80] Kate is not unaware of these associations in the western mentality. She sees Teresa as "the Harem type", and Ramón as her "Sultan" (TPS, 433) revelling in his "pasha satisfaction" (TPS, 435). In her feminist mood, sounding now like her later feminist namesake, Kate is damning of the "male conceit and haughtiness swelling his blood and making him feel endless" (TPS, 436), but equally damning of the "ancient female power, which consists in glorifying the blood-male". Was it not "degrading?" (TPS, 435). She, though, is no longer certain. Here, Lawrence is drawing on the clichés of popular literature, just as he will in *Lady Chatterley's Lover* with the common story of the lady and the servant.[81]

The orientalist stereotypes are just one among many types of cultur-ally centred stories. The signifiers: "blood" and "dark" shift their connotations through a number of stories. There are two further signifiers which are subject to the process of dissemination. First, there is the signifier: "serpent". Kate reads up about *Quetzalcoatl*, the ancient "plumed serpent" (TPS, 90). She also reads about "the potency of the snake upon the Aztec and Maya imagination", and sometimes feels like a bird might feel, mesmerized by the watching snake (TPS, 100). She feels from the start that her destiny lay in Mexico as a "doom .... [s]omething so heavy, so oppressive, like the folds of some huge serpent that seemed as if it could hardly raise itself" (TPS, 56). Mexico has a "heavy reptile-like evil" with its "dark undertone, the black, serpent-like fatality" (TPS, 82). Its more ancient, "elaborate rituals of death" are opposed to the death of modern Mexico, "ragged, squalid, vulgar, without even the passion of its own mystery" (TPS, 82). The drums and the ritual chanting of the hymns awaken the "snake of the coiled cosmos" (TPS, 212). Cipriano has a snake-like power to mesmerize Kate (TPS, 346), and the new image in the temple is the carved serpent of the *Quetzalcoatl* cult (TPS, 375). The signifier keeps in play connotations from Christian, pagan, and Lawrentian creeds.

---

[80] For a critique of women as voyeurs admiring the naked bodies of men see Linda Ruth Williams (1993).

[81] Cf. Simpson (1982), 125, where she suggests that *The Plumed Serpent*, but also *Lady Chatterley's Lover* "show traces of some of the most well-worn clichés of the popular literature." See also Linda Ruth Williams (1993), 82.

Likewise, the signifier: "volcano", whose "lava rock" beneath the earth's crust is the deepest trace of history (TPS, 64), threatens the stability of the earth, and acts as metaphor for an ancient vibration, underground and beyond the control of modern man and his science, and a reminder of impending seismographic explosion. It becomes a symbol of Lawrence's deep wish to blow up the modern world and start again, as Ramón is given to say: "Oh! If only the world would blow up like a bomb." (TPS, 307). Also, Kate is "swept away in some silent tide, to the old, antediluvian silence" (TPS, 324), which by association, refers to the clean-sweep made in the proverbial flood, and also implicates the cultural crisis in renewal through destruction. As in all mythology, a prelapsarian paradise (as in the lost city of Atlantis) is a powerful image.[82] As motif of cosmic vibration, the volcano, by extension, encapsulates the theory of a new authority, and a new self-discipline as the people learn the natural vibration with the earth through perfecting "animistic dancing", which Cipriano prefers to imposing "machine discipline" on his men. The old Indians danced "to gain power ... over the *living* forces or potencies of the earth".[83] The volcano represents the earth's potency. Its vibration is felt by the people (TPS, 87). Furthermore, it is a sign of death, a threat of imminent catastrophe, which influences the fatalistic attitude of the people. Kate senses this volcanic menace in the spirit of the place. After witnessing the ritual dancing and the incantatory chanting of the hymns, Kate feels that "here and here alone ... life burned with a deep new fire" (TPS, 156). When she first loses her will to resist Cipriano, we read: "her will, her very self gone, leaving her lying in molten life" (TPS, 356). The core of the novel is the rebirth of Cipriano as Pan, assisted by Kate in the role of the newly reconstructed woman. The shock-waves of this volcanic eruption will be registered most by feminist criticism.

Thus, the text disseminates the key signifiers: "blood", "dark", "serpent", and "volcano" into a play of connotations establishing a structure of recurrent *leitmotifs*. Through this "aesthetic structure" is inscribed a surplus of meaning. Meanings are unfixed as any one signifier slides between several possible connotations, so that cultural understanding

---

[82] Cf. Walker, in notes, TPS, 499.

[83] In "Indians and Entertainment" (1924) Lawrence describes the dance:
The men tread the rhythm into the centre of the earth. The drums keep up the pulsating heart-beat .... [P]erhaps they are giving themselves again to the pulsing, incalculable fall of the blood, which forever seeks to fall to the centre of the earth, while the heart like a planet pulsating in an orbit, keeps up the strange, lonely circulating of the separate human existence ... the strange falling back of the dark blood into the downward rhythm, the rhythm of pure forgetting and pure renewal. *Mornings in Mexico* (London: Penguin, 1986. First published 1927), 56.

becomes an interplay of constructions, Christian and anthropological, literary or philosophical. Thus at the semiotic and narrative levels the text keeps in play a series of connotations which work against single, transparent meaning. That Lawrence tries to abolish dissemination, difference and irony through the increasing dominance of myth and ritual is a generic and ideological assertion that is only partly held in check by Kate's continued resistance, the undecidability of the ending, and the truth emerging throughout the text that myth and ritual, above all, are constructions.

Yet the question remains: is the adventure of writing an effective enough deconstructive force to undermine the mythology of masculine supremacy? The one thing on which most critics agree is that when Kate admits to herself that she "didn't really want it (orgasm), that it was really nauseous to her", (TPS, 459) it is difficult to believe. Lawrence seems to have confused his generic values; the sex with Cipriano works on two levels: the mythic and the realistic. Kate's acceptance of the superiority of the man's sexuality only makes sense within the masculinist mythology. Unfortunately, her reaction is expressed within the realism, which subjects it therefore to conditions of plausibility not necessary to the mythic level. Indeed, a major problem in the text is the clash of these two levels.

Lawrence tries to establish a level of plausibility through the psychological realism of Kate's instabilities, her volatile moods, and her changing cultural understanding. She becomes less cynical, just as the text moves away more and more from satire. But the realism, and many of the sub-genres (travelogue, romantic or expressionist description, essayistic discourse), continue to surround the increasingly dominant ritual and myth. The latter never quite manages to abolish realism altogether in the text. In the passages of ritual ceremony, the mythic is its own, exclusive explanation. However, as Worthen[84] puts it, there is always the ordinary Kate, and her focalization is reinstated after the hymns and sermons, the dances and drums have ceased. She remains critical of the new masculinity. When Kate, famously, thinks: "How wonderful sex can be, when men keep it powerful and sacred, and it fills the world! Like sunshine through and through one", the next sentence is invariably omitted by critics:[85] "But I'm not going to submit, even there. Why should one give in, to anything!" Although we are used to her changing her mind, the force of her critical stance towards macho men,

---

[84] Worthen, 95.
[85] Significantly only partly quoted by Foucault in *The History of Sexuality Volume 1* (London: Penguin, 1984. First published 1976), 157.

and submissive women like Teresa, places a strain on the plausibility of her giving in to the exclusively male sexual pleasure. Lawrence has tried to prepare for this moment by having Carlota, and therefore another critical woman's voice, killed off; by having Teresa speak for the new submissive wife, and Kate become more like Teresa, and thus less feminist. "Frictional sex" has been the label on which to hang much that is wrong in the culture, and the "wilful woman" has been consistently blamed. When Kate is given to think that it was right to get beyond "her own old desire for frictional, irritant sensation" (TPS, 473, 485), the orgasm is described as "beak-like" (TPS, 459). Ursula's destruction of Skrebensky is described in similar terms in *The Rainbow*. However, the earlier female character was able to learn from this experience to be more together with her sexual partner and not exploit him for her own destructive sexual pleasure, even when it needed another novel to do so. Lawrence returns to the potential of mutual sexual pleasure in *Lady Chatterley*. In *The Plumed Serpent*, however, the balance has shifted decidedly towards a phallic priority. But the careful narrative preparation, through character development, action, symbolism and recurrent motif that makes *The Rainbow*, by general agreement, Lawrence's most successful novel — in traditional and in Lawrentian terms — is largely missing from this novel.

The sexual theory has become too sexist for most tastes today. Some critics have chosen to ignore this in order to promote the novel as modernist, with its Frazerian myth and ritual. Deconstruction ignores nothing. Marginal details, the play of figures, generic shifts — indeed, the logic of textualization that disperses into so many subgenres belies any unity, even when promoted by any one genre (as is the case in myth). On the positive side, we have seen how there is a dissemination around key signifiers which keeps several connotations in play. On the negative side, however, the attempt to insist on a doctrinaire masculinity and a spiritual revival as the solution to the post-war cultural crisis is undermined by the textual instabilities of genre and meaning. The adventure of writing clashes with the "thought-adventure". More so than in the other two novels discussed in this and the previous chapter, *The Plumed Serpent* deconstructs the very doctrine it wishes the reader to believe in, by drawing attention to the cultural construction of meanings and values at different levels; and by its own disseminatory process of writing. Once framed in the genres of myth and ritual, the doctrine becomes one among several literary constructions, albeit overdetermined, and Lawrence's attempts to give it priority may be understood as a last ditch gesture to enforce the doctrine of leadership.

7. Conclusion

In this chapter and the previous one, I have attempted to approach the novels of Lawrence's "leadership" period, first, through masculinity theory and, second, through deconstruction. The novels have been read for their processes of dissemination and their generic instabilities. I hope to have shown how much more radical this approach is than the ideologically narrow approaches which have read the texts as doctrinally transparent works. I have not denied the sexism and misogyny in those texts. I have, however, sought to demonstrate the differing extents to which the masculinist ideas in them are questioned by the texts which try to promote them. Lawrence is at his most sceptical in parts of *Aaron's Rod* and practically all of *Kangaroo*, his most adventurous writing. The doubts are played down in *The Plumed Serpent*, yet the deconstructive approach has teased out the contradictions in the text to an extent that the earlier feminist readings, for instance, could not achieve by exclusively concentrating on the sexual politics. As we shall see in the next chapter, the feminist reception has a long history, part of which records its own internal disputes as some feminists reworked the developments in post-structuralism into their agenda.

What has emerged is the recognition of a writing which, while seeking to express a doctrinaire masculine supremacy in reaction to the perceived wilfulness of modern women and the general post-war cultural disintegration, represents degrees of modernist experiment. Thus it is that textual instabilities undermine the assertions of ideology. In this, the "leadership" novels belong to the whole play of writing that began with *Women in Love*, and includes *The Lost Girl* and *Mr Noon*, which I discussed in chapter 3. Post-structuralist criticism brings out the warring contradictions in the text because it is not hampered by an older paradigm of textual unity, as so many Lawrentian critics have been.

Methodologically, the deconstructive approach works in two ways that are difficult to disentangle. First, reading the essential oppositions against their assumptions is a strategy of reappropriating the text in an understanding that goes beyond its own self-understanding, and, at the same time challenging those readings which are parasitic on that self-understanding. Second, the text is read as self-deconstructing, as a self-conscious play of writing that always already rehearses the critical disputes of its reception. Monologic, narrowly ideological reading is deconstructed by the play of meaning in the text, by the destabilizing strategies of writing. Deconstruction, however, tends to become a hall of mirrors when the text as an object of its criticism is at the same time a reflection of the truth of deconstruction.

6

Lady Chatterley's Lover: Sexual Politics and Class Politics

1. Introduction

In this the last of the main chapters, I shall revisit the feminist critique of Lawrence with the aim of showing that the more radical positions within feminism have had little purchase on Lawrence studies. While American and British feminist critics have approached the works through a sexual politics, they have generally relied on older critical paradigms. Thus the author's reputation and his views from the non-fiction have been the starting point for transparent readings of the fictional texts, so that while the approach has been radical as sexual politics it has been conservative as textual criticism. I shall explain this point in more detail when I discuss Kate Millett. Her sexual politics derived from Simone de Beauvoir's reading of Lawrence. Millett shares her unhistoricized approach, even though de Beauvoir is working within a different critical paradigm, that of Sartrean existentialism.

A quite different French feminism, represented by Hélène Cixous and Luce Irigaray, has re-read sexual politics through the radical textual theories of post-structuralism. I shall be putting their concepts of "*écriture féminine*", "*jouissance*", and the insistence on a new language of the body to work on *Lady Chatterley*. I shall argue that it is here, in post-structuralist French feminism that we find a critical approach which could do justice to Lawrence's poetic representation of female sexuality. Moreover, in the textualisation of "*jouissance*", Lawrence gives female sexuality a moment of autonomy and a value that serve to prioritize it over male phallicism, even while the phallus remains the transcendental signifier. Reading such moments as instances of "*écriture féminine*" should enable us to avoid the ideological reductionism of American and British sexual politics.

I want, though, to take things one step further, and bring the problem of class into the discussion of sexuality. Indeed, a major criticism of post-structuralist French feminism is its general lack of politics. It is accused of preferring instead to remain within the closed complexities of textual criticism and the cultural generalizations of semiotics. Within feminism broadly defined, Toril Moi, Cora Kaplan and Catherine Clément have posed the questions of class and ideology in considerations of sexuality and politics. Drawing on their work, I shall suggest ways in which *Lady Chatterley* problematizes the relationship between class and sexuality. This will involve revisiting the instances of the problematic in *Sons and Lovers*, *The Rainbow*, and *Women in Love*. Furthermore, I shall suggest, in conclusion, that we need a post-Althusserian approach to the relationship between text and ideology, which would insist on the ways in which the workings of ideology become visible in the narrative forms of literature and myth. This should enable us to understand the complex relationship between the class ideologies and the sexual ideology that seeks to abolish them as Lawrence attempts to write class out of the text and mythologize history and social relationships — a process clearly visible in the differences between the three versions of *Lady Chatterley*, as many critics have noted. But also there are complexities between the text and ideology which go beyond the description of the text's internal contradictions towards its future, a future which lasts a long time, as text-for-criticism and cultural object: the scandal in the text has become a scandal of the text.

In what follows, I work with the assumption that a sexual politics without a textual theory is no better than a post-structuralism without politics.

2. Feminist criticism in Lawrence studies

"'You are very conceited, Monsieur,' she mocked. 'How do you know what my womanly feelings are, or my thoughts or my ideas? You don't even know what I think of you now'". (WL, 147) Ursula's challenge to Birkin is a proto-feminist moment that raises the key question: how can a man know what a woman thinks or feels? Yet there are plenty of men who have researched and written about woman's sexuality. But whereas Freud admitted defeat, asking Marie Bonaparte late in his life: "*Was will das Weib?*" ("What does woman want?"),[1] Lawrence has represented female characters as sexual beings, directly revealing their thoughts and feelings. At worst, he has been legislative about sexual behaviour. For feminist criticism, Lawrence is indeed very conceited. (And, of course, he gets his female character to accuse him through the male figure who most represents the author's views.)

Simone de Beauvoir set in train the feminist attack on Lawrence by categorically maintaining that he detested self-conscious modern women, "passionately" believed in male supremacy, and promoted the ideal of the

---

[1] "The great question that has never been answered and which I have not yet been able to answer, despite my thirty years of research into the feminine soul, is 'What does woman want?'" Cited in Ernest Jones, *Sigmund Freud: Life and Work Volume. 2* (London: Hogarth Press, 1955), 468.

"true woman" as the one who "unreservedly accepts being defined as the Other". Thus women are called upon to surrender their hard-won freedom, because to become man's other "takes the shape of an alien consciousness and will", [2] which is also a return to a pre-modern position of subjugation. For de Beauvoir, the Sartrean dictum *"l'enfer, c'est les Autres"* ("hell is other people")[3] has a specifically gendered twist to it: if for Lawrentian man modern woman has become that opposing other, then he will reassert his supremacy in a new phallocracy whose starting point is the return to the phallus as the defining principle of sexuality. Thus, for feminism, man becomes the hellish other imposing his wilful pattern on woman. This has since become a familiar argument — a feminist consensus. Lawrence is the object of an ideological critique, part of the general case about the subjugation of women in patriarchy.

It could be argued, though, that the attack on Lawrence's attitude to women starts long before this. In chapter 4, I mentioned Murry's character assassination, in which the works are used as evidence to prove that Lawrence feared women, only thinly disguised his latent homosexuality, and was sexually retarded thanks to his mother's smothering influence. Carswell was the first to defend Lawrence against Murry. Nevertheless, some critics go back further to those who knew the author as a young man, to Jessie Chambers or Helen Corke whose memoirs are often drawn upon as evidence against Lawrence. Faith Pullin quotes Helen Corke:

> These three women [in the early novel *The White Peacock*] are fully drawn, but Lawrence is not interested in them as individuals. He sees them only in relation to their men. "Take", he would seem to say to his reader, "a male creature! We shall now study its reactions to the various forms of feminine stimuli".[4]

A feminist reading of *Sons and Lovers* could draw liberally on Helen Corke's claims. They would be more difficult to maintain in *The Rainbow*. Here, Lawrence has reversed the structure and has given priority to the women, Anna and Ursula, who use others — the men in particular — to achieve greater self-understanding. The feminist counter-argument is that Ursula is merely Lawrence thinly disguised, speaking his new theory about the need for feminization of the culture; and that, in the

---

[2] Simone de Beauvoir, *The Second Sex* (London: Vintage, 1997. First 1949), 254.
[3] Cf. Sartre's play *Huis Clos* (*In Camera*) (Paris: Gallimard, 1968. First published 1947; first performed 1944), 75.
[4] From *D.H. Lawrence: The Croydon Years* in Anne Smith ed., *Lawrence and Women* (London: Vision Press, 1978), 57.

post-war fiction, the New Woman, which Kate Leslie in *The Plumed Serpent* and Constance Chatterley in *Lady Chatterley's Lover* epitomize, is given to voice approval of her submission to the revived phallic man.

Kate Millett, as is well known, has been enormously influential on the development of a radical sexual politics. Moreover, she has changed the fortunes of Lawrence and Lawrence studies irrevocably. Widdowson assesses Millett's chapter on Lawrence as:

> still one of the wittiest and savagely ironic pieces of literary demolition one could hope to find .... Angry, engaged, assertive, "distorted" it may be, but few would disagree that somehow along the line she rings a bell that is still tolling for the pretensions of Phallic Man.[5]

One cannot overestimate Kate Millett's impact. As Mary Eagleton argues, the relationships between the sexes were henceforth "intrinsically political", a matter of the unequal relations of power, as men dominate women in all kinds of ways in patriarchy. Feminist criticism as sexual politics insists on the "need to explore a text in terms of its gender ideology".[6] John Worthen has reiterated the problem of sexual politics for Lawrence studies: "it has now become impossible to address Lawrence's work without either going on to the defensive or the attack in relation to his attitude to sexuality".[7] The battle over Lawrence was at its most fierce in the 1970s, Norman Mailer leading the defensive camp. However, Lydia Blanchard was already claiming in 1975 that the Millett-Mailer dispute was history. Hers is a rare woman's voice at the height of the most doctrinaire period of radical feminism, speaking for Lawrence as "extraordinarily sensitive to the problems of women".[8] Nevertheless, we can see with hindsight that this was an optimistic assessment of the situation. Blanchard, as one who has taken account of the developments in critical theory,[9] was one of the first in the new era of feminism to insist that you had "to separate the work from the author's reputation".

---

[5] Peter Widdowson ed., *D.H. Lawrence* (London: Longman, 1992), 14-15.

[6] Mary Eagleton ed., *Feminist Literary Criticism* (London: Longman, 1991), 135.

[7] John Worthen's review of L.R. Williams, *Sex In the Head* in the *Journal of the D.H. Lawrence Society*, 75 (1996).

[8] Lydia Blanchard, "Love and Power: A Reconsideration of Sexual Politics in D.H. Lawrence" in *Modern Fiction Studies*, 12 (1975), 432.

[9] See for instance her paper "Lawrence, Foucault and the Language of Sexuality" in Michael Squires and Dennis Jackson eds, *D.H. Lawrence's Lady: A New Look at Lady Chatterley's Lover* (Athens, Georgia: University of Georgia Press, 1985), and reprinted in Widdowson ed., (1992).

Moreover, she argues the case for the works to be read in three phases: up to *Women in Love*, where there is the male-female conflict and the critique of industrial urbanizing England, beginning with the call for the feminization of the culture and ending with questioning the New Woman. Second, the resolution for the cultural crisis in male leadership, a phase ending with *The Plumed Serpent*. And, finally, the rejection of leadership for a new tenderness in *Lady Chatterley's Lover*. Her conclusion is that if you reduce Lawrence's works to one type of relationship between the sexes, then you miss his portrayal of "intelligent women trapped by a society that provides them inadequate outlets for their talents and energies", [10] and the critical and rebellious female figures, those who already rehearse the arguments for a proto-feminist rejection of the dominant male voice (I discussed examples in chapters 4 and 5). However, the most ardent feminist criticism has rejected this reading of Lawrence's *oeuvre*, seeing continuity where others see change.

Judith Ruderman is a case in point (see my comments in chapter 4). She argues against the consensus that Lawrence turned against women in the post-war fiction but returned to his pro-women stance of the earlier work in *Lady Chatterley* through the concept of tenderness: because of his obsessional mother-fixation from his earliest writing, he is misogynist throughout his work. *Lady Chatterley* is not therefore a repudiation of male leadership and misogyny. The leadership novels are an extreme reaction to domineering women, and the last novel continues the tirade. Ruderman continues the sexual politics that Kate Millett began, reading sexual relations as gender power struggles, and Lawrence as male supremacist. [11]

Anne Smith may be taken as representative of the spectrum of arguments about Lawrence and women. Most of the essays in this collection link biography to thematics, yet only Faith Pullin speaks for the post-Millett view. Her conclusion is that "what Lawrence actually wrote about was the relationship between man and a series of female stereotypes". [12] All the other essays are either undecided or defensive. The most defensive is Harry T. Moore's accusing Millett of oversimplifying the texts, missing all the complexities of Lawrence's symbolism. But the most useful is Kinkead-Weekes who demonstrates that the novels only make sense in the textual detail. In a series of examples from different novels he shows that Lawrence at his best represents sexuality in poetic but unstable tropes. The conclusion is that, "one cannot extrapolate

[10] Blanchard, 431-443.
[11] Judith Ruderman, *D.H. Lawrence and the Devouring Mother: The Search for a Patriarchal Ideal of Leadership* (Durham, N.C.: Duke University Press, 1984).
[12] Faith Pullin in Anne Smith ed., 73.

authorial attitudes, because generalizations suggest a relationship between author and fiction that is false to Lawrence's art".[13] This is especially the case in *The Rainbow* and *Women in Love* because of an insistent metaphoricity, and less the case in *Lady Chatterley's Lover* which approaches the genre of fable and is therefore more explicitly doctrinaire. The case for the attention to textual detail I have been promoting throughout this book; and often enough, as I hope to have shown, that detail has revealed degrees of self-criticism and experimental Modernism which have destabilized the authorial doctrine.

The work of Blanchard, Kinkead-Weekes, and others is more convincing than the less helpful defence of Lawrence by Carol Dix. She, like the more recent anti-feminist Peter Balbert, recommends Mailer's riposte that "never had a male novelist written so intimately about women". And contrary to the claim that Lawrence feared and hated women, Dix maintains that he praises women, and was ahead of his time in "creating female characters who were finally to emerge as real people in the sixties and seventies".[14] Indeed, this woman reader endorses Mailer's view that Lawrence "understood women as they had never been understood before".[15]

However, a woman reading is different from reading as a woman; and reading as a woman may be different again from reading as a feminist. As Stephen Heath put it: "To read *as* is to make the move of the construction of an identity in which the diverse, heterogeneous relations of experience are gathered up in a certain way, a certain form". What is clear is that "reading as a feminist involves reading as a woman (it involves a knowledge of what it is to be a woman both negatively, the assigned place of oppression, and positively, the force of the struggle against oppression)".[16] It is therefore problematic for a man to be a feminist; and to say that Lawrence was pro-feminist in *The Rainbow* is quite different from saying that he knew the intimate and sexual needs of a woman. A feminist reading that statement would add that he can only fantasize a woman's needs from a man's desires.

A more convincing way of reading Lawrence is to appreciate the full extent of what he is saying about men and women in relation to how he is expressing such ideas in the fiction. Sheila Macleod acknowledges the difficulties a woman faces writing about Lawrence: "I have scarcely been

---

[13] Mark Kinkead-Weekes, "Eros and Metaphor: Sexual Relationship in the Fiction of Lawrence", 106. First published in *Twentieth Century Fiction*, 2 (1969).
[14] Norman Mailer cited in Carol Dix, *D.H. Lawrence and Women* (London: Macmillan, 1980), 17.
[15] Norman Mailer cited in Dix, 18.
[16] Stephen Heath, "Male Feminism" in Mary Eagleton, 218.

able to find a woman in the 1980s who had a good word to say about him". But she adds that accusing him of sexism and male-centred sexual theories is not the whole story, because his work, "especially the later fiction, is riddled through and through with paradox". Macleod's is another rare woman's voice (like Blanchard's) in the mid-1980s not limited strictly to the post-Millett feminist attack. She promotes detailed and sympathetic readings which manage to get through to the essence of Lawrence's writing even while sharing some of the feminist views about the less acceptable, misogynist moments: "Although Lawrence's fiction is often marred by his obtrusive moralising, it seems to me that the sure instinct of the novelist just as often works to subvert the easy polarities — and, indeed, the hubris — of the moralist". [17]

But we should not take everything away from Kate Millett. Her intervention in the late sixties was nothing less than polemical and controversial. Toril Moi reminds us how significant and audacious her book *Sexual Politics* was: "In courageous opposition to the New Critics, Millett argued that social and cultural contexts must be studied if literature was to be properly understood". This view, not uncontroversial then, is now not just shared by feminists. Moi continues: "The most striking aspect of Millett's critical studies, though, is the boldness with which she reads 'against the grain' of the literary text". [18] Her readings defiantly oppose the author's perspective. She certainly upset the development of Lawrence studies.

Millett's notion of "sexual politics" is the elaboration of the statement: "the process whereby the ruling sex seeks to maintain and extend its power over the subordinate sex". However, her theory of patriarchal power is limited because it cannot account for the exceptional women who "have indeed managed to resist the full pressure of patriarchal ideology, becoming conscious of their own oppression and voicing their opposition to male power". Moreover, patriarchal oppression has more than the one single cause argued for by Millett, namely misogyny. On this level, her approach is reductionist because she attempts "to explain all cultural phenomena *purely* in terms of power politics". The rhetorical force of her argument leads her towards selective quoting, sometimes neglecting the full context, and also the simplification or even misrepresentation of the theories she opposes. Her reading of Freud has since become a notorious case in point. She reduces psychoanalytic theory to biological essentialism, and Freud's whole work to her understanding of

[17] Sheila Macleod, *Lawrence's Men and Women* (London: Heinemann, 1985), 5, 229.
[18] Toril Moi, *Sexual/Textual Politics: Feminist Literary Theory* (London: Methuen, 1985), 24.

"penis envy", "female narcissism" and "female masochism".[19] Sadly, feminism has often gone along with this reductionist dismissal of Freud. But there have been voices within feminism that have challenged this reading of Freud: Juliet Mitchell, Jacqueline Rose, and Cora Kaplan, to name the most prominent.[20]

Kaplan, like Moi, criticizes Millett for her misreading of Freud, where for instance she misunderstands the Oedipus complex as pathological instead of an essential stage of normative development.[21] For Mitchell, Millett's reading of Freud is reductive because she extracts comments on femininity out of the broader arguments and concepts of psychoanalysis thus "making them sound absurd and/or reactionary". Without careful understanding of Freud's theories of sexuality and the unconscious, sexual difference looks like prejudice once its significance in relation to his principal arguments is overlooked. Millett's empiricist critique of sexuality leaves out of account Freud's theories of desire, phantasy, and the unconscious. The outcome of this is that she "denies any attribute of the mind other than rationality".[22]

Millett misreading Freud is bad enough. Her literary criticism is even more obviously faulty in its reductionism. As Moi rightly argues, "Millett's critical readings, like her cultural analysis, are guided by a monolithic conception of sexual ideology that renders her impervious to nuances, inconsistencies and ambiguities in the works she examines". Millett reads Lawrence's works transparently and biographically, finding evidence in the content, selectively, of his sexism and misogyny, and leaving the textual ironies, parodies, and disruptive narrative strategies generally out of account. Moi concludes that *Sexual Politics* "can hardly be taken as a model for later generations of feminist critics". [23] Cora Kaplan's critique of Millett demonstrates the extent to which feminist criticism settles its own accounts. Kaplan usefully locates Millett's critical practice in its formation in American sixties New Left radicalism, counter-culture, Civil Rights, and anti-imperialism. Then, patriarchy was first defined as a political institution, a hierarchical relation of power, alongside other such repressive institutions like "the State, the Family,

---

[19] Moi, 26-28.

[20] Juliet Mitchell, *Psychoanalysis and Feminism: A Radical Reassessment of Freudian Psychoanalysis* (London: Penguin, 1975); Jacqueline Rose, *Sexuality in the Field of Vision* (London: Verso, 1986); Cora Kaplan, *Sea Changes: Culture and Feminism* (London: Verso, 1986).

[21] Cora Kaplan, "Kate Millett's *Sexual Politics*" reprinted in Mary Eagleton, 166.

[22] Mitchell, 351-53.

[23] Moi, 30, 31.

the University, the Mental Hospital or the Army".[24]

Now, it may be surprising that so many radical feminists turned to literature for their revolutionary struggle. It has, nevertheless, caused a fundamental shift in the understanding of the depiction of sex in literature from a libertarian counter-cultural attack on the prudery of State censorship to an ideological issue in itself. Fortunately for Lawrence studies, the change came well after the trial of *Lady Chatterley's Lover*, where the case for the defence argued for healthy and wholesome sex, (ironically ushering in promiscuity and a sex industry that Lawrence would have abhorred). The Millett-effect, though, changed the terms of the debate away from censorship and health towards pornography, less as an issue of obscenity (a moral argument), but more fundamentally as an issue of sexual politics — women being represented as sex-objects for male pleasure in a new subjection, a commodification typical of the dominant ideology of both capitalist and patriarchal social formations. Yet Kaplan takes Millett to task for her limited theory of ideology as false consciousness, her insistence on patriarchy as the dominant ideology, and on gender difference as the condition of modern existence. Millett is not personally responsible for such limitations; they derive from her formation in sixties radical feminism. Considerations of class and material and historical conditions, fundamental to radical social thought, are reduced to the monolithic ideology of patriarchy in a sexual politics concerned exclusively with unequal relations of gender. Moreover, as Kaplan suggests, Millett's argument could have benefited well from Althusser's reinscribing psychoanalytic theory in a theory of ideology where the unconscious is central to the workings of ideology. Kaplan has also drawn attention to the naive assumption in *Sexual Politics* that, "literature is always a conscious rendering of an authorial ideology". This raises the vexed issue of the relationship between text and ideology, and one elided by Millett in her unquestioned assumption that the text simply reflects ideology. Althusser insisted that literature made ideology visible by its determinate absences, its silences about the conditions of ideological coherence. The literary text has a critical relationship to ideology, consciously or unconsciously, by definition. But to understand this you need to look carefully at its narrative and stylistic processes — which is

---

[24] Kaplan, 157-8. The most representative writing of the period is Herbert Marcuse (1964), *One Dimensional Man* where it is argued that institutionalized democracy is covertly totalitarian because although the people are persuaded they are free, their protest is contained by the State and the University in what Marcuse calls a "repressive tolerance". His arguments may be much more complex than Millett's, but the ideological thrust is similar. However, her exclusive focus is the institution of patriarchy.

what Millett does not do. Because her critical method is limited to transparent content analysis, she does not "stay with a single text long enough to let the contradictory elements in its ideological inscription play themselves out in her analysis". [25] I shall return later in this chapter to the relationship between text and ideology, working with a concept of the "gendered imaginary" in an analysis of the relationship between class and sexuality in *Lady Chatterley*.

3. French Feminism

With the notable exception of Linda Ruth Williams, whose study draws on the Lacanian-influenced feminist film theory, there has been a telling absence of French feminist critical approaches in Lawrence studies. Yet, I would have thought that deconstructing the binary hierarchies that have dominated the essentialisms of gender difference, and redeploying the notion of an "*écriture féminine*" might pay off as critical approaches to texts which represent female sexuality.

Hélène Cixous in "*Sorties*" asks the question: "Where is she?" in the key oppositions of western culture: "activity/passivity, sun/moon, culture/nature, day/night, father/mother, head/heart, intelligible/sensitive, logos/pathos ...". As Derrida has insisted, the first term in the binary is the privileged one, which Cixous understands as a male privilege, "which can be seen in the opposition by which it sustains itself, between *activity* and *passivity*. Traditionally, the question of sexual difference is coupled with the same opposition: activity/passivity". [26] Cixous is not simply distinguishing between man and woman, but between the cultural constructions of the masculine and the feminine. In this she is close to Lawrence's conceptualization in the "Study of Thomas Hardy" (1914) of an essential bisexuality, and one to which he returns in the characterization of Mellors in *Lady Chatterley's Lover*. Cixous is also close to Freud's fundamental belief in our bisexuality, which once recognized would discredit those who see Freud as a biological essentialist, because for him too, gender differentiation became largely a matter of the constructions of culture and society.

Reading literature through the structures of sexual difference will tend to draw attention to phallocentrism. But how different would a Cixous reading of Lawrence be from Kate Millett's? The crucial difference is that Cixous links phallocentrism to logocentrism in the rather cumbersome term, "phallogocentrism". Derrida defines logocen-

---

[25] Kaplan, 159-168.

[26] From, Hélène Cixous and Catherine Clément (1975), *The Newly Born Woman*, and reprinted in Elaine Marks and Isabelle de Courtivron eds, *New French Feminisms.: An Anthology* (Brighton: Harvester, 1981), 90, 91.

trism as the western tradition of thought which believes the truth of the word is fixed in speech, understood as unmediated access to meaning. In Aristotle's formulation: "Spoken words are the symbols of mental experience and written words are the symbols of spoken words". In this, the dominant tradition of western thought, speech is a reflection of the workings of the mind, the psyche; it is a truer expression than writing. However, for Derrida, writing is more than the expression of speech, and more than its supplement. Writing is a challenge to speech because it is subject to the process of *"différance"*, never settling on final meaning, always figuratively unstable. Metaphoricity "cannot have an ultimate referent". [27] The play of dissemination in *The Plumed Serpent*, which I discussed in the previous chapter, is an illustration of writing as *"différance"*.

Cixous's concept of *"écriture féminine"* — defined by Elaine Showalter as "the inscription of the female body and female difference in language and text"[28] — is meant to subvert both the phallocentric and the logocentric. Moreover, it is here that the most fundamental difference between Cixous and Millett is to be found. In Derrida's words:

> Some texts signed by women can be thematically anti-phallocentric and powerfully logocentric .... This is what is at issue in some debates, real or virtual, with militant feminists who do not understand that without a demanding reading of what articulates logocentrism and phallocentrism, in other words without a consequential deconstruction, feminist discourse risks reproducing very crudely the very thing which it purports to be criticizing.[29]

Mary Jacobson defines *"écriture féminine"* as a writing-effect, asserting not "the sexuality of the text but the textuality of sex". It is not a matter of women's writing, necessarily, but of a textual play of meaning which derives from Derrida's notion of writing. The tyranny of hierarchical oppositions essential to patriarchal discourse is deconstructed in a writing characterized by an unstable metaphoricity that tests the limits of representation. In its most extreme and poetic form, "the eruption of female *jouissance* can revolutionize discourse and challenge the Law of the Father", by getting beyond essentialism to "the conditions of

---

[27] Derrida cited in Peggy Kamuf ed., *A Derrida Reader: Between the Blinds* (Hemel Hempstead: Harvester Wheatsheaf, 1991), 31, 32.

[28] Elaine Showalter (1981), "Feminist Criticism in the Wilderness" reprinted in David Lodge ed., *Modern Criticism and Theory: A Reader* (London: Longman, 1988), 335.

[29] Interview with Derek Attridge in Derek Attridge ed., *Jacques Derrida: Acts of Literature* (London: Routledge, 1992), 60.

representability". [30]

Now it seems to me that the representation of female "*jouissance*" in Lawrence's fiction would benefit from such a reading. Moreover, as I hope to have shown in the last two chapters, ostensibly phallocentric texts, as Derrida puts it, "produce deconstructive effects, and precisely against phallocentrism, whose logic is always ready to reverse itself or subvert itself". [31] "*Écriture féminine*" is thus similar to Derrida's notion of "*différance*", which is "to struggle to undermine the dominant phallogo-centric logic, split open the closure of the binary opposition and revel in the pleasures of open-ended textuality". Furthermore, it is also "firmly located within the closure of the Lacanian Imaginary: a space in which all difference has been abolished". [32] This should be very productive for reading "*jouissance*" in Lawrence's writing as sites of feminine autonomy within a general phallocentricity; a metaphorization that exceeds the encoding of femininity in patriarchal discourse.

Cixous's concept of "*écriture féminine*" — for all its faults of privi-leging avant-garde writing, and of using a term of gender differentiation to define what is a process of abolishing fixed gender differences — has enabled feminist criticism, in Moi's words, "to escape from a disabling author-centred empiricism", so that bringing together sexuality and textuality has opened up "a whole new field of feminist investigation of the articulations of desire in language, not only in texts written by women, but also in texts by men". [33]

Luce Irigaray goes further than Cixous in demanding an historical analysis of "the repressed female imaginary". [34] Patriarchy has defined female sexuality as a closed zone of few possibilities "within the dominant phallic economy". Female pleasure must get beyond the privileged phallomorphism, indulge in autoeroticism to rediscover pleasure "almost everywhere". Her radical programme calls on women to "tacitly go on strike, avoid men long enough to learn to defend their desire" [35] — and develop that language which Irigaray calls "womanspeak", which, as Moi explains, "emerges spontaneously when women speak together, but disappears again as soon as men are present". The problem with this radical programme is that Irigaray's idea of

[30] Mary Jacobson, "Is There a Woman in this Text?" Reprinted in Mary Eagleton, 190.
[31] Interview with Derek Attridge, 59.
[32] Moi, 108, 117.
[33] Moi, 126.
[34] Luce Irigaray (1977), "This sex which is not one", reprinted in Marks and de Courtivron, 102.
[35] Irigaray, 100, 103,106.

woman is idealist and essentialist because she fails "to consider the historical and economic specificity of patriarchal power, along with its ideological and material contradictions".[36]

In an interesting exchange between Hélène Cixous and Catherine Clément, the limits of French feminism emerge. Clément accuses Cixous of remaining within the closure of the poetic. In a timely reminder, Clément states that "*cultural* oppression of women coincides with economic evolution and is accentuated by the development of capitalism". She goes on to say that, "there is a class struggle, and, within it, women's struggle". She accuses French Left intellectuals of living the class struggle "mythically" because "they are in a position where work on language and work on the Imaginary have fundamental importance and can put blinders on them".[37] This is a trenchant critique of Theory — of a post-structuralism without politics.

However, the literary and philosophical *avant-gardism* of Cixous's brand of French feminism is a welcome return to writing and the text after the naive critical paradigms of Millett's sexual politics. It certainly offers us an approach to the libidinized inscription in Lawrence's fiction, as we will see later. It is, though, élitist in its privileging high Modernism over popular culture, expressionism over realism. Moreover, it is a loss of political reality. Not all feminists share the belief in a revolution at the level of poetic language. It may be, though, that the changing of consciousness at the level of the imaginary — that release of the repressed female imaginary called for by the French feminists — is the closest we can come to changing "the imaginary in order to be able to act on the real".[38] I would add that to date the most enabling analysis of the relationship between the imaginary and the real conditions of existence has been Althusser's. And although his work has been discredited within Marxism, it has continued to exercise a fascination in literary and cultural studies, not least because it does suggest ways in which texts may be read through keeping both the imaginary and the real in play.

4. Sexuality, gender and class

If there is one key slogan from feminism, especially in its Anglo-American varieties, it is that the personal is the political. But, as Mary Eagleton points out, "the political isn't only the personal; an untheorized politics of personal experience may never get us beyond subjectivism". The insistence of French feminism on textual theory and Lacanian

[36] Moi, 144, 148.
[37] Hélène Cixous and Catherine Clément *The Newly Born Woman* (1985), extract reprinted in Mary Eagleton, 116, 132-33.
[38] Clément quoted by Gayatri Spivak in Mary Eagleton, 97.

psychoanalysis runs the risk of being too exclusively universalist, while refusing the category of the personal. Feminist work outside the rigour of post-structuralism has researched the history of women, forgotten lives and personalities, and women's writing previously marginalized by male canon formations. Mary Eagleton also insists that French feminism has tended to idealize textuality at the cost of a disengagement from "the particularities of the historical and political world". This is not to say that all French feminists are pure theorists. For instance, Catherine Clément has tried to link the two areas, relating "politics to the poetic, the social and the collective to the personal and the familial, the class struggle to the language of desire". [39] And, as I hope to have shown in the last two chapters, theorizing textual effects makes visible a sometimes disjunctive relationship between text and authorial doctrine which should send out semiotic and deconstructive messages to those who wish to reduce Lawrence's fiction to their own ideological parameters. Lawrence seems, at times, to be challenging the essentialisms of gender difference by problematizing the conventions of representation; at other times, he replaces one set of essentialisms with another. In *Lady Chatterley*, "*jouissance*" is proposed as the resolution of class conflict; yet the class problem cannot be wished away — and I shall return to the problem of transcending class boundaries through sex.

Feminism, therefore, has not always avoided the issue of the relation-ship between class and sexuality. Kate Millett, as you might expect from her formation in the political revolt of the 1960s, was conscious of class in Lawrence's works. She describes *Sons and Lovers* as "probably still the greatest novel of proletarian English life";[40] and *Lady Chatterley* as a reversal of the conventional class relations of the eighteenth and nineteenth century novel where "gentlemen entered into exploitative social relations with serving maids". Lawrence, instead, brings the lady and the manservant together, and thus attempts to assert that the class system is an "anachronism".[41] Millett is good on the class positions in the novel, although — consistent with her critical method — she tends to draw conclusions about the author's class attitudes as the key to understanding the text: for Lawrence (thinly disguised as Mellors), "women of his own class and kind are beneath his contempt; the cruellest caricatures in the novel are Bertha Coutts and Mrs Bolton," who are seen

---

[39] Mary Eagleton, 6, 14, 15.

[40] Kate Millett, *Sexual Politics* (London: Virago, 1977. First published 1969), 247.

[41] Millett, 244. The last point is not strictly true — it is in the second version, *John Thomas and Lady Jane*, where class is declared out of date; there is of course an urge in the final version towards transcending class barriers through sex, as I argue later in this chapter.

by Mellors to be "unbearably 'common'". Sir Clifford may be a critique of the ruling classes, but Lawrence still wants a ruling, but "natural" aristocracy; and Mellors will lead the way as "Lawrence senior [i.e. Walter Morel/Lawrence's father], rehabilitated and transformed into Pan". Millett mentions the anti-industrialism, and the influence of the mother in *Sons and Lovers* to get the boys educated and upwardly mobile. However, it is strange for a feminist reading that she does not go into any more detail on the class positions of Lawrence's women characters except in passing reference to Connie Chatterley and Mrs Morel. She reduces the complexities of sexuality and class to generalizations about sexism.

British feminists have done more work in this area of class and gender, especially in film and media studies from the early 1980s; but also in literary studies.[42] Hilary Simpson's study is exemplary as a feminist reading of Lawrence which draws attention to the details of the social and gender contexts of Lawrence's writing, the contemporary attitudes and debates about the New Woman and the masculine reaction. I discussed her book in chapter 4, but here I want just to re-emphasize her documentation of women's history with which she wants to "provide a fresh basis for literary analysis". Lawrence was writing during "one of the most crucial periods in that history". [43] Pre-First World War feminism and the post-war reaction against the women's movement are both registered by Lawrence. In this approach, his works are not read through the different feminist concerns of today, but instead are located in their historical determinations in relation to women's history. It is an object lesson for feminist criticism, showing the extent to which Lawrence was part of the controversial debates about sexuality and gender in the early twentieth century. As Worthen puts it: "Lawrence's contemporaries found him remarkably advanced in his attitudes towards men, women and sexuality." Furthermore:

> over and over again, Lawrence surpassed in insight and understanding everything that might have been expected of a man of his generation, class and cultural background; and that he saw, seventy years ago, more clearly into many of our continuing dilem-

---

[42] Examples include: Michèle Barrett, *Women's Oppression Today* (London: Verso, 1980); Rosalind Coward, *Patriarchal Precedents: Sexuality and Social Relations* (London: Routledge, 1983); and *Female Desire: Women's Sexuality Today* (London: Paladin, 1984); Terry Lovell, *Pictures of Reality: Aesthetics, Politics and Pleasure* (London: British Film Institute, 1982); Janet Wolff, *The Social Production of Art* (London: Macmillan, 1981).

[43] Hilary Simpson, *D.H. Lawrence and Feminism* (London: Croom Helm, 1982), 14.

mas about sexuality than most of our contemporaries, even though
his positions were clearly historical and seem to some extent historically defined.[44]

Lawrence was not, however, sympathetic to the political ambitions of the
Suffragettes, even though he was close to politically committed women
like Sallie Hopkin and Alice Dax. Pragmatic and collective concerns
were less important to Lawrence than individual and spiritual ones.

Nevertheless, his fiction registers some of the key gender and class
issues of his day. Mrs Morel in *Sons and Lovers* represents in particular,
as Simpson explains, "many of the material conditions of women's
oppression which inspired the women's movement".[45] The first part of the
novel is, in a sense, a document of details about working-class life and
the conditions of women's oppressive and limited existence. Much has
been written about the biographical source of the story. Feminists like
Hilary Simpson have been more concerned with the accuracy in which it
registers women's history. Mrs Morel, for instance, belongs to the
Women's Guild. The men resent the political activities of the women.
Later, after the children have grown up, she returns to her education by
reading more and sharing her interests with her son, Paul, but no matter
how much effort she makes, she and the rest of the working-class women
are powerless against their men, and against the capitalist system. When
they are shown to be a radicalizing force, their power is limited to their
domestic sphere. They are not the breadwinners, they have no financial
independence, and they are wary of the threat of domestic violence and
personal tragedy. At such moments, like when the next child is due, the
women close ranks to help each other. The men are portrayed as hard-
working, heavy-drinking, prone to both violence and illness. The life of
the working-class women is mostly joyless. Sex for Mrs Morel was
passionate at the beginning of her marriage, but soon degenerated into
childbearing and near penury. Clara Dawes represents the women of the
new generation, educated, feminist, and reasonably independent,
financially and sexually. However, as Simpson explains, in the character
of Clara, "the novel betrays little appreciation of the relationship between
the personal and the political". Indeed, Paul Morel tries to dissuade her
from feminist activism. Here, feminism is only a detail of character, and
the personal world is not connected, as it is in the situation of Mrs Morel,
to the "material forces which have a part in shaping it".[46]

---

[44] Worthen 75.
[45] Simpson, 26.
[46] Simpson, 29, 37.

In *Sons and Lovers* it is already becoming evident that Lawrence is giving priority to sex over class. His attitude to class, and to class politics is ambivalent. Jeremy Hawthorn reminds us of the standard view that although Lawrence came from the working classes he stands apart from it in his work.[47] His father was a miner for fifty-six years in Nottinghamshire; his mother came from lower middle-class origins, and it was she who encouraged the son from beginning to end in education, to move away into school teaching, and then writing. In *Sons and Lovers* we see working-class culture from the outside, even though there is a distinctive focus "upon the life of a well-defined region ... a workplace". Indeed, *Sons and Lovers* — like *Lady Chatterley* — does have a strong sense of region, of locale. Yet, although there is much emphasis on spoken dialect, on the behaviour of the working men and their womenfolk in the coal-mining community, on their hardships and material penury, it is not a working-class novel. Admittedly, Lawrence has had a significant working-class readership, and has exerted "a very considerable influence upon the development of working-class fiction". [48] Indeed, by the mid-1930s Lawrence, as Andy Croft puts it, "had somehow come to be seen as the archetypal working-class writer .... [A]ny aspiring working-class writer, particularly a miner, and particularly one from the East Midlands" would want to follow his example. Reviewers of such novels would more often than not compare them to Lawrence's novel.[49] Such an aspirant would of course always be advised to tone down the political emphasis in his writing.

Lawrence, however, "does not take us down the pit". Paying the workers' wages is only observed by the young Paul. His work experience will be quite different, as clerical (white collar) worker. Typically, the division of labour leaves the women at home where they can, in their isolation, play out their fantasy of higher class aspiration for their children. The division becomes a split in the Morel family, the children taking the mother's side, represented through the social dimensions of speech registers, attitudes, and behaviour. What starts out as a breakdown of the relationship between husband and wife, becomes a conflict of class only marginally. Lawrence demonstrates already in the first of his major novels, that he is neither a working-class writer nor a socialist, more

---

[47] Jeremy Hawthorn, "Lawrence and working-class fiction" in Brown (1992). See also Jeremy Hawthorn, *The British Working-Class Novel in the Twentieth Century* (London: Arnold, 1984).
[48] Hawthorn, 68-69.
[49] Andy Croft, "Lady Chatterley and D.H. Lawrence", *Artery*, viii (1985), 50, cited in Hawthorn, 69.

"socio-intellectual than political". [50] It is not simply a choice between the sophisticated codes of educated middle-class life and the restricted, brutalized existence of the workers in the mining community, despite Paul Morel's snobbery. Indeed, perhaps because of it, and the sophisticated soul-searching and emotional atrophy that *Sons and Lovers* and the subsequent novels dramatize, there are moments where a more solid, stable working-class community comes off best. It is never that straightforward in the novel. Paul is chided by his mother for always talking about the "common people". He justifies it as follows:

> Because — the difference between people isn't in their class, but in themselves. Only from the middle classes one gets ideas, and from the common people — life itself, warmth. You feel their hates and loves. (SL, 298)

It is that word, "common" which signifies, in its emphasis and its recurrence, Paul's developing attitude. And Lawrence will return to the terms of this understanding of class difference in *Lady Chatterley*.

In *Sons and Lovers* class plays its role in so far as it affects the family, and the upwardly mobile development of the children. But it begins gradually to recede from view as the middle-class, educated point of view of mother and son are foregrounded. Class conflict gets reworked into the struggles between the passion and the intellect, between spontaneity and rationality, until the material presence of class disappears altogether, only to return in the end as a kind of pre-capitalist idyll in *Lady Chatterley's Lover*.

Raymond Williams argued that Lawrence adopted a nineteenth-century critique of industrial capitalism which derived from Carlyle's Romantic humanism, and from William Morris's socialism. In Lawrence, this critique consistently takes the form of dramatizing the killing of the instinctual, spontaneous self — a feeling that someone of his ambitions would have located deep in the place of his origin, a place and a way of life from which he escaped. It is an attitude of mind, a whole "structure of feeling" (Williams), a "forcing of all human energy into a competition of mere acquisition" (Lawrence). Williams points to the key words in the Lawrence lexicon: "mechanical", "disintegrated" and "amorphous", to describe the effect of industrial capitalism on individuals and on society as a whole. In Lawrence's words: "The real tragedy of England ... is the tragedy of ugliness. The country is so lovely: the man-made England so

---

[50] Hawthorn, 75.

vile". [51] His revolution would be personal liberation (the great appeal of Lawrence to the 1960s). Moreover, Williams stresses that perhaps the only use of looking to the author's life and background, "with its emphasis on the restless wanderings and the approach to any way of life but his own, lies in the fact that these things were only contingencies". The opening chapters of *Sons and Lovers* are drawn from such contingencies. They represent details in the history of working-class family life in a mining community in the East Midlands before the First World War; and are also, in their generalizing capacity, "an indictment of the pressures of industrialism". [52] As the example of *Sons and Lovers* shows, working-class life and the pressures of industrialism were "mediated by the experiences of family and locality" — as Williams puts it in a later essay. [53] Lawrence is, therefore, "never in any danger of writing a reductive novel about working-class life, since what first materialized was not the class but family, neighbours, friends, places". He appreciated class relations better once he had moved away, written *The Rainbow* and *Women in Love*, and lived through the experience of the war. These are not so many details for a transparent biographical reading, but belong to the raw materials from which one of Lawrence's main concerns throughout his work derives: that recurrent story of "individuals who were moving out and away from their origins". [54]

The Rainbow, too, is very much a history of family and locale, as I described in some detail in chapter 2. It also emphasizes individual development, but with a well-documented historical reference. The changing class positions of the Brangwens, from farm labourers to tradespeople, and to colliery manager (Uncle Tom), or technical college teacher (Will Brangwen), are now more than just contingencies. For the improved social and economic conditions of the family enable the daughters, and Ursula in particular, to be educated into a position of greater freedom. Yet, true to her representative status as a modern woman, Ursula decides to enter the man's world — the world of work. The conditions of that employment foreground class differences (the pupils are from some of the poorest and most deprived working-class

---

[51] "Nottingham and the Mining Country" (1929) in *Selected Essays* (London: Penguin, 1974), 120; cited in Raymond Williams, *Culture and Society* (London: Penguin, 1958), 119, 201.

[52] Raymond Williams, 204, 206.

[53] "Region and Class in the Novel", in *Writing in Society* (London: Verso, 1983), 235.

[54] And one especially reflected in the stories written during or just after the war, and collected in *England, My England and Other Stories* (Cambridge: Cambridge University Press, 1990). The stories were written between 1913 — 1922, and first published in 1922).

backgrounds), and gender politics — as she is subjected to the sadistic authority of Mr Harby, the Head teacher. The gender conflict is exacerbated by her pedagogic idealism and her association with the Women's Movement through Winifred Inger, Maggie Schofield, and Dorothy Russell. She is briefly involved in a discussion of *Women and Labour*.[55] However, as Simpson rightly insists, radical feminism is rejected in the novel, because Winifred Inger betrays her principles by marrying Uncle Tom, and Dorothy Russell is a caricature of a Suffragette: "Lawrence was consistent in his antipathy to reformist politics".[56] Yet although he may have been against the vote for women, and he gets Ursula to say so, he was in favour of a broadly conceived feminism in 1915.

In the early works, a persistent theme is the New Woman. Sally Ledger traces her origins to the 1890s. The "Woman Question" had emerged by about mid-century, represented in fiction (Dorothea in George Eliot's *Middlemarch*, 1872), and reached its heyday by the end of the century, when the New Woman was the object of pathological men's fiction. Gender categories were destabilized, the institution of marriage was seen to be under threat. Indeed, the very health of the nation, if not the race itself, was endangered by the new self-conscious, independent-minded woman. Detractors were quick to associate her with decadence, and the Oscar Wilde scandal from the mid-1890s. The Women's Movement was at pains to dissociate itself from sexual libertarianism, and encouraged at its worst a new puritanism, and at best a public campaign for equality within marriage. Because of the need to distance herself from the many disparaging discourses that pathologized her as the cold, "masculinized" woman, blue stocking, lesbian, harpy, blood-sucking vampire (Bram Stoker's *Dracula* was published in 1897), the early feminist never developed a discourse of female sexuality. It was left to the men like Carpenter, Ellis, and Freud to begin the discussion of sexual difference. Lawrence belongs to that discussion in the early twentieth century.

In their historical moment, the men who first addressed the sexuality of women, against the taboos of nineteenth-century morality, were both controversial and daring. Freud was so worried about being publicly demonized that, especially in his early work, he was careful about his choice of words when discussing the sexual implications of dreams.

---

[55] Cf. *The Rainbow* (London: Penguin edition of the Cambridge D.H. Lawrence, 1994), 379. The reference is to Olive Schreiner's radical work — although it was not published until 1911. For further discussion see Sally Ledger *The New Woman: Fiction and Feminism at the Fin de Siècle* (Manchester: Manchester University Press, 1997).

[56] Simpson, 42.

Lawrence, of course, invented a whole lexicon of indirection, which is easily parodied today. He did not write explicitly about sex until *Aaron's Rod*, and the second version of *Lady Chatterley (John Thomas and Lady Jane).*[57] Feminists today should be more conscious of these historical pressures, and appreciate what was radical about Freud or Lawrence — which is not to excuse them for their errors, but to understand the history of the emergence of their truths.

As Simpson also pointed out, in *Sons and Lovers*, Clara is an example of the independent-minded woman, employed, and challenging traditional gender and sexual codes. Miriam is perceived by Paul as the Pre-Raphaelite "dreaming woman", more spiritual than passionate. He blames her for their sexual failure, but this view is challenged by Clara in the novel. She suggests the whole business needs approaching differently; or maybe, as Simpson suggests, "Miriam resists the yielding of identity that passion seems to demand".[58] She succeeds in resisting Paul's domination, and finally achieves a certain independence by becoming a teacher. In *The Rainbow*, Anna fights her battle in the relationship with Will, and represents the struggle for equality within marriage. The battle may be fierce but the outcome is traditional. As Sally Ledger puts it, her personality is allowed "to collapse into contented, bovine maternity". It is left to Ursula to incorporate the new self-awareness in sex and gender difference. Her coming of age in the novel is coincidental with the heyday of the New Woman in the late nineteenth century (the story ends in 1904). She represents Lawrence's call for the feminization of the culture, against the accusation commonly levelled against the New Woman of causing the "effeminacy of culture" (especially after the Wilde scandal).[59] Within the terms of early feminism, Lawrence's novel is radical. It is utopic, but not as fanciful as that other utopic novel of the same year, Charlotte Perkins Gilman's *Herland* (1915). In Lawrence's fiction, the New Woman begins to go wrong from *Women in Love*. Hermione is too cerebral, Ursula too sexually self-conscious, and Gudrun too destructive. Here, Lawrence has begun his turn against the New Woman.

There is from the outset, though, a "relatively narrow class identity of the archetypal New Woman". She was essentially "middle class, educated, literary". Sometimes in Lawrence she comes from the upper classes. Moreover, the revolutionary impact of the Women's Movement

---

[57] And then the passages in *Aaron's Rod* were cut; and Lawrence probably felt freer to write explicitly about sex in the second *Lady Chatterley* as he was planning to publish the novel privately.
[58] Simpson, 56.
[59] Ledger, 27, 97.

was limited because of its "solid middle class, bourgeois ideology".[60] There was a brief association of feminism with socialism through the work of Eleanor Marx, Olive Schreiner, and Beatrice Webb. Working-class women only gradually got involved in the campaign for women's suffrage in the late 1890s. However, there was ideological conflict within the movement; the Pankhursts being essentially conservative and evangelical Christian. The forces against them were so great that even the socialist utopic fiction of the day was often defeatist, proposing emigration as the only alternative to failure.[61] Lawrence also recognizes the problems of establishing a utopia in England, and often ends his fiction with characters making plans for emigration (Canada is a popular choice).

A significant moment in the history of early feminism is the shift in the 1890s from class to gender. In Ledger's words: "in the feminist fiction of the 1890s it is the male body, rather than the working-class body, which threatens English society".[62] Gender politics became a disruptive force as conventional codes of femininity were deconstructed. However, through the work of Carpenter, Ellis, Freud, and Stopes, sexuality entered the debate. For Lawrence, sexuality was an ontological force, and as Simpson puts it, "sexual pleasure and self-realization are more important than the reproductive process".[63]

Thus it seems to me that once you appreciate the historical determinations of Lawrence's writing, like the significance of the women's histories in *The Rainbow*, and his invention of a discourse of sexuality out of "a pool of common notions and theories available for the discussion of sexuality at this time",[64] then it is limiting (and ideological) to accuse Lawrence of the many sins of chauvinist man from the exclusive view of post-1960s feminism. The work of Simpson and Ledger is instructive.

5. The *Lady Chatterley* novels

i. Introduction
The Chatterley novels are in many senses a summary or culmination of a life's work, as it is now easy to see with hindsight. They are State of England fiction *circa* 1926-1928. The changes in the three versions,

---

[60] Ledger, 15, 35, 42.
[61] For a full discussion of socialism in the Women's Movement, and examples of socialist utopic fiction see Ledger, chapter 2.
[62] Ledger, 115.
[63] Simpson, 84.
[64] Simpson, 83, 84.

especially with their different attitudes towards class, reflect the evolution of a utopian fiction which has to bear the full weight of a resolution to the cultural crisis. "*Jouissance*" will only be achieved in a version of the English pastoral. But the novels are also a return to familiar territory: the industrial Midlands of *Sons and Lovers*, *The Rainbow*, *Women in Love*, *The Lost Girl*, and the first part of *Mr Noon*. Lawrence had revisited in August and September 1926 "the country of [his] heart",[65] and was shocked by the changes brought about by the General Strike to the mining communities. He became aware of the political radicalization of the dispute and the extent of class resentment. Lawrence's impressions were recorded in the essay, "Return to Bestwood", written once he was back in Italy. There is no better place to begin this discussion.

According to Graham Martin, "Return to Bestwood" may be understood "as the first notes for the Chatterley novels ... [making] a valuable prolegomenon" to the three novels. I would add that in his observations on the industrial unrest, Lawrence's ambivalence towards the miners emerges in the essay. Moreover, as Martin rightly argues, Lawrence's explanation of the political crisis, and the threat of class war, is not "the immediate political and economic struggle of which the Strike was the culmination", but instead the "psychological change in the miners themselves".[66] They have been changed by the experience of the war. Lawrence does not have a political solution. Instead, he calls for better contact between people; a solution which he will develop into a full-blown utopia by the third version, *Lady Chatterley's Lover*, but not before he has visited the "Etruscan places" and found a model civilization that existed before the destructive influence of modern rationalism and the machine principle. In "Bestwood" Lawrence sees the world of his childhood gone forever; and "the women seem to have changed the most in this, that they have no respect for anything".[67] The signifier: "respect" will take on a particular class resonance in the novels, as the ruling classes sit in judgment on those they have exploited. Lawrence recalls that his mother's generation believed "so absolutely in the ultimate benevolence of all the masters, of all the upper classes. One had to be grateful to them, after all!" (PII, 260) — and the tone here is clearly

---

[65] Lawrence cited in David Ellis, *D.H. Lawrence: Dying Game 1922-1930* (Cambridge: Cambridge University Press, 1998), 316.
[66] Graham Martin, "'History' and 'Myth' in D.H. Lawrence's Chatterley Novels" in Jeremy Hawthorn ed. (1984), 65, 66.
[67] D.H. Lawrence, "Return to Bestwood" (1926). First published in *Phoenix II: Uncollected, Unpublished and Other Prose Works* (London: Heinemann, 1968), 258. Further references in text [PII].

affected by the class resentment he has experienced. In *Women in Love* it is Gerald's father who represents the old, benevolent ruling classes, as the responsible large employer concerned with the welfare of the people (WL, 215). But the great houses have spawned ugly mining settlements, and the industry that gives them their wealth has ruined the countryside and the health of the people, with the coal dust that settles everywhere and the sulphurous smell on the wind. The miners themselves, once "men from the underworld" when the author was a boy, have lost that "strange power of life", their vitality, and have become the ghosts of themselves since the war (PII, 263). They drink in their club "with a sort of hopelessness". Lawrence comes away with a feeling of "doom over the country, and a shadow of despair over the hearts of the men" (PII, 264). He knows that "we are on the brink of class war", and that the key question is the ownership of property; and even suggests a socialist programme: nationalization of land, industry and transport. However, his solution is a new conception of life, quality not quantity, a vitalist morality (PII, 265). It is not immediately clear how people are going to change their whole way of being, nor how this will resolve the class conflict and industrial unrest. It will take him the three Chatterley novels to work it out in fictional form.

There is one other essay on class that was written just after Lawrence finished the final version of *Lady Chatterley*. In July 1928 he wrote "Autobiographical Sketch".[68] You would expect that the writing of the last fiction would have clarified some new understanding of class difference. Lawrence (in 1928) characterizes the middle classes as educated, often charming, but "shallow and passionless". The working classes are "narrow in outlook, in prejudice, and narrow in intelligence", but they are also "fairly deep and passionate". In either case, he feels that the "vital vibration" is limited, and he can belong to neither the class of his origin nor the one into which he was educated (PII, 595). Lawrence's attitude to class has not changed since the early fiction. He consistently sees it in psychological terms. We are reminded again of Paul Morel's pronouncement:

> Because — the difference between people isn't in their class, but in themselves. Only from the middle classes one gets ideas, and from the common people — life itself, warmth. You feel their hates and loves. (SL, 298)

In the Chatterley novels Lawrence is not only concerned with the

---

[68] Published posthumously and collected in PII.

working classes or the middle classes. The three versions, in their different emphases, are a critique of the English ruling class, the aristocracy, represented by Sir Clifford and his cronies. In the final version, *Lady Chatterley's Lover*, Mellors is seen to be the "natural aristocrat", a superior being above social class-distinctions, because he has a "*vital* relation to the universe" (Lawrence's emphasis).[69] Thus, "the true aristocrat is the man who has passed all the relationships and has met the sun." (PII, 482) He envisages a new aristocracy, going beyond national and class boundaries, of "men who have reached the sun", who will rule the world in a kind of pagan utopia. It should become clearer in what follows that Lawrence's displacement of class politics by a pastoral mythology and utopian fantasy — a tendency already evident in *The Rainbow*, and one which I discussed in chapter two — is contradicted by the detailed description and representation of political and class realities.[70] Sir Clifford's class still has the power at the end of the novel, despite Lawrence's attempts to displace class by sex.

It is a further contention in this chapter that Lawrence returns to the "*jouissance*" of female sexuality after rejecting it altogether in the leadership novels, even though he does not abandon all the phallocentric sexual ideology. Indeed, as I shall argue later, there is a tension between a sexual theory discredited today and "*jouissance*", expressed in an "*écriture féminine*". It is in these poetic moments that the representation of the "female imaginary" as a physical experience threatens to upset the theories of phallic man.

ii. *The First Lady Chatterley* (the first version of *Lady Chatterley's Lover*)

As many critics have noted, *The First Lady Chatterley* is Lawrence's most explicit representation of the crisis of class in post-war England. The story of the love-affair between the gamekeeper and the Lady — a common enough fiction — is a focus for the question of class. Parkin is very working class, and is also politically active as Secretary of the local Communist League. The affair is resonant with class implications, and reflects the explosive situation in the industrial unrest and the general class resentment in the mining communities of the Midlands and in the

---

[69] "Aristocracy" in "Reflections on the Death of a Porcupine" (1925) reprinted in PII, 478.
[70] For further discussion of the pastoral and mythic tendencies see Kingsley Widmer (1973), "The Pertinence of the Modern Pastoral: The Three Versions of *Lady Chatterley's Lover*"; Michael Squires (1974), "*Lady Chatterley's Lover*: 'Pure Seclusion'"; both reprinted in Ellis and de Zordo, *Volume III* (1992); Pinkney, ch. 3; Hyde, ch. 7.

steel works of Sheffield. It is clear from the outset that Lawrence was writing just after he had returned from "Bestwood". The realism of locale is matched by the detail of class culture. We begin in the upper classes with the intellectual differences between Connie and Clifford: the one educated in the German tradition of cultural critique, the other a Cambridge intellectual. Connie's life of the body opposes Clifford's life of the mind. She rejects his neo-Platonism and aestheticism. He represents reactionary Tory values, while she is more flexible ideologically, aware of the "cold distance between herself and the people". Like Paul Morel before her in *Sons and Lovers*, the common people sometimes make her angry.[71] She can resort to the ease of high culture and upper-class privilege she shares with Clifford, but her phallic dreams tell another story (FLC, 14-15), and it is one that Lawrence will draw out more explicitly in subsequent versions.

In this first version it is Clifford who suggests that she take a lover, and not "suppress" her sex (FLC, 21). But for him it is only an abstract proposition. Her desire is roused by the sight of Parkin's naked body. It is a moment of physical attraction which awakens her interest in her own body, so that studying her naked body in the mirror — a sort of belated "mirror stage" — she becomes conscious of the body as libidinal site, and as defining her sense of being as being-seen. After this, the polarization of Clifford's high cultural pleasure (*plaisir*) and Connie's bliss (*jouissance*) at discovering her female sexuality is first a crisis of language. In the mirror, her body "spoke in another, silent language, without the cheapness of words" (FLC, 30). The chatter at Wragby is cultivated, mannered and superficial. It also acts as a safe zone in which Connie can keep at bay "those lunatic ideas about her body" (FLC, 30). Lawrence readers should appreciate the connotation that female sexuality is akin to lunacy, the woman's totem being the moon. There is a whole set of associations, that we are familiar with from *The Rainbow* and *Women in Love*, with losing control, with unconscious forces that rationality and polite manners may not be able to contain, with a creative-destructive instinct. Female sexuality in Lawrence's fiction has a power that makes it superior to male sexuality.

We need to appreciate the extent to which, already in the first version of the Chatterley novels, "*jouissance*" has to carry the full weight of the social and cultural critique. The upper classes are not fit to rule and to lead the culture into regeneration because they have denied themselves

---

[71] *The First Lady Chatterley* (London: Penguin, 1973), 27. All subsequent page references in text [FLC] are to this edition. The text was first published in 1944 in the USA.

the full creativity of the life of the body. Through Connie we discover what that might mean. Moreover, sex and class are linked from the start. Upper-class woman is frustrated, when allowing herself to be honest, because she has never been really satisfied. Lady Eva represents this condition, lead astray by the very politeness her class promotes along with its purer forms of romantic love, and its sophisticated speech manner of indirection, which is here stigmatized as a crippling subtlety. The insinuation is that aristocratic men are poor lovers, and good sex is only possible in the lower classes. It is a doctrine predicated on an impossible situation: the lower classes are vulgar and uneducated, but they have a less complicated relationship to their bodies and to each other; while the upper classes keep the culture going, yet polite society makes rigorous demands which destroy the natural sex instinct in them. For Lawrence, then, class difference is understood in sexual terms, even in the one novel where the material and historical conditions of class are represented in the greatest detail.

Clifford is a gentleman, as Connie's sister Hilda explains (speaking for Lawrence): "Yet he never felt Constance really as another flowing life, flowing its own stream. He idealized her, perhaps". He was a devoted husband, and Hilda is tired of such devotion in her own husband, a man who could never come "forth naked to her out of his amiable and would-be manly shell" (FLC, 34). She leads the woman's revolt by leaving her husband (at least in this version), and taking more care of her sister. Connie is medically examined and diagnosed as suffering from "neuralgia of the nerves" — a representative hysterical woman in the age of Freud. The causes of her suffering are the tensions of civilized society combined with a life without sex in the cold-hearted upper classes. Yet, even while Clifford persists in promoting the life of the mind as the key to their marriage, she is gravitating towards the life of the wood. There, the "gamekeeper's garden" with its magic "fairy-tale atmosphere" (FLC, 41) stirs up her suppressed unconscious desire, mirrored no longer as self-conscious sexuality but as the "rushing wind" and "wild flowers" of the natural world. Her rational mind, however, still vies for control of the situation as she approaches the gamekeeper.

The realities of class conflict are never left out of the picture for long. The Ted Bolton story casts a shadow over the imminent love affair between the Lady and the gamekeeper from the lower classes. She may need a better lover, but the consequences of crossing class boundaries are unthinkable. Parkin is suspicious from the start, and Connie knows that behind his efforts at politeness he was "at war, really, with Clifford and herself". Here, Lawrence redeploys the language of "Return to Best-wood", and goes further by dramatizing contempt in the aggressive use of dialect on the part of the gamekeeper. And, throughout the three versions,

dialect ("talking broad") will have a double function: either as a class
weapon, or as a language of tenderness (a function already seen in *Sons
and Lovers*). At its best, the relationship will only succeed in overcoming
class difference when it is beyond speech, relying on the ineffable
communications of desiring bodies.

Class difference is also marked by the attitude to nature. For Clifford,
nature is aestheticized: "we should care half so much for flowers if it
weren't for the lovely things poets have said about them". Yet the same
poets idealize women: "Thou still unravish'd bride of quietness". Connie,
in one of her many feminist interventions, questions the violent
implication of the signifier: "ravished". Nature and women are misrepresented; even worse, they are kept at a distance, and controlled by the
poetry of men. She rejects Clifford's aestheticism just as she rejects his
Platonism (on behalf of Lawrence). And it is surely crucial to notice that
Lawrence gives the aesthetic and the philosophical ideas a precise class
location. Education and upbringing has made the upper classes too
cerebral: life is only "in the head". Connie feels "the flowers were more
flowerily unspoken than ever" (an awkwardness of expression that speaks
volumes against the over-sophistication of the language of the aesthetic).
Clifford's literary allusions are, for her, his "way of making abstract love
to her in words and suggestion" (FLC, 46). Parkin, of course, is close to
nature and short on words. The wood is his domain, away from the
difficulties of society. He is everything Clifford is not. Connie is already
in sympathy with Parkin's direct access to nature, and extends this
through the perspective of her sexual desire to his natural, instinctual
physical life. But class is still in the way. His initial resistance to her is
complicated by his early sex life, which is only briefly told in this
version, but given more importance in the later versions. It is not only
that she is the Lady, but also simply that she is a woman threatening his
self-imposed celibacy. What this implies is that sex for Parkin is as
powerful and disruptive a force as it threatens to be for Connie.

When it comes to sex, it is beyond words. In contrast to Clifford who
makes love with words (through his incessant chatter), the love-making
of Parkin and Connie is not described. The greater sexual explicitness for
which Lawrence is famous first occurs in the second version. The cold-
hearted reasoning of Clifford contrasts with the warm-hearted tenderness
of Parkin's dialect speech, which flows "soft, warm". She, for her part,
discovers passion for the first time as a "body consciousness", a new
speech of "short wild cries", "unconsciously" — a "*jouissance*". And
characteristic of Lawrence's (rather telegraphed) structure of oppositions,
we are next with Clifford reading Racine, seventeenth-century classical
French tragedy, where overpowering passion destroys the genteel and
mannered life of the Court (FLC, 52). It is of course the greatest irony

that, while his voice drones on, we are listening only to Connie's thoughts about being filled "with an unspeakable pleasure, a pleasure which has no contact with speech". Instead of Racine's measured verse maintaining control of the passion in the abstract, Connie's pleasure-text is a celebration of the body as nature. She feels alive like the buds in the wood in spring. The body of the man (regardless of his working-class status), has breathed new life into her: "All her body felt like the dark interlacing of the boughs of an oak wood ... in the vast interlaced intricacy of the forest of her body." By contrast, Clifford's speech, emptied of content by the newly-born woman, is just a voice going on and on "clapping and gurgling with strange sound ... like the uncouth cries and howls of barbarous, disconnected savages dancing round a fire somewhere outside of the wood" (FLC, 53). Her new physical awareness is expressed in her "*écriture féminine*", writing the body in a neo-Romantic poetry that displaces the Classicism of Racine and the classically allusive Romanticism of Keats. Her class has banned sex from speech, and controls it in the public sphere (to protect the moral health of the nation, as Lawrence found to his cost). But Lawrence reverses the dominant system of values by having the cultivated, civilized, post-Enlightenment man play the savage to Parkin's natural man. Her powerful apprehension of him is perception through desire, and her rejection of Clifford follows the new priorities of her female sexuality. She does, however, have an instinct for survival in the social world too, and in a moment of pure irony smiles at the chattering Clifford, the "cultured gentleman".

That real world returns to haunt her as he takes an obsessive interest in improving the mines, and Mrs Bolton, despite her class resentment, displaces Connie as companion to the master. She keeps Connie's secret, but wonders why she had not "looked a bit higher" (FLC, 58) for a lover. And as if to emphasize the full impact of what it could mean to be in the lower classes, Connie's car-drive around the district of Tevershall — which is significant enough to be in all three versions — is a device to give us a panorama of industrial ugliness and class difference at a moment of crisis in English social history. Although ambivalence always resurfaces — there is, for instance, in the "awful region" a "feeling of blind virility" (FLC, 60) — the country estate and the new colliery are prominent sites of class difference and potential conflict. Lawrence, however, rewrites politics as cultural allegory as the new industrialism is opposed to the old rural England, a tradition in the English novel which includes George Eliot, and which was first seen in *The Rainbow* (as I described in chapter two). The good old world was, of course, as harmonious as any myth. It, like Clifford, has been destroyed by the modern machine principle. Connie now truly represents her class perspective: the stately homes of England are doomed; lineage is imperative to keep things going. The irony is that the Lady will conceive the child from the proletarian man who wants to abolish private property and the unequal distribution of wealth. In this version of the Chatterley novels Parkin is a communist.

Lawrence's ambivalence resurfaces in a nostalgia for the old class relations, on the one hand, where the patrician ruling classes maintained social harmony through mutual respect; and, on the other, the expansion of industry and its workforce, necessary to maintain the stately home, now threatens to destroy the country. In short: "One meaning blotted out another" (FLC, 61).

The ambivalence goes right into the heart of Connie's relationship with Parkin. Whereas Clifford would turn Connie into "Greek marble", Parkin turns her into "a volcano". Yet she could not even contemplate living with the man from the lower classes, neither as his working-class wife, nor in her own class with him as her husband. Sexually, he makes her erupt like a volcano (an image for the power of the female "*jouissance*" often used by Lawrence). Socially, she would suffer because of his lack of conversation. Passion is opposed to culture (in the sense of high culture). Moreover, the cultural difference is defined in racial terms, in the sense of breeding and pure ancestral blood. Culturally and socially she fears "they would humiliate one another". Yet, if she had his children they would be like "a fresh fountain of life" (FLC, 82). When Clifford gives her permission to breed, he expects the surrogate father to be of acceptable stock.[72]

Class and sex seem irreconcilable. Lawrence would only find a solution to his problem by changing the character and class position of the gamekeeper in the third version of the novel. In this first version, however, class and sex separate off even more. On the one hand, Connie reflects on the possibility of class war in historical terms: could the Bolshevik Revolution of 1917 happen in England? Such thoughts bring about a resurgence of class loyalty in her; she and Clifford were, after all, "on one side in the division" (FLC, 93). Growing class animosity is further encouraged by Parkin's attitude to Connie when he accuses her of not taking him as seriously as she would one of her "own sort", and of looking down on him (FLC, 95). She, for her part, feels he is mocking her. They do not even speak the same language. The situation is impossible. But we have known this for some time. It is the sex that is

---

[72] The contemporary debate about eugenics lies near the surface of this discussion. It is, though, ironic that, apart from the class problem, the aristocracy is presented as incapable of regenerating the enfeebled men of England.

supposed to resolve all conflict by transcending such mundane differences. However, it seems that sex is not able to do that in the first version; or, perhaps, that Lawrence sets up the affair only to imagine the consequences of class conflict as he witnessed them in his last visit to "Bestwood".

Class cultural difference and sexual ideology only merge around Connie's developing feminist perspective. Sexually, "she had never realized till now that a man could be, in his body, the living clue to all the world to a woman" (FLC, 86). And later she comes to realize the "mystery of the phallus", because "every woman knows, that the penis is the column of blood, the living fountain of fullness in life ... which washes away the old corruptions" (FLC, 156-57). Lawrence's phallocentric doctrine is writ larger in the next two versions, and it is the focus of Millett's attack. But it is only a partial reading which leaves the irresolvable conflict between sex and class out of account. Connie wants to feminize the class conflict with "warmth" and "heart" (FLC, 172). But it will be a daunting, even impossible task.

If Clifford's attitude to sex is either Platonic or poetic, his poetry reveals a latent male power which will "ravish" the innocent virgin. Classical order is threatened by his mental virility. Parkin is able to let himself go, and is by Connie's account all she needs as a lover. Yet he cannot resist understanding it as "cunt" and "fucking". Whatever Lawrence's theory may have been about returning the obscene words to their original meaning (displacing the idealization of femininity and the romanticizing of love), and despite the defence of *Lady Chatterley's Lover* at the trial in 1960, the words are still degrading for women because the man reduces her to the genital sexual act, she becomes an object and a function of his phallic desire. However, we should notice that these obscenities are only words after the sex, in the head not in the body, as it were. Connie's "*jouissance*" and the new life that flows through her could never be matched by the words that men use to understand or rationalize sexual love. Indeed, it is because Parkin's obscene words are shocking and vulgar to her that Connie is made aware of the limits of class culture. When Lawrence has Connie describe the gamekeeper's passion as "vulgar healthiness" (FLC, 204) he keeps in play the senses of "in poor taste", "crude", "offensive", "indecent" and "obscene"; but also "of the common people", "ordinary", even "earthy", and this brings class and sex together in a positive valuation. It does well against the nervous tension, the "*sang froid*" of cultivated, upper-class life. Lawrence does invent better words for her attraction to Parkin: "sex glamour" (FLC, 216) and "sex warmth" (FLC, 217). But these are rationalizations.

The language of "*jouissance*" does not rely on any single formula, but on a whole textualisation of the sexual in metaphors of natural process, of flow and rhythm. Lawrence will develop this "*écriture féminine*" much more in the subsequent versions. We should, though, listen to Connie's feminist voice. For when the "sex glamour" is "in abeyance", she can see the man for what he is at his worst: "A ridiculous little male, on his guard and wary in his own self-importance!" (FLC, 216) However, Lawrence cannot resist putting in his creed about post-war modern women who look down on men through their "contemptuous superiority". If it was not for the instinctual, unconscious "sex warmth" between men and women, their assertive egoism would keep the sexes at war:

> The woman, feeling for some reason triumphant in our day, man having yielded most of the weapons into her hands, looks on her masculine partner with ridicule. While the man, knowing he has given up his advantage to the woman and not having the strength to get it back, looks on her with intense resentment. (FLC, 217)

The sex war uses the terms of the class war: superiority and inferiority, suspicion and mistrust, contempt and ridicule, resentment. Connie is doubly vulnerable: both as a member of the ruling class and as a woman. The critique of the capitalist system of ownership and inequality is matched by the critique of patriarchy and "the curious freemasonry of men" (FLC, 111). She perceives that men are "all gentlemen when it comes to preventing a woman from living" (FLC, 181). Connie may attain a level of freedom in her "*jouissance*", but the fixed positions of class and gender are in the end immovable. The scene where this is brought most explicitly to the surface is when Connie goes to tea at the Tewsons in Sheffield.

Like the device of the drive around Tevershall, Connie's visit to Sheffield allows for an outsider's view of an industrial town and working-class life. It is an upper-class perspective, but less judgmental, more limiting. The streets are "decent", however the poky, dark interiors are a culture shock for one used to life at the Hall. Her ignorance of working-class culture is exposed as soon as she makes the mistake of trying to gain access to the terraced house through the front door, which of course is bolted (FLC, 186). Class exploitation is written on the body of Parkin, now a scarred, health-damaged factory worker. He challenges her with his working-man's status. Yet she notices his fragile health, which undermines his pride (FLC, 187). She plays the Lady with her superior social confidence, while Bill Tewson and his wife apologize for the cramped conditions. The best china is on the table, and everyone is feeling awkward; yet in this version Lawrence resists the comic potential of the scene. The situation is charged with class difference. When Connie refuses the bland food, Mrs Tewson tells her she will cause offence if she does not eat something — in a direct manner that contrasts markedly with the elaborate subtleties of upper-class conversation. Inevitably the discussion turns to class differences, understood as way of life (in the general sense of class culture) (FLC, 191). Bill Tewson provokes the discussion in a rather naive way by reducing class to differences in refinement; deep down, we are all the same really; if we are all in the one nation, why should the Sir Cliffords be living in such a different world? Connie becomes very uncomfortable as the tirade develops into real class hatred. Parkin is more politically articulate and leads the discussion into the key areas of the ownership of property, the distribution of wealth, and the greed of the profit motive. Connie as modern woman is articulate and forthright enough to be a match for the men, in contrast to the more traditional housewife represented by Mrs Tewson who tries to calm the men down. The working-class men are radicalized because of their personal resentment. The talk is now of Socialism, even Communism. Later Parkin will reveal to Duncan Forbes that he is Secretary of the local branch of the Communist League, so that despite Connie's proposal at the end of the novel that they live together on a farm he will continue his political work. At the Tewson's, though, much of the class conflict is understood in personal, psychological terms. For Parkin the upper classes have "always got a door shut in your face, an' they're always behind the door, laughing at you" (FLC, 198). For Connie, the man who was the object of her desire has become a stranger reduced to the metonymy of his occupation: "his swollen hands". The huge cultural divide between the upper and lower classes is now what divides them (FLC, 199). She feels sorry for him, but is relieved to be back at Wragby, where the shooting party offers a rather obvious contrast to tea at the Tewsons; as do Clifford's political views. For him any threat of strike action by the miners would depreciate the coal market (FLC, 201). Politically, he has already made it clear that the few should rule the many in "a mild, benevolent form of slavery" (FLC, 103). Once Connie is pregnant, Clifford wants to exercise his rights and bring up his heir. She cannot expect a divorce from him (FLC, 251).

The artist-figure, Duncan Forbes promises a thematic and narrative resolution. He represents a modernist bohemianism, and reminds Connie of her origins as daughter of an R.A., and clashes quite obviously with Clifford. The artist exercises his privileged position and mocks the emptiness of modern life. But, in his attitude to Parkin, he indulges a superior cynicism that exposes him to the very hollowness he criticizes. Indeed, he has an upper-class contempt for the common people (FLC, 215). His attempts to mediate between Connie and Parkin are not convincing. His chic radicalism cannot really be expected to cope with Parkin's politically committed work. When he tells Connie that Parkin, like themselves, is also beyond class, an exception, we might want to ask for the evidence. He may be sexually different; but he has achieved a measure of pride in his class solidarity. Moreover, it is Duncan Forbes who, after several whiskies, envisions the new democracy with "men kindled to this glow of human beauty and awareness, opened glowing to another sort of contact" (FLC, 239). But we are not convinced, as it is the drink that has relaxed him from "his usual nervous tension" (FLC, 240). His past socialist sympathies, like Connie's, seem to have been eroded by the pressures of society. And already there is a hint of things to come in the subsequent versions, as Connie believes the English working man "too human" to get involved in violent revolution. Duncan Forbes reiterates Lawrence's message: it is "some sort of passionate human contact ... the life-flow with one another" that the English need (FLC, 242). The resolution to the cultural crisis does not apparently lie with politics — yet this is Lawrence's most explicit novel about class politics. As Connie waits out her pregnancy, the novel ends with her thoughts about Wragby as a symbol of "generations of superiority, centuries of conceit!" She decides that she must learn to take Parkin's "manly fucking" more seriously. They plan to marry, yet this seems implausible, and the ending is left open.

The First Lady Chatterley has the rudiments of the story, but we should not forget that it was only the first of three versions. Lawrence seems to have changed his mind about the explicit class content, and placed much more emphasis on the sex in the second version. The first version, then, is a political novel about the threat of class war, in response to Lawrence's visit to "Bestwood", but the diagnosis is not so much socio-economic as sexual: the ruling classes disqualify themselves as leaders because they cannot let themselves go. The solution proposed — the feminization of the culture in a democracy of "touch" — is not well worked. The second version develops these themes in much more detail; and it also quite deliberately moves away from class towards the explicit description of sex itself.

iii. *John Thomas and Lady Jane* (*The Second Lady Chatterley*)
The second version has much more detail about character, sex, and class culture. Yet it establishes a distance from class as a category even while demonstrating once again that English culture is divided by class. That division goes right into the psychology of Connie whose passionate sex with the gamekeeper causes a split self — her critical spirit deriving from her superior class and intellectual position, on the one side; her instinctive body-knowledge experienced in her "*jouissance*" on the other side.

The textualization of these polarized differences takes on more generic significance, characteristic of late Lawrence. Clifford and his cronies are subjected to satire, filtered through Connie as focalizing agent, which is both a trenchant critique of the ruling aristocracy and a feminist perspective on the inflated self-importance of chattering men. The high cultural register as speech genre (which I discussed in chapter three) is a focus for the satire, as Lawrence overplays the speech mannerism to undercut the grand ideas expressed by these upper-class men. Tommy Dukes, for instance, an old soldier, is "frightfully cultured, and extremely nice to a woman but didn't care for women, and was most happy when cornered alone with Clifford in a bachelor privacy". These men are only really happy when they are "manly and masculine and womanless".[73] Thus, through the woman's focalization, a sharper feminist edge is added to the social and class satire, rewriting the post-war masculinity represented in *Aaron's Rod* through the detached and cynical perspective of Connie Chatterley, and one previously represented by Johanna in *Mr Noon* and Harriett in *Kangaroo*. The shift away from sympathy towards cynicism changes the tone of the story. The third version will take this much further. However, we should notice that satire is only generically commensurate with the level of social critique — like courtly romance, satire targets the culture of the refined upper classes. Because it is an intellectualizing process it will cede precedence to the poetry of "*jouissance*" because that has a higher value in Lawrence's writing.

Another aristocratic genre is the gothic horror, a popular development in the novel in the Romantic era, and one already redeployed by Lawrence in the novella, *The Ladybird* (1923). Connie feels imprisoned at Wragby Hall by the tyranny of Clifford over her as his voice seems disembodied: "What creature was this?" (JTLJ, 31). He begins to fit the part well as he becomes more neurotic, even hysterical; more interested in "the problem of immortality and the reality of mystical experiences" (JTLJ, 87). To escape his overbearing egoism and will-to-power (as substitute-gratification for his lack of sex), she escapes to her own room, which takes on the role of a feminine space, a sanctuary — at least until she can escape to the woods and the phallic awakening (in another subgenre noticed by many critics, the Cinderella fable). The "Wild Woman" (JTLJ, 196) is played by Bertha Coutts, who, like her namesake in *Jane Eyre* (1847), is the hysterical woman from the sexual history of the gamekeeper, and who will return to haunt him like Bertha does to

---

[73] *John Thomas and Lady Jane* (London: Penguin, 1974. First published 1972), 13. Subsequent references in text [JTLJ].

Rochester. Lawrence's version draws out the Freudian implication that the sexually voracious woman is self-destructive, and adds his own theory that she is dangerous for men because of her strong-willed "frictional" (JTLJ, 196) sex. Moreover, the sexual history has a lower-class location, and Connie is "silent with dread, thinking of the awful lives people led: there in Clifford's village" (JTLJ, 201). Public scandal will also return to haunt her. Clifford is power-mad: he has a master-slave mentality, and expects total respect and subservience from the miners, from the servants, and from his wife. Her only chance of an acceptable relationship with him is through high cultural discussion. But she rejects this, finding his incessant chatter, like his Platonism, deadening. As she says of the contemporary neo-Platonist, Whitehead: "He's another windbag .... I expect he's one of these intellectuals with a dead body so he wants to kill everything and have a universe of abstract forms." (JTLJ, 265)

When Connie returns to Wragby from France she is shocked by the contrast with "the old clarity of southern Europe". Middle England was "grey, weird ghoulish" and eternally "sunless". It was a twilight world of "real ghoulishness and the after-death". Wragby Hall is the gothic castle, and Mrs Bolton has become Clifford's right hand, with her "long, pale cheeks" and "flashing" eyes, in the "region of dread dreams" (JTLJ, 316-318). The gothic atmosphere of the place transfers itself to the whole Midlands region, and the colliers of Tevershall seem like "ghosts, ghouls, not men", as Clifford seeks to impose his will on the mines to "make them pay". He is described as no longer human, because of his "long-enduring ecstasy of the struggle with uncanny matter" (JTLJ, 339-340). We are reminded of the fate of Gerald Crich in *Women in Love* who is destroyed by the very process of seeking to impose his will on matter. Once Connie is pregnant she is in mortal fear: "She was in the most subtle danger, the danger of being dragged under water by these two uncanny creatures" (i.e. Clifford and Mrs Bolton). Weeping and fretting, she faints in Clifford's presence "like a heroine, in the eighteenth-century" (JTLJ, 346).

The generic shifts are not just a matter of parody, as they were in *Mr Noon*. Here, genre has class location. The description of Connie's visit to the Tewsons in Sheffield takes on, in this second version, a Dickensian register (similar to some of the writing in *The Lost Girl*, as I described it in chapter three). Here is an example, with the characteristic personification and repetition: "mean, rigid dwellings, the mean doors and the mean windows that repeated themselves identically so rapidly, in the utter aridity of stone and black pavement". The poky interior of the terraced house is now, "the dressed-up little hole" (JTLJ, 350). The comedy in the situation Connie finds herself in is emphasized more in this version:

... into the small passageway, where it was dark ... and from another dark doorway ... Connie found herself running into the coats
that hung from the pegs on the wall of the passage, and a hat, a
bowler hat, fell with a rattle. (JTLJ, 352)

As there is so little room, she is concerned she might break something.
Her perspective has a distancing effect that is potentially comic. All her
careful efforts to fit in and become invisible are upset by her class-
cultural ignorance when she talks of Parkin instead of Mr Seivers or
Oliver, a class-code slip which she soon realizes might be seen as an
insult. But it is worse coming from a woman, as the gender positions are
quite rigid (JTLJ, 359). When they leave together, they walk down the
"hideous street". In the tram she notices "the depressing ugliness of the
other passengers, poorish working-class, without colour, grace, or form:
or even warmth of life. It was too gruesome." (JTLJ, 367) If the
Dickensian register verges on the patronizing, the ethical and aesthetic
values through which Connie assesses the quality of working-class life
are expressions of her upper-class distaste. Lawrence has abandoned the
socialist sympathies of the first version. This is consistent with the whole
scene at the Tewsons, where the class diatribe has been reduced to some
comments about the haves and the have-nots, and whether the upper
classes feel guilty about being rich. Parkin has been depoliticized, and
takes on the role (given to Mrs Tewson in *The First Lady Chatterley*) of
trying to shut Bill up.

The generic shifts are a new development in the *Lady Chatterley*
novels, and especially with their link to class. But as many critics have
noted, there is at the same time an explicit and deliberate refusal of the
socio-economic and political implications of the category of class itself.
Later in the novel, Connie is given to think: "There was no longer any
such thing as class." Class position is now only a state of mind. Therefore, Clifford is proletarian and Parkin is not. Moreover, class is "an
anachronism. It finished in 1914." (JTLJ, 294) What she (and Lawrence)
means by this is that: "[v]itally, organically, in the old organic sense of
society, there were no more classes. That organic system had collapsed".
Therefore, "she need not have any class-mistrust of Parkin, and he need
have none of her." (JTLJ, 301) So despite all the social realism of class-
cultural difference in the novel, Lawrence now seems to understand class
in the same organic terms with which he values the instinctive self.
Before 1914, culture was nature. Then, the social world was an organism;
now it is a mechanism. The new capitalists, like Clifford, value science
and technology and the life of the mind. Connie stands for nature and the
organic principle and the life of the body. Philosophically, Lawrence's
vitalism is consistent and plausible. But the transference of the organicist

values to the social sphere is simply a form of mystification of the real historical and material processes which the novel, in any case, makes visible. 1914 is a watershed in history, in many senses. And Lawrence, like any writer of his generation, tried to come to terms imaginatively with the Great War. But history cannot be reduced to an organic and a post-organic era.

We have been here before: in *The Rainbow*, as I argued in chapter two, history tends to give way to myth. At least there the organicism is established on a number of levels in the narrative. Here, in the second version of *Lady Chatterley*, the organic understanding of class is less plausible because it has not been established in the narrative. Lawrence appears to confuse what happens to exceptional individuals (who are not, in any case, always typical of their respective class) and the state of England. *Sons and Lovers* and *The Rainbow* offer glimpses of a real history in the gaps between the family stories. *Women in Love* gives us the example of Gerald Crich's father as a caring mine-owner from the old world. But it is more usual to call this a benign patrician than organic rule. Lawrence's organic social theory wants the return to the pre-industrial country estate (a Great Houses theory of English culture), so that he can imagine a social unity where everyone knew their place in an unquestioned hierarchy that was, presumably, ordained by Nature — a kind of organicist Great Chain of Being, now reinscribed as a social eco-system. However, the narrative continually tells a different story, and we should conclude that the abolition of class conflict through a return to a putative organic order is nothing less than utopic.

Yet, as in the first version of the novel, class resentment or "grudge" resurfaces: in the Ted Bolton story; in Mrs Bolton's attitude to the upper classes where her increased importance in Wragby seems at times as a kind of revenge; the hardened class attitude of Parkin, which is only overcome in the end once his confidence in Connie is established and he can work on a farm; the view of Tevershall in the famous car-ride, and the visit to Sheffield — all in a novel that wants to move away from class as a category, transcending it with sex itself. It is Connie's sister, Hilda, who reminds her, and us, that in England class is everything, and that she should use her money to maintain her status. (cf. JTLJ, 311-12)

The state of England that is preferred is always framed in its literature or in a traditional landscape painting. The English park on the country estate in autumn is "a vision from the past ... from the late eighteenth century, a day such as lingers in the old English aquatints" (JTLJ, 26). Connie prefers to think of the southern counties and London as the England of Shakespeare and Chaucer, Jane Austen and Dickens. The real, industry-ruined country is sooty and sulphurous (which is a lingering memory for Lawrence as it appears in several of his fictions); it is a "grey-coffin England". Yet the mines are mythologized: "The monstrous new colliery was the Eleusis, the sacred place of the terrific modern demon". The colliers are underground creatures, "trolls" with an "elementary tribal instinct". It is an instinct that Parkin shares too (JTLJ, 156). The future is grim, because it belongs to the industrial machine; the past feudal, mythological, and literary.

Heritage England is breeding and lineage. The ruling families need heirs, and Clifford's disability takes on greater significance. The sense of impending doom and apocalypse is talked up from the initial loathing Clifford has for "a swamp of common people, profane vulgarity". Wragby represents "decency, dignity, and beauty" (JTLJ, 207). What he wants is to find "enough strong men to form a small aristocracy, and put the rest back into slavery where they belong" (JTLJ, 27). For Connie, though, a return to the distant past would be to the Celtic origins of Britain (and not for the first time in Lawrence). Once again, it is the culture itself which is at stake. But despite the presence in the text of class-cultural differences that divide the nation, Lawrence persists in positing a unified idea of the national culture — which is of course consistent with his organicist beliefs.

What has to carry the full weight of the cultural regeneration is sex. And in this second version of the novel, there is, as John Worthen has put it, "a wholly prepared for explicitness" in the representation of sex (for the first time in the English novel).[74] Sex is linked with health as Connie shows all the symptoms of repression. In this version, it is her father who warns Clifford of the dangers: "her nerves will suffer". At Wragby, "the tick-tock of mechanistic monotony became an insanity to her" (JTLJ, 16). Sexual repression and class are clearly linked because Connie has "a very high sense of duty" as the Lady of Wragby Hall (JTLJ, 23). Lawrence is much more explicit about her growing sexual frustration, making her into a Freudian case of hysteria. In a moment of irony (intended?), her father tries to explain things through a car-motor analogy which closely resembles Freud's "hydraulics" (the pressures and drives that play off desire against the superego): "You've got your brake jammed .... [Y]ou'd better get help to get it taken off, or your axle's going to break" (JTLJ, 24). The situation is exacerbated by Clifford's firm belief in the superiority of the life of the mind, but, as in the first version, he does give his consent for her to take a lover and try for a son (JTLJ, 31), provided she does not cause a scandal and stays married to him. She persists in disciplining herself by keeping busy: "she had very little time for herself, no time at all" — and here the text captures the growing hysteria through

---

[74] John Worthen, *D.H. Lawrence* (London: Arnold, 1991), 107.

its stylistic over-determination of her mind-style which is represented by compulsive repetition and sequences of exclamation marks (JTLJ, 41). Her restlessness is transferred into her dreams of violent storms, as the self-destructive sex-drive is imaginatively re-enacted. Yet, it is tempting to ask how serious we should take this, given Lawrence's declared rejection of Freudianism as sexual determinism. It is close to the clichés of popular Freudianism. We do get all the classic conditions for Freud's "*Spaltung*" — the split personality: "She was at the mercy of her two selves" (JTLJ, 173). Her unconscious desire demands one thing from her; her "critical spirit" (*superego*) demands another. The Lacanian dictum, "the unconscious is the discourse of the Other" is also illustrated: "The woman of the evil moods was not herself at all. It was some other, unreal, abstract personage." (JTLC, 44) As in the first version, she becomes more physically self-conscious once she studies herself naked in the mirror — in a belated "mirror stage" she apprehends herself as a libidinized body-to-be-seen by the other, a moment where she escapes the closed world of her mental torment in defiance of Clifford's wish to banish nakedness. It is the precondition of her wanting to be physically touched. (cf. JTLJ, 57)

What Connie discovers unconsciously, Tommy Dukes rationalizes into "the democracy of touch" (JTLJ, 65). Lawrence gives more space in the text for the new doctrinal formula for rescuing the doomed culture. The "*noli me tangere*" of *Aaron's Rod* is now displaced by "*voli me tangere*". Connie's passionate sex with Parkin will, of course, be exemplary; and the detailed description of their lovemaking will have to carry the full weight of the doctrine. The new resurrection will take the form of the new erection: "a new fire to erect [the] phallus" (JTLJ, 71). The psychoanalytics of desire will give way to the sacredness of sex, as the novel returns to familiar late-Lawrentian territory. The Lady and the gamekeeper will show us how sex can take on greater spiritual signifi-cance and become the key to cultural regeneration. It begins with abandoning self-assertion and approaching the other "as the flower does, naked and defenceless and infinitely in touch" (JTLJ, 115).

In this second version, Lawrence constructs the prehistory of the love affair in greater and careful detail. The lovers seem to grow organically towards each other: "he felt himself streaming towards her, and the flow gradually growing stronger, even while he was unaware of it". What holds them up is a quite plausible reticence, deriving in his case from the bad experience with his estranged wife, and in her case from her senses of duty and refinement. Both are also wary of the other for obvious class reasons. However, all these rationalizations are no match for the force of desire, because "the desire he had was in his body" (JTLJ, 118). Yet even after they have become lovers, they are both in dread of the mass reaction of society were they to be found out. What lingers in the memory for her is that "the man loved her with his body" (JTLJ, 124).

However, she is only really transformed or newly-born once she experiences her "*jouissance*":

> ... thrills ... wilder and wilder, like bells ringing pealing faster and faster ... when everything within her turned to fluid, and her life seemed to sway like liquid in a bowl, swaying to quiescence. (JTLJ, 133)

This is how Lawrence imagines the female orgasm. It is an explosion or eruption from deep within, "like a volcano" (JTLJ, 135). It is the first time she experiences it, and it therefore changes her irrevocably. But how accurate is Lawrence's representation of the female orgasm? Writing the woman's experience of her own body, Hélène Cixous uses figures similar to Lawrence:

> I, too, overflow; my desires have invented new desires, my body knows unheard of songs. Time and again I, too, have felt so full of luminous torrents that I could burst ... I said to myself: You are mad! What's the meaning of these waves, these floods, these outbursts?[75]

The images of water, waves, floods, bursting, and of unheard of sounds coming from deep within the body are common to both texts. For Lawrence, such imagery deliberately brings sexuality and nature together as organic process: she grows or blossoms as woman, and the seed is in her womb.

There is, of course, a world of difference between Lawrence's doctrine of phallus-worship and Cixous' promotion of female masturbation as a crucial process of self-discovery and a defiant rejection of "parental-conjugal phallocentrism". The waves of pleasure in Lawrence's text are brought about by the man's action:

> And her own flesh quivered and seemed to melt, in wave after wave of new moltenness, as he entered her and melted her in successive sharp, soft waves of unspeakable pleasure, molten and for ever molten, while her voice uttered sharp, strange cries, till she reached the climax and was gone, in the pure bath of forgetting and of birth. (JTLJ, 240)

---

[75] Cixous in Marks and de Courtivron, 246.

The man is the phallic agent and the active party; the woman is submissive and passive. Yet, we should notice that Connie sees the man as only the "guardian and keeper of the bright phallus", because it was "pure ecstatic servant to the woman". The phallus is "hers, her own". This can be understood on two levels. First, it is an instrument of her pleasure (a kind of sacred vibrator?), implying a *"jouissance"* all of her own (and we do not get any description of the man's orgasm). Second, we are close to Lacan's transcendental signifier, from which all significance in sexual ontology derives. Furthermore, Lawrence returns to a more ancient idea of the phallus as a totem or symbol of fertility, a life-giving and life-enhancing force (an anthropological connotation in Lacan too).

Nevertheless, Lawrence values female sexuality; it has a kind of priority status. In *A Propos of "Lady Chatterley"* (1930), he writes:

> When a woman's sex is in itself dynamic and alive, then it is a power in itself, beyond her reason. And of itself it emits its peculiar spell, drawing men in the first delight of desire.[76]

His descriptions of female orgasm — his *"écriture féminine"* — are detailed and poetic; indeed, within the western cultural hierarchy of discourses, the poetic has always had a high ranking. It has also been stigmatized, like female sexuality, as mad and dangerous. We must not forget that Clifford wants sex and emotions controlled by the aesthetic and the Platonic. Lawrence is on the side of the Romantics. The poetry of female *"jouissance"* challenges the scientific discourses of sexuality. Its representation, however, only thinly veils a doctrinaire, cosmic significance.

But is that significance any more than symbolic? The realism is fuller in its circumstantial detail than it is in the first version, and the fixed class positions of the characters still stand in their way. Connie's gender position makes her doubly vulnerable: crossing the class divide for an adulterous affair leaves her open to an awful treatment, given both Clifford's attitude to the common people and the way they treat Parkin in any case. As he puts it: "If they knowed we was like this ... they'd want to kill us." (JTLJ, 260) And yet at those moments when she fears being dominated by the will of men, she feels on safer ground with Clifford: "she was really more afraid of Parkin, or of herself under Parkin's influence, than she was of Clifford." (JTLJ, 255) She is afraid of Parkin awakening her otherwise dormant sexuality — her *"jouissance"* is so

---

[76] Reprinted in *Lady Chatterley's Lover* (London: the Penguin edition of the Cambridge D.H. Lawrence, 1994), 316.

powerful and disruptive. Once back in the rational light of day, she knows there is also the question of economic dependence. She has a small income of her own inherited from her mother, but it would mean a considerable drop in life-style marrying Parkin.

The more detailed presentation of character psychology and sexual content renders the relationship of the Lady to the working-class man much more plausible. Parkin is now more articulate and less proud of being helped by a woman; Connie defiantly shows more sympathy for the servants. She is, after all, consistently an outspoken, modern woman critical of the fixed social positions. She is even more of a feminist who understands the workings of the masculine mind: "If Clifford knew she was going to the gamekeeper, what a night of fever, excitement, pornographic imaginings, and jealous torment for him!" (JTLJ, 222) The principal link between sex and society is scandal. Although Lawrence was used to imagining marriage across class barriers (his mother's and his own, and those like Tom Brangwen to Lydia, or Alvina to Ciccio), the class positions of the Lady and the gamekeeper still make the match implausible on all but the sexual level. As Hilda crudely but effectively puts it: it is not Parkin's penis, but Clifford's baronetcy that rules the world! (JTLJ, 311-312) Lawrence will need to resolve this if he is to bring his story to a satisfying end. As we shall see, he will have to make the gamekeeper's class position more ambivalent in the third version. But the changes will go much further than that, affecting the narrative itself. Significantly, the second version ends with the lovers being caught "necking", as Connie plays the collier's girl.

iv. *Lady Chatterley's Lover* (The Third Lady Chatterley)
The third version is in many respects different from the second. After finishing *John Thomas and Lady Jane* in February 1927 Lawrence went on his tour with Brewster of the "Etruscan places".[77] His account was not published until 1932. But it is generally accepted that the differences in the final version are partly clarified by his imaginary recreation of the ancient Italian civilization which now represents all the values that Lawrence promotes in his late doctrine: vitality, fullness of life, spontaneity, harmony with the natural world, delicate sensitivity, and above all, "the natural beauty of proportion of the phallic consciousness". The Etruscans are everything the Romans are not (and this has a contemporary agenda too, as the Italian Fascists promoted everything Roman). The tombs are symbolically gendered, as the phallus or the ark or arx (i.e. womb) are still visible by the doors of tombs, male or female

---

[77] For a brief account see David Ellis, 348-63.

respectively. Lawrence opposes these symbols to the dominant Roman values of empire, dominion, riches, social gain: "You cannot dance gaily to the double flute and at the same time conquer nations or rake in large sums of money".[78]

It should not be surprising, then, that Clifford represents the Roman Emperor, wanting to impose his will on the mines and turn the workers into his slaves. It was an idea already emergent in the second version, but discussed now in more detail. In *Lady Chatterley*, Clifford's political views are encapsulated thus: "The masses are always the same, and will always be the same. Nero's slaves were extremely little different from our colliers or the Ford motor-car workmen."[79] Rylance describes how Clifford's politics reflect the solutions entertained by the authoritarian Right in England in the late 1920s after the General Strike, "based on firm perceptions of class role, national — and racial — purpose, and the need for a Caesarist leader for England".[80] The Etruscan civilization, as Lawrence understood it, gave him a model for a utopian alternative to the growing fascism in Europe. (There was little archaeological evidence with which to counter his version.) Tenderness is now quite explicitly opposed to all forms of masculinist will and power. Mellors, the third version of the gamekeeper, will represent this new but ancient mode of being.

For Lawrence, then, the Etruscans are the antipathy of the people of Tevershall and Wragby Hall. They were "a vivid, life-accepting people, who must have lived with real fullness ... dancing in their coloured wraps ... dancing and fluting along through the little olive trees, out in the fresh day".[81] It is an image projected onto Mellors' utopia which ends the novel. It seems that the Etruscans believed in the power of nature, the cosmic forces of the earth — derived from their lived experiences of volcanoes, earthquakes, the power of the sea, the roots of plants, and the life of trees. Knowledge is derived from the experience of living naturally, and not by scientific formula or the abstractions of aesthetics. It is all familiar Lawrence doctrine. But thinking the Etruscans enabled him to clarify his theory of "touch" before writing the third version of the Chatterley novel. However, what it also does is to make this last version more explicitly doctrinal. And this goes right into the sexual explicitness, which now takes on even more transcendent significance, losing some of

---

[78] D.H. Lawrence, *Etruscan Places* in *D.H. Lawrence and Italy* (London: Penguin, 1997. First published 1932), 10, 14, 23.

[79] *Lady Chatterley's Lover* (London: the Penguin edition of the Cambridge D.H. Lawrence, 1994), 182. Subsequent references to this edition in text [LCL].

[80] Rick Rylance, "Lawrence's Politics" in Brown, 177.

[81] *Etruscan Places*, 38-9.

the lyricism of the second version.

The opening chapters are a thematic overture in a more detailed and explicit way. There is more family history. Moreover, the early sexual history of Connie turns her into a more experienced woman than in the other two versions, even when the point is being made that it is the wrong kind of experience, and that she will have to learn a different sexual practice. Lawrence has returned to his legislative role, only implicit in the other versions: the wrong kind of sex is "frictional"; but now the men themselves are to blame. Indeed, before Mellors enters her life, men seem to have little patience with the time it takes the woman to achieve her orgasm. Connie learns to take her pleasure where she can, and Lawrence gives us the intimate details. There is so much sympathy for her part that she herself is not castigated for "frictional" sex. It is merely part of her learning experience, and not just another example of her modern-woman's wilfulness. Lawrence gets Michaelis — a new character, there for the purpose of her sexual development — to say what the author would have said in earlier fiction: that women hold themselves back, and "try to run the show". Connie speaks for the women: "like so many modern men, he was finished almost before he had begun. And that forced the woman to be active". As for Michaelis placing the fault with the women, this was for her a "piece of novel, masculine information" (LCL, 54). When, much later, Mellors discusses the same issue in recounting his experiences with Bertha Coutts, the man is no longer the guilty party: "She had to work the thing herself, grind her own coffee." (LCL, 202) In this case, sex is a wilful and mechanical act on the part of the woman. Mellors proves himself to be better at sex than Michaelis. However, he who is the promoter of the new tenderness is driven by the memory of the bad experiences in his sexual history to make terrible generalizations about women, and with such forceful sexism, concluding that all sexually active women are lesbians, and he would kill them if he could! (LCL, 203) But is he wholly free of blame? Connie once again speaks for the women: "And perhaps the women *really* wanted to be there and love you properly, only perhaps they couldn't. Perhaps it wasn't all their fault." (LCL, 205) Sexual politics is now carried into the very activity of sex itself, losing much of its metaphysical significance for the moment. But it is easy to misread if you do not appreciate the context of these masculinist outbursts. The simple message is that a heterosexual couple who are truly together accept their differences, do not impose their selfish will on the other, and relate to each through tenderness. Then, as Michael Squires explains, "[a]t the emotional centre of their

encounter is a reciprocity that dismantles their sexual politics".[82]
Admittedly, it is a difficult message to take if the "emotional centre" is
framed in a sexual theory which is unacceptable today, and not just to
feminists. Lawrence may insist, once again, on the woman's submission
to the male phallus, with all the cosmic significance that we saw in the
second version; yet this insistence often comes over as a particularly
limited form of sexual practice, with the woman submitting to the man's
wishes, and only being able to achieve her orgasm through his phallic
activity. Lawrence even justifies anal penetration by giving it a transforming function for the woman. She is even given to think "she had
secretly wanted it", because it was necessary "to burn out false shames"
(LCL, 247).[83]

What Connie has learnt in her sexual education is a further development from the "mirror stage", when she studied her naked body as it
might be seen by the male other. Now: "the fluid, male knowledge of
herself seemed to flow to her from his eyes and wrap her voluptuously"
(LCL, 248). Yet, sometimes this begins to read like popular romance
fiction. She is always asking for a kiss, and wants him to say that he
loves her. His replies are always indirect, kissing her anywhere but on the
lips, and telling her that she should know instinctively — in her body-
knowledge — how he feels. Connie does not seem to be able to translate
the experience of herself in her "*jouissance*" into the rational, mental
understanding of their relationship. This takes nothing away from the
"*écriture féminine*" of her "*jouissance-text*". But it seems there is no
language available in which to translate it after the experience. Usually
the lovers do not speak much after sex — which is often contrasted
sharply with Clifford's incessant chatter, with which Connie becomes
increasingly impatient. However, talking about sex is a theme throughout
the novel.

For Clifford and his cronies sex is an overrated, irritating necessity, a
bodily function like going to the toilet. They would prefer having babies
bred in bottles so that the whole awkward business would no longer be
necessary. Clifford is in favour of selective breeding (eugenics).
Winterslow suggests: "It's quite time man began to improve on his own

---

[82] Introduction to the Penguin (1994) edition of the Cambridge D.H. Lawrence, xxix.
[83] For a scathing critique of Lawrence's "enthusiasm for sodomitic solutions" see
David Holbrook (1988), "Sons and Mothers: D.H. Lawrence and *Mr Noon*" reprinted
in Ellis and de Zordo eds (1992), Volume III, where he also endorses Kate Millett's
attack on Lawrence. Holbrook continues his tirade in "Exorcist on an Unholy
Crusade" in *Times Literary Supplement* (July 9 1993), 15, in which he argues that
"D.H. Lawrence's advocacy of sodomy masks a deep violence to women rather than a
sexual liberation."

nature, especially the physical side" (LCL, 78). Yet the upper classes often reproduce in thought and manners their own quaint and archaic allegories of femininity. In the right company, Connie knows when to appear as the "demure, submissive" maiden. Winter "called her: dear child! and gave her a rather lovely miniature of an eighteenth-century lady ... much against her will" (LCL, 129). Clifford claims he gets all he wants from Racine. Echoing that other neo-classicist of the day, T.S. Eliot, he insists that: "[e]motions that are ordered and given shape are more important than disorderly emotions". Emotions have become "vulgarized" in the modern world, and what we need is "classic control" (LCL, 139). Clifford's attitude towards women ranges from outright chivalry towards Connie, through Madonna-worship — a state to which he regresses with his surrogate mother-love for Mrs Bolton, to a total rejection of the life of the body for the life of the mind, and finally to a violent rejection of Connie once she tells him about Mellors: "you ought to be wiped off the face of the earth! ... [I]s there any end to the beastly lowness of women ... the *nostalgie de la boue*" (LCL, 296). Sex for him is now atavistic behaviour; and his reaction is the more extreme because of his expectations of loyalty and her class betrayal. A child from a man of the lower classes is the end of civilization as he knows it.

Mellors, the other man, talks of women in crude sexual or sexist terms. He can say "she shits and pisses", and "arse", and explain to Connie the difference between "fucking" (which animals do) and "cunt" (which a man does with a woman when she is really aroused). But instead of vagina he (and Lawrence) says "secret opening" or "mound of venus"; clitoris is "beak" or "tip" (always with negative connotations); pubic hair is "maiden hair", and "loins" is the euphemistic, poetic word used for genitals (as it is throughout Lawrence). The male organs — "penis" and "balls" (the latter used as a swear-word too) — are directly expressed and sometimes on display for the woman to admire. And, of course, the penis is promoted to the transcendental signifier: the phallus — except that in this third version Lawrence uses the more ancient Greek spelling, "*phallos*" (perhaps to avoid the anthropological association of phallus), when he is not personifying both male and female genital organs as "John Thomas" and "Lady Jane". Mellors' vulgar discourse has a shock value that has had a long after-life (the obscenity trial was in 1960). It is meant to debunk all the higher aesthetic, philosophic, and scientific discourses of sexuality in the text. Yet, there is an obvious contradiction between his anti-romantic discourse — Mellors says to Connie: "You love your fucking all right: but you want it to be called something grand and mysterious, just to flatter your own self-importance" (LCL, 207) — and Lawrence's evasive and poetic language when it comes to the female genitals. Moreover, Mellors' critique of

Connie can be extended to Lawrence, who wants sex to be exemplary, and more than ever in *Lady Chatterley's Lover* gives it a cosmic significance that goes beyond the initial opposition in the text between "warm-hearted fucking" and "cold-hearted fucking" (LCL, 206) to the rejuvenation of the culture itself.

Mellors' sex-talk is not, though, voluble, and it is superseded by a physical sexuality which speaks a different language. He communicates directly with the woman through his body and sexuality. He is kind to the woman in Connie, while the other men talk sex and are destructive to women even when being kind. Mellors puts into practice what Tommy Dukes theorizes: "Real knowledge comes out of the whole corpus of the consciousness; out of your belly and your penis as much as out of your brain and mind. The mind can only analyse and rationalize." (LCL, 37)

In the Chatterley novels, as in most of his fiction, Lawrence gives priority to the life of the body by attempting to represent it in a language of the body. French feminism, as I argued above, has been calling for a writing that would express the woman's imaginary and her sexualized body, a writing which would displace the essentialisms of conventional femininity. Approaching Lawrence's writing (as opposed to his reputation) through French feminism draws out these aspects of his fiction; but it also demonstrates the extent to which he tends to replace one set of essentialisms with another: the different conventional discourses of female sexuality, whether literary, scientific, or vulgar, in the talk of men (especially amongst men, when Connie is a silent but ironic observer), and the models of the feminine the women live by as lovers, wives and mothers, are all rejected, only to be replaced by a much more ancient idea of Patriarchy, but now with a new, partly feminized man who promotes tenderness. Lawrence has reinstated the feminization of culture from the early works while not abandoning male leadership. Indeed, he is at pains to demonstrate what bad male leadership looks like: Clifford's "Caesarism" is rejected for Mellors' "democracy of touch", bullying for tenderness.

Connie's romantic discourse of love is inconsistent with her modern woman's self and her feminism; and above all with her "*jouissance-text*", itself a kind of writing that was radical in its day — and, in comparison with Cixous' writing quoted above, still is today. As Sally Ledger claims, there was no discourse on female sexuality in the early feminism of the late nineteenth and early twentieth centuries. There were no models for such a discourse because women's sex-desire was not recognized before the 1890s, when lesbianism became an object of discourse (predominantly as a pathology).[84] Once women's sexuality became no longer exclusively a subject of procreation and mothering, a new discourse had to be invented. The work of Carpenter, Ellis, and Freud (all men) has enabled the feminists of today to construct a discourse of female sexuality, even while starting with a critique of the limits of these early theorists. Lawrence invented an *"écriture féminine"* out of the poetic, biblical, and psychoanalytic discourses in circulation. All the other talk about sex in his writing is put into perspective by his representation of the female *"jouissance"*:

> ... there awoke in her new strange thrills rippling inside her. Rippling, rippling, rippling, like a flapping overlapping of soft flames, soft as feathers, running to points of brilliance, exquisite, exquisite, and melting her all molten inside. It was like bells, rippling up and up to a culmination. She lay unconscious of the wild little cries she uttered at last. ... [H]er womb was open and soft and softly clamouring, like a sea-anemone under the tides, clamouring for him to come in again and make a fulfilment of her ... pure, deepening whirlpools of sensation, swirling deeper and deeper through all her tissue and consciousness, till she was one perfect concentric fluid of feeling. (LCL, 133-34)

Such textual moments are aesthetically superior to all the inadequate talk and unacceptable sexual theory that circulates through the novel.

The principal difference, therefore, between the third version and the other two is the attention to writing (*écriture*). Lawrence returns to the self-conscious Modernism of the other 1920s fiction, which I discussed in chapters 3, 4 and 5. In the Chatterley novels, letter-writing dominates the latter part of all the versions. Mellors is a more articulate gamekeeper than Parkin, and Lawrence gives his closing letter the function of communicating the central message, in a kind of coda — as if the author was not confident that the narrative had finally clarified things. Here, his model is his own letter-writing to Rolf Gardiner (a genuine Lawrence disciple),[85] especially the letter of the 3 December 1926 where Lawrence encourages Gardiner to establish an alternative community, perhaps on a farm, with a different life-style based on colourful clothing, dance and mass music. It is a development of "Rananim" first tried out by Ramón in *The Plumed Serpent*. Also in the letter to Gardiner, 7 January 1928, Lawrence praises his involvement with the German *Bünde*, the Youth

---

[84] Ledger, 111, 125.
[85] As Ellis explains, 308.

Movement which promoted outdoor activities, farm-work, and the "*Freikörperkultur*".[86] Connie has already experienced the German Youth Movement, the "*Wandervogel*", when she was younger (as described in the beginning of the novel); and Mellors has explained his utopia to her: as a leader he would tell his men to take their clothes off and look at themselves, come alive, wear more colourful clothes, clean up the countryside, rebuild Tevershall, and restrict birth as the world is already overcrowded (LCL, 219-220).

Other characters write letters, and their styles contrast as markedly as their characters. Mrs Bolton's gossip-text contrasts with Clifford's high cultural, essayistic style. In *Lady Chatterley*, Lawrence has made him a successful writer of modern short stories; but a writer of the wrong (i.e. not Lawrentian) sort: "Clever, rather spiteful, and ... meaningless ... [T]he stories were curiously true to modern life, to the modern psychology" (LCL, 16). Connie's father thinks Clifford's writing has "nothing in it" (LCL, 17). Michaelis, the Irish playwright, wrote "smart society plays", but is snubbed by the metropolitan literati for being anti-English, and makes a fortune in the USA instead (LCL, 20). Clifford's obsession to become known throughout the world "as a first-class modern writer" (LCL, 21) is eventually displaced by the ambition to impose his will and new scientific knowledge on the matter of the very earth itself, through getting the mines to become more efficient. But before that, he does become famous as a writer, makes some money, and has an additional set of literary admirers visit Wragby. His writing is "really clever at that slightly humorous analysis of people and motives which leaves every-thing in bits at the end" (LCL, 50). Just like the personal revelations of the letters characters write, these critical evaluations of Clifford's or Michaelis' writing are transparently biographical. They also throw into relief Lawrence's own aesthetic: not the cool, detached writing of social observation (in the tradition of the novel of manners); but the great novel of ideas — satiric, poetic and utopian (more European than English at times).[87]

What is most noticeably different in the third version is the often cynical tone, made all the more effective by the use of a narrator. The first two versions use Lawrence's common device of telling the story

---

[86] Lawrence was, however, cautious of the *Bünde*'s "drift into nationalistic, and ultimately, *fighting* bodies". He felt that German militarism was not a model for the English. *The Selected Letters of D.H. Lawrence* compiled and edited by James T. Boulton (Cambridge: Cambridge University Press, 1997), 376-77. Gardiner himself later sympathized with the Nazis.

[87] Described by Lawrence: "It seems to me it was the greatest pity in the world, when philosophy and fiction got split." "Surgery for the Novel — or a Bomb" (P, 520).

through character-focalizing agents as narrators. Here, he reintroduces the cynical narrator more typical of his post-*Mr Noon* writing. This device makes the third version more consistent with the tone of Lawrence's fiction in the 1920s. In fact, he employs both devices; the narrator being more prominent in the satirical passages, for instance. Interjections like: "Heaven knows why" (LCL, 8), and cynical comments like: "Both sisters ... mixed with the young Cambridge group, the group that stood for 'freedom' and flannel trousers, and soft shirts open at the neck, and a well-bred sort of emotional anarchy" (LCL, 9); or the familiarizing direct address to the reader about the choice of words: "or perhaps rebel is too strong a word; far too strong" (LCL, 10). There are those direct addresses to the reader more common in popular fiction: "Poor Connie! As the year drew on ..." (LCL, 50). Then the often-quoted meta-fictional comment on the theory of the novel: the novel is important because it can "inform and lead into new places the flow of our sympathetic consciousness ... can reveal the most ... passional secret places of life" (LCL, 101). Moreover, it is here that the narrator and the author are indistinguishable, as Lawrence reiterates his principal thesis on why the novel matters. This novel, *Lady Chatterley's Lover*, is inclusive enough to contain Mrs Bolton's gossip-text, Clifford's politics, Mellors' utopian thought, and Connie's "*écriture féminine*". In this, the third version of the car-ride through Tevershall, Connie's focalization is sometimes interrupted by the narrator, showing the limits of her view: "But if you looked"; and: "But as a matter of fact, though even Connie did not know it" (LCL, 154). The omniscience sometimes breaks the flow of her consciousness during sex, for the sake of a doctrinal point: "Cold and derisive her queer female mind stood apart" (LCL, 172). Or it sometimes interjects general statements of truth (as in the convention of the nineteenth-century novel): "And that is how we are. By the strength of will we cut off our inner intuitive knowledge from our admitted consciousness" (LCL, 288). The comic Sternean narrator from *Mr Noon* reappears in the farcical scene when Clifford loses control of the wheel-chair, and thus undermines his confident claim that he is riding upon "the achievements of the mind of man" (LCL, 179). The burlesque through literary parody (as in the eighteenth-century convention of the mock-heroic) is familiar to readers of *Mr Noon*:

> Oh last of all ships, through the hyacinthine shallows! oh pinnace on the last wild waters, sailing in the last voyage of our civiliza-

tion! ...Oh captain, my Captain, our splendid trip is done![88]

Moreover, here the persona of the narrator as literate and humorously critical emerges. His sense of comedy unsettles any attempt to take the novel seriously at times. Like the minor incident when Mellors seems about to say something momentous to Connie: "Maybe". Then he sneezes, and forgets what he was going to say. The narrator comments: "And it was one of the disappointments of her life, that he never finished" (LCL, 228).

Lawrence manages a fine balancing act between the comic, satiric writing where the narrator plays a key role, and the more explicit doctrine, and the poetry of "*jouissance*". Lydia Blanchard sums up the achievement as follows:

> By the time Lawrence comes to write *Lady Chatterley's Lover* , he is able to perform the extraordinarily difficult artistic feat of simultaneously parodying his own canon and reaffirming his belief in life and growth, trusting the reader to understand the complex play that underlines his final novel.[89]

But as the reception of the novel has shown, not all readers can be trusted.

6. Conclusion: text and ideology

The texts of the *Lady Chatterley* novels, as I have argued, are concerned to articulate the relationship between sexuality and class. The first version attempts to represent class most transparently, as a recognizably radical critique of positions of power and privilege (the ruling classes) and resentment (the working classes). It also gives us the details of class cultures as different ways of life. Although seen from an outside, upper-class perspective, there is some sympathy for the lower classes from a more socialist-minded Connie. Moreover, the text clearly and objectively represents the views of the proletarian Left at a time of militancy and the threat of class war. In *The First Lady Chatterley*, Lawrence's vivid impressions from his visit home prevent him from imagining a narrative resolution to the problem of a lasting relationship between the Lady and

---

[88] LCL, 185.The last words are recognizably adapted from Walt Whitman. For a detailed discussion of the literary allusions see Dennis Jackson, "Lawrence's Allusive Art in *Lady Chatterley's Lover*" in Ellis and De Zordo, Volume III, 145-70.

[89] Lydia Blanchard, "D.H. Lawrence and the 'gentle reader': the furious comedy of *Mr Noon*" in Paul Eggert and John Worthen eds, *Lawrence and Comedy* (Cambridge: Cambridge University Press, 1996), 103.

gamekeeper. In the second version, the politics of class are overshadowed by the more explicit and lyrical sex, and although class differences stubbornly refuse to go away, the discussion turns against class as a category. Lawrence has an unusual notion of class as organic relation within a closely-knit, paternalistic social unit based around the Great Houses of England. He dates the end of this, largely mythic, golden age of social harmony at 1914. The second version also adds a more unsettling generic diversity to the text, and this results in Connie's visit to the working-class family in Sheffield being presented as comedy, giving the impression of a patronising view from a distance — a superior, literate, class position. In his attempts to write class out of the picture, Lawrence resorts to literary precedence in the English novel tradition of Dickens. Although Parkin has become more articulate and flexible, as well as less politically committed on the Left, the future of the relationship between the Lady and the gamekeeper is still left uncertain. The life styles of the different classes, and the scandal that is waiting to become public, speak against it. Even though Parkin may have become more flexible and therefore more acceptable to Connie as a husband, it seems she would miss the sophistications and luxuries to which she has been accustomed in the leisured classes. The final version, *Lady Chatterley's Lover*, further attempts to resolve the class problematic by transforming the gamekeeper into Mellors, a local man with a grammar school education, formerly an army officer, with more experience of the world, and an early sexual history. He, like Connie now, has sexual experience. But does the novel resolve the class problematic once and for all? Mellors' class position is ambivalent: he passes for a gentleman, speaks the King's English when he chooses, but shows all the signs of lower-class resentment and working-man's pride. In trying to make the gamekeeper a more plausible future husband for Lady Chatterley, Lawrence has turned him into his own image. Someone of working-class origin, educated and travelled, who can promote a sexual theory and practice that transcends all social differences, and promises to be a model for a new social harmony based on the alternative principles outlined in Mellors' closing letter, and ones which Lawrence discovered were confirmed by the ancient Etruscans. But will anything be changed other than the lives of the two lovers?

In all three versions the most consistent connection between sex and society is scandal. There is one certainty that the open-ended, unresolved narrative cannot mention: the future will be dominated by scandal. The logic of the narrative, even as it tries through the three versions to abolish the class problematic and the force of social pressure, predicts the sex scandal. Versions of what will happen are already reported in Mrs Bolton's gossip-text, Clifford's letters, and also Mellors' letters. The

Mellors-Bertha Coutts' public scandal, the revelations of the postman who heard voices in the cottage, the reactions of Connie's sister, of Duncan Forbes and, above all, of Clifford to the affair and the pregnancy indicate that the future will be far from utopian.

The future lasts a long time. The future as scandal already predicted in *Lady Chatterley's Lover*, returns to haunt it in its subsequent publication history, and especially its cultural impact in the 1960s. Even before the interventions of feminist criticism reinscribing the novel as a text-for-criticism, the obscenity trial made it into a cultural object which would set in train another set of scandalous futures. The failure to successfully prosecute the book ushered in an era of licence and a sex industry whose decline is not in sight. This is not Lawrence's utopia. Admittedly, there was in the 1960s a brief period of sexual liberation, and Lawrence was its high priest (he would have castigated it for being too self-conscious). Sex and health were tied together once again, just as they were in the early twentieth century when Lawrence was writing. From 1969, though, the future took a different turn, the scandal in the text has become a scandal of the text. The sex scandal of Lady Chatterley and the gamekeeper became the scandalous readings of sexual politics.

What this illustrates is that the relationship between text and ideology is not restricted to the internal representations and contradictions of the text. In *Lady Chatterley's Lover*, political ideologies with their specific class locations are challenged by the sexual ideology, which is made possible by turning history into myth, the future into utopia. However, the text does not continue to exist in isolation. It becomes a text-for-criticism, an object of competing critical practices with their own ideological assumptions — political and aesthetic. If you approach the mythic and utopic tendency in Lawrence through Barthes' notion of "mythology" then you can see that once ideology enters the text as a narrative, its processes of mystification become visible:

> In passing from history to nature, myth acts economically: it abolishes the complexity of human acts, it gives them the simplicity of essences, it does away with all dialectics, with any going beyond what is immediately visible, it organizes a world which is without contradictions because it is without depth, a world wide open and wallowing in the evident, it establishes a blissful clarity: things appear to mean something by themselves.[90]

Paradoxically, in attempting to simplify complex processes, myth, like

---

[90] Roland Barthes, *Mythologies* (London: Paladin, 1989. First published 1957), 156.

ideology, draws attention in its narrative to what it has to exclude to remain coherent.[91] In *Lady Chatterley's Lover*, class and the force of social conventions hover around in the margins of the text refusing to go away. In the sexual ideology, Connie's sexuality is simplified more and more into an essence to fit better the new phallic tenderness. To do this, Lawrence has to abolish her critical consciousness, and her feminism. But the moments of *"jouissance"* defy her reduction to the second sex, as they are high points of aesthetic as well as sexual value. The female imaginary is foregrounded in the text because Connie is so often the focalizing agent. The feminist critique is already articulated in the text. Lawrence does not convince us that the future perfect is masculine. It seems more likely to be feminist: the newly-born, blissful woman; the feminized culture; and the feminist reader.

---

[91] This is one of the principal claims of French structural Marxism. See Althusser, *Lenin and Philosophy and Other Essays* (London: New Left Books, 1971), especially "A Letter on Art"; and Macherey, *A Theory of Literary Production* (London: Routledge, 1978) for the attempt to apply Althusserian concepts to literature. For a recent, if rather generalized use of an Althusserian approach see Said, *Culture and Imperialism* (New York: Alfred A. Knopf, 1993): "Jane Austen and Empire".

Conclusions:
Modernism, Modernity, and Critical Theory

In this last chapter, I shall draw some conclusions from my study of D.H. Lawrence and critical theory. Contrary to the fears of those who resist theory because it has its own agendas, and therefore would use Lawrence for its own purposes, I hope to have demonstrated that once the fictional narratives become texts-for-criticism in the newer paradigms of post-structuralism, their coherences are understood differently. An older notion of textual unity is displaced by the proposition of an aesthetic structure characterized by degrees of generic and linguistic destabiliza-tion. I described Lawrence's writing as expressionist in the representation of key moments of the self in crisis, and the subject-in-desire in *Sons and Lovers* and *The Rainbow*, but more "writerly" in the fiction from *Women in Love* onwards.[1] Thus I take up a position contrary to those who see *The Rainbow* as *the* Lawrentian novel, with its prose rhythms and repetitions, and its intricate organic form, and who then subsequently declare the writing in the early 1920s chaotic and incomprehensible.[2] What I hope to have shown is that post-structuralist critical paradigms — the psycho-analytic, the discursive, the dialogic, the deconstructive, and *"écriture féminine"* — in producing different senses of coherence than those that have dominated Lawrence studies, have done greater justice to Law-rence's writing. Furthermore, what is clear from the different approaches in this study is that there are complex processes of textualization in Lawrence's writing, and therefore nothing is achieved without textual detail. The conclusion I come to is that closer re-reading and theorizing of that detail enables a displacement of the monolithic relationship of Lawrence to Modernism in the critical reception, not least because critical theory has problematized the concept of Modernism itself. Therefore, in this concluding chapter, I shall offer a few suggestions

---

[1] For those who doubt Lawrence's "expressionist turn" around 1912 see Hans Ulrich Seeber, "D.H. Lawrence und der deutsche Expressionismus" in *Sprachkunst*, 13 (1982), 151-172. Also, Sheppard, "German Expressionism" and "German Expres-sionist Poetry" in Malcolm Bradbury and James McFarlane eds, *Modernism: A Guide To European Literature 1890-1930* (London: Penguin, 1976).
[2] Like Terry Eagleton's comment: "novels like *Aaron's Rod* and *Kangaroo* are signally incapable of evolving a narrative, ripped between fragmentary plot, spiritual autobiography and febrile didacticism." *Criticism and Ideology* (London: New Left Books, 1976), 160.

about an expanded relationship between Lawrence and the problematics of Modernism, which go beyond the formal experiments of the narrative fiction to include the question of modernity itself.

Indeed, Lawrence's own critique of modernity, and one which emerges in the main body of this study, is in tune with the modernist responses to it of his contemporaries — Conrad and Eliot, Kafka and Mann. The terms of that critique are argued out between the post-Nietzschean and the post-Marxist social theorists of the early twentieth century. Frisby quotes Siegfried Kracauer as representative of the anti-modernity position: the human being "is a cog in a powerful soulless machine which rests upon the interlocking of countless little wheels. The goal that is striven for vanishes from the inner gaze".[3] It is a position Lawrence himself adopted. Kracauer's description is reminiscent of Mark Gertler's painting, "Merry-Go-Round" (1916), which impressed Lawrence as the best articulation of the mechanization and spiritual emptiness of modern existence.[4] Fictional versions of this critique appear throughout Lawrence's work, as the previous chapters have shown. Many Lawrence scholars have discussed his rejection of modernity. However, what this study has sought to demonstrate is that the methodologies deriving from the newer critical paradigms enable a rethinking of Lawrence's relationship to the artistic response to the crisis of modernity called Modernism.

The concept of Modernism is much more problematic than that of modernity. Indeed, there is a general consensus of what the latter means. As Frisby explains, modernity in its modern understanding originated in Baudelaire's slogan from the mid-nineteenth century that modern life was characterized by the "transitory, the fugitive, and the contingent".[5] Modern society had become unstable, traditional values were being questioned, conventions seemed an empty shell, and social relations were subject to instrumental reason and reification. These are the terms of the critique of modernity argued for variously in the work of Weber, Simmel, Kracauer, and Lukács. Much of this condemnation of modernity is registered by Lawrence, as the main body of this study has shown. The loss of traditional beliefs and community were famously exemplified by

[3] David Frisby, *Fragments of Modernity: Theories of Modernity in the Work of Simmel, Kracauer and Benjamin* (Cambridge: Polity Press, 1985), 113.
[4] The painting is reproduced on the back cover of Mark Kinkead-Weekes' biography, *D.H. Lawrence: Triumph To Exile 1912-1922* (Cambridge: Cambridge University Press, 1996).
[5] Frisby, 2.

Benjamin in the disappearance of the traditional storyteller.[6] Lawrence, for his part, suffered from the loss of the reader — as I argued in chapter 3 — as he transgressed what he saw as the moribund aesthetic of impersonality promoted by the *English Review*, and then by T.S. Eliot. Lawrence transformed the crisis of the old stable ego into an assault on the prudish reader. He pulverized a traditional English culture of understatement and reticence with a growing explicitness, which diagnosed the crisis of modernity as a sexual crisis. Attempting to represent the crisis of the culture in these terms entailed degrees of textual complexity that I have sought to describe and theorize through the reading strategies of recent psychoanalytic criticism, Foucauldian discourse theory, Bakhtinian dialogics, masculinity theory, deconstruction, and French feminism.

Lawrence's aesthetic and his tendency to turn to mythic solutions for the cultural crisis seem to be a compensation for fragmentation in life. As Jameson put it: "Modernism can ... be read as a Utopian compensation for everything reification brings with it".[7] At such moments he has a darker apocalyptic reaction to modernity, and one that may be characterized as post-Nietzschean and neo-Romantic with its valorization of peasant cultures and primitivism — as Lawrence scholars have said before. However, what I hope to have shown in this study is that Lawrence's modernist writing, in its various forms, has deconstructive effects on his myth-making, his essentialist notions of the self, and his sexual ideologies — a creative contradiction which the preceding chapters have sought to elucidate in bringing together Lawrence and critical theory.

The general response to modernity was twofold. In the one camp, it was celebrated as a great advance in man's control over nature in technology and science (Futurism, early Vorticism); in the other, (the vast majority) it was condemned as a greater loss to the culture: a life empty of meaning as the greater massification and rationalizations of modernity were perceived as having swept away the traditional values that had given the self its senses of identity. Lawrence's position was ambivalent. He celebrated the loss of the old stable ego on which to base his characters, because he saw it as an illusion grounded in false notions of identity, and thus opened up his textualizations to the problematics of

---

[6] Walter Benjamin, *Illuminations* (Glasgow: Fontana, 1970. First published 1955): "The art of storytelling is reaching its end because the epic side of truth, wisdom, is dying out." (87) "A great storyteller will always be rooted in the people, primarily in a milieu of craftsmen." (101).

[7] Fredric Jameson, *The Political Unconscious: Narrative as a Socially Symbolic Act* (Ithaca and London: Cornell University Press, 1981), 236.

modern subjectivity. Yet, he called for a revival of a more instinctual relationship in a consummate marriage whose paradigms were based on his reading of the ancient civilizations of Britain, Mexico, and Italy — pre-modern worlds which were the radical alternatives to the spiritual depredations of modernity. Mythic solutions and the attractions of primitivism were, of course, widespread in literary and artistic Modernism. Lawrence's case is unusual because he wants to displace the stability of the traditional ego with a greater instinctuality which, in the age of Freud, was bound to lead to greater degrees of instability — although ones that would be regenerative. Despite the doctrinaire assertions in his fictional and essayistic writing, Lawrence's attempts to represent new senses of the self in a sexual ontology result in a contradiction that emerges throughout his work, and is variously made explicit by post-structuralist readings in this study. The writing itself is more radically modernist than Lawrence studies has often given credit. When representing the unconscious, the discourses of modern sexuality, the problematics of femininity and masculinity, the insincerity of social intercourse, the destruction of the countryside by the industrial machine, or the end of old class certainties without the emergence of a new aristocracy to lead the culture into regeneration, Lawrence's writing experiments with different modernist paradigms. His works are sometimes examples of expressionism, symbolism, organic form, parody and collage, myth, and impressionism (exemplified, for instance, in Connie Chatterley's drive through Tevershall), as Lawrence deconstructs the broader conventions of the English novel. His narrative resolutions are both utopic and inconclusive; his stylistic Modernism deconstructive.

The modernist solutions to the chaos, decadence and instrumentalities of modernity were to assert the aesthetic order as the only alternative. Fragmentation and loss of value would be overcome by aesthetic and formal values.[8] Lawrence, however, objected to the purely aestheticist doctrine of the modernists — the autonomy of art promoted by his contemporaries, Clive Bell and Roger Fry.[9] Yet his most complete attempt at organic form, *The Rainbow*, with its aesthetic structure of recurrent motifs (first tried out in *Sons and Lovers*) was deconstructed by its sequel, *Women in Love*, for largely personal reasons. The instabilities of character were carried over into the instabilities of the form of the novel. As I argued in chapters 3, 4 and 5, Lawrence tried out more experiments

---

[8] What Jameson calls "aestheticizing strategies" (230) or "strategies of containment" (242), when describing Conrad's stylistic impressionism.

[9] For a discussion of Lawrence's relationship to the aesthetics of Clive Bell and Roger Fry see Anne Fernihough, *D.H. Lawrence: Aesthetics and Ideology* (Oxford: Clarendon Press, 1993), chapter 4.

in writing to rival those of Joyce — parody and self-parody, self-conscious authorial intrusion, broken text and collage — commensurate with his loss of confidence in the organic novel which had no reader after the banning of *The Rainbow* in 1915. This phase of his Modernism reached its high point in *Kangaroo* (1923). The appreciation of the very deliberate experiment in that novel has been slow to emerge in Lawrence studies because, as I argued in chapter 5, critics have mostly been working with older, less flexible notions of textual unity, and a monolithic concept of Modernism.

Lawrence's work, which begins (like Freud's) in the examination of his own case, establishes its place amongst the great modernists because it is a continual and persistent reflection on the cultural crisis of modernity (understood in the senses given to it by Nietzsche, and by Freud in *Civilization and Its Discontents*). Wherever his travels took him, Lawrence was principally concerned with the state of English culture. The critique was given a greater focus by the effects of the Great War, which was a watershed in Lawrence's Modernism, as it was for many of his contemporaries. As Harvey puts it:

> The trauma of world war and its political and intellectual responses ... opened the way to a consideration of what might constitute the essential and eternal qualities of modernity that lay on the nether side of Baudelaire's formulation. In the absence of Enlightenment certitudes as to the perfectibility of man, the search for a myth appropriate to modernity became paramount. ... But it also seemed possible to build metaphorical bridges between ancient and modern myths.[10]

One thinks immediately of Joyce's *Ulysses*, T.S. Eliot's *Waste Land*, and Lawrence's *Phoenix*; and the enormous influence of Frazer and Weston on the mythic imagination of the modernists.

It is as if Lawrence's work corresponds to the two phases of Modernism: the philosophical critique of modernity (in Nietzsche, Conrad, and Weber) — often designated as early Modernism; and the problematics of representation in the parodies and ironies, the play of writing, exemplified *in extremis* in the avant-garde movements of Dada and Surrealism, and in literature in Joyce — often designated as late Modernism. Of course, this account is always too schematic to account in detail for the stylistic impressionism of Conrad's *Heart of Darkness*, or Thomas

---

[10] David Harvey, *The Condition of Postmodernity: An Enquiry into the Origins of Cultural Change* (Oxford: Blackwell, 1989), 30.

Mann's philosophical novels. But the general terms do help us to question the often hitherto monolithic account of Lawrence's relationship to Modernism. His audacious insistence on publishing novels whose content was explicit about sex to differing degrees has made him immortal for all the wrong reasons. We need to acknowledge the extent to which his work belongs to an emerging crisis of representation in artistic and literary Modernism. To quote Harvey once again:

> The articulation of erotic, psychological, and irrational needs (of the sort that Freud identified and Klimt represented in his free-flowing art) ... had to recognize the impossibility of representing the world in a single language. Understanding had to be constructed through the exploration of multiple perspectives.[11]

The discourses of sexuality in Lawrence's writing do not produce a smooth, unified, organic sense of the modern self. The clash of discourses — as I demonstrated in my Foucauldian reading of *The Rainbow* — is exemplary of that crisis of representation in Modernism to which Harvey refers. And those discourses are both ancient (mythic or biblical) and modern (scientific or psychoanalytic).

Sheppard has produced the most extensive and thorough critical discussion of the concept of Modernism. The critical formation of the concept may be traced to the explosion of interest in the 1960s. Since then, different national academic traditions — especially the French, the German, the American and the British, and their uneven influences on each other — have approached the concept in such different ways that it is now impossible to come to terms with Modernism "as a total phenomenon".[12] Leavis's categorical distinction between Joyce and Lawrence now seems at best quaint.[13] Sheppard usefully suggests three common strategies for approaching the question: what is Modernism? First, through the common traits of relativism, anti-democratic ideology, nihilism, alienation, and the use of myth. But, as he points out, the weakness here is that generalized common ground pays scant attention to the details of specific contexts, and is therefore reductionist. Thus we need "to reconstruct the dynamic, not to say cataclysmic context which generated them [the common traits] in their specifically modernist

---

[11] Harvey, 30.

[12] Richard Sheppard, , "The Problematics of European Modernism" in Steve Giles ed., *Theorising Modernism: Essays in Critical Theory* (London and New York: Routledge, 1993), 1.

[13] F.R. Leavis, *D.H. Lawrence: Novelist* (London: Penguin, 1985. First published 1955), 10.

combinatoire".[14] The second strategy is to approach Modernism through a more broad-based historical, or literary historical, or sociological context. Thus Modernism is a continuation of Romanticism; a rejection of Realist conventions; or a precursor of postmodernism. All these positions are "more or less tenable", depending on your examples. But the approach tends to concentrate exclusively on "purely aesthetic considerations" (like Barthes' celebrated claim that the whole of modern literature since Flaubert is concerned with the "problematics of language"). The third strategy is what Sheppard calls a "matrix approach", which compares ostensibly disparate works by demonstrating their responses to a common underlying *"problématique"* — a concept derived from Althusser. Thus, for Adorno the problematic is imperialism, while for Lukács it is reification[15] — I would add that the latter is reworked by Jameson in his reading of Conrad's "will-to-style".[16] Sheppard endorses this third strategy. And the approaches in my study have demonstrated the problematic of the transvaluation of values combined with the experience of modernity as cultural crisis. At times, especially after the war, Lawrence's apocalyptic response was Spenglerian, understanding himself as the prophet of cultural decline. Yet within his own work, Lawrence's response to the problematic varies in degree of complexity. Sheppard mentions the late novels of D.H. Lawrence like *The Plumed Serpent* as "relatively simple" versions, "notwithstanding the portentous weight of their rhetoric". Thus the concept of Modernism becomes more elastic, and also, through the "matrix approach", enables a more effective mediation between a variety of Modernisms and modernity.

As this study has sought to demonstrate, a variety of Modernisms has been played out in the texts of Lawrence's major narrative fiction. For example, there are moments when the stress on elemental, cosmic forces in *The Rainbow* and *Women in Love* brings Lawrence closer to the early German Expressionists; but also the nihilist tendencies of a whole series of fictions — *Heart of Darkness, Death in Venice, The Trial, A Passage to India.*[17] Or, when the whole problematic of perception is represented in the narrational discontinuities of multi-perspectivism, parodies, speech mimicry, and even in that quintessential modernist technique: *collage* (as in *Kangaroo*), which thus foreground the problematic itself. Here

---

[14] Sheppard, 2.

[15] Sheppard, 3-5. For Roland Barthes' famous claim see *Le degré zero de l'écriture* (Paris: Seuil, 1953). Translated as *Writing Degree Zero* (London: Cape, 1967).

[16] Jameson, chapter 5: "Romance and Reification: Plot Construction and Ideological Closure in Joseph Conrad".

[17] Sheppard, 12, 16-17.

Lawrence, like many of his contemporaries, is modernist[18] in the Russian Formalist sense of "defamiliarization", challenging conventional perspectives. And if for Shklovski *Tristram Shandy* was the most typical example, then so was Lawrence's *Mr Noon* in its proto-Brechtian assault on the reader. Additionally, as I argued in chapter 1, Jakobson's "poetic function" (the creative metaphor), or what Lawrence called "art-speech",[19] is a principal textual feature of Modernism. It marks Jakobson's loyalty to the origins of his thought in the Russian Formalism of the 1920s. In chapter 1 the poetic function was given a psychoanalytic value as the expression of the imaginary, creative subject; in chapter 2 it represented the new female subject's challenge to the discursive formations of late nineteenth-century femininity; in chapter 3 it functioned as self-parody of the author's metaphysical and poetic gestures; in chapters 4 and 5 as deconstructive effect; and in chapter 6 as the poetry of *"jouissance"*. The metonymic, the second of the two key functions of Jakobsonian rhetorics, is designated as central to the language of Realism, as the text tries to capture the essential attributes of a world open to description. For Lawrence, those attributes are libidinized, as others and landscapes serve as objects of projections for the subject's unconscious symptoms or desires. Indeed, in the later fiction, the symbolic and symptomatic landscapes of the travel writing play an ever greater part. Narratives of travel have destabilizing effects on cultural identities.

Attention to such textual detail has demonstrated that Lawrence's Modernism is not only thematic. His *"Kulturpessimismus"* carries over into the writing itself, which undermines the old novelistic certainties through the play of style and structure. This modernist process begins in the disruptions of realism and narrative closure through expressionism, symbolism, and open-endedness in *Sons and Lovers* and *The Rainbow*; and then with *Women in Love* turns into a more thorough-going destabilization of the organic text as the crisis of identity of the characters is reflected in the form of the novel itself. Even as *The Lost Girl* strives to become a traditional novel, it resorts to parody of the genre, only finally

---

[18] Lawrence is modernist in this sense also in his theory of poetic language. Anne Fernihough comments: "Lawrence sees in free verse a way of dehabitualizing language: 'We can get rid of the stereotyped movements and the old hackneyed associations of sound or sense. We can break down those artificial conduits and canals through which we do so love to force our utterance. We can break the stiff neck of habit'." ("Preface to the American edition of *New Poems*", in *Phoenix*, 221. Cited in Fernihough, 111).

[19] *Studies in Classic American Literature* (London: Penguin, 1971. First published 1923), 8.

Conclusions   351

to abandon the attempt altogether and become travel writing as the central protagonists move to the barren Abruzzi mountains and an uncertain future. Much of the writing of the 1920s is travel writing. The novels, *Mr Noon*, *Aaron's Rod, Kangaroo* and *The Plumed Serpent* are all characterized by travel and the detailed description of exotic places and symbolic landscapes — as if, once Lawrence had abandoned the old stable ego of the character, and attempted to represent the modern libidinized subject in poetic figures, the poetic landscape itself remained the only focus for a stable sense of truth. Lawrence's attraction to primitivism as a response to modernity is best represented in the primitive landscape. Jameson encapsulates the representationalist crisis of Modernism in a way that may be applied pertinently to Lawrence:

> By this suspension, in which representation undermines itself, Modernism hopes to preserve and keep open the space of some genuine Experience beyond reification, the space of the libidinal and Utopian gratification of which the Frankfurt School speaks, a space in which the failure of the imagination, cancelled by the form itself, can then release the imaginary to some more intense second-degree fulfilment and narrative figuration.[20]

Modernism has been seen as having significant parallels with post-structuralist theories. Giles reiterates a now not uncommon claim that, "modernist art pre-empted conditions of meaning and logic associated with the deconstructive critique of logocentrism, as well as rejecting humanism and anthropocentrism".[21] Moreover, the agendas of post-structuralist theories are similar to Modernism's self-understanding predominantly as a critique of modernity, a crisis of representation and language, a displacement of the essentialist self with the subject, a deconstruction of the traditional discourses of gender, and a rewriting of the history of sexuality. With this affinity between Modernism and post-structuralism in mind, we should consciously go beyond the narrowly English focus of the critical formation deriving from Leavis when approaching Lawrence, not least because Lawrence himself was not narrow in his focus, belonging clearly to the problematics of European Modernism. Indeed, as Eysteinsson claims, "it would be possible to approach Jacques Derrida as a theorist as well as a practitioner of Modernism, and to see Modernism in its totality as a deconstructive

---

[20] Jameson, 171.
[21] Giles, 177.

practice in the Derridean sense".[22] The dispersal of desire, the decentring of the subject, and the process of dissemination bring Lawrence's Modernism and post-structuralist theory productively together.

The relationship between Modernism and post-structuralist theory raises methodological issues. As Eysteinsson rightly insists, Modernism "is not a concept that emanates directly from literary texts; it is a construct created by the critical inquiry".[23] Modernism is the object of different critical formations. For Roland Barthes it is "*écriture*" (the problematics of language); for Lukács it is decadence, for Ortega y Gasset the dehumanization of art; for Adorno a radical attack on modernity in the realm of the aesthetic, while for Jameson aestheticizing strategies are a compensation for reification; for Shklovski it is de-familiarization, and for Brecht "*Verfremdungseffekt*"; for Eliot in his reading of Joyce's *Ulysses* it is a necessary imposing of the order of the aesthetic on the chaos and futility of contemporary history. The German academic tradition, following Habermas, reads Modernism as a continuation of the Enlightenment tradition, and one that has still not completed its project; while the American and British now argue for a clear separation between the modernist and the postmodernist, which reads the former as élitist and conservative. Raymond Williams argued for many years that the radical nature of the early twentieth-century *avant-garde* Modernists had been commodified by the very business community it was attacking. Radical art techniques are now the common currency of the advertising companies.[24]

While recognizing the complexities of the critical formations of Modernism, both in its self-understanding and in the belated readings of critical approaches, this study endorses the view that, as Eysteinsson puts it, it is only with the emergence of post-structuralism that "theory 'catches up with' the literary practices of Modernism".[25] In other words, post-structuralist theories have a specially privileged relationship to Modernism, drawing the lessons from it in its own practice. Thus the often lamented lost subversive nature of early twentieth-century Modernism, including the narrative fiction of D.H. Lawrence, is recovered in the radicalizing re-readings of post-structuralist critical theories. Moreover, the newly reformulated radicalness of Modernism

---

[22] Astradur Eysteinsson, *The Concept of Modernism* (Ithaca and London: Cornell University Press, 1990), 48. This study is particularly instructive for its thorough discussion of the critical formations of the concept in different national traditions.
[23] Eysteinsson, 100.
[24] Raymond Williams, *The Politics of Modernism: Against the New Conformists* (London: Verso, 1989).
[25] Eysteinsson, 47.

should challenge the conservativeness of certain critical formations which continue to dominate Lawrence studies even when their critical paradigms have for a long time been untenable, subverted by the deconstructive effects of the very texts they were reading. Even the old opposition between Realism and Modernism is undermined in Lawrence's fiction by his use of several narrative and stylistic codes (itself not uncommon in modernist writing). Furthermore, we have understood at least since Todorov's early structuralist work that, in Eysteinsson's words, "each subgenre operates its own kind of verisimilitude, a reader-contract".[26] As I have demonstrated in this study, fragmentation and collage in *Kangaroo* was an implicit critique of the organic form of *The Rainbow*, which in any case was destabilized by its moments of expressionism. With such examples, it becomes clear that the crude polarization of Lawrence's writing into Realism or Modernism is reductive.

Finally, let me comment, in summary, on what I think approaching Lawrence through critical theory has achieved.

In chapter 1, a Lacanian reading of *Sons and Lovers* brought together the poetic and the psychoanalytic in a way that went beyond the impasse of the polarization between the Freudian and the Lawrentian unconscious by demonstrating that the figurative representation of the creative unconscious in Lawrence was prescient of the Lacanian Imaginary which would resist the prescriptions of the Law of the mother (in Lawrence's version). The poetic metaphor, which Lacan develops for his psychoanalytic rhetorics from Jakobson's "poetic function of language", is a key term in modernist defamiliarization.

In chapter 2, a Foucauldian approach enabled a critical mediation between the various discursive representations of modernity and its discontents. However, Lawrence's history of sexuality as a challenge to scientific materialism was seen to rely on the discourses of the very science it was critiquing. Nevertheless, the transgressive effects of *The Rainbow* were revealed in the epiphanic moments of its expressionism and symbolism which marked the limits of being. Eroticism and instinctive sexuality thus undermined the conventional and stable foundations of the self.

The analysis of these two texts showed that Lawrence was developing an aesthetic structure based on the recurrent motif that would attempt to integrate the text into an organic whole. But just as the effects of expressionism destabilized the newly sexualized subject, so the subject-problematic began to break up the organic form. This disintegration of

---

[26] Eysteinsson, 197, note 35.

stable form was already evident in the latter parts of *Sons and Lovers* as the breakdown of the central protagonist was represented as broken text. *Women in Love* was then read as a final but atrophied attempt to hold organic form together, but once it was read through Bakhtinian dialogics, a completely new sense of textual structure enabled the comic to emerge as a wholly different creative and destabilizing force. Lawrence's work would now develop a different kind of Modernism.

The satirical play on speech genres in *Women in Love,* as an assault on the over-intellectualized and self-conscious modern self, has specific class and cultural reference. The dialogics in this text establish the kinds of parody and self-parody that were taken to new levels in *The Lost Girl* and the anarchic comedy of *Mr Noon,* as Lawrence turns the crisis of his writing into a problematics of writing — a characteristic of Modernism itself. The formal instabilities of the narrative fiction of this period of Lawrence's writing-life reflect his own instabilities, his loss of direction and his loss of a reading public. Bakhtin enabled detailed readings of the three novels that productively drew attention to a dialogic textual structure, intertextual and parodic, as Lawrence turned his anxieties into a comic reflection on the state of the novel. Thus a different kind of Modernism to that of *The Rainbow* emerged, and one which challenges any monolithic understanding of Lawrence's relationship to Modernism.

Lawrence never abandoned these destabilizing tendencies, even when he was at his most doctrinaire in the "leadership" novels. The narrative fiction became an experiment, a "thought-adventure" (Lawrence's own description), in which the ideas from his more prescriptive essays were "tested out". Moreover, as I argued in chapters 4 and 5, the "thought-adventure" becomes an adventure of writing as the play of linguistic and representational codes serves to trouble the very possibility of fixing meaning in grand narratives. In approaching *Aaron's Rod, Kangaroo* and *The Plumed Serpent* through deconstruction, the charactcrological and textual instabilities were seen to undermine the doctrinal assertions of a new masculinity and male leadership. Thus, against the feminist consensus, I argued that Lawrence's turn against women was expressed in texts with degrees of deconstructive effects, so that the leadership novels contained their own critique, reminding us to heed Lawrence's own warning: "Never trust the artist, trust the tale. Trust the tale. The proper function of a critic is to save the tale from the artist who created it".[27] Furthermore, if his masculinist doctrine has failed the test of the "thought-adventure" because the deconstructive effects of writing have thrown it into contradiction, then Lawrence has already saved the tale

---

[27] *Studies in Classic American Literature*, 8.

from himself. A narrowly ideological reading necessarily misses these complexities. Instead, a deconstructive approach drew attention, in some detail, to the effects of dissemination (a more unsettling version of the structure of the recurrent motif in *Sons and Lovers* and *The Rainbow*) and (generic) play — both as destabilizing forces on the strident assertions of gender essentialism. The "leadership" novels turn out to be much more radically modernist than previously thought. As I argued in the conclusion to chapter 5, Lawrence is at his most sceptical in parts of *Aaron's Rod* and practically all of *Kangaroo*, his most experimental text. *The Plumed Serpent* is not as obviously deconstructive as the two previous novels. It is, though, the best example in the Lawrence corpus of the modernist attraction to primitivism and ancient civilizations as a reaction to western European modernity. Yet even here, textual detail revealed instabilities on a number of levels which undercut the assertions of ideology. Furthermore, what is now clearer is the extent to which there is a continuity with the play of writing that began with *Women in Love*. Textual play and serious thought seem to co-exist in a strangely unsettling way. We know that Lawrence held strong and often disturbing views, but how committed was he to them if his fiction deconstructs them?

In chapter 6, I argued that the more radical positions within feminism have had little purchase on Lawrence studies. Post-structuralist French feminism offered a critical approach to the *Lady Chatterley* novels. The concepts of "*écriture féminine*' " and "*jouissance*" and the insistence on a new language of the body enabled a theorizing of Lawrence's poetic representation of female sexuality. The textualization of "*jouissance*" gave a moment of autonomy to female sexuality, a higher creative and ontological value than male sexual experience, even while the phallus remained the transcendental signifier. However, as I argued, despite Lawrence's attempts progressively through the three versions to write class out of the story, there is a complex relationship between the class ideologies and the very sexual ideology that wants to abolish them. The Lawrentian sexual subjects are supposed to transcend class barriers, yet, it is clear that this can only be plausible in a utopian fiction, and one that may be understood as the author's wish-fulfilling fantasy. Lawrence's mythic tendency now turns back from the primitivism of *The Plumed Serpent* to the pastoral of a familiar kind, re-imagining the ancient Etruscans as the model for the revival of English traditional life.

Lawrence's last novel is a kind of last movement, reworking motifs and themes, styles and characters from the whole corpus, and as if in defiance of his reception, the most persistent connection between sex and society in all three version of *Lady Chatterley* is scandal. Utopic gestures notwithstanding, the future promises only scandal. The sex scandal in the novel would become the scandal of the novel — in the courts, and in the scandalous readings of sexual politics. Perhaps it has been the one Lawrence text that best illustrates the assumption central to this study that meaning and significance never exist in isolation — in "the text itself". As a text-for-criticism, or -prosecution, or -demonization, it is an object of competing critical formations with their different ideological assumptions. It has been the purpose of this study to bring that discussion about formations of reading and reception into a post-structuralist reassessment of the narrative fiction of D.H. Lawrence. In doing this, I have been less concerned to save the tale from the author than to save it from the critic who is still working with older critical paradigms, and has thus failed to do justice to Lawrence's radical Modernism.

Bibliography

1. Lawrence bibliography

Only works cited in the text or in the notes have been included in this bibliography. Wherever it was available at the time of writing, the Penguin edition of the Cambridge D.H. Lawrence has been listed. First date of publication appears after the title.

Aaron's Rod (1922) (London: Penguin, 1995).

Apocalypse (1931) introduced by Richard Aldington (London: Penguin, 1974).

D.H. Lawrence: Selected Essays, introduced by Richard Aldington (London: Penguin, 1974).

D.H. Lawrence: Selected Literary Criticism, edited by Anthony Beal (London: Heinemann, 1967).

England, My England and Other Stories (1922) (Cambridge: Cambridge University Press, 1990).

"Etruscan Places" (1932) in *D.H. Lawrence and Italy* (London: Penguin, 1997).

Fantasia of the Unconscious and Psychoanalysis of the Unconscious (1922) (London: Penguin, 1971).

John Thomas and Lady Jane (The Second Lady Chatterley) (1972) (London: Penguin, 1977).

Kangaroo (1923) (London: Penguin, 1997).

Lady Chatterley's Lover (1928) (London: Penguin, 1994).

Mornings in Mexico (1927) (London: Penguin, 1986).

Mr Noon (1984) (London: Penguin, 1996).

Phoenix II: Uncollected, Unpublished and Other Prose (London: Heinemann, 1968).

Phoenix: The Posthumous Papers of D.H. Lawrence (1936) (London: Heinemann, 1967).

Reflections on the Death of a Porcupine and Other Essays, edited by Michael Herbert (Cambridge: Cambridge University Press, 1988).

Sons and Lovers (1913) (London: Penguin, 1994).

Studies in Classic American Literature (1923) (London: Penguin, 1977).

Study of Thomas Hardy and Other Essays, edited by Bruce Steele (Cambridge: Cambridge University Press, 1985).

The Boy in the Bush (1924) in collaboration with M.L. Skinner (London: Penguin, 1996).

The Complete Poems of D.H. Lawrence, edited by Vivian de Sola Pinto and Warren Roberts (London: Penguin, 1977).

The First Lady Chatterley (1944) (London: Penguin, 1973).

The Letters of D.H. Lawrence, Volume I, compiled and edited by George J. Zytaruk and James T. Boulton (Cambridge: Cambridge University Press, 1979).

The Letters of D.H. Lawrence, Volume II, compiled and edited by George J. Zytaruk and James T. Boulton (Cambridge: Cambridge University Press, 1982).

The Letters of D.H. Lawrence, Volume IV, compiled and edited by George J. Zytaruk and James T. Boulton (Cambridge: Cambridge University Press, 1987).

The Lost Girl (1920) (London: Penguin, 1996).

The Plumed Serpent (1926) (London: Penguin, 1985).

The Rainbow (1915) (London: Penguin, 1994).

The Selected Letters of D.H. Lawrence compiled and edited by James T. Boulton (Cambridge: Cambridge University Press, 1997).

The Symbolic Meaning: The Uncollected Versions of 'Studies in Classic American Literature', edited by Armin Arnold (Fontwell, Arundel: Centaur Press, 1962).

Twilight in Italy and Other Essays, edited by Paul Eggert (Cambridge: Cambridge University Press, 1994).

Women in Love (1920) (London: Penguin, 1995).

2. General bibliography

Adamowski, T.H., "The Father of all Things: The Oral and the Oedipal in *Sons and Lovers*", *Mosaic* (Fall 1981).

Althusser, Louis, *Lenin and Philosophy and Other Essays* (London: New Left Books, 1971).

Bakhtin, Mikhail and P.N. Medvedev, *The Formalist Method in Literary Scholarship* (Cambridge, Massachusetts and London: Harvard University Press, 1985. First published 1928).

Bakhtin, Mikhail, *Problems of Dostoevsky's Poetics* (London and Minneapolis: University of Minnesota Press, 1984. Translated from the 1963 version).

Bakhtin, Mikhail, *Rabelais and his World* (Bloomington: Indiana University Press, 1984. First published 1965 from work done in the 1930s).

Bakhtin, Mikhail, *The Dialogic Imagination: Four Essays* (Austin: University of Texas Press, 1981. First published 1975 from work done in the 1930s and 1940s).

Bakhtin, Mikhail, *Speech Genres and Other Essays* (Austen: University of Texas Press, 1986. First published 1979).

Balbert, Peter, *D.H. Lawrence and the Phallic Imagination: Essays on Sexual Identity and Feminist Misreading* (London: Macmillan, 1989).

Barrett, Michèle, "Discoursing with Intent", *Times Higher Education Supplement*, 12 (May 1995).

Barthes, Roland, "The Death of the Author", in *Image-Music-Text*, edited and introduced by Stephen Heath (Glasgow: Fontana, 1977. Paper first published 1968).

Barthes, Roland, *Mythologies* (London: Paladin, 1989. First published 1957).

Beauvoir, Simone de, *The Second Sex* (London: Vintage, 1997. First published 1949).

Becket, Fiona, *D.H. Lawrence: The Poet as Thinker* (London: Macmillan, 1997).

Bell, Michael, *D.H. Lawrence: Language and Being* (Cambridge: Cambridge University Press, 1991).

Benjamin, Walter, *Illuminations* (Glasgow: Fontana, 1970. First published 1955.).

Bennett, Tony, *Outside Literature* (London: Routledge, 1990).

Bernheimer, Charles and Claire Kahane eds, *In Dora's Case: Freud-Hysteria-Feminism* (New York: Columbia University Press, 1985).

Black, Michael, *D.H. Lawrence Sons and Lovers* (Cambridge: Cambridge University Press, 1992).

Black, Michael, *D.H. Lawrence: The Early Philosophical Works: A Commentary* (London: Macmillan, 1991).

Blanchard, Lydia, "Love and Power: A Reconsideration of Sexual Politics in D.H. Lawrence", *Modern Fiction Studies*, 12 (1975).

Bloom, Harold, *The Anxiety of Influence: A Theory of Poetry* (New York and London: Oxford University Press, 1973).

Bowie, Malcolm, *Lacan* (Glasgow: Fontana, 1991).

Boyne, Roy, *Foucault and Derrida: The Other Side of Reason* (London: Unwin Hyman, 1990).

Brooks, Peter, "The Idea of a Psychoanalytic Criticism", *Critical Inquiry*, 13 (Winter 1987).

Brown, Keith ed., *Rethinking Lawrence* (Buckingham: Open University Press, 1990).

Burden, Robert, *The Critics Debate: Heart of Darkness* (London: Macmillan, 1991).

Burden, Robert, "Lawrence and Germany: An Introduction", in *Lawrence and Germany: A Bibliography*, compiled by Michael Weithmann and Regina Hoffmann (Passau: University of Passau Library, 1995).

Burke, Seán, *The Death and Return of the Author: Criticism and Subjectivity in Barthes, Foucault and Derrida* (Edinburgh: Edinburgh University Press, second edition 1998. First published 1992).

Carswell, Catherine, *The Savage Pilgrimage: A Narrative of D.H. Lawrence* (Cambridge: Cambridge University Press, 1981. First published 1932).

Carter, Angela, "Lorenzo the Closet-Queen", in *Nothing Sacred: Selected Essays* (London: Virago, 1992. Article first published 1975).

Chaitin, Gilbert D., *Rhetoric and Culture in Lacan* ((New York and London: Cambridge University Press, 1996).

Chambers, Jessie (E.T.), *D.H. Lawrence: A Personal Record* (London: Frank Cass, 1977. First published 1935).

Clarke, Colin, *River of Dissolution: D.H. Lawrence and English Romanticism* (London: Routledge, 1969).

Cousins, Mark and Athar Hussain, *Michel Foucault* (London: Macmillan, 1984).

Cuddon, J.A., *A Dictionary of Literary Terms and Literary Theory* (Oxford: Blackwell, 1991).

Culler, Jonathan, *The Pursuit of Signs: Semiotics, Literature, Deconstruction* (London: Routledge, 1981).

Daleski, H.M., *The Forked Flame: A Study of D.H. Lawrence* (London: Faber and Faber, 1965).

Deleuze, Gilles and Félix Guattari, *Anti-Oedipus: Capitalism and Schizophrenia* (London: The Athlone Press, 1988).

Derrida, Jacques, *Positions (3 Interviews)* (London: The Athlone Press, 1981. First published 1972).

Derrida, Jacques, *Margins of Philosophy* (Hemel Hempstead: Harvester Wheatsheaf, 1982. First published 1972).

Derrida, Jacques, *Dissemination* (Chicago: Chicago University Press, 1981. First published 1972).

Derrida, Jacques, "That Strange Institution Called Literature: An Interview with Jacques Derrida" in *Jacques Derrida: Acts of Literature*, edited and introduced by Derek Attridge (New York and London: Routledge, 1992).

Derrida, Jacques, "To Do Justice to Freud: The History of Madness in the Age of Psychoanalysis", *Critical Inquiry*, 20 (Winter 1994) .

Dix, Carol, *D.H. Lawrence and Women* (London: Macmillan, 1980).

Doherty, Gerald, "White Mythologies: Lawrence and the Deconstructive Turn", *Criticism*, xxix/4 (Fall 1987).

Dollimore, Jonathan, *Sexual Dissidence: Augustine to Wilde, Freud to Foucault* (Oxford: Clarendon Press, 1991).

Donald, James ed., *Psychoanalysis and Cultural Theory: Thresholds* (London: Macmillan, 1991).

Draper, R.P. ed., *D.H. Lawrence: The Critical Heritage* (London: Routledge, 1979).

Dube, Wolf-Dieter, *The Expressionists* (London: Thames and Hudson, 1972).

During, Simon, *Foucault and Literature: Towards a Genealogy of Writing* (London: Routledge, 1992).

Eagleton, Mary ed., *Feminist Literary Criticism* (Harlow: Longman, 1991).

Eagleton, Terry, *Criticism and Ideology* (London: New Left Books, 1976).

Eagleton, Terry, *Literary Theory: An Introduction* (Oxford: Blackwell, 1983).

Eggert, Paul, "Opening Up the Text: the Case of *Sons and Lovers*", in Keith Brown ed. (1990).

Eggert, Paul, and John Worthen eds, *Lawrence and Comedy* (Cambridge: Cambridge University Press, 1996).

Ellis, David, *D.H. Lawrence: Dying Game, 1922-1930* (Cambridge: Cambridge University Press, 1998).

Ellis, David, and Ornella De Zordo eds, *D.H. Lawrence: Critical Assessments*, 4 Volumes (Mountfield: Helm Information Ltd., 1992).

Evans, Dylan, *An Introductory Dictionary of Lacanian Psychoanalysis* (London: Routledge, 1996).

Eysteinsson, Astradur, *The Concept of Modernism* (Ithaca and London: Cornell University Press, 1990).

Felman, Shoshana ed., *Literature and Psychoanalysis: The Question of Reading: Otherwise* (Baltimore and London: Johns Hopkins University Press, 1982).

Fernihough, Anne, *D.H. Lawrence: Aesthetics and Ideology* (Oxford: Clarendon Press, 1993).

Fjagesund, Peter, *The Apocalyptic World of D.H. Lawrence* (Oslo and London: Norwegian University Press, 1991).

Forrester, John, *The Seductions of Psychoanalysis: Freud, Lacan and Derrida* (Cambridge: Cambridge University Press, 1991).

Foucault, Michel, *Madness and Civilization: A History of Insanity in the Age of Reason* (London: Routledge, 1992. First published 1961).

Foucault, Michel, *The Birth of the Clinic: An Archaeology of Medical Perception* (London: Routledge, 1991. First published 1963).

Foucault, Michel, *Death in the Labyrinth: The World of Raymond Roussel* (London: The Athlone Press, 1987. First published 1963).

Foucault, Michel, "A Preface to Transgression" (1963), in D.F. Bouchard ed., *Michel Foucault — Language, Counter-Memory, Practice: Selected Essays and Interviews* (Ithaca: Cornell University Press, 1977).

Foucault, Michel, *The Order of Things: An Archaeology of the Human Sciences* (London: Routledge, 1991. First published 1966).

Foucault, Michel, "Politics and the Study of Discourse" (1968), in *Ideology and Consciousness*, 3 (1978).

Foucault, Michel, *The Archaeology of Knowledge* (London: Routledge, 1992. First published 1969).

Foucault, Michel, "What is an Author?" (1969), in D.F. Bouchard ed., *Michel Foucault — Language, Counter-Memory, Practice: Selected Essays and Interviews* (Ithaca: Cornell University Press, 1977).

Foucault, Michel, "The Order of Discourse" (1970), in Robert Young ed., *Untying the Text: A Post-Structuralist Reader* (London: Routledge, 1981).

Foucault, Michel, *Discipline and Punish: The Birth of the Prison* (London: Penguin, 1986. First published 1975).

Foucault, Michel, *The History of Sexuality Volume 1: An Introduction* (London: Penguin, 1984. First published 1976).

Foucault, Michel, *The Care of the Self: The History of Sexuality Volume 3* (London: Penguin, 1990. First published 1984).

Fowler, Roger, *Linguistics and the Novel* (London: Methuen, 1977).

Fowler, Roger, *Linguistic Criticism* (Oxford and New York: Oxford University Press, 1986).

Freud, Sigmund, *Introductory Lectures: The Penguin Freud Library Volume 1*, edited by Angela Richards and Albert Dickson (London: Penguin, 1974).

Freud, Sigmund, *On Sexuality: The Penguin Freud Library Volume 7*, edited by Angela Richards and Albert Dickson (London: Penguin, 1977).

Freud, Sigmund, *Art and Literature: The Penguin Freud Library Volume 14*, edited by Angela Richards and Albert Dickens (London: Penguin, 1990).

Freud, Sigmund, *Civilization and Its Discontents* (London: The Hogarth Press, 1975. First published 1930).

Frisby, David, *Fragments of Modernity: Theories of Modernity in the Work of Simmel, Kracauer and Benjamin* (Cambridge: Polity Press, 1985).

Frow, John, *Marxism and Literary History* (Cambridge, Massachusetts: Harvard University Press, 1986).

Genette, Gérard, *Narrative Discourse* (Ithaca: Cornell University Press, 1980. First published 1972).

Giles, Steve, *Theorizing Modernism: Essays in Critical Theory* (London and New York: Routledge, 1993).

Grigg, Russell, "Metaphor and Metonymy", *News Letter of the Freudian Field*, 3/12 (1989).

Gunn, Daniel, *Psychoanalysis and Fiction: An Exploration of Literary and Psychoanalytic Borders* (Cambridge: Cambridge University Press, 1990).

Gutting, Gary ed., *The Cambridge Companion to Foucault* (Cambridge: Cambridge University Press, 1994).

Habermas, Jürgen, *Knowledge and Human Interests* (London: Heinemann, 1968).

Harvey, David, *The Condition of Postmodernity: An Inquiry into the Origins of Cultural Change* (Oxford: Blackwell, 1989).

Harvey, Geoffrey, *The Critics Debate: Sons and Lovers* (London: Macmillan, 1987).

Hawthorn, Jeremy, *The British Working-Class Novel in the Twentieth Century* (London: Arnold, 1984).

Heath, Stephen, *The Sexual Fix* (London: Macmillan, 1982).

Hoffmann, Frederick J., *Freudianism and the Literary Mind* (Baton Rouge: Louisiana State University Press, 1957).

Holbrook, David, "Exorcist on an Unholy Crusade", *Times Literary Supplement* (9 July 1993).

Holderness, Graham, *D.H. Lawrence: History, Ideology and Fiction* (Dublin: Gill and Macmillan, 1982).

Holland, Norman, *The Dynamics of Literary Response* (New York: Oxford University Press, 1968).

Holquist, Michael, *Dialogics: Bakhtin and his World* (London: Routledge, 1990).

Holub, Robert, *Reception Theory* (London: Methuen, 1984).

Hough, Graham, *The Dark Sun: A Study of D.H. Lawrence* (London: Duckworth, 1956).

Howe, Marguerite Beede, *The Art of the Self in D.H. Lawrence* (Athens, Ohio: Ohio State University Press, 1977).

Hoy, David Couzens ed., *Foucault: A Critical Reader* (Oxford: Blackwell, 1986).

Hyde, G.M., *D.H. Lawrence* (London: Macmillan, 1990).

Iser, Wolfgang, *The Act of Reading* (Baltimore and London: Johns Hopkins University Press, 1978).

Jackson, Rosemary, *Fantasy: The Literature of Subversion* (London: Methuen, 1981).

Jakobson, Roman and Morris Halle, *Fundamentals of Language* (The Hague: Mouton, 1956).

Jakobson, Roman, "Linguistics and Poetics" (1958), in David Lodge ed., *Modern Criticism and Theory: A Reader* (London and New York: Longman, 1988).

Jauss, Hans Robert, *Aesthetic Experience and Literary Hermeneutics* (Minneapolis: University of Minnesota Press, 1982).

Jauss, Hans Robert, *Towards an Aesthetics of Reception* (Minneapolis: University of Minnesota Press, 1982).

Jameson, Fredric, *The Prison-House of Language: A Critical Account of Structuralism and Russian Formalism* (Princeton, New Jersey: Princeton University Press, 1972).

Jameson, Fredric, "The Imaginary and the Symbolic in Lacan: Marxism, Psychoanalytic Criticism, and the Problem of the Subject" (1978), in Felman, Shoshana ed. (1982).

Jameson, Fredric, *Fables of Aggression: Wyndham Lewis, the Modernist as Fascist* (Berkeley and London: University of California Press, 1979).

Jameson, Fredric, *The Political Unconscious: Narrative as a Socially Symbolic Act* (Ithaca and London: Cornell University Press, 1981).

Jones, Ernest, *Sigmund Freud: Life and Works, Volume 2* (London: The Hogarth Press, 1955).

Kamuf, Peggy ed., *A Derrida Reader: Between the Blinds* (Hemel Hempstead: Harvester Wheatsheaf, 1991).

Kaplan, Cora, *Sea Changes: Culture and Feminism* (London: Verso, 1986).

Kazan, A., "Sons, Lovers, and Mothers", *Partisan Review*, 29 (1962).

Kermode, Frank, *Lawrence* (Glasgow: Fontana, 1973).

Kinkead-Weekes, Mark, *D.H. Lawrence: Triumph To Exile, 1912-1922* (Cambridge: Cambridge University Press, 1996).

Knights, Ben, *Writing Masculinities: Male Narratives in Twentieth-Century Fiction* (London: Macmillan, 1999).

Kuttner, Alfred Booth, "*Sons and Lovers*: A Freudian Appreciation", *Psychoanalytic Review* (July 1916).

Lacan, Jacques, *Écrits* (Paris: Éditions du Seuil, 1966).

Lacan, Jacques, *Écrits: A Selection* (London: Routledge, 1977).

Lacan, Jacques, *The Seminar. Book III. The Psychoses, 1955-56*, edited by Jacques-Alain Miller (London: Routledge, 1993).

Laclau, Ernesto, "Psychoanalysis and Marxism", *Critical Inquiry*, 13 (Winter 1987).

Leavis, F.R., *D.H. Lawrence: Novelist* (London: Penguin, 1985. First published 1955).

Leavis, F.R., *Thought, Words and Creativity: Art and Thought in Lawrence* (London: Chatto and Windus, 1976).

Ledger, Sally, *The New Woman: Fiction and Feminism at the Fin de Siècle* (Manchester: Manchester University Press, 1997).

Lodge, David, "D.H. Lawrence: Genius, Heretic, Classic", in *Write On: Occasional Essays 1965-1985* (London: Penguin, 1986).

Lodge, David, *After Bakhtin: Essays on Fiction and Criticism* (London and New York: Routledge, 1990).

Lyotard, J-F., *The Postmodern Condition: A Report on Knowledge* (Minneapolis: University of Minnesota Press, 1984. First published 1979).

Macey, David, *The Lives of Michel Foucault* (London: Vintage, 1994).

Macherey, Pierre, *A Theory of Literary Production* (London: Routledge, 1979. First published 1965).

Macleod, Sheila, *Lawrence's Men and Women* (London: Heinemann, 1985).

Magnusson, M. ed., *Chambers Biographical Dictionary* (Edinburgh, fifth edition, 1990).

Marks, Elaine, and Isabella de Courtivron eds, *New French Feminisms: An Anthology* (Brighton: Harvester, 1981).

McCracken, Scott, "Blinded by Intense Revelation: Peter Balbert, *D.H. Lawrence and the Phallic Imagination*", *Times Higher Education Supplement* (11 May 1990).

Meyers, Jeffrey ed., *Lawrence and Tradition* (London: The Athlone Press, 1985).

Middleton, Peter, *The Inward Gaze: Masculinity and Subjectivity in Modern Culture* (London: Routledge, 1992).

Millett, Kate, *Sexual Politics* (London: Virago, 1977. First published 1969).

Mitchell, Giles, "Sons and Lovers and the Oedipal Project", *The D.H. Lawrence Review* (Fall 1980).

Mitchell, Juliet, *Psychoanalysis and Feminism: A Radical Reassessment of Freudian Psychoanalysis* (London: Penguin, 1975).

Moi, Toril, *Sexual/Textual Politics: Feminist Literary Theory* (London: Methuen, 1985).

Møller, Lis, *The Freudian Reading: Analytical and Fictional Construc- tions* (Philadelphia: University of Pennsylvania Press, 1991).

Muller, John P., and William J. Richardson eds, *The Purloined Poe: Lacan, Derrida and Psychoanalytic Reading* (Baltimore and London: Johns Hopkins University Press, 1988).

Murry, John Middleton, *Son of Woman: The Story of D.H. Lawrence* (London: Jonathan Cape, 1931).

Neu, Jerome ed., *The Cambridge Companion To Freud* (Cambridge: Cambridge University Press, 1991).

Panken, Shirley, "Some Psychodynamics in *Sons and Lovers*: A New Look at the Oedipal Theme", *Psychoanalytic Review*, 61 (1974).

Pinkney, Tony, *D.H. Lawrence* (London and New York: Harvester Wheatsheaf, 1990).

Poplawski, Paul, *The Works of D.H. Lawrence: A Chronological Checklist* (Nottingham: D.H. Lawrence Society, 1985).

Preston, Peter and Peter Hoare eds, *D.H. Lawrence in the Modern World* (London: Macmillan, 1989).

Preston, Peter ed., *D.H. Lawrence: The Centre and the Circles* (Nottingham: D.H. Lawrence Centre, Occasional Papers No.1, 1992).

Rand, Nicholas and Maria Took, *Questions for Freud: The Secret History of Psychoanalysis* (Cambridge Massachusetts and London: Harvard University Press, 1997).

Rose, Jacqueline, *Sexuality in the Field of Vision* (London: Verso, 1986).

Ruderman, Judith, *D.H. Lawrence and the Devouring Mother: The Search for a Patriarchal Ideal of Leadership* (Durham, N.C.: Duke University Press, 1984).

Russell, Bertrand, *The Autobiography of Bertrand Russell* (London: Unwin, 1975).

Rylance, Rick, *New Casebook: Sons and Lovers* (London: Macmillan, 1996).

Said, Edward, *Culture and Imperialism* (New York: Alfred A. Knopf, 1993).

Salgado, Gamini, *Casebook: Sons and Lovers* (London: Macmillan, 1979).

Salgado, Gamini, *A Preface to Lawrence* (London: Longman, 1982).

Salgado, Gamini and G.K. Das, *The Spirit of D.H. Lawrence: Centenary Essays* (London: Macmillan, 1988).

Schmidt, Johann N., *D.H. Lawrence: 'Sons and Lovers'* (Munich: UTB-Verlag, 1983).

Seeber, Hans Ulrich, "D.H. Lawrence und der deutsche Expressionismus", *Sprachkunst*, 13 (1982).

Sheppard, Richard, "German Expressionism" and "German Expressionist Poetry", in Malcolm Bradbury and James McFarlane eds, *Modernism: A Guide to European Literature 1890-1930* (London: Penguin, 1976).

Sheppard, Richard, "The Problematics of European Modernism", in Steve Giles ed. (1993).

Simons, Jon, *Foucault and the Political* (London: Routledge, 1995).

Simpson, Hilary, *D.H. Lawrence and Feminism* (London: Croom Helm, 1982).

Smith, Anne ed., *Lawrence and Women* (London: Vision Press, 1978).

Squires, Michael and Dennis Jackson eds, *D.H. Lawrence's Lady: A New Look at Lady Chatterley's Lover* (Athens, Georgia: University of Georgia Press, 1985).

Stanton, Domna C. ed., *Discourses of Sexuality: From Aristotle to Aids* (Ann Arbor: University of Michigan Press, 1992).

Stewart, Jack F., "Expressionism in *The Rainbow*", *Novel*, 13/3 (Spring 1980).

Stoltzfus, Ben, *Lacan and Literature: Purloined Pretexts* (Albany, New York: State University of New York Press, 1996).

Tallack, Douglas ed., *Literary Theory at Work* (London: Batsford, 1987).

Todorov, Tzvetan, *The Fantastic: a Structural Approach* (Ithaca, New York: Cornell University Press, 1975. First published in 1970).

Toolan, Michael, *Narrative: A Critical Linguistic Introduction* (London: Routledge, 1988).

Weber, Samuel, *Return to Freud: Jacques Lacan's Dislocation of Psychoanalysis* (Cambridge: Cambridge University Press, 1991).

Weiss, D.A., *Oedipus in Nottingham: D.H. Lawrence* (Seattle: University of Washington Press, 1962).

Widdowson, Peter, "Post-Modernizing Lawrence", Introduction to the *Longman Critical Reader: D.H. Lawrence*, edited by Peter Widdowson (Harlow: Longman, 1992).

Wiener, Gary, "Lawrence's 'Little Lost Girl'", *D.H. Lawrence Review*, 19/3 (1987).

Wilden, Anthony, *Speech and Language in Psychoanalysis: Jacques Lacan* (Baltimore and London: Johns Hopkins University Press, 1981. First published 1968).

Wilden, Anthony, *System and Structure: Essays in Communication and Exchange* (London: Tavistock, 1980. First published 1972).

Williams, Linda Ruth, *Sex in the Head: Visions of Femininity and Film in D.H. Lawrence* (Hemel Hempstead: Harvester Wheatsheaf, 1993).

Williams, Linda Ruth, *Writers and their Work: D.H. Lawrence* (Plymouth: Northcote House Publishers in association with the British Council, 1997).

Williams, Raymond, *Culture and Society* (London: Penguin, 1958).

Williams, Raymond, *Writing in Society* (London: Verso, 1983).

Williams, Raymond, *The English Novel from Dickens to Lawrence* (London: The Hogarth Press, 1984).

Williams, Raymond, Foreword to Gamini Salgado and G.K. Das eds (1988).

Williams, Raymond, *The Politics of Modernism: Against the New Conformists*, edited and introduced by Tony Pinkney (London: Verso, 1989).

Woolf, Virginia, *Collected Essays Volume 1* (London: Chatto and Windus, 1966).

Worthen, John, *D.H. Lawrence and the Idea of the Novel* (London: Macmillan, 1979).

Worthen, John, *D.H. Lawrence: The Early Years, 1885-1912* (Cambridge: Cambridge University Press, 1991).

Worthen, John, *D.H. Lawrence* (London: Arnold, 1991).

Worthen, John, "Review of Linda Ruth Williams" (1993), in *The Journal of the D.H. Lawrence Society* (1996).

Wright, Elizabeth, *Psychoanalytic Criticism: Theory in Practice* (London: Methuen, 1984).

Young, Robert, *White Mythologies* (London and New York: Routledge, 1990).

Young, Robert, "Psychoanalysis and Political Literary Theories", in James Donald ed. (1991).

Index

sex/power relations, 127
sexual essentialism, 125, 137
sexual ontology, 108, 112
sexual politics, 1, 19-21, 101, 133,
 208, 210, 220, 231, 244, 263, 264,
 269, 271, 272, 285, 287, 288, 290,
 291, 293, 295, 299, 331, 332, 340,
 355
sexuality, 9, 12, 13, 15, 16, 20, 21, 33,
 34, 41, 52, 53, 58, 65, 81, 82, 84,
 88, 89, 99-101, 103, 112, 114, 115,
 117, 120, 121, 125-128, 131, 135-
 137, 144, 145, 207, 213, 215, 216-
 218, 224, 238, 267, 269, 278, 283,
 287-290, 292, 294, 296-298, 300-
 302, 306, 308, 311-313, 315, 327,
 328, 333, 334, 338, 341, 346, 348,
 351, 353, 355
Shakespeare, William, 51, 91, 163,
 166, 231, 260, 324
Sheppard, Richard, 348, 349
Shklovski, Victor, 158, 350, 352
Showalter, Elaine, 297
Sillitoe, Alan, 13
Simons, Jon, 145, 146
Simpson, Hilary, 207, 209, 210, 212,
 213, 220, 267, 301, 302, 306-308
skaz, 154, 164, 185
Smith, Anne, 291
Smollett, Tobias, 164
socialist utopic fiction, 308
sociological poetics, 157, 161, 201
solar plexus, 233, 273
speech genres, 18, 153, 158-160, 169,
 170, 172, 175, 184, 186, 191, 195,
 197, 201, 354
speech mannerism, 321
Spengler, Oswald, 95
Spilka, Mark, 11, 222
spiritual aristocracy, 106
spiritual degeneration, 87, 102, 103,
 110, 118
spiritual journey, 102
spiritual rebirth, 123
spiritual renewal, 96, 104, 266, 270
Squires, Michael, 331
star-equilibrium, 235
Sterne, Laurence, 155, 164, 166, 171,
 197, 201
Stewart, Jack F., 114

Stoker, Bram, 306
Stoltzfus, Ben, 63
Stopes, Marie, 213, 217, 308
Storey, David, 13
Stravinsky, Igor, 240, 241
structuralism, 3, 4, 6, 8, 9, 10, 13, 20,
 21
structure of feeling, 304
stylistics, 119, 165, 168, 170, 172,
 201, 202
stylization, 18, 152, 153, 158, 164,
 168, 170, 172, 173, 175, 176, 195,
 200
Suffragette, 306
Suffragettes, 133, 207, 302
Surrealism, 347
Symbolic, 35, 40-43, 45, 46, 56, 64,
 67, 69-71, 76, 85
Symbolic Order, 35, 41-43, 46, 67, 69-
 71, 76, 85
symbolism, 82, 107, 123, 128, 246,
 263, 284, 291, 346, 350, 353
symbolist poetry, 246
symptomatic imagery, 34
symptomatic reading, 47, 64
synechdoche, 72, 73, 79

Tantric yoga, 267
tenderness, 121, 131, 291, 314, 330,
 331, 334, 341
the Real, 41-45, 47, 64, 71, 85, 299,
 324
"thought-adventure", 5, 9, 18, 205,
 213, 214, 230, 245, 250, 251, 261,
 262, 273, 275, 284, 354
Tindall, William York, 264, 265, 271
Todorov, Tzvetan, 353
Torok, Maria, 30
touch (theory of), 320, 326, 330, 334
transference, 34, 39, 85
transgression, 16, 89, 143, 145, 146
transvaluation of values, 349
Tristram Shandy, 152, 166, 350
Tristram, Philippa, 223

Ulysses, 152, 245, 261, 347, 352
utopia, 95, 236, 247, 259, 308, 309,
 311, 330, 336, 340
utopian fiction, 355